PEASANTRY
THEIR PROBLEM AND PROTEST IN ASSAM
(1858-1894)

PEASANTRY
THEIR PROBLEM AND PROTEST IN ASSAM
(1858-1894)

KAMAL CHANDRA PATHAK

PARTRIDGE
A Penguin Random House Company

To order additional copies of this book, contact
Partridge India
000 800 10062 62
www.partridgepublishing.com/india
orders.india@partridgepublishing.com

CONTENTS

The book unravels the theoretical framework of the peasant uprisings with definition on unrest, uprising and movement. The peasant uprisings in India and abroad from ancient to modern time, the British agrarian policy with reaction of the peasants, emergence of middle class in the 19th century with their opinions and activities on various socio-economic and political problems, role of the *Raijmels*, root causes of the uprisings of Phulaguri of Nowgong (1861), Rangia and Lachima of Kamrup, and Patharughat of Darrang (1893-94) have been discussed in this book thoroughly. Attempt has also been made by pointing-out the gap period (1862-92), making it a systematic, comprehensive and total study in place of either narrative or stray one.

PREFACE

Discontentment of the peasants against the high trend of revenue of the British was a common feature of the 19th century India. The uprisings of Assam draws attention not only of all the parts of India, its echo was reflected even in the Imperial Legislative Assembly of Britain also. The uprisings was aimed at not for freedom from the colonial yoke, but for emancipation from exploitation and revenue-hike.

The book, specially, deals with the peasant unrest and uprisings in the erstwhile three districts of Assam viz. Kamrup, Darrang and Nowgong from 1858 to 1894. The year 1858 has been taken as a starting point, as it has a special importance in the history of the British India. After the'Great Mutiny of 1857, 'Assam like other parts of India went into the hands of the British Crown in 1858. The Colonial Government decided to augment the rate of revenue on land from this year with a view to removing the loss of the 'Great Mutiny.' Hence, this year may be termed as the '*CONFRONTATION YEAR*' between the peasants and the government, which continued upto 1894 and even beyond that.

The peasant unrest of Assam have fetched some new aspects in to focus, and some of them have been referred here at proper places. The specific period (1858-94) has yet not been studied, notwithstanding lots have been done in this field. It is because of that it has received not due attention, as is given to the same phenomena in other parts of India. This book is an endeavour to give as far as possible a comprehensive, accessible and a crystal picture of a series of complex scenario. The book is chiefly built up on the primary as well as the secondary datas, both published and unpublished, the details of which are appended in the bibliography.

For my father Umesh Chandra Pathak (Uma) who grew me up and Lakshi Pathak, my elder sister who loved me enough.

This book has grown out of my doctoral thesis, submitted to the University of North Bengal, Darjeeling (West Bengal) in 2010 under the supervision of Dr. B. K. Sarkar, the then Head, Department of History of North Bengal University. I owe a great debt to him. I am equally grateful and indebted to Dr. J. B. Bhattacharjee, former Head, Department of History of NEHU, Shillong and former Vice-Chancellor of Assam University, for his constant encouragement and blessings apart from the interest that he had infused in me for the completion of the book. I am also equally grateful and beholden to Dr. S. D. Goswami, former Professor of the Department of History, Dibrugarh University; Dr. S. D. Dutta, former Professor of History and Dean, Faculty of Social Sciences, Rajiv Gandhi Central University; Professor Dr. M. K. Sharan, Department of History of Magadh University, for their valuable suggestions at the initial stage of progress of my book. In the completion of this book, I have been helped by many others in more ways than one, and my acknowledgements are due to all without mentioning any particular name. My sincere thanks are due to the Directors, Librarians and also to the Staff members of North Bengal University Library, Indian Council of Historical Research Library of Gauhati University, K. K. Handique Library of Gauhati University, NEHU Library, Omeo Kumar Das Institute of Social Change and Development Library, Directorate of Archives of Guwahati and a few other similar institutions for their help and co-operation.

My thanks of gratitude are due to my honourable college authority and colleagues irrespective to teaching and non-teaching for their assistance during my long journey of the work. I do wish to thank . . . . for publishing the book.

I devotedly express my deep respect and gratitude to my *aie* Jamila Pathak for her blessings, good wishes and endless inspiration, especially, for this book. Last but not the least, no words suffice to offer my love and best wishes to my *sahadharmini* Purabi and my *jiyari* Sukanya (Daisy) who always revived my spirit enough to complete the book by giving constant support and enormous co-operation in innumerable ways.

Despite proper guidance and care, there may be omissions or errors of judgment. For that, author eveready to bear the onus of this.

Kamal Ch. Pathak

Pratap-villa, Hatigaon, Guwahati-38

GLOSSARY

A

Abkari	***The excise on drugs and liquors***
Ahat	A kind of tree
Ahu	Short maturing rice suitable for dry farming
Ahu-toli	Land growing Ahu-rice
Amlah	Bureaucrat
Angamee	A tribe of Nagaland
Anna	Six paisa
Assam Dipak	A monthly journal published from the river island Majuli of Assam
Athbhaga	A tax of ancient India at the rate of 1/8
Ayasa	Copper

B

Bakijai	Recovering loans or revenue arrears from defaulter
Bali	An ancient tax at the rate of 1/6
Baniya	Trader
Bao-toli	Land growing bao-rice
Baris	Garden land
Barun-baan	Arrow of rain
Basti	Homestead
Bazaar	Market
Beel	Lake like
Bhaga	A tax
Bhoga	An additional levy

Bhogapati	Tax collector
Bhritya	Hired servant
Bigha	1/3 of an acre (land)
Boka-chaul	Soft and husked rice taken just soaking them in unboiled water
Brahmanas	Priests
Brahmottar	Revenue free land granted to brahmanas
Bunker	Tax for cutting reeds

C

Chakua	A variety of rice
Charsani	Aryan folk
Chaul	Rice
Choudhury	A revenue officer in charge of a purganah
Corvee	Service to land lord in medieval Europe
Cutcherry	Court of justice

D

Da	Bill hooks
Dak-system	Postal system
Dakowals	Postmen
Dal	Pulse
Dalimari	Mallets
Daroga	Officer in charge of police station
Dasas	Slaves
Dasyu	Demon, pirate
Demesne	Land under direct occupation of the lord in medieval England or Europe
Devottar	Revenue free land granted to temple
Dhanah	Rice
Dharmottar	Revenue free land granted for religious purpose
Diwan-i-kohi	Agriculture related department founded by Md. Bin Tughluq
Doloi	Head of a Hindu temple, chief priest
Duli	Big bamboo container
Dun	Bamboo container, normally, of three seers capacity

F

Faringati	Dry land, land growing dry crops viz. mustard
Farman	A declaration

G

Gaon burah	Village Head man
Ghar duwari paiks	Auxiliary footmen
Gorkhati	Tax on timber
Gosain	Spiritual guide

H

Hat	Market
Haladhara	Wielder of the plough, another name of Balorama, the elder brother of Lord Krishna
Hathikheda	Elephant chasing
Havildar	Non-commissioned officer corresponding to a sergeant
Hindoos	Hindus, a community

I

Indra Puri	Land of Lord Indra, Heaven

J

Jobaka	Wooden rakes
Jaha	A variety of rice
Jalkar	Water tax
Janapadas	Tribes
Japi	A wicker hat made of the dry leave of 'tokou' tree and with split bamboos. It protects head and neck from sun-shine and rain
Jarmoni	A wild green and thin plant having medicinal value.

Jiziya	A kind of tax specially imposed on the Hindus

K

Kabuliala	A money-lender whose business is to give money on interest
Kacharees	Kacharis, a major tribe of Assam
Kachi	Sickles
Kaivartas	A low caste of Assam and Bengal
Kalar dal	A kind of pulses
Kalazar	Black fever
Karori	Revenue collector
Kar shakas	Cultivators
Keya	Merchant from Marwar
Kharahi	A bamboo basket
Kharaj	A medieval land tax
Kharikatana	A house tax
Khat	A small estate including arable land
Kheldar	Head of a Khel
Khesari	A kind of pulse
Khetra karma	Cultivation field
Khetri Kasya	Cultivator
Khiraj	Full revenue paying land
Khot	Village head man
Khusary	Grazing tax
Khusury	Do
Kodavas	Coorgs
Komal chaul	Soft and husked rice, taken just soaking them in unboiled water
Kookees	Kukis, a tribe
Kristi	Aryan folk
Ksetrapati	Master of the field
Kshatriya	Second varna
Kulai dal	A kind of pulse
Kutcherry	Court of justice

L

Lakhiraj	Land free from payment of revenue

Lakhirajdar	One who enjoyed revenue free land
Laloongs	Lalungs, a tribe of Assam
Lathi	Club, stick
Lathials	Armed retainer
Lovita	A female character of an Assamese play 'Lovita' by J. P. Agarwala

M

Machwagiri	Fisherman
Mahadroha	Great rebellion
Mahajan	Village money-lender
Mai	A rough bamboo harrow
Mal	A medieval land tax, land revenue
Mandal	A village surveyor in govt. employ
Manor	Lord
Manorial	Feudal
Mans	Maunds, 40 seers equal to one maund
Masjid	Mosque
Matikalai	A black pluse
Matimah	Do
Mau	An Assamese periodical
Mauza	A fiscal unit
Mauzadar	In charge of a mauza
Mel	An assembly of the village people of Assam
Melkies	Local judges of the village corps
Mer	Bamboo basket
Mikir	A tribe of Assam
Moamoria	A religious sect of the Vaishnava faith of Assam
Mowa	Small local fish
Mug	A kind of pulse
Mustajir	Revenue farmer
Musuri	A kind of pulse

N

Namghar	Vaishnavite prayer hall
Nangal	Wooden plough

Nihilists	Revolutionary Russians of Czarist regime believed in absolute skepticism
Nisf khiraj	Land paying revenue at half
Non-rupit	Non-arable, Non-cultivable

P

Paan	Betel leaf/betel leaves
Pachi	A bamboo basket
Paguri/ Pugris	Turban
Paik	An Assamese ryot under the Ahom kings
Panchayat	Village assembly
Pargunnah	A revenue division
Parijat	A kind of flower believed to be available in heaven
Patta	A lease deed
Patwari	A village accountant
Phal	Iron tipped share
Phul	Flower
Phulaguri	Land of flower
Phulaguri-hat	Phulaguri market
Pura/ Purah	A measurement of land, equivalent to 32/3 Bengal bigha/four bighas

Q

Qamargah	Enclosure

R

Raijmels	Assembly of the village people
Raj	Country
Rajanyas	Aristocrats
Rayat Sabha	Assembly of the ryots
Reza riaya	Small peasant
Rupit	Arable, cultivable
Ryot	Peasant whose main occupation is cultivation
Ryotwari	The system where land settled directly with the ryot

S

Sali	A long maturing variety of rice requiring transplantation
Sali-toli	Land growing Sali rice
Samurai	A warrior class of Japan
Sapta Sindhavah	Upper Indus basin
Satra	A vaishnava monastery of the Brahmaputra valley
Satradhikar	Head of a satra
Satya Yug	Age of truth
Seristadar	A keeper of records
Sira	Plough
Sudra	Fourth varna
Sumathira	A thick-skinned fleshy fruit that tastes sour
Swami	Master, lord
Swaraj	Freedom

T

Tahsil	Fiscal unit bigger in size than mauza
Tahsildar	In charge of Tahsil
Takeli	Earthen jar
Tarh	The standard measure from 111/2 to 121/2 in length
Telis	Producer and seller of oil, specially, of local mustard oil
Thakuria	A minor fiscal officer to collect temple and other dues.
Thana	Police station
Tup	A high sand land, mound

U

Upadrava	Trouble

V

Vaishya	Third varna
Vehmgercht	Secret court
Virar	Levy
Vis	Peasant
Vistikarma	Forced labour

Y

Yava	Barley

Z

Zamindar	Landlord

COLONIAL ASSAM

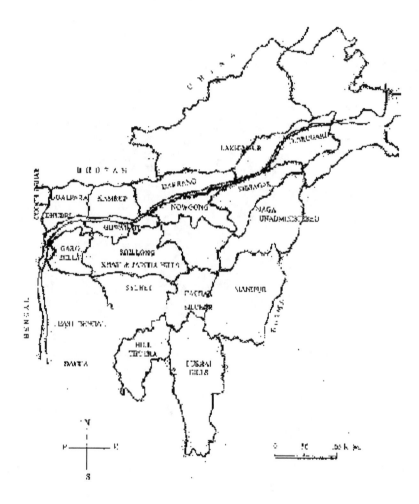

Sketch drawn under the shade of H. K. Barpujari's (ed)
'The Comprehensive History of Assam', Vol. IV (1826-1919)

KAMRUP, DARRANG AND NOWGONG (ERSTWHILE)

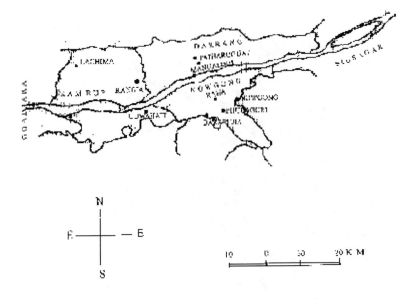

Sketch drawn under the shade of H. K. Barpujari's (ed)
'The Comprehensive History of Assam', Vol. IV (1826-1919)

CHAPTER – ONE

INTRODUCTION

The peasants, who constitute the largest single segment of mankind, play a special role in shaping our destinies. Chayanov and Mao Tse-tung have interpreted the historical qualities of the peasantry and they offer two widely different, even opposite, views. Yet, they inspired in to the past of the peasantry for discovering its capacity for change and resistance. In order to reconstruct the peasant-history in India, D.D.Kosambi and R.S.Sarma, together with Daniel Thorner, brought peasants in to the study of Indian history for the first time.

Literally, a peasant is one who tills the land. Raymond William says that peasant, a word of French origin, came to be widely used in English from the 15th century for one, who worked on land and also lived in the village.[1] Oswald Spengler portrayed the peasant as an organic, rather than historical figure. The peasant in the legal sense was not an ancient figure unaffected by history but rather a historical figure that emerged in the high middle ages. Evidence reveals that the word 'peasant' did not appear before those engaged in agriculture became legally distinguishable.[2] But such a definition is not so simple as it appears to be. It is naturally elusive to give a rigorous definition of the peasant. Habib takes the peasant to mean a person who undertakes agriculture on his own, working with his own implements and using the labour of his family.[3] This definition is acceptable to Marxists as well as to Chayanov. In general, a peasant is one who generates income out of the land owned by him.

Revolutionary transformation has become a world-wide process. Hardly a year passes without a revolutionary change in some or other part of the world.[4] This change began to attract the attention of the social scientists since 1960. Prior to that, there was only political history as historians had concentrated their attention on that. Recently, some social scientists turn their attention on peasant-study in a class framework that is rooted in Marxism.[5]

Sometime, on the contrary, movements hope to preserve the status-quo in the face of threatened changes. In this case, social movement can play a vital role in changing the pattern of society according to its desire.

The terms like rebellion, revolution, revolt, uprising, movement and insurrection have been used synonymously. Dictionaries, encyclopedia and glossaries have given different meaning to the term 'movement.' According to Chamber's Dictionary, movement means 'general tendency of current thought, taste, opinion or action or mere drift.' So, a series of combined action and endeavour of body of persons for a special object is called movement. According to Lenin, revolution is a profound, difficult and complex science.'[6] Revolutions are not made to orders; they cannot be timed to any particular moment. They mature in a process of historical development and break-out at a moment determined by a whole complex of internal and external causes. Revolution breaks out when tens of millions of people come to the conclusion that it is impossible to live in the old way any longer.[7]

Revolutions are inevitable in the process of social development. Political and social revolutions are not the same thing. 'Every revolution dissolves the old society and to that extent, it is social,' wrote Marx. 'Every revolution overthrows the old power and to that extent, it is political.' Revolutions affect the foundations of the rule of one or another class, but coups only replace persons or groups of persons in power. Similarly, reforms help to overcome social contradictions but revolutions not.[8]

The peasants throughout the world have displayed a great role in various movements, and their participation in all such movements catapulted the movements to a new height. Indian scholars were largely influenced by various peasant movements that took place within and outside India. Chinese revolutions and number of agrarian movements in Latin America are special among them. Naxalite movement in the second half of the 20th century also provided more scope to Indian sociologists, political scientists and scholars. The peasants played a predominant role in bourgeois revolutions which helped in ushering capitalist society in England and France, and communist societies in China and Russia. Regarding the rebellious nature, Barrington Moor Jr. said that the Chinese peasants were more rebellious than the peasants of India. But A.R.Desai in 1979, Dhanagare in 1983, R.Guha in 1983 and Kathlene Gough in 1974 disagreed with Moore's comment. Gough counted 77 revolts and classified them in terms of their 'goals, ideology, methods and organizations as restorative, terrorist, mass, religious and social banditary.'[9] But she overlooked some peasant movements which were linked with the nationalist movement in some ways or other.

According to Marx, peasant movement took place in response to extraction of surplus by landlords, money-lenders and the state. In the rural society of India, caste and economic interest play an important role in all respects. 'Class conflict is based on exploitation of peasantry,' Marx said. He treated the peasantry as a secondary social class, and criticized the French peasantry for not taking side with the industrial proletariat in their struggle against the bourgeois in 1848.

It is noteworthy to explore why Indian peasants couldn't achieve their goal what the European and the Chinese peasants could. Scholars in their studies find the fact. Caste system and the Hindu religion is an obstacle for which poor peasants could not organize against the exploitation. Like Marx, Ranajit Guha also mentioned about the primary and secondary discourse, terrible insurgencies and elite leadership. He in order to understand the peasant movement gives importance to exploitation on peasantry. Some scholars want to explain the peasant movement as predominantly middle-class movement. But it is not true in the case of the south. The poor peasants and the labourers are the 'backbone of resistance from the beginning till the very end.'[10]

The emergence of innumberable social movements with a multitude of issues, values and demands are very noticeable phenomenon in all contemporary societies. With the gradual transformation of the economic and social structure of the society and as a result of industrial revolution, various social movements emerged. Industrial revolution tore the structure and relations of feudalism and replaced it with capitalism. Development of capitalism and its inherent contradictions gave birth to many social movements in history. Fundamental rights have also played a significant role in the emergence of various contemporary social movements. Most of the historically significant political movements by nature and implication are social movements.

Many social scientists have attempted to provide definition of social movement. The earliest definition perhaps was provided by Lorenz Vonstein, the Danish historian 1852. In his analysis of the French revolution, he defined social movement as people coming together to change the conditions of society. According to him, masses were the volatile element in society which was capable of bringing about social disruption and political change.

In order to reach its goal, a social movement needs collective action, a social mobilization. For social mobilization, a social movement needs to depend on some kind of organization to provide leadership and direction. For this, the leadership needs some kind of ideology to explain a situation convincingly which it wants to change through mobilization. With the help of ideology, the leadership justifies the existence and continuity of a social movement. A social movement cannot exist without some goals, social mobilization, organization, leadership and ideology. These are the foundations on which 'the edifice of the movement stands; the stronger the foundation, the stronger is the movement and its impact on society and history.'[11]

The term 'peasant movement' and 'agrarian movement' refer to all kinds of collective attempt of different strata of the peasantry either to change the system which they felt, was exploitative or to seek redress for particular grievances without necessarily aiming at overthrowing the system. The rural sociologists have analyzed the peasant unrest in different terms. For instance, A.R.Desai calls the unrest as 'the peasant struggle.' Kathlene Gough terms it as 'peasant uprising', for N.G.Ranga again, 'it is a struggle of the peasantry' and according to Hamza Alavi, 'it is a peasant revolution.' It appears that the sociologists who are oriented to Marxism have analysed the peasant agitation as struggle on the pattern of class struggle and class war. These sociologists look at the peasant agitations from the perspective of class antagonism. D.N.Dhanagare reviews the peasant agitation as 'a peasant movement.' The dictionary meaning of 'agrarian' means anything related to land, its management or distribution. Agrarian system also includes land tenure system. Andre Beteille says that agrarian system does not mean only peasantry.[12]

It is argued by economists and sociologists that the present agrarian problem of rural India is the outcome of the colonial policy adopted by the British in Pre-Independent India.[13] The process of Sanskritisation and Westernisation brought socio-cultural change in India which broadened the mental horizon of the people, and brought a revolutionary change in their socio-economic life. Imbibed by this, they tried to break hitherto prevailing obsolete system. This gave birth to confrontation. It does not mean that the people never sought change before the starting of the process of westernization. But it became imminent after that.[14]

In recent years, the peasants study receives much importance at the hands of Subaltern groups. It may be noted that earlier the historians, particularly, the Imperialist and the Nationalist historians have paid less importance on the role of the peasants in their movements. They emphasized to study their history through the eyes of the elite leadership.

Those who believe in Marxist-Leninist-Maoist formulations regarding peasant movements, they assign the role of motive force in such movements to the urban proletariat, and in the rural areas, to the poor peasantry. Middle peasants are taken to be firm allies and on occasions, alliance is envisaged even with the rich peasants. Counter to this, in recent years, a school of peasant studies has sprung-up which sees the middle peasant as the class most liable to rise in revolt and feels that the socio-economic condition handicaps the poor peasants, including agricultural labourers and it makes them more revolutionary. To these social scientists, 'assigning primacy in peasant movement to the poor peasantry is no more than conforming to Marxist orthodoxy.'[15]

II

The land known as Assam is situated to the extreme north-east of India. Assam in different periods was known in different names. Her earliest name was Pragjyotishpur. The name Pragjyotishpur is found mentioned in the Mahabharata and the Puranas. Narakasur, Bhagadatta, Ghatotkacha and Bana, the father in law of Lord Krishna's grandson Aniruddha, all were hailed from Pragjyotishpur. The great king Bhagadatta took part in the battle of Kurukshetra. Pragjyotishpur later came to be known as Kamarupa. The earliest reference to the name of Kamarupa is found mentioned in the Allahabad Prasasti of Samudra Gupta engraved about 360 A.D. Regarding the origin name of Kamarupa, there is a legend in the Purana, but this has no historical value. The more reasonable view is that the term Kamrup is derived from Kambru or Kamru, the name of a non-Aryan God. According to *Yogini Tantra*, Kamarupa in ancient time was divided in to four parts: Ratnapith, Kamapith, Svarnapith and Soumarpith. The first three historical and royal dynasties of Kamarupa: the Varmanas, the Salastambhas and the Palas ruled over Kamrupa from the 4th century to the beginning of the 12th century. The name Kamarupa continued to be used till the advent of the Ahoms in the Brahmaputra valley in the 13th century. With the coming of the Ahoms, Kamrupa came to be known as Assam. The arrival of the Ahoms is a decisive factor in the history of Assam. The Ahoms, a Shan tribe from Burma, wandered in to the Brahmaputra valley about the year 1226. Established once firmly in the upper Brahmaputra valley, they followed a policy of expansion and by 1700, had conquered the territories once included in the kingdom of Kamarupa. The Ahoms had to fight a series of battles against the Koches and the Mughals; against the Kacharis and the Jayantias; against the Chutias and the Barabhuyans and thus, had to defend and sometime to offend the hill tribes. Not withstanding that, Assam did not become a part of other and thus, they proved their might. The Moamoria uprising shook the very foundation of the Ahom kingdom and in utter distress, the king had to seek the help of the British in quelling the uprising. Moreover, internal dissension, feud, internecine conflict, intrigues, maladministration and sycophancy, all these made the foundation of Ahom kingdom fragile and topsy-turvy. There also prevailed social inequalities, like the kings could only build houses of bricks and mortars, nobles could wear shoes, ride on horses, travel in palanquin but same were denied to the ordinary people. The people of humble birth were obliged to fold *chaddar* over the left shoulder, not over right like the nobles. All these social disparity gave birth to discontentment amongst the subjects. This and such type of environment encouraged the Burmese to interfere in to the internal affairs of the Ahom kingdom and thus, precipitated her collapse as the time marched.[16]

III

On the north-east corner of the Republic of India, lies the present state of Assam, situated between the twenty-fourth and twenty-eighth degrees of north latitude, and eighty ninth and ninety-seventh degrees of east longitude. The long alluvial valley of the Brahmaputra or Assam proper extended at the beginning from the river Manah on the north bank of the Brahmaputra to the foot of the Himalayas close upon the frontier of China. On the north, it is bounded by the hills inhabited by the tribes of various groups that separate Assam from China and

Burma. On the south-east lie the states of Cachar and Manipur. From the Patkai hills, which form the natural boundary with Burma, runs the irregular chains of mountains commonly known as the Assam Range occupied by the Nagas, the Jayantias, the Khasis and the Garos westward in succession. Guarded, thus, almost on all sides by mountain barriers, Assam remained practically isolated. Geography had imposed a 'formidable barrier on her contact with the rest of the world.' Navigation along the river Brahmaputra before the steam-age was always uncertain and at times extremely hazardous.[17]

The interference of the Burmese in the internal affairs of Assam is a dark chapter in the history of Assam who unleashed a region of terror. Plunder, devastation, murder and desecration became the order of the day. There was wholescale depopulation, industry collapsed, agriculture was neglected and trade, if any, was at a standstill. Major John Butler and Maniram Dewan described the outrages of the Burmese, 'the dreadful atrocities perpetrated on the helpless Assamese could better be imagined than described.'[18]

In 1825-26, the British appeared on the scene in the guise of saviours, and expelled the Burmese from Assam. So, people at large naturally welcomed their advent and expected that their troubles would end; and peace, prosperity and normalcy would return soon to the land. But the hopes entertained by the people with unbounded joy were soon turned to bitter disappointment, and the first flush of popular enthusiasm gave way to growing discontent while it dawned in their mind that the British had come to stay and their motto was to turn the land in to an agricultural estate of tea-drinking Britons, transform local traditional institutions to suit the colonial pattern of exploitation. The people found-out from experience 'the new master's immediate concern was extortion of land revenue, even to the detriment of the welfare of their subjects.'[19] Shorn of their power and privileges, the official aristocracy of the former Ahom Government 'gave vent to their bitter feelings and hostility in a number of abortive attempts to overthrow the alien rule.'[20]

The disaffected section of the nobility was the first to strike at the alien rulers, albeit with the avowed purpose of restoring its own social status and privileges. Upper Assam was the mainstay of the Ahoms and the haunt of the European tea planters; the anti-British uprisings occurred in Upper Assam within a few years of British occupation.[21]

The old aristocracy which had lost its offices of profit was the first to react violently to the alien rule. The first revolt was at the initiative of

Gomdhar Konwar, a prince of the Ahom royal family in 1828. Dhananjoy Borgohain, his son Haranath and many members of the dispossessed nobility were a party to this rebellion. But the ill-organized revolt was suppressed by Lt.Rutherford in October, 1828. The second revolt took place in 1829 under Gadadhar Singha, but this also met failure. The third attempt was made in 1830. The British crushed the third attempt too. Some leaders were sent to Dacca for detention, and Piyali Barphukan and Jiuram Dihingia Barua were hanged in August, 1830. The revolt of 1830 was much more organized than the 1828 and the 1829's.

Within four years of the treaty of Yandaboo, revolts began in Assam. The Khasis fought under the leadership of UTirat Singh, and the Singphos under a Khamti Chief. Thus, alongside the dwellers of the plains, the hillmen also made their mark as rebels. The Khasis fought the British for four years from 1829 to 1833. As for the Singphos, they were in contact with the leaders of the Khasi insurrection and of the 1830 of Assam.[22]

The system of British administration reduced vast masses to poverty. The result was mal-administration as the foreign government cared more for revenue than for the philanthropic work. For example, Nowgong became depopulated in 1832-33 due to the hike of revenue, and ¼ of the total population abandoned their houses and took asylum in Jayantia, Kachar and Yamunamukh. Four years later in 1836, some peasants of Nowgong revolted against revenue-hike. 'The attempted reform and reorganization of the administration could not eradicate the evils of an alien government and their satellites whose interest was more of economic exploitation than improving the lot of the masses or redress of their augmented grievances.'[23]

Like the other parts of India, the echo of revolt of 1857 was felt in Assam also, and it was fuelled by Maniram Dewan. The revolt of 1857 had imposed severe financial strain on the British Indian Government. Local authorities in Assam began to tap new sources of revenue to meet their increasing expenditure. The government increased the revenue demand by 3 to 4 times. Stamp duties and income tax were introduced in 1858 and 1861 respectively in addition to excise duties and taxes for grazing and cutting timber and reeds. To make the large number of opium-eaters dependent entirely on government opium, cultivation of poppy was totally banned in 1861. Already, the increase of land revenue on dry crop lands in 1861 was much resented in Nowgong. But as the news of the ban on the poppy cultivation reached Nowgong, the fury of the peasants burst-out, as it affected their economy the most. The people were also apprehensive about the imposition of tax on betel nut and *paan* cultivation. All these, however, led to an agitation, mainly, among the Lalung tribe of Phulaguri in Nowgong in 1861. All sections came out in support of the rebels, but finally met fiasco.

In 1868-69, the government had increased the rates of revenue on *rupit* and non-*rupit* lands from 25 to 50%. The people particularly in the districts of Kamrup and Darrang reacted against this enhanced through the *Raij-mels*. The people launched no-tax campaign against ruthless imposition of higher rates of assessment in Kamrup (Lachima, Rangia and neighbouring areas) and Darrang (Patharughat) towards the close of the 19th century. Both the Hindus and the Muslims met together in the *mels*, and nauseated their protest against the revenue-hike on land. Anyway, the movements of Rangia, Lachima and Patharughat lost their edge and met ultimate fiasco. Indeed, all revolts against the British from 1828 onward failed to achieve their goals. P.N.Gohain Barua, the founder of the Ahom Sabha said, 'the period from 1838 to 1893 was a season of dead-march for the Ahom community.' Within these years, he said, they became 'insignificant and neglected.'[24]

IV

Though the movements of Patharughat (Darrang); Rangia and Lachima (Kamrup) and Phulaguri (Nowgong) are the main areas of this book, the persistence of these movements were seen in other segment also, which were within and beyond the periphery.

The period 1858 to 1894 has been chosen for two major considerations: The peasant movements of Kamrup, Darrang and Nowgong particularly of this specific period have not been studied systematically, though lots have been made in brief, narrative and casual type. That's why, they have not received its due attention, as is given to the same phenomena in other parts of India. So, attempts have been made to give a systematic and clear-cut picture of this. The North-Eastern regions including Assam had fiercely resisted the colonial domination. But little is known of the peasants of this region, who resisted revenue hike of the colonial government; and the year 1858 has a special importance in the history of Assam. After the great mutiny of 1857, Assam also like other parts of India went in to the hands of the

British Crown in 1858. The Crown contemplated and finally, decided to increase revenue on land in this year (1858) so as to remove their loss in the mutiny of 1857. Augmentation of revenue gave birth to direct confrontation between the government and the peasants. As a result, there took place peasant movements in Assam, which came to an end in 1894.

The peasant movements of colonial Assam have some peculiar aspects. The movements did not get adequate momentum in all districts, except three viz. Kamrup, Darrang and Nowgong. Instead of zamindari system, ryotwari system was prevalent there. Moreover, distinction was very much less between the rich and the poor peasants. Both agricultural and non-agricultural classes took active role in the movements. The peasant movements of Assam, unlike the south, were open rebellion against the state, open rebellion not for freedom from colonial yoke, but for emancipation from revenue burden and exploitation. The movements of Assam could be termed as popular movements, as all sections irrespective to caste and creed took active part in that. Another noticeable feature is that the peasants organized themselves through the *Raij-mels*. The *Raij-mels* were, mainly, the peasants mobilization campaign. The peasants and non-peasants assembled for a common purpose under the leadership of *Gossains, Dolois, Gaonburhas* or land-owners. Numerical strength to the movements was given by them. Non-political character of the union was another feature of the peasant movements of Assam, and it was the starting point for the peasants to enter into system of organization. Unfortunate is that though the peasant-related matters were discussed in the *Raij-mels,* but less number of them could become their leaders.

Notes & References

1. *cf.* Jha, Hetukar   'Understanding peasant-Its low-classness' in *Peasants in Indian History-I*, Thakur V.K. and Aounshuman A. (eds), Janaki Prakashan, Patna, Delhi, 1996, P. 4.

2. *cf.* Rösener, Werner   *Peasant in the Middle ages*, Polity Press, Cambridge, 1996, PP. 11-12.

3. Habib, Irfan   *Essay in Indian History—towards a Marxist perception*, Tulika Books, New Delhi, 2001, P. 109.

4. Sertsova, A., Shishkina, V. & Yakovleva, L.   *What is revolution?* Progress Publishers, Moscow, 1986, P. 5.

5. Dhanagare, D.N.   *Peasant movements in India* (1920-50), Oxford University Press, Bombay, Calcutta, Madras, 1983, P. 1.

6. *cf.* Sertsova, Shishkina & Yakovleva   *op. cit.*, P. 11.

7. *Ibid.*   P. 7.

8. *Ibid.*   PP. 9, 20-21.

9. Gough, Kathlene   'Indian peasant uprising' in *Economic and Political weekly*, Vol. IX, 32-34, Special number, Aug, 1974, P. 1393.

10. Dhanagare   *op. cit.*, P. 509.

11. Hussain, M.   *The Assam movement—class, ideology and identity*, Manak Publications Pvt. Ltd. in association with Har Anand Publication, New Delhi, First Edition, 1993, See-Introduction.

12. *cf.* Doshi, S.L. & Jain, P.C.   *Rural Sociology*, Rawat Publications, Jaipur and New Delhi, Reprinted, 2006, PP. 115-16, 229-30.

13. *Ibid.*   P. 119.

14. Srinivasa, M.N.   *Social Change in Modern India*, Orient Longman Ltd. Delhi, 1995, P. 1.

15. Das, A.N.   *Agrarian Unrest and Socio-Economic Change* (1900-80), Manohar, New Delhi, 1983, P. 13.

16. *cf.* Bose, M.L.   Social History of Assam, Concept Publishing Company, New Delhi, 2003, P. 44.

17. Barpujari, H.K. (eds)   Political History of Assam (1826-1919), Vol. I, Publication Board of Assam, Guwahati, Second edition, 1999, P. 1.

18. *Ibid.*   P. 4.

19. Guha, A.   *Planter Raj to Swaraj* (1826-1947), Tulika Books, New Delhi, 2006, P. 2.

20. Barpujari (eds)   *op. cit.*, Preface-xi, xii.

21. Dutta, A.K.   'The Background of National Awakening in Upper Assam' in A.Bhuyan's (ed), *Nationalist Upsurge in Assam*, Government of Assam, Guwahati, 2000, P. 66.

22. Dutta, Anuradha   'Aspects of Growth and Development of Nationalism in Assam in the 19th century' in A. Bhuyan's (ed), *op. cit.*, PP. 59-60.

23. Barpujari (eds)   *op. cit.*, Preface-xi, xii.

24. *cf.* Saikia, Rajen   *Social and Economic History of Assam* (1853-1921), Manohar, New Delhi, 2001, P. 38.

CHAPTER – TWO

THE PEASANTS AND THEIR UPRISINGS IN AND AROUND THE GLOBE

To conduct wars, to promote religion, to cultivate art and literature and to maintain administrative staff, enormous resources are needed. According to R.S.Sarma, 'these were apparently provided by the peasantry.'[1] This peasantry originated within society then when agriculture became main provider of food. Agriculture gave a family more time to spend on cultivation and harvesting. This way, the food-gatherers turned into food-producers and family became a social organization. There was no agriculture because seed-plants were realized in the jungles. A good example of pre-history of agriculture was 'Chopni Mando, a Megalithic community of Vindhyan foothills who consumed wild rice.'[2] The Neolithic revolution brought with it the domesticated plants and two crop-zones within India. The first zone is within the period of 6500-4500 B.C. in the Belan valley, and the second is within the period of 6th to 3rd millennium B.C. in the Bolan pass.

A notable stage in human progress marked with the domestication of plants and animals, though a full-fledged agricultural revolution was yet to come. Till then, there was no trace of plough and 'cultivation might still be a continuation of food-gathering.'[3] The first urban and agricultural revolution took place in India coincidently in the Indus basin

(Harappa) within 2600-1800 B.C. Indus agriculture, no doubt, rested on plough cultivation. The Indus people sowed seeds in the flood-plains in November and reaped their harvest of wheat and barley in April, before the next flood. 'No hoe or ploughshare has been discovered but the furrows discovered in the pre-Harappan phase at Kalibangan indicate that the fields were ploughed in Rajasthan during the Harappan period.'[4] Scholars believe that in olden times, Sind received copious rainfall and 'the presence of a great river must have made the problem of irrigation easy solution.'[5] Establishment of two harvest system, agriculture as a full time occupation and peasantry as a social class; the Indus culture, thus, gave India her first peasantry which was firm and settled.

The Aryans directly succeeded the Indus culture. The Rigvedic people practised agriculture. Reference to term '*Krishi*' occurs rarely in Rigveda. The well known term '*hala*' for the plough is not found, but two other terms for plough '*langala*' and '*sira*' are mentioned. Ploughs were drawn by oxen, and ploughshares of wood were used for cultivation. The early Aryans also possessed some knowledge of season which promoted agriculture.[6]

The Aryan technology was still Chalcolithic, and the Rigvedic '*ayasa*' is generally thought to mean copper, not iron. Agriculture was primitive but there is no doubt about its wide prevalence. The Satapatha Brahmana speaks at length about the ploughing rituals. According to ancient legends, 'Janaka, the king of Videha and Sita's father, lent his hand to the plough. In those days, even kings and princes did not hesitate to take to manual labour. Balarama, Krishna's brother, was called *Haladhara*. Eventually, ploughing was assigned to the lower orders and prohibited for the upper castes.'[7]

The Aryans seemed to have regarded with scorn the mound-based (ditch-based) agriculture of their enemies and therefore, brought certain changes in agricultural conditions. The Aryans method of preserving cattle and cultivations were learnt by the tribal peasantry.[8]

There is no doubt that the surplus still came from the peasants. The peasants were the *kshetrapati*. But all peasants were not *kshetrapatis*, as there was division and variations among them. The *varna* scheme of the Rigvedic hymns seem to reflect the deep division of the peasantry in to free '*viz*' and the servile '*dasyus*' who transmuted as *vaisyas* and *sudras* respectively the third and fourth *varnas*. The '*dasas*' were in the lowest level.

After the Indus basin, the long transition in the history of Indian peasantry began in the Gangetic basin. The first clearings began in the

Gangetic basin with the appearance of copper. The Copper Hoard People established few settlements in the Doab and Rohila-khand during the earlier half of the second millennium and extended upto western Bihar. They like the Rigvedic people raised rice and barley, but not wheat. Two pulses gram and *khesari*, also appeared with black gram.[9]

Arrival of iron in the Upper Gangetic basin took place around 1000 B.C., and it was a boost to agriculture and industry and also to human civilization.

Agricultural conditions in the Gangetic basin were vastly different from those of the Indus basin. The cultivators shifted from one field to another virgin land and thus, they improved their yield in the Gangetic plains. The '*jhum*' method required collective action which led to the formation of tribes like the *Sakya* who were peasants. In the late Vedic and Brahmana literature, there was reference of ploughs drawn by six, eight or even twelve oxen. This might be because of hard nature of the soil full of roots and stone.[10]

By the middle of the first millennium B.C., long period of agricultural penetration towards east had created a complex social problem. Emergence of Mahajanapadas with the kings' powers restricted by the powerful aristocracies and Brahmanas created the problem. They had control over large areas of land but paid no levy to the king. It was the peasant alone who paid the levy. That's why, king was called 'the devourer of peasants.'[11]

For almost 500 years (from around 500 B.C.), there was tremendous acceleration in the process of change which universalized peasants' production, and created a caste-divided peasantry. Extensive use of iron was adopted to clear fresh land and to break stony ground with iron-axes and iron-plough shares, which according to Gordon Childe 'cheap iron democratized agriculture.' Growing multiplicity of crops from 6th century B.C. contributed to the growth of the urban markets resulting from the rise of towns. The new method of cultivation like rice transplantation, questions of skilled labour and knowledge of soil and crop both, all these brought revolutionary change in agriculture from 6th century B.C. onwards.[12]

Pressure for surplus extraction reinforced agriculture expansion which led to the establishment of peasant agriculture. The peasants were the basic tax-payers, and in 5th and 4th centuries B.C. and finally, the Mauryan empire intensified the tax-drive. According to Megasthenes, the peasants paid to the king a land tribute. According to Kautilya, *Sudra*

Karshakas and other lower classes were more amenable to exploitation. The Mauryan period did witness the emergence of fairly well-organized agrarian economy in the upper and middle valleys of Ganges; and the dissemination of this knowhow to outlying regions of the subcontinent inaugurate a phase of peasantisation in this part of the world.[13]

One exceptional case which was widely prevalent in Mauryan and Post-Mauryan period was that some peasants (owners) rented or leased-out the water from their tanks and ponds to the needy. But for that, the needy had to give a stipulated produce. Of course, permission was required for that from the state. The peasants who had enough resources to mobilize men and money could do their own irrigation works. Their control over water must have led to the establishment of some sort of an exploitative relationship between the rich and the poor peasants in the villages.[14]

The lord or *swami* leased-out the land to *karshakas* rather than he tilled it under his own direct management. But in second century B.C. as Patanjali mentioned, lord or *swami* supervised ploughing by five labourers.

The Kushana rulers were more interested in tolls from trade. They paid, probably, little attention to the organization of agricultural production, and some organizations in rural areas would play an important role in this context.[15]

Deliberate attempts, on the otherhand, were made to extend the arable land by means of grants. It was realized that barren tracts could be of no use to the owners unless these were made cultivable, and so grants were made to priests and temples with the object of bringing such lands under cultivation.[16] The social changes disintegrated the *janapadas*, and the *jatis* replaced the *janapadas*. The *janapadas*, naturally, broke-up into separate segments while occupational *jatis* were formed. Not a single peasant *jati* but a large number of peasant *jatis* resulted from this break-down of the *janapada*-system. The peasants were relegated to a *sudra-jati*. According to Manu, the Hindu law-maker, 'agriculture was one of the *vaishya* occupation and the labourer in tillage was *sudra*.' But Kautilya's theory of *sudra karshakas* more properly defined the actual status of the peasants. By the 7th century, Yuan Chwang classified the peasants simply as '*sudras*.'[17]

The co-existence between agriculture and hunting broke down during the long-transition in the Gangetic basin due to the increasing size of population in the forest. The raising of leguminous crops reduced the villager's dependence on animal meat or fish, and growing use of cotton affected the demand for animal skins. The areas of forest that the hunters had to have for their subsistence started to dwindle which jeopardized peace and solitude hitherto prevailed in the region. As a result, clash for subsistence among several groups became inevitable.[18]

The peasants searched for more land but obstruction came from the forest people. As a result, they had to entertain a bitter hostility towards the forest people. The peasants had a bitter disdain towards the hunting tribes of the forests. The prejudice against the animal killings was likely to have derived in much larger measure from the peasantry. Edicts of Asoka and the Buddhist texts explain this. Even the occupation of peasants too not spared, and it was termed as sinful and lowly one as the plough with its iron point injures the earth and the creatures living in it. According to I-tsing, the sage (Buddha) is said to have forbidden the monks from engaging in cultivation because this involved destroying lives by ploughing and watering field.[19]

Gradually, the tribal moorings with their customs and superstitions collapsed, and peasant became an invincible part of society. The literal significance of the name 'Krishna' (*krishi, krihsak, krishti, krishna, keshab*) and the anecdotes of his childhood proclaim clearly the rustic elements in the great *Bhakti*-cult. A kind of peasant Hinduism, thus, developed.[20]

In its early social evolution, southern India followed an independent line of development dawn to the Mauryan conquest in 3rd century B.C. The plough appeared in south in the second millennium B.C. was, basically, a Neolithic culture. Though various crops were raised but rice and *bajra*-millet began to be cultivated after the coming of iron. This type of agriculture implied the existence of peasantry from the late Neolithic times.

The arrivals of north-culture on the south along with its effects were important. An important index of the contemporary status of the peasants in India is that the peasants were classed as *sudras,* and it is difficult to admit that there was ever an alliance between the Brahmanas and peasants which served as 'the keystone of local south Indian societies.'[21]

Kosambi propounded a sombre view on the cultural and economic performance of entire period of first millennium, and described it deadlier than any invasion. Agriculture declined during this period, and the concept of peasant society became a 'constant factor' in accordance of Burton Stein's postulation.[22]

The Sudarsana lake in Saurashtra and its history from the Mauryas to the Guptas marked the beginning of the recorded history of tank and bund irrigation. The construction of irrigation tanks seemed to have become well-established in the south by the Chola times and contributed to the extension of cultivation throughout the Indian peninsula. During the first thousand years after Christ, agriculture production increased considerably. Every step was taken to improve peasant production, and agrarian slave became superfluous during this period.

There was a considerable degree of stratification within the peasantry. There were large numbers who were 'mere share-croppers on the fields of others.' Manu says that 'the owner of the field' have priority over the actual tiller. Yajnavalkya supports this when he says that the owner of the field has the right to assign it to a cultivator of his choice.[23]

From the 4th century onward, the donees took land on lease to cultivate or get it cultivated subject to certain bindings. Usually, the Buddhist monasteries leased-out their lands to share croppers but gave nothing except sometime oxen. Some monasteries even did not divide the produce.

Some segments of the peasantry imply a serf-like status of the peasantry. According to Manu, *kshetrikasya* employed *bhritya* in his field. The *Milindapanho*'s (1st century B.C. to 5th A.D.) husbandman; *Kamasutra*'s (4th century A.D.) youngson of a peasant who employed *vistikarma* in his *kshetrakarma*, all these reveal 'exploitation of peasants by peasants' in ancient Indian societies.[24]

This type of peasant-stratification raises questions about the real nature of the village community of India. Private property might not have arisen due to the abundance of land. In 9th and 10th centuries, much of the land might have been held to be vested with the community. But this does not imply lack of stratification. In the earliest village community, only the upper stratum mattered in the community, where power lay in the hands of the non-peasant landowners.[25]

Economic autonomy of the village developed once agriculture had been universalized by the iron-pointed plough. According to Kosambi, Post-Mauryan villages gave surplus in kind to the rulers while the village became self-sufficient. This first developed in north and then in the south. Kosambi talks of the growth of virtually self-contained villages and a close village for the Gupta period. Sarma sees villages and towns as more self-sufficient between the 3rd and 9th century.[26]

The benefits of the dominance came mainly through the fiscal system. A large part of the surplus had to be alienated by the village in payment of taxes. The strong in the villages used to shift the burden on to the weak. Tax amounting, normally, to 1/6 of the produce had little reality behind it. This was prescribed as the maximum for '*bali*' in the *smritis*, but the *Arthasastra* has prescribed *bali* and *sadbhaga* as separate taxes. The Rummindei pillar inscription of Asoka confirms the existence of this double tax. He remitted the *bali* for the holy village and continued the other tax at the reduced rate of *athbahaga* (1/8). Megasthenes Greek accounts also speak of two taxes: land tribute and a land tax of ¼ of the produce. The two taxes occur in Rudra Daman's Girnar inscription of 150 A.D., where after there is 'an increasing multiplicity of taxes.'[27]

It is said that the agrarian taxation was at higher rates in the Mauryan days than in the Gupta-days, which is hardly justified. The increasing number of taxes like *bhaga-bhoga* appearing in inscriptions indicate a real increase in the fiscal burden on the peasants. A passage ascribed to Varahamihira (6th century A.D.) describes the sight of 'desolate villages abandoned by peasants owing to the oppression of the *bhogapatis.*'[28] Agriculture was the main occupation of the Rashtrakutas of Manyakheta (753-973 A.D.) and it received encouragement from the kings. The dynasty ruled over Karrnataka for about 250 years enjoyed political supremacy over Deccan.[29]

The villages granted to the Brahmanas by the Pallavas were exempted from payment of all taxes, and forced labour to the state. This implied that these were collected from the cultivators by the Brahmanas for their personal use and profits. Thus, the Brahmanas emerged as an important class at the expense of the peasantry, from whom they collected their dues directly. Land grants seem to have stimulated agrarian expansion under the Pallavas in south Andhra and north Tamilnadu from the end of the 3rd century onward, but they seem to have adversely affected the peasants.[30]

While tax extraction had an immediate terror for the peasantry, its mode of distribution also affected it in the long run. Sarma's theory of 'Indian Feudalism' rests essentially on the mode of alienation of the tax resources by the rulers. A more important source of feudalism was the decay of commerce and decline of towns, which seems to have continued down to the 11th century. 'This synchronized with a ruralisation of the ruling class and the creation of hereditary tax collecting potentates placed one over the other in some hierarchical order.'[31]

Cavalry supported such dispersed political power. Chariots were obsolete in India, and when the Arabs faced Dahir in the battle in

712-13A.D., the ruler of Sind was accompanied by sons of kings numbering 5,000 horsemen. These horsemen were the knights of Indian feudalism. The horsemen represented the armed and warrior clans and their members dispersed among the villages to extract taxes and keep the peasants subjugated. The powers and the rights, that these feudal warriors carved-out for them, long survived the polities within which they had originated. The zamindars class of medieval India, continuing in to modern times was created out of these deeply entrenched elements.

II

The revolt led by the Kalabhras in the 6th century is an important event in the history of south India. They seem to have been a tribal people, who captured power at the cost of the Cholas and ruled for seventy five years. The Kalabhras are the foes of humanity and whip of civilization. They were charged with resumption of *Brahmadeya* lands. They overthrew many kings and established their hold in Tamilnadu. The revolt was a powerful peasant protest directed against the landed Brahmanas. They put an end to the *Brahmadeya* rights granted to the Brahmanas in numerous villages. Their revolt was so widespread that it could be quelled only through the joint efforts of the Pandyas, the Pallavas and the Chalukyas of Badami. By the last quarter of the 6th century, according to a tradition, the Kalabhras had imprisoned the Chola, the Pandya and the Chera kings, which underlines how formidable their revolt was. The Confederacy of the Kings formed against Kalabhras, who had revoked the land grants made to the Brahmanas, shows that the revolt was directed against the existing social and political order in the south. The Pandyas brought an end to the so-called dark period inaugurated by the Kalabhras.

Sometime, the peasants took advantage of royal visits so as to register their complain to the king. For example, a large number of rural folk came out to welcome Harsha when his army was passing through the country side, but at the same time, they complained to him against the oppression of the *bhogpatis* who had been placed in enjoyment of revenue from the villages.[32]

Sometime, the officials of the government found it difficult to collect taxes which created problem to remunerate priests, warriors and officials. To remove the problems, land grants were made on a large scale leading to the adversion in production. Some land grants indicated the possibility of conflicts. A 9th century's grant from Garhwal advised the people not to create *upadrava* for the grantee and considered disobedience to be *mahadroha*.[33]

There was a peculiar form of protest prevalent particularly in south India. By killing themselves in public, people registered their protest. A dancing girl threw herself from the temple tower to assert the right of her relatives to plough the land assigned to her for maintenance. This methods was adopted by the peasants of south India in protest against their exploitation by the landlords.[34]

'The *Brahmavaivarta purana*' for the first time mentioned that the Kaivartas were a mixed caste born of *kshatriya* father and *vaishya* mother.[35] Traditionally, a low mixed *jati* of boat men held plots of land in North Bengal.[36] They were divided in to two sub-communities. One section took to agriculture and another pursued fishing. They were a powerful war-like community of North Bengal who cultivated land. Some of them were powerful feudal chiefs. The Buddhist Palas restricted the fishing occupation of the Kaivartas due to their faith in non-violence which alienated the Kaivartas. This is propounded by B.C.Sen. A literacy account 'Ramacharita' says that upon being subjected to heavy taxation, they revolted under Divya. Fighting naked with bows and arrows and riding on buffaloes, Divya headed the revolt against king Mahipala II. Finally, the king was killed and Divya captured the throne of Varendri (modern Rajshahi district). The revolt, by nature, had a feudal character. The social significance of the Kaivarta revolt is that a non-*kshatriya* caste revolted against the upper caste rule of the palas, who were probably *kshatriyas*.

Some dreadful revolts between the landlords and the peasants rocked the south in the 11th and the 12th centuries. The peasants of Andhra and Karnataka launched armed attacks against the landlord Brahmanas; and the landlords, in retaliation, burnt many villages and crops.[37]

III

The intrusion of Islam in to Indian history opened the gates for the admission of technique from external sources. There were certain improvements in agricultural tools and methods which can be ascribed to the medieval centuries. The medieval land tax, *kharaj* or *mal*, came into its own with Alauddin Khalji (1296-1316). Until then, except in some localities, the sultans or their assignees had taken the *kharaj* as 'a kind of tribute extorted from the chiefs of the defeated regimes.'[38]

The imposition of land-tax remoulded the relations of the peasant with their superiors. The land tax was no longer seen in the nature of tribute but as levy directly assessable upon each cultivator whether he was a *khot* or other. Authorities forced the peasants (says a 14th century 's document) to cultivate the land and it was asserted on various occasions during the Mughal period. Finally, if the peasants failed to pay the tax, they would become subject to raids and enslavement by the king's troops.[39]

Lands sometime brings power, honour and prestige to its owner. Control over land was a matter of social prestige in an essentially feudal society.[40]

The hereditary magnates of the days of Indian feudalism, after an inevitable process of conflict, confusion of rights and nomenclature; obtained the universal designation 'zamindar' in the Mugal Empire. Thus, a triangular relationship came to exist between the peasantry, the zamindars and the ruling class. The fact is that in medieval India, the surplus was extracted mainly for consumption by the king and his revenue assignees. The cash nexus appears to have been fairly well-established early in the 14th century during Alauddin Khalji's time. In the Mughal empire, the cash-nexus was almost universal even when the tax was fixed in kind, it was most often commuted into money payments. One important thing to be noticed is that Aurangzeb exempted the *rezariaya* from the *jiziya* in a *farman* who engaged in cultivation but depended upon entirely on debt for their subsistence, seed and cattle.

The medieval peasantry was beset by a dual exploitation of the ruling class and the zamindars. The peasants not only became victims of the zamindars raids, but sometime they sought protection from them.[41] The upper class was enormously wealthy. Wealth was taken from the lower class by force or threat of force in the form of tax or revenue. 1/3 of the produce were taken from the villagers who by the sweat of their brow produced it. They were concerned for revenue but much of the time unconcerned with the plebians.[42]

Life for most peasants was a battle for bare survival. The 17th century witnessed recurring cycles of famine with immense mortalities. Calamities of nature underlined men's oppression. The heaviest burden that the peasants had to bear was the land tax, an arbitrary confiscation of such a large part of his produce. Payment of the land tax was the root of all major social conflicts involving the peasantry. The land tax represented the principal, and the other seemed secondary.[43] The immediate provocation of the peasant uprisings of medieval India seems uniformly to have been the demand for payment of land-revenue. Numerous instances of peasant protest of Chola period in the first half of the 13th century are found. The strong reaction of the peasants to the oppression of the landlords and occasionally of the royal agents was one of the best examples during the time of Rajaraja III.

The ponds and tanks formed the chief means of irrigation. Sources unearthed speak that there took place conflict for the possession of tanks. An inscription from Hasan district in Karnataka shows that in 1212., the Chief of Hanche died fighting the people of Kerehalli for a pond.[44]

In 13th century in Karnataka and Andhrapradesh, several violent conflicts between the peasants and the landlords rocked the lands. The peasants launched armed attacks against Brahmana landlords, and the landlords also in retaliation, burnt the whole villages and the standing crops; and thus, carried on their war against peasant-villages.

Widespread rebellion occurred in the Doab about 1330 when Muhammad Bin Tughluq (1325-51) increased the demand of revenue. Resourceless and weak peasants completely made prostrate, but the rich and wealthy peasants turned hostile. The sultan wanted to punish the *khots* and the *muqaddams*, by killing or blinding them. Those who were left, they gathered bands and fled into the jungles. The troops of sultan did *gherao* the jungles and slaughtered everyone whom they found. Increasing the revenue was an ill-advised measures as the region, at that time, was in the grip of a severe famine.[45] Finally, Bin Tughluq sought to bring change in agriculture. He established *'diwan-i-kohi'* with the object of bringing uncultivated land under the plough cultivation and also under the direct state management. But the experiment, one of the best in the history of the revenue administration, had, therefore, to be abandoned.[46]

The revolt of Sanatan Sardar (1614-16) began mainly at Khuntaghat, situated on the south bank of the river Brahmaputra and within the erstwhile district of Goalpara. It occurred during the time of Jahangir. Sanatan, a headman of the *paiks,* emerged as its leader in 1615. The *karoris* and the *mustajirs* began to tyrannize the peasants and abducted their beautiful daughters and sons for the harem of Muhammad Zaman Tabrizi, the *karori* of Khuntaghat pargana.

Mir Safi, the *diwan* and *bakshi* of Kamrup did not pay any heed to the discord and sedition of the cultivators. The officials were busy in increasing the revenue for their own benefits and expenses which augmented the discontent of the ryots.[47] The Mughal annexed the north-eastern kingdom and deported the local princes. Their deportation aroused the nobles leading to the outbreak of the revolt at Khuntaghat. The nobles also joined with the peasant rebels and killed many Mughals. Finally, the rebels were defeated and their forts at Putamari and Takunia were destroyed. Despite that, the peasants of Khuntaghat were not completely subdued. It was at this moment, Sanatan, the Koch chief of the *paiks*, began to harass Shaikh Ibrahim, the *karori* of Kamrup and declared his revolt in Kamrup. His alliance with the local peasants created terror in the hearts of the Mughals and finally, Mirza Nathan sent proposal for peace but Sanatan gave him several terms which was impossible to accept for him. After getting continued resistance, Mirza Nathan in retaliation, razed the neighbouring villages and many food-suppliers were killed. The fortress of the rebels fell to the Mughals; Sanatan was forced to flee, though he continued his resistance against the Mughals.[48]

Khuntaghat was sparked-off once again in 1621. This uprising was, popularly, known as the '*hathikheda*' uprising. The elephants, at that time, carried war materials into the jungles of Assam and were used to seize forts in the hill tracts. Because of this, they were important for the army. The army of Mughal captured elephants and it was one of the duties of the ryots to help them in capturing the elephants. The services of the *palis* were necessary in order to keep the elephants confined within the *qamargah* while those of the *gharduwari paiks* were required to drive the elephants in to the enclosure. The government officers were sent with special instruction to draft the *gharduwari paiks* from their lands. This practice disrupted the ryots' work on their own lands and was, naturally, resented by them.

Baqir Khan, a Mughal officer, carried out a '*hathikheda.*' Some of the elephants escaped while being put in chains. In consequence, the leading elephants drivers among the *palis* and *gharduwari paiks* were sentenced to death and the others were whipped. Baqir Khan ordered 'either bring the escaped elephants here or pay rupees one thousand for each elephant.' This was the immediate cause of the revolt. State demanded service for catching elephants. The ryots who trapped and tamed elephants as a profession were first to react and rose in revolt, and were then joined by other oppressed cultivators. It appears that the leadership lay in the hands of ryots of the lower strata.[49]

The revolt spread to other classes. Bhaba Singh, a Koch noble, became involved in it. The tyranny of Balabhadra, the Hindu *diwan* of Mirza Nathan, had roused the peasants to join in the insurrection. The rebels imprisoned the family of Qulij Khan, the Mughal Commander of Koch Bihar. Jahangirbad was raided and stockades were built at Bangaon and Madhupur on either side of the river at Goalpara. Mirza Nathan suppressed this after much trouble. The words of his rival suggests that this revolt was conducted by the ordinary people belonging to a group of *machwagiri*.[50]

The villagers and cultivators of the other side of the river Jamuna sheltered behind dense jungles, and constantly engaged in thieving due to their poor condition. They passed their days with fastnesses and became rebellious and declined to pay land revenue to the jagirdars. In 1622, Jahangir received the report and army, thereupon, was sent to curb the revolt with killings, rapine and enslavement.

The peasant uprisings of earlier time formed a prelude to the revolt of the Jat peasants. The Jat peasants under the leadership of a succession of zamindars revolted with certain aims. The uprising, in formal terms, was a successful one ending in the establishment of Bharatpur state. It resulted in a very great expansion of Jat zamindari in the Doab at the expense of other zamindar clans. A number of upper Jat peasants moved in to the ranks of zamindars. It had no other sequel as far as the ordinary peasants were concerned. One noticeable feature was that the zamindars tended to feed on peasant unrest during the 17th century or merged with the peasants revolts in many areas. The revolt of the Jat peasants bears the good example of it. The power of the Maratha also fed on peasant unrest in its formation in the 17th century.

The revolt of the Satnamis (a peasant class) in 1672 deserves particular notice. It was combined with religious movements emanating from the great monotheistic preaching of the 16th century. In the verses of Kabir and Arjun, 'God's faithful worshipper appears as a peasant as well as a village headman.'[51] Abul Fazi Mamuri says that they were peasants and carried out trade in the manner of *baniyas*. Their revolt in 1672 in the Narnaul region shook the Mughal empire. The Satnamis were defeated and crushed. Though it failed out, but Delhi was affected because the Satnamis interrupted the grain supply of the capital.[52]

The revolt of the Sikh peasants was also like the Satnamis emanated from the great monotheistic preaching of the 16th century. The peasants appeared as rebels under the monotheistic leadership. Their revolt was successful. Inspite of its undisputed peasant composition, the community admitted men of the low and menial castes as well. This is an important social movement. But while it lifted sections of the community from a lowly status, it did not yet change the major elements of the social order. Even, there is no reference to the oppression of the peasants in Guru Gobind Singh's Persian poem which was composed in criticism of Aurangzeb. It may be said that though the peasants might fuel a zamindar's revolt (Marathas) or might rise in a locality (the Doab) or as a caste (Jats) or as a sect (Satnami Sikh), they failed to attain recognition of any common objectives that transcended parochial limits.[53]

The fiscal demands on the peasants of different *parganas* began to increase from mid 17th century onwards. The peasants of Chatsu were asked to pay a *patwar* cess at the rate of 10 *annas* per 100 rupees, but the peasants declined to pay on the ground that in the past they had never paid it. Obviously, the peasants had lost their caste which was based on an appeal to custom.

The peasants of Kotla and Bawal (1646) were asked to pay an additional cess called *seri* at the rate of 4 ser per maund. The peasants of Malpura and Niwai (1663-64) were also forced to pay heavy tax which led to dismal and anarchy in that *parganas*. The famine of 1663-64 aggravated the situation. The peasants of Salawad *pargana* (1691) were asked to pay two fresh taxes. Again, a new tax was imposed in the *pargana* in 1691. The peasants of Niwai were forced to pay twice the amount of existing class in 1691. *Jizya* at the rate of 4 percent of the *mal* began to be collected from the cultivators of *parganas* of the Mughal north India. The peasants of some 40 villages were asked to pay a lump-sum *virar* but refused to pay it on the ground that there was no such custom in the *pargana*. In 1693, the peasants of Toda Bhim complained that the revenue rates mentioned were in excess to the customary limit.

There are many more instances of fresh fiscal demands being made from peasants. The peasants of eight *parganas* under different jagirdars, complained about their bleak economic condition due to the heavy burden of revenue demand. In order to highlight their terrible plight, they gave the example of Akahera in Rinsi *pargana*. The peasants of this village produced 16,000 maunds of grains in the Khariff season of 1665. The peasants paid 8000 maunds to the jagirdar as land revenue out of this gross produce. They paid other cesses totalled 4500 maunds from the remaining 8000. They were left 3500 maunds only. These figures clearly show that the peasants had paid 78% out of their total output as revenues to the jagirdars.

$$16000 \times 78 = 1248000 \div 100$$
$$= 12480$$
$$16000 - 12480 = 3520$$

In the revenue literature of the period, there is clear official recognition of the widening ambit of poverty among peasants.[54]

The Mughal empire owed its collapse largely to the agrarian crisis which engulfed it. The massive fiscal pressure on the peasantry led to increasing indebtedness in the villages, causing peasants flights. Though the tendency to demand more from the peasant was inherent in the jagir system, there was a conflict between the long-term interest of imperial administration and the short-term calculation of jagirdars. The imperial policy was to set the revenue demand to approximate to the surplus. But the individual jagirdar, being aware of his impending transfer after 3 to 4 years was less interested in the development of his jagir and more concerned to maximize tax collection from the peasants. Thus, the system of jagir transfers led to a reckless exploitation of the peasantry. The increasing burden on the peasantry began to encroach upon their means of survival. As oppression increased, the number of absconding peasants grew, sluggishness in agriculture augmented and peasants took to arms giving birth to rural uprisings of varying intensity. Consequently, the empire fell prey to the wrath of an impoverished peasantry. 'The apparatus of the empire' which was responsible for initiating an endless process of raising revenue demand, was the first to fell the tremor of its diminishing income.[55] The revenue system evolved by the Mughals did provide stability for some time, but it was full of so contradictions that consequently it generated a series of conflicts, leading to the collapse of the system itself.[56]

IV

Indian peasantry has witnessed many ups and downs in its long history. There was a time in ancient and medieval history when the country experienced long battles and constant bloodshed. But these long-term disturbances did not affect our peasantry. The wars were fought by the warriors and the peasants with plough on their shoulders to the field for cultivation. Even during the feudal rule, the causes of land eviction were few and far between. But, this peaceful and quiet peasantry has now been transformed into an agitating peasantry. A.R.Desai has very rightly observed that our peasantry today are 'up in arms.'[57]

The peasant movements had been a part of national movement since 1920. With the emergence of agricultural capitalism, unrest among the peasants has increased. The tribals of the country who are late comers to agriculture have also raised their head high to agitate against the government for the fulfillment of their demands. Land and agriculture is the state subject, and therefore, the peasant movement is the concern of the state government. The root of peasants' unrest, therefore, lies in the social structure of peasantry, its history and process of agricultural modernisation. The peasants are a dominant force in the society. But unfortunately in a period of less than 40 years, 'the peasantry ceased to be a unipartite body.'[58] Agriculture has become capitalistic and with the commercialization of agriculture and transformation in agriculture, the situation and condition of peasants has also undergone tremendous change. And this change has given birth to many peasant uprisings in India.

In 18th and 19th centuries, some major peasant movements broke-out in India. Most of them, by nature, are tribal peasant uprisings. The most militant outbreaks in earlier or later periods, tended to be of tribal communities. This community revolted more often and far more violently than any other community including peasants in India. The term 'tribal' is used to distinguish people 'so socially organized from 'caste' and should not convey a sense of complete isolation from the mainstream of Indian life.'[59]

The British land settlement eroded the tribal traditions of joint ownership, and ended their relative isolation within the ambit of colonialism. It introduced some instruments like money-lenders, traders, *mahajans* which fetched the tribals within the vortex of colonial exploitation. Moreover, the influx of Christian missionaries created varied reactions among the tribals.

Demobilized soldiers and displaced peasants of Bengal led by estranged religious monks and dispossessed zamindars were first to rise-up in the Sanyasi rebellion that lasted from 1763 to 1800. The British could curb this popular revolt only after prolong military action. B.C. Chatterjee made this revolt famous through his novel '*Anand math.*'

Enhanced land revenue demands, famine and economic distress goaded the Chuar indigenous tribesmen of Midnapur to take up arms. Finally, it engulfed five other districts of Bengal and Bihar from 1766 to 1772 and then again from 1795 to 1816. The Ho and Munda tribesmen of Chhota-nagpur and Singbhum had their own scores to settle and they challenged the Company's forces in 1820-22, again in 1831 and thus, the area remained disturbed till 1887.

The Pagal-Panthis, a semi religious sect founded by Karam Shah, lived in the northern district of Bengal. Tipu, the son and successor of Karam Shah was inspired both by religious and political motives. He took-up the cause of the tenants against the oppressions of the zamindars. In1825, Tipu captured Sherpur and assumed royal power. For two decades from 1813 to 1833, Tipu continued to defy the British authority for the favour of the Pagal Panthis.

The Bhils, an aboriginal tribe, lived in the Western Ghats with their strongholds in Khandesh. During 1817-19, the Bhils revolted against their new master, the East India Company. Agrarian hardships and fear of the worst under the new regime were their apprehensions. Several British detachments ruthlessly crushed the revolt. However, the Bhils were far-from being pacified. Encouraged by the British reverses in the Burmese war, they again revolted in 1825 under their leader Sewaram. The unrest erupted in 1831 and again in 1846 signifying the popular character of the discontent.

The Ahom nobility in Assam accused the Company's authorities of non-fulfillment of pledges of withdrawal from their territory after the conclusion of the Burmese war. The attempt of the British to incorporate the Ahoms territory in the Company's dominion and imposition of land revenue in the villages sparked-off a rebellion. In 1828, they (the Ahoms) declared Gomdhar Konwar as their king and planned to march to Rangpur. The superior military power of the Company aborted the move. A second revolt was planned in 1830. The Company this time also crushed the revolt, but finally in 1838, handed over Upper Assam to Purandar Singha.

The Kols of Chhota-nagpur resented the gradual extension of British authority in their soil and the transfer of soil from Kol headmen (Munda) to outsiders like Sikh and Muslim farmers. In 1831, the Kol rebels killed or burnt about a thousand outsiders. The rebellion spread to adjoining areas and orders could be restored only after large-scale military operations.

As a result of the Burmese war, the British got possession of the Brahmaputra valley and conceived the idea of linking-up this territory with Sylhet by a road passing-through the entire length of the Khashi domain. Tirat Singh, the Khasi leader, resented it and won-over the support of the Garos, the Khamtis and the Singphos to drive away the strangers. This revolt developed in to a popular revolt, but met failure in 1833.

The Fairazis were followers of a Muslim sect founded by Haji Shariatullah of Faridpur in Eastern Bengal. They advocated radical religious, social and political changes. Haji's son Dadu Mian took-upon himself to expel the English intruders from Bengal and supported the cause of the tenants against the exactions of the zamindars. This continued from 1838 to 1857. The Santhals are a group of tribes largely concentrated in Bihar. They are mainly agriculturists. This massive revolt took-place in 1855-56. The revolt covered the districts of Birbhum, Singbhum, Bankura, Hazaribagh, Bhagalpur and Monghyr in Orissa and Bihar. The zamindars, money-lenders, traders and European employees oppressed the Santhal peasants to such an extent that there was no alternative left for them rather than to take resort to revolt.[60] These money-lenders and zamindars were outsider Diku who got the blessings of the British. 'Along-with class exploitation, there continued social torture and harassment' in the Santhal region.[61] Two brothers, Sidhu and Kanhu took the leadership of this revolt. But, the British crushed the revolt with iron hand. However, the government pacified them by creating a separate district of Santhal pargana.

Mention may be made of other tribal and peasant revolts like Koli disturbances in Maharashtra (1784-85); Chauri revolt in Bihar (1798); Munda rising (1820-32-37); Gond rising in Bastar (1842); Jivo Vasuo revolt in Gujarat (1850-57-58); Munda rising (1899-1900); Khonda Dora revolt (1900); Bhil rising in Rajasthan (1913); Bastar rising (1910) etc.

The indigo revolt (1859-60) was directed against the British planters, who forced peasants to take advances and sign fraudulent contracts and forced them to grow indigo under terms which were least lucrative for them. The revolt began in Govindpur village in Nadia district, Bengal and was led by Digambar Biswas and Bishnu Biswas who organized the peasants in to a counter force to deal with the planters *lathiyals*. In April,

1860, all the cultivators of Barasat sub-division and in the districts of Pabna and Nadia resorted to strike. They refused to sow any indigo. The strike spread to other places in Bengal. The revolt enjoyed the support of all categories of the rural population, missionaries and the Bengal intelligentsia which led to the appointment of an Indigo Commission in 1860 by the government through which some of the abuses of indigo cultivation was removed. Din Bandhu Mitra vividly portrayed the picture of indigo planters and peasants in his famous play 'Neel darpan.'

In 1870, the agrarian unrest broke-out in East Bengal where peasantry was oppressed by zamindars through frequent recourse to ejection, harassment and use of force. The newly emerging village oligarchies even forcibly drove-out inferior ryots in order to get hold of more land. Having secured the lands of the expelled ryots at a low rate on the ground of 'desertion,' these rich villagers then employed their dependents as share-croppers in order to bring the lands under cultivation again.[62] The zamindars also tried to prevent them from acquiring the occupancy right under the Act of 1859. In May, 1873, an Agrarian League was constituted in the Yusuf Zahi *pargana* of Pabna district of East-Bengal. Payment of enhanced rents were refused and the peasants fought the zamindars in the courts. Similar leagues were formed in the adjoining districts of Bengal. The leaders of the league were Ishan Chandra Roy, Shambhu Paul and Khoodi Mullah. The unrest continued till 1885, when the government through the Bengal Tenancy Act of 1885, enhanced the occupancy rights.

The revolt of the Marathas (1875-78) was mainly directed against the excesses of the Marwari and Gujarati money-lenders, excessive government land revenue demand, slump in the world cotton prices at the end of the American Civil War that led to the peasant indebtedness. The peasants organized a complete social boycott of the 'outsiders' money-lenders to compel them to accept their demands in a peaceful manner. The social boycott was soon transformed in to agrarian riots when it did not prove effective. The peasants attacked the money-lenders' houses, shops and assets. Their chief targets were the bond documents deeds and decrees that the money-lenders held against them. By June, 1875, nearly a thousand peasants were arrested and the revolt was completely crushed. The government appointed Riots Commission to enquire in to the causes of the uprising. The ameliorative measure passed was the Agriculturists Relief Act of 1879 which put restrictions on the operations of the peasants land and prohibited imprisonment of the peasants of the Deccan for failure to repay debts to the money-lenders.

Rural indebtedness and the large scale alienation of agricultural land to non-cultivating classes led to the peasant unrest in Punjab. The Land Alienation Act of 1900 prohibited the sale and mortgage of lands from peasants to money-lenders. The Punjab peasants were given partial relief against oppressive incidence of land revenue demand by the government and it was not to exceed 50% of the annual rental value of land.

The attempts of the British to hike the land revenue in temporarily settled ryotwari areas provoked rural protests in 1861 and in 1893-94 at Phulaguri, Rangia, Lachima and Patharughat of erstwhile Nowgong, Kamrup and Darrang districts of Assam province. But, the attempts of the peasants were dashed to the ground and ultimately, met decisive fiasco at the hands of the colonial government.

The peasantry on the indigo plantations in Champaran of Bihar was oppressed by the European planters. They were forced to grow indigo and sell it at prices fixed by the planters. Gandhiji along with Rajendra Prasad investigated the real condition of the peasants and taught them the virtue of Satyagraha. The district officials ordered him to leave Champaran but Gandhiji defied the order. Later, the government appointed an Enquiry Committee (June, 1917) with Gandhiji as one of the members. The Agrarian Act of Champaran freed the peasants from the imposts levied by the indigo planters. Regarding the nature of punishment to the peasants by the government, Rajendra Prasad describes, 'peasants were forced to embrace a *neem* tree with both hands tied together. On such occasions, the planters used to be present on the scene. On the other hand, the red ants on the tree would bite the man tied to the tree, but he could do nothing as his hands were tied'.[63]

The Kheda campaign was, mainly, directed against the government. In1918, crops failed in the Kheda district of Gujarat, but the government refused to remit land-revenue and insisted on its full collection. Gandhiji along with Ballabh Bhai Patel supported the peasants and advised them to with-hold payments of revenue till their demands for its remission was met. The Satyagraha lasted till June, 1918. However, the government had to concede the just demands of the peasants.

In the post first world war period, peasant movement was started in Rae-Bareilly and Faizabad districts of Uttar Pradesh where the condition of the peasants was really appalling. Most of the peasants did not possess any rights and were treated as serfs and tenants, and their plight was, indeed, miserable. Even the Royal Commission of Agriculture observed that there was far more pauperism in the United Provinces than in other Indian provinces. In 1920-21, the failure of the crops encouraged the peasants of Rae Bareilly and Faizabad districts to organize a revolt against oppression. The peasants not only rose against taluqdars but also thought of defying the British rule. However, the British crushed the peasant movement by using all types of violence methods.

In late 1932 and early 1933, a popular rising broke out in the region of Mewat in north Central India. Although this occurred in opposition to the political power of the princely states of Alwar and Bharatpur, as a peasant revolt, it spread over and was supported from areas of British India. According to Harold Laski, 'it was not merely an instance of peasant rebellion in an area of indirect British rule.' Popular protest in Mewat arose within the totality of an historical context made up as much of developments in British India as of features that were specific to areas of indirect rule.[64]

In August, 1921, peasants' discontent erupted in the district of Malabar of Kerala. It was more revolutionary than the Te-bhaga of Bengal since the latter only sporadically used violence where as Moplah organized a full-scale rebellion.[65] Their grievances related to lack of any security of tenure, renewal fees, high rents and other oppressive landlord exactions. In 1920, the Khilaphat movement took-over the tenants rights agitation after the Congress Conference held at Manjeri in April, 1920. The arrest of the established leaders of the Congress and the Khilaphat movement, left the field clear for the radical leaders. In the first stage of the rebellions, the Moplahs sacked the police stations, looted government treasuries and destroyed the records of debts and mortgages in the courts and registries. Soon, the British declared martial law and thus, they wanted to curb this. Unfortunately, the movement acquired communal colour and the rebels killed about 500 Hindus, sacked about 100 temples and forcibly converted 2500 Hindus to Islam. The movement was suppressed by December, 1921.

The revolt of Rampa took place in the Eastern Ghats in Jeypore on the borders of Narsipatam taluk. Alluri Sitarama Raju provided its leadership. He could not bear the sufferings of these people who were exploited by the forest and excise officials and appealed to the authorities to adopt more humane attitude. The people of the area were not allowed to carry on jungle cultivation and were forced to pay various kinds of dues which posed a serious threat to their traditional mode of life. When he was convinced that justice could not be procured through appeals, he gave a call for spontaneous rising. The response was so favourable that it soon developed into a violent revolt and the government then resorted to most brutal policy towards them and killed a large number of Koya and Savara people. Raju and other leaders were killed and remaining were sent to jail. The revolt was 'as more revolutionary or radical than the Kisan Sabha movement in Coastal Andhra which organized wide sections of peasants, including tenants and agricultural labourers.'[66]

Enhancement of land revenue by 22% in the district of Bordoli of Gujarat by the British Government led to the organization of a no revenue campaign by the peasants of Bordoli under the leadership of Ballabh Bhai Patel. The Bordoli movement of 1928 which demonstrated heroic non-violent resistance electrified the entire country and inspired the peasants all over the country.[67] Unsuccessful attempts of the British to suppress the movement by large scale attachment of cattle and land resulted in the appointment of an Enquiry Committee. The enquiry conducted by Maxwell and Broomfield came to the conclusion that the increase had been unjustified and reduced to 6.03%.

The Te-bhaga movement which started in North Bengal and gradually, engulfed the districts of East Bengal, found its natural way into the Barak and Surma Valley due to its geographical continuity and ethno-linguistic affinity as well as similarity in the nature of peasants' problems which 'attracted the attention of peasant leaders of Bengal to unite the peasants to a common cry of Te-bhaga.'[68] The Te-bhaga in Bengal (Now in Bangladesh) offered the most formidable blow to the foundation of the colonial state and hastened up the British exodus from Indian territory. It was the first politically organised mass peasant revolt led by the Communist Party as well as the Kisan Sabha. In September, 1946, the Bengal Provincial Kisan Sabha gave a call to implement the Floud Commission's recommendation of 2/3 share of the crops (Te-bhaga) instead of half, even less, for the share-cropper on land rented from Jotedars. The revolt was against the Jotedars, not against the colonial state. Like the most successful movements in Indian history, Te-bhaga also had a spread which even its organizers failed to record. The course of Te-bhaga is known to have erupted in North Bengal and then spread to certain parts of Eastern Bengal. It erupted with equal intensity and perhaps for longer period than Bengal in certain parts of North East India like Goalpara and Cachar.[69]

Dewan C.P.Ramaswamy Iyer in January, 1946, announced an 'American-Model Constitution' with assemblies elected by universal suffrage but an executive controlled by a Dewan appointed by the Maharaja. The ambitious Dewan was clearly working for an independent Travancore under his own control when the British left. While the State Congress was willing to a compromise with Ramaswamy Iyer, the Communist launched a massive campaign with the slogan '*throw the American model in to the Arabian Sea.*' From September, 1946, the state government began an all-out campaign against the Communist and trade unions. The Conservative estimates speak of about 800 killed in this bloody rising. The massacre prevented any alliance with between the totally discredited Dewan and the Congress, though the latter was careful next year to bring about the integration of Travancore with India 'blocking the road towards Balkanisation.'[70] According to Mridula Mukharjee, it was not a peasant movement, otherwise, the similarities with Patiala and Telengana.[71]

The Telengana peasant-uprising (1947-51) was launched in Andhra Pradesh against the former Nizam of Hyderabad. The agrarian social structure in Nizams' Hyderabad was of feudal order, ryotwari and jagirdari. The causes of this movement are exploitation of the jagirdars and deshmukh; and the bhagela system (slavery system). The bhagela was required to serve the landlord for generations. Moreover, the poor peasants did not get irrigation facility. As a result of growing land alienation, many actual cultivators were being reduced to tenants-at-will, share-croppers or landless labourers.[72] The Telengana rising did not erupt over-night. It took about three to four decades. Actually, till 1930, the poor condition of the peasants had reached its culmination. There was enough discontent among the lower-strata of peasantry. They were only waiting for some opportunity to engineer insurrection. It was engineered by Communist Party of India. However, the movement had to be withdrawn after receiving a death-blow at the hands of the police. According to Mridula Mukherjee, 'in Telengana, it was the landlords' attempts to use armed hoodlums to break peasants' resistance. In many ways, this movement was most radical and revolutionary than that of the other Indian peasant movements.'[73]

The peasant struggle in Naxalbari was launched in March and April, 1967. The Te-bhaga of 1946 had acted as its torch-bearer. The chief aim of this insurrection was to alter the entire society, not merely the condition of peasants. The ideology of Naxalbari movement was highly charged by the ideology of violence. The idiom of the movement was that the power comes from the barrel of the gun, not by slogans and non-violence. The total annihilation of the big farmers, landlords and the jagirdars were the aims of this movement. Naxalbari is a police sub-station in the Darjeeling district of West Bengal. It is in the name of the police sub-station that the movement is known all over the world. At later stage, it took an ideological flavour. It was essentially a movement launched by share-croppers. In the beginning, the movement was restricted to Khoribari, Naxalbari and Phanisidewa, having a population of about one lakh. The Rajbansis are the most preponderant community of the region. In the process of political development which took place in the Tarai region, the Rajbarnsis acquired larger portion of land and came to be known as jotedar, a peasant proprietor. Below to them were small farmers, *adhiars* who cultivated land on equal share basis. Under this system, cultivators were reduced to the status of share-croppers who suffered exploitation and succumbed to bondage. The Naxalbari movement was, basically, against the big farmers, jotedars. Albeit, there was no immediate gain of the struggle, it apparently influenced the course of peasant movement in the country. It was a specific struggle, ideologically, oriented to Marxian socialism.'[74]

The Krishi Rakshak Sangha, the peasant organization of the Patels of Mehsana district of Gujarat, blocked roads and railways and fought pitched-battles with the police. They also demanded better prices for groundnut and milk.

In Maharashtra which abounds in the production of onion and sugarcane, Sharad Joshi led an independent agitation in the regions of Nasik and Pune. His movement of peasants took off in 1977-78. The peasants mobilized as a group to effect change in the face of resistance. Sharad Pawar of Maharashtra with the alliance of other six parties, took out a long march from Jalgaon to Nagpur with a peasant strength of 8000.

In Tamilnadu, Narayan Swamy organized the peasants under the form of Tamilnadu Agriculturists Association in December,1983. His demands included a hike in paddy prices, writing off loans and remunerative prices for produce. The movement started by the peasants of Karnataka demanded a hike in support of price of *jowar* and maize.

The peasants of Uttar Pradesh and Bihar have also expressed their grievances against the increase in the price of input. Movement in the pattern of Nasik was launched by cane growers in both the states. Their demands included a fair share in the crops grown on the land owned by the Mahants.

There is lot of controversy among the scholars regarding the extent of the peasant uprising in India. Barrington Moore Jr. is of the opinion that the Indian peasant uprisings have been very weak in comparison to the Chinese peasant uprisings. He attributes the weakness of the Indian peasant uprisings to the caste system with its hierarchical divisions among villagers; and to the strength of bourgeois leadership against landlords and the British. Kathlene Gough does not agree with this view. She conducted a survey and discovered 77 revolts. 34 of these were solely or partly by the Hindus which caused her to doubt that the caste system has seriously impeded peasant uprisings in the time of trouble.[75]

Prof. Bipan Chandra has also admitted the limited character of the peasant uprising in India during the 19th century. He says that at no stage did the peasant uprising and popular uprisings of the 19th century threaten the British supremacy over India. Their anger was often directed against the indigo planters, the zamindars or the money-lenders. But, they also stoutly resisted the British efforts to bolster the colonial agrarian structure in the name of maintaining law and order.[76] Due to the paucity of the authentic source materials, we are too feeble to understand the peasant uprisings of India. There are hardly any records of the details of peasant resistance to the British colonialism. It is again complicated as most of the peasant uprisings have been listed as acts of lawlessness and robbery in the official records. Often they are also stated as 'communal riots' between the major religious cults or activities of 'criminal castes and tribes.' Credit goes to the scholars and researchers for whose labour we are able to have a clear idea about the peasant uprising during the colonial period.

Basising on the methods of organization, goals and ideology; Kathlene Gough classified the peasant uprisings in five categories, viz. mass insurrections for the redress of particular grievances; social banditary; terrorist revolt with ideas of meeting out collective justice; restorative revolts to drive out the British and restore earlier system and rule; religious revolts for the emancipation of a religion or an ethnic group under a new form of government.

The peasants organized certain mass insurrections with a view to seek redress of a particular vengeance. These mass insurrections were spontaneous, sporadic, sudden and lacked the religious or ideological basis. They often started in a peaceful manner, but assumed violent shape in the face of policy of oppression resorted to by the authorities. The chief factors which led to these risings were economic deprivation and exploitation due to the British policy and exactions by the landlords and money-lenders. The repeated outbreaks of the peasant struggles of Assam against the tax policy of the colonial government, viz. the *Raij mels* of 1861, 1868 and 1893-94 as well as the Jayantia people's war of resistance in 1861-63 were in line with broadly similar peasant and tribal revolts in many parts of India.[77]

VI

After studying the different peasant insurrections during the 18th and 19th centuries, we find that there was a growing consciousness among the Indian peasants to emancipate themselves from the oppression of money-lenders and zamindars. It also convinced them that the organized power of the government also solidly stood behind them, and they had to exert necessary pressure on the government before they could achieve anything substantial. Another feature of these uprisings was that they were sporadic and spontaneous; and in no way aimed at ending the British supremacy over India.[78]

The insurrections also contributed to the founding of the Indian National Congress. The massive fights put-up by the peasants shook the confidence of the British in their ability to hold on to their dominion in India. Scaring that the small bands of discontented peasants in different parts of their empire would coalesce with each other and assume the shape of a national revolt. A.O.Hume motivated by these considerations, took a lead and initiated action for the formation of the Indian National Congress.

The peasant uprisings of the 20th century unlike the 18th and 19th century lead us to some observations. The leadership of the peasant uprisings of the 20th century rests with the left-oriented political parties. The objective of these parties is to gain political power by mobilizing the peasant masses as their support base. The peasant uprisings in the 20th century in different parts of India are rooted in the process of modernization. Their leadership is provided by the Kulak peasants, rich peasants and the boggy of ex-jagirdars and zamindars. The struggles are mobilized to fulfil the vested interest of better off segments of the country. The struggles of the peasants are not the struggles of the deprived and relentlessly exploited landless labourers or untouchables; it is the localized caste-based rural resurgence. It also reveals that the demands of the peasant uprisings revolve round the interest of the rich peasants. Finally, the present day ills of the country manifesting themselves in poverty, famine, unemployment and economic inflation; can be wiped-out only through peasant-based revolution.

VII

While dealing with the nature and basic traits of the peasant movements in ancient, medieval and modern India; we have come across several instances projecting the impact of peasant movements in other countries beyond the jurisdiction of Indian territory. Hence, it is an endeavour to present a brief note about the peasant movements in ancient world.

The year of 579, saw a major peasant insurrection which was directed against the rule of Chilperich, the Merovingian king, in the course of which many peasants in the vicinity of Limoges left their holdings to escape excessive tax burdens. Tax collectors were threatened with death by the infuriated mob. So, at the end, military force was used to stop the rebellion. The biggest peasant rebellion in Carolingian times occurred in 841, when the peasants of Stellinga in Saxony protested against the Frankish type of feudal rule. In Saxony which had only recently been subjugated by the Frankish rulers, the process of feudalization was much slower than in the other provinces of the Frankish empire. Therefore, the conventional social structure of nobles, freemen and half-free survived longer in Saxony than elsewhere in the empire. The position of freemen and half-free who had fought most persistently against the Frankish conquerors, had deteriorated markedly with the invasion of the Franks and the introduction of their rule. Encouraged by open dissent among the sons of king Louis 'the Pious', the Saxon freemen and half-free arose in a big rebellious movement between 841 and 843. This Stellinga movement encompassed both dependent and free peasant groups, and was, primarily, directed against lay and ecclesiastical manorial lords whose position had improved since the Frankish conquest to the detriment of the peasantry. It took king Louis and the Saxon nobility several extremely violent campaigns to suppress the insurrection, which had spread over large parts of Saxony.

The resistance of the peasants against the heavy demands of the manorial lords grew in the medieval period with the rise of urban centre and the intensive development of landed resources. The frequent disputes of peasants with their lords concerning rights to woodlands and pastures lasted for several years. In 1210, a conflict was, finally, settled concerning the use of the woodlands between the monastery of Salem and the peasants of Oberzell, a village to the north of Lake Constance, which had lasted for several years. It had escalated particularly in 1198 when the inhabitants of Oberzell devastated a farm of the monastery at Adelsreute, an action for which they were sentenced to heavy punishment. A conflict which was also related to the use of the Commons was recorded between the abbey of Himmerode and a number of its villages. It was above all the peasants of Dudeldorf, Pickliessem and Gindorf who felt defrauded of their traditional right to use a large stretch of woodland, as a result of which they attacked a farm belonging to the monastery, seized its cattle and threw stones at the lay servants of the monastery. It was only after the inhabitants of the villages concerned faced with the possibility of being excommunicated, a compromise between the conflicting parties was reached in 1228, which put an end to the aggression on both sides. Similar struggles between assertive peasant communities and manorial lords, who tried to restrict their rights to the Commons, were also recorded in many other regions during the 13th century. The number of conflicts grew as arable land became scarce with the intensified development of land resources, a trend which incited many feudal lords to try and raise their revenues by limiting peasant rights to the Commons.

In the 13th and 14th centuries, peasants communities clashed with ambitious rulers, especially, in the Alpine provinces and along the coastlines of the North Sea where the rural population had fought hard to obtain a relatively independent social position and far reaching autonomy in communal matters. In the 13th century, the peasant insurrections and even the long peasant wars shook particularly such regions as Drente, West and East Frisia, the Stedingerland and Dithmarschen. The insurrection of Stedingers was one of the most impressive peasant revolts of the medieval ages. The Stedinger communities in the lower Weser area waged a major war against the archbishops of Bremen and the counts of Oldenburg in an effort to preserve their freedom. Yet although they fought for years; they were not as successful and the Frisians and eventually lost against the combined forces of their enemies.[79]

The Flemish revolt lasted for several years from 1323 to 1328. The principal targets of this revolt were lay manorial lords and administrative abuses by tax collectors and administrative officials. The centres of the revolt were the coastal areas of Flanders where the peasants had won considerable independence in the high middle ages. It started in the vicinity of Bruges during the winter of 1323, and was, at first, directed against the excesses of the judicial authorities who charged taxes and court fees in an arbitrary manner. The struggle against these individual abuses soon developed into a universal protest of assertive peasant communities who held much more far-reaching goals. In their rage, the rebels launched their assaults, mainly, on the castles of the nobility, which were often pillaged and destroyed in the course of revolt. Without meeting any serious opposition, the revolt soon affected the entire province and found the support of all towns except Ghent. The office-holders of the courts were replaced by representatives from the peasant estate, who maintained the normal administration for years. The decisive blow against the rebels, eventually, came from an army sent by the king of France at the request of the count of Flanders. After a big battle near Cassel in 1328, the Flemish peasant army was forced to surrender to the French Knights and 'this defeat marked the final collapse of the insurrection.'[80]

The Jacquerie of 1358, which was essentially a revolt caused by peasant destitution, was unique because of its surprising geographical spread over a very small time span. Heavy tax demands, the vast devastation of the country as a result of the hundred years war and innumerable lootings by impoverished mercenaries had driven the defenceless peasantry to despair. Faced with the wretchedness and insecurity of their condition, the peasants were allowed to form their own defence units to repulse the assaults of vagrant mercenary gangs. In the last days of May, 1358, an open insurrection started in the Beauvais region which soon spread into Picardy and other neighbouring areas. In many places, the rebellious peasant troops, which for the most part operated independent of each other, forced procrastinating individuals to join them. Great bitterness was felt towards a nobility which only pursued its own interests and often participated in pillaging the countryside rather than protecting the peasants and their villages. Hence, the peasants answered with destruction of many castles and mansions, often driving away the owners. Most towns, however, were undecided and only a few of them were active supporters of the revolt. It was soon plain

41

that the insurrection was highly spontaneous in character and lacked a political perspective, for it collapsed after a few months despite its vast geographical extent.[81]

The German peasant revolts in the late middle age became much more frequent in the late 14th and 15th centuries, and had a much greater political impetus than their forerunners. In the 14th century, only 4 major peasant revolts were recorded while this number increased to 15 in the first half and then to 25 in the second half of the 15th century. These revolts mainly occurred in the south of Germany.

In south-west Germany, the grave consequences of the agrarian crisis induced many lords to strengthen the ties of personal lordship over their peasants so as to prevent them from moving elsewhere as well as to compensate for losses in income by charging higher dues. But around the year 1370, a serious conflict developed between the monastery at Hauenstein and its peasants concerning the terms of serfdom which, finally, culminated in an insurrection. The peasants had sought to escape from the monastery by moving into towns and refusing to pay the dues connected with their status as bondsmen. After years of conflict, a legal agreement was reached in 1383 which permitted the peasants to move in to those towns which acknowledged that it was legitimate for the monastery to demand the payment of heriot. In cases where a bondsman failed to obey this rule, the monastery was entitled to confiscate both his movable and immovable property.

There was scarcity of labour following the depopulation after the Black-Death in England. The land-owners had a lot of land in their hands which required tilling. Many land-owners had to take recourse to hired labour whereas they relied on the manorial villeins before the plague. Hired labourers were not abundant at that time which put them in a very commanding position. The landlords found it difficult to cope with the situation and therefore, they appealed to parliament to eradicate the problem through some form of legislation. 'The Statute of Labourer' passed by parliament in 1351, sought to offer remedies in the event of the situation precipitated by the Black Death, but in reality, it was an indirect attempt to give the land-owners control over labourers even in the changed conditions. Indeed, the statute was highly impractical in the context of the situation that existed after the plague. In the course of the implementation of the statute, there was a strong ignition as it forced the labourers to be tied to the land. Once again, labourers who fled their employers were branded as falsity. The Statute of Labourer was one of the instruments that provoked the peasants to revolt against the oppressive working standards. Such provocation touched its pinnacle when another oppressive poll tax was imposed on the peasants. The rising originated from an unpopular poll tax. Its oppressive and corrupt administration caused local revolts in Essex and Kent which became the signal for a national rebellion.[82]

In 1377, the parliament imposed a poll tax of a groat or four-pence on all English people above 14 years, except beggars. Two years later in 1379, there was an enhancement to the tax which was now increased on the wealthier nobility while a peasant was required to pay a groat as earlier. In 1380, however, the matters became worse when a new tax of three groats was imposed on all persons above fifteen, irrespective of their condition. The peasantry was incensed by this tyrannical poll tax and within months there was a consolidation of the public against it. The first outbreak of the revolt took place in Kent when one Wat Tyler murdered a tax-collector and marched to Canterbury. He headed a large group of protestors who destroyed many manorial records that came to their way. According to Trevelyan, 'the revels invaded the manor houses and abbeys, extorted the right they claimed and burnt obnoxious charters and manor rolls.'[83]

Spontaneous revolt took place in Hertfordshire and Essex. Riots started entire England and the basic demands of the rioters were the abolition of the institution of villeinage, freedom to the peasants and access to markets. One of the drawbacks of the revolt was that it took place in the towns. The Archbishop of Canterbury was murdered, the tower of London was looted and countless justices and manorial heads were assaulted or manhandled. Such violence did not help the peasants to arrive at their objects. The murder of Wat Tyler by London's Mayor caused the spark for the revolt to run-out. Soon, Richard II, the king of England was able to quell the revolt within three weeks of Tyler's death. The king and the nobility did not keep the promises that they made and the abolition of villeinage was pushed further in to the future.

According to Trevelyan, the rebellion had been a great incident and its history throws a flood of light on the English folk of that day. Historian cannot decide whether it helped or retarded the movement for the abolition of serfdom, which continued at much the same pace after 1381 as before. But the spirit that had prompted the rising was one of the chief reasons why serfdom died out in England as it did not die out on the continent of Europe.[84]

The Knights revolt of 1523 was followed by a peasant revolt in Germany. Leopold Von Ranke called the peasant war of 1525 as 'the outstanding natural phenomenon in German history.'[85]

The peasant class in Germany had been fully exploited and the clergy too had a share in this. The peasants had social and economic grievances and finally, the religious ferment added fuel to the fire on it. As a result of which, the movement assumed serious proportions. Headed by fanatics, various groups of peasants freely indulged in ghastly acts of crimes. Martin Luther saw in this revolt the possibility of a danger to the reform movement and so, it was put-down. The peasants did not like the protestants as they suppressed their revolt with the help of the princes of German states. The medieval peasant was not a tenant in the modern sense of the term; rather he was dependent on or subject to his lord in a variety of ways. A powerful factor of peasant existence in medieval feudal society was the bondage to the feudal lord. Until German peasants were emancipated in the 19th century, majority of them depended on feudal lords who were entitled to various tributes and services. Taxes had to be paid upon marriage and death; on St. George's and St. Martin's Day; and in spring and in autumn. Pathetically, little remained for the peasants in years of bad harvests and even in normal years, the remaining supplies only allowed for a modest livelihood.[86]

G.Franz regards each and every peasant revolt of the 14th and 15th centuries 'as a precursor of the peasants' war of 1525.' Even, Peter Blickle, the author of the most recent comprehensive study of this event has also endorsed this view.[87]

Predominantly, during the Tokugawa period, Japan was an agricultural country. More than 80% of the total population accepted agriculture as their principal profession. The government revenue was, mainly, collected from the poor peasants to maintain the government and support the idle *samurais*. This led to a chronic economic distress in the country which, ultimately, culminated in peasant uprisings. The economic growth of the merchants was highly responsible for the deterioration of the peasants economy. The stability of a society depends mainly upon its sound economic system. But the history of Tokugawa period was a stay of growing dissatisfaction with economic conditions. It, gradually, undermined the era of stability inaugurated by the early Tokugawas. With the emergence of township and merchant community, the peasant economy met a great set back. These economic discontent found their expression in numerous peasant uprising in

Japan. These peasant uprisings, gradually, gained momentum during the time of floods, drought and adverse price of commodities. No provision was made 'for import of food grains from other countries to relieve the starving millions at the time of the failure of crops' which culminated their anger.[88]

Abolition of feudalism in 1871 in Japan directly affected the farmers. The peasants were now freed from the feudal obligations and became free holders. There was also a drastic change in the system of revenue collection. During the feudal regime, taxes were collected in kind, according to the value of the crops; and the peasants were left with no more than just enough to live on. Thus, the feudal lords were the real care-takers of the peasants in the sense that in the time of need, they used to help the peasants under their jurisdiction. But under the new government after the abolition of feudalism, the taxes were collected in cash, according to the value of the land. Moreover, the peasants were not forced to stick to their land. They were at liberty either to remain on their land or sell it out and leave for the city.

The Agricultural conflicts popularly known as 'Swing Riots' took place in England in 1830-31. The production of agriculture came down heavily following the Napoleonic wars and even after that. The matter was far from improving. Poor harvests and increasing prices bitterly affected the British economy which led to labour-unrest creating a complicated and difficult situation. Unemployed number had risen and a collective dissatisfaction found manifestation in the agricultural disorders, the first of which began in Kent in 1830. The unrest speedily spread to other areas of England. The name 'Swing' associated with the riots was derived from Captain Swing, who led the rioters by writing anonymous letters. Loss of property and the destruction of equipment was common. About 2000 of the protestors were arrested and 19 were hanged. Though the riot was quickly curbed, but despite that, it brought some issues relating to agricultural and working conditions into sharp focus and was influential in bringing the Reform Act of 1832. The Swing Riots also highlighted other social discrepancies by involving the general population in the affected areas.

The economic condition of China during the Manchu rule was, partially, responsible for the outbreak of Tai-Ping rebellion in China, which continued from 1851 to 1864 under the leadership of Hung Hsiu-Chuan. It was, basically, a peasant movement. There was economic dislocation due to accumulation of land in large holdings. There was no equal distribution of land; and the poor peasants, the real tillers of the soil, were put to the mercy of the landlords for a piece of land. The situation was further aggravated by the profit-mongering merchants who used to hoard food-grains in huge quantity until the price was raised abnormally. The situation was worst confounded by the increase of population. This increase of population without corresponding increase of arable land caused acute food-shortage which affected the poorer section of the people most. Large scale importation of finished foreign goods also shattered the rural economy of china. It affected cottage industries which was subsidiary to agriculture of the local craftsmen and small traders. Another economic factor which was especially injurious to the tax payers was the sudden increase of the value of silver in comparison to copper. As the agricultural tax was calculated in silver but paid in copper, the tax burden of the peasants increased heavily. Thus, the economic mal-adjustment in the country infuriated millions of poor and unprivileged, who were out to join the rebellion.

The economic distress was further worsened by floods and famine in South China. The people of Kwangshi, Kwantung and Hunaor provinces suffered a lot due to recurring floods which caused constant failure of crops. Finally, starvation and malnutrition broke the morale of the people. The corrupt government machinery failed to tackle the situation to redress the minimum grievances of the hungry millions. The people came out to join the rebels in large number out of utter dejection. It made the confusion more confounded. This revolt was, practically, a crusade against feudalism; and its aims and objects was to re-distribute land among the Chinese, taking into consideration its productivity. The rebels attempted to dissolve the big land-holdings for improving the condition of the poor peasants, but failed miserably!

Notes & References

1.	Sarma, R.S.	*India's Ancient Past,* Oxford University Press, New Delhi, 2008, P. 272.
2.	Habib, I.	*Essays in Indian History-towards a Marxist perception,* Tulika Books, New Delhi, 2001, P. 110.
3.	*Ibid.*	P. 111.
4.	Sarma	*op. cit.,* P. 78.
5.	Tripathi, R.S.	*History of Ancient India,* Motilal Banarsidass, Delhi, Reprinted, 1987, P. 18.
6.	Jha, D.N.	*Ancient India in Historical outline,* Manohar, New Delhi, Reprinted, 2001, P. 46.
7.	Sarma	*op. cit.* P. 120.
8.	*Ibid.*	P. 273.
9.	Choudhury, K.A.	*Ancient agriculture and forestry in Northern India,* Bombay, 1977, PP. 60-63.
10.	Habib	*op. cit.* P. 118.
11.	*Ibid.*	PP. 119-120.
12.	*Ibid.*	PP. 120-121.
13.	Thakur, V.K.	'The peasant in early India problems of identification and differentiation' in *Peasants in Indian History-I,* Thakur V.K. (eds), Patna, Delhi, 1996, P. 137.
14.	Jain, V.K.	'Dynamics of Hydraulic Activity and Agrarian formation during the Mauryan and Post-Mauryan period', *op. cit.,* Thakur & Aounshuman (eds), P. 254.
15.	Liu, Xinru	'Some Kharosthi records concerning irrigation co-operatives in the Kushana period', *op. cit.,* Thakur & Aounshuman (eds), P. 262.
16.	Sarma, R.S.	*Indian Feudalism (c. AD 300-1200),* Macmillan India Ltd., Madras, Reprinted, 1996, P. 32.
17.	Habib	*op. cit.,* P. 123.
18.	*Ibid.*	P. 124.
19.	*Ibid.*	P. 126.
20.	Jaiswal, Suvira	*The origin and development of Vaishnavism,* Delhi, 1967, PP. 110-115.

21. Stein, Burton — *Peasant, state and society in medieval South India*, Oxford University Press, Delhi, 1999, PP. 70-71, 83.

22. *Ibid.* — PP. 16,24.

23. Sarma, R.S. — *Aspects of political ideas and institutions in ancient India*, Delhi, 1959, PP. 22-23.

24. Habib — *op. cit.*, P. 133.

25. Burton — *op. cit.*, P. 145.

26. Parasher, Aloka — 'Writing on villages and peasants in early India—problems in historiography', *op. cit.*, Thakur & Aounshuman (eds), P. 81.

27. Jha, D.N. — 'Land revenue in India' in *Historical Studies*, Sarma R.S.(eds), Delhi, 1971, P. 5.

28. Sarma, R.S. — *Indian Feudalism*, PP. 265, 267.

29. Sequeira, G. & Quadres, S. — *History of Ancient India-I*, J.J.Publications, Mangalore, First Edition, 2001, P. 326.

30. Sarma, R.S. — *India's Ancient Past*, PP. 268-269.

31. Sarma, R.S. — *Indian Feudalism*, PP. 156,209

32. — *Early medieval Indian society*, P. 215.

33. *Ibid.* — PP. 214-215.

34. *Ibid.* — PP. 215-216.

35. Maiti, P. — *Studies in ancient India*, Sreedhar Prakashan, Kolkata, 2007, P. 551

36. Sarma — *Indian Feudalism*, P. 298.

37. — *Early medieval Indian society*, P. 216.

38. Habib — *op. cit.*, P. 146.

39. *Ibid.* — P. 147.

40. Chandra, Satish — 'The Mughal state-review of the crisis of the Jagirdars system' in *the Mughal state* (1526-1750), Alam M.& Subrahmanyam (eds), Oxford University Press, New Delhi, 2008, P. 347.

41. Alam, M. — 'Aspect of agrarian uprisings in North India in early 18th century', *op. cit.*, Alam & Subrahmanyam (eds), P. 471.

42. Smith, Wilfred Cantwell — 'Lower class uprisings in the Mughal empire', *op. cit.*, Alam & Subrahmanyam (eds), P. 325-326.

43. Habib — *op. cit.*, PP. 154-155.

44. — *Early medieval Indian society*, P. 216.

45. Mukherjee, L.   *History of India*, M. L. Mukherjee, Clacutta, 29th Edition, P. 61.
46. Srivastava, A.L.   *The Sultanate of Delhi*, Agarwala & Company, Agra, 1971, PP. 189-190.
47. Bhuyan, S.K. (ed)   *Kamrupar Buranji*, Calcutta, 1930, P. 27.
48. Gautam, Bhadra   'Two frontier uprisings in Mughal India,' *op. cit.*, Alam & Subrahmanyam (eds), P. 480.
49. *Ibid.*   P. 485.
50. *Ibid.*   P. 481.
51. Habib   *op. cit.*, P. 157.
52. Banerjee, A.C.   *A New History of Medieval India*, S. Chand & Company Ltd., P. 289.
53 Habib   *op. cit.*, P. 159.
54. Rana, R.P.   'Was there an agrarian crisis in Mughal North India?' in *Social Scientist*, Vol. 34, Prabhat Patnaik (ed), Tulika, New Delhi, Nov-Dec, 2006, PP. 25-26.
55. *Ibid.*   PP. 22-23, 27.
56. Pande, Rekha   'Writings on peasants in medieval India—historiographical critique', *op. cit.*, Thakur & Aounshuman (eds), P. 99.
57. *cf.* Doshi, S.L. Jain, P.C.   *Rural Sociology*, Rawat Publications, Jaipur & New Delhi, Reprinted, 2006, P. 229.
58. Saikia, Rajen   Social and Economic History of Assam (1853-1921), Manohar, New Delhi, 2001, P. 110.
59. Sarkar, Sumit   *Modern India* (1885-1947), Macmillan, Delhi, Reprinted, 2008, P. 44.
60. Doshi & Jain   *op. cit.*, P. 232.
61. Sarma, Dr. Debabrata   'Saotal Ganasangramar Itihash', in *Asomiya Khabar*, Dr. Khiren Roy (ed), 6th. Feb., 2008.
62. *cf.* Sen, Ranjit   'The peasant question in Bengal in the second half of the 19th century—a note on the marginal peasants', *op. cit.*, Thakur & Aounshuman (eds), P. 462.
63. *cf.* Doshi & Jain   *op. cit.*, P. 237.
64. Siddiqi, M.H.   'History and society in a popular rebellion Mewat (1920-1933)' in *the Past in the present*, Dr. Kumkum Roy (Co-Ordinator), Academic Staff College, JNU, New Delhi, 2001, P. 442.

65. Mukherjee, M.   'Peasant resistance and peasant consciousness in colonial India-Subalterns and beyond', in *Economic and Political weekly*, Oct. 8, 1988, P. 2113.

66. *Ibid.*   P. 2113.

67. *Ibid.*   P. 2113.

68. Biswas, G.R.   *Peasant movement in N.E.India* (1946-50), Regency Publication, New Delhi, 2002, P. 17.

69. *Ibid.*   P. 6.

70. Sarkar, Sumit   *op. cit.,* P. 442.

71. Mukherjee, M.   *op. cit.,* P. 2113.

72. Doshi & Jain   *op. cit.,* P. 252.

73. Mukherjee, M.   *op. cit.,* P. 2113.

74. Doshi & Jain   *op. cit.,* P. 259.

75. Gough, Kathlene   'Indian peasant uprising' in *Economic and Political weekly*, Vol. IX, 32-34, Special Number, Aug. 1974, P. 1393.

76. Chandra, Bipan   *India's Struggle for Independence* (1857-1947), Penguin Books, New Delhi, 1998, PP. 50-51.

77. Guha, A.   *Planter Raj to Swaraj* (1826-1947), Tulika, New Delhi, 2006, P. 274.

78. Raychaudhury, S.C.   *Modern India*, Surjeet Publications, New Delhi, P. 354

79. Rösener, Werner   *Peasant in the Middle Ages,* Polity Press, Cambridge, 1996, P. 246.

80. *Ibid.*   P. 250.

81. *Ibid.*   P. 249.

82. Trevelyan, G.M.   *English Social History*, Orient Longman Ltd., Mumbai, 2001, P. 14.

83. *Ibid.*   P. 14.

84. *Ibid.*   P. 14.

85. Werner   *op. cit.,* P. 8.

86. *Ibid.*   PP. 7, 16.

87. *Ibid.*   PP. 241-242

88. Singh, A.K.   *History of Far-East in Modern times*, Surjeet Publications, New Delhi, PP. 5,7.

CHAPTER – THREE

THE AGRARIAN POLICY: THE BRITISH VIS-A-VIS THE PEASANTS

Su-ka-pha founded the Ahom rule in 1228 and the Ahoms dominated the Brahmaputra valley for about six centuries prior to the inclusion of Assam by the East India Company in 1826. Instead of organizing the land system on the basis of areas of land, it was organized on the basis of the people engaged in it. Wet-grounds and swamps were brought into the state of cultivation by the Ahoms through collective efforts, and made them fit for the cultivation of rice. It is agriculture that besieges a dominant place in the economy of the state of Assam. Assam is a peasants' land par excellence; not only her economy but also her social and cultural patterns are determined by this avocation.[3] Agricultural lands during the Ahom regime were distributed amongst various families. This type of land became the foundation and support of the entire Ahom state.

During the early part of the Ahom occupation of the valley, almost major part of the region except some selected areas, was under shifting cultivation pursued by the tribes, mostly of the Bodo Kachari origin. Insptite of the best efforts of the Ahom rulers, agricultural extension was sometimes handicapped in the valley by natural as well as human factors. But, the Ahom rulers fully utilized the existing manpower and every possible advanced technology to overcome them, and thus, brought considerable amount of land under cultivation even at the initial stage of their rule. New lands were either made revenue free or were given to the peasants for a lump sum of its produce as revenue. This policy encouraged the peasants to open new lands time and again.[4] As a result, ¾ of the total land area in Upper Assam came under the cultivation prior to the *Moamariya* rebellion.[5]

In north-eastern region and as such in Assam, methods of cultivation, mainly, depended on ethnic heritage and geographical situation of the lands. As a matter of fact, agriculture system as a whole was largely marked by tribal ways of farming. In subsequent period, the Ahoms had developed agricultural tradition. Anyway, the period witnessed tribal and non-tribal, both methods of cultivation.

All the tribes were adapted to shifting rice cultivation. Crops were produced with less utilization of labour and use of very ordinary tools. The native set fire in the jungle to clear the land of cultivation. The jungle was burnt down and for three successive years, two crops were annually realized from it. After the land had been, thus, impoverished, it was allowed to remain fallow for three years; and fresh jungle land was prepared in the same primitive way and with most simple implements of husbandry.[6]

According to M'Cosh, 'the grain is first sown on a piece of well manured garden land and when about a foot high is transplanted in masses into large *khates* previously ploughed and in a state of inundation.'[7]

Early records show that the Ahom kings built large number of embankments, spurs cum roads with *paik* labourers to prevent floods and protect the agricultural field from the raids of the Brahmaputra and her tributaries. The Bhuyans of Assam built embankments on the river Tembuwani and Magurijan for protection of crops and houses.[8]

Assam, where rainfall is copious throughout the year, provides a fertile soil for cultivation and rice is raised extensively throughout the state.[9]

The system of irrigation essential for wet rice culture was in some form prevalent since early times among some people of Assam, and it is known from some contemporary foreign accounts. For example, Yuan Chwang, the Chinese traveller who visited Kamrup in the middle of the 7th century described in his account that water led from the rivers or from banked-up lakes flowed round the towns. During the Ahom regime, irrigation and flood control work were undertaken as a state policy so that the flat level lands opened up for rice cultivation could contain only that amount of water which was actually needed for good cultivation.[10]

Fertilizer in the modern sense of the term was only a recent development in Assam. Gunabhiram Barua in the last part of the 19th century remarks that the people of Assam did neither use fertilizer nor artificially irrigate their fields for the improvement of the fertility of the soil.[11] Chemical fertilizer was hardly in use in Assam even as late as the 20th century. Natural vegetation and soil fertility made the use of manure in Assam a matter of secondary importance.

Implements of cultivation in Assam during ancient and medieval period were simple. The implements included a *nangal* with a *phal, jabaka* and *dalimari*, a *mai, juwali* (yoke), *kachi, da,* knives etc. Different types of bamboo baskets like *dulie, mer, kharahi, pachi* etc. were used to keep the products.[12] The inhabitants of the lower Brahmaputra valley had possibly the knowledge of the use of plough drawn by a pair of bullocks much earlier to those of the upper valley. The Ahoms inherited the use of domestic buffalo in ploughing from their earlier abode in South East Asia.

The *Yogini Tantra,* an early 16th century Sanskrit work of Assam, speaks of as many as twenty varieties of rice. The *Katha Guru Charit* contains numerous references to rice cultivation, and mentions its varieties. The *Fathiya-i-Ibriya* and the *Alamgirnama,* both speak of extensive rice cultivation in Assam.

The Statistical Account of Assam by Hunter mentions as many as eighty-seven varieties of rice.[13] Of these, the most peculiar three varieties were *chakua, bara* and *jaha. Chakua* and *bara* were so soft that people in Assam used to take them un-boiled just soaking in water which was then called *komal chaul* or *bokachaul.* It should be mentioned that the *paik* militia while in the battle field, mostly depended on *komal chaul* with ripe banana.[14]

Land revenue formed the basis of the state's existence in the medieval period. In a society of self-sufficient economy, where money hardly played any serious role in state maintenance; land, labour and the produce of the soil formed the major sources of meeting the state expenditure. Rulers of medieval Assam, therefore, took every care to register quality lands and the peasantry who worked on it. The Ahoms rulers had a peculiar system of collection of revenue. Here, not only the soil, but its people were also considered as property of the state.[15]

During the initial stage of the Ahom period, revenue was in form of manual labour, but later on, as a result of the extension of the state machinery and growth of different profession, non manual working groups also became necessary.[16]

There was the system of paying revenue in kind and cash also. A *paik* peasant, on rare occasions could avail the option to pay revenue in cash at the rate of Rs. 2 or 3 per head instead of giving his personal service.

Revenue system of Lower Assam was somewhat different from that of Upper Assam. This was due to the fact that there was already a well established system of administration in Mughal pattern which was almost impossible to be replaced by a new one entirely. When the Ahom rulers occupied Kamrup, they did not abolish the former structure of land revenue. Instead, keeping the old system almost intact, it was provisioned that land and properties of the revenue officers in Kamrup were to be increased proportionately to the amount of revenue they could actually deposit to the state treasury. As a result, when in Upper Assam every peasant possessed a piece of land and had collection of paddy to meet the needs of his family for the whole year; the peasant in Lower Assam, on the contrary, had accepted bondage as a way of living.[17]

The peasants got incentive from the state to clear new lands for cultivation of some seasonal crops like mustard, pulses, sugarcane, gourds etc. With no revenue or little, they possess temporarily certain amount of additional fertile lands. According to Goswami, no land revenue was imposed during the Ahom rule excepting the cleared jungles.[18] If anyone cleared jungles for cultivation, he was allowed to hold that land on payment of one or two rupees per annum per *pura*. But he could enjoy it till then so long it was not required for settlement to other *paiks*. Moreover, some time some settlers were permitted to cultivate inundated lands on payment of a nominal plough tax to the state. Artisans and others had to pay a higher poll tax as they did not cultivate land. Thus, even though the Ahom revenue and civil administration possessed many characters of a feudal society, it had some safety—valves in the form of liberty and possession so that the peasants were not like the serfs in a typical feudal social system.

Regarding revenue free grants of lands, it can be said that such grants were given to the nobles, officials and the priests. This system was developed and maintained all through the entire period of Ahom rule until the 19th century.[19] Land donation practice for charitable rule and religious purposes was prevalent in Ahom period, and it became popular after the Ahoms embraced the Hinduism. The *lakhiraj* estates which were granted for religious and other related purposes were of three classes, viz. (i) *debottar* lands appropriated and dedicated to temples and idols, (ii) *dharmottar* lands dedicated to religious purposes and (iii) *brahmottar* lands granted to priests and learned people. It remains expressed that the *lakhiraj* estates were revenue free estates.

The families of Parbatia Goswami had 41,000 acres of *nisfkhiraj* and *lakhiraj* land spread over to 31 *mauzas*. It was estimated in 1883 that Parbatia Goswami and *Madhav Devalay* (a shrine) accounted for no less than 1,000 tenants, and they did not enjoy occupancy rights anywhere in the Brahmaputra valley.[20]

The process of systematic and regular land survey and measurement under the Ahoms started since the inception of the 17th century. One chronicle states that king Pratap Singha introduced the system of measuring lands by using a bamboo pole which was 7½ cubits and 4 fingers long, a system which was used in measurement of land in the Mughal Bengal. Different units of land measurement denoting different measures were in use in medieval Assam.[21]

Except the nobles, priests and persons of high caste; the male population between the age group of 15 and 50 was required to render services to the state. The Ahom rulers of medieval period organized the peasantry in such a way that the state could obtain the maximum use of its labour force through the *paiks*. Such persons known as *paiks* were personally allotted to the high officials, priests and elites in lieu of allowances and regular salary. Two *puras* (about 3 acres) of good quality land free of charge was given to each *paik* in return for his services. A *paik* could also pay Rs.2 per annum instead of rendering personal services. *Paiks* were also granted land for homestead called *bari,* for which they were to pay a poll or hearth or house tax of about one rupee per annum. The *bhaktas* loyal to Neo-*vaishnavite satras* were exempted from rendering physical services in royal house and even their name had been excluded from the *paik* list.[22] This was an example of social-injustice existed in the society.

The *paiks* paid throughout the country a poll tax, variously named in Kamrup as house tax; in Nowgong, Lakhimpur proper and Sibsagar as body or poll tax, both at one rupee for each *paik* of full age. In Darrang, a hearth tax upon every party looking separately high or low, of one rupee was imposed.

The *paik* system had assumed a complete and elaborate structure. Four *paiks* were grouped under a *got* (unit), but the number was, finally, reduced to three in Upper Assam. One member of each *got* was forced to be present in rotation for work as might be required of him and during his absence from home, the other members were expected to cultivate his land and keep him supplied with food. In times of war, two members of a *got* or three if situation demanded, might be called on to attend the war field and it was the tradition, in times of peace, to employ the *paiks* on public and philanthropic works. Like a bondsman, a *paik* had to render his compulsory manual service and other kinds of duties to the state. But in regard to possession of certain political rights, he was sometime treated as free citizen. This was a most valuable privilege whereby the *paiks* were saved from much of the oppression of . . . . [23].

The *paiks* were further grouped under the *khels*, which ultimately developed in to a full-winged part of the state instruments. There was regular gradation of officers. A *Bora* commanded twenty *paiks*; a *Saikia* hundred; *Hazarika, Rajkhowa* and *Phukan* likewise commanded one, three and six thousand *paiks*. The system maintained a rigid discipline like a regular army.

Many elements of tribal economy crept in to the Ahom land system, which could be stated as feudal in character. In the words of Guha, 'these were indeed feudal estates in a largely semi-tribal, semi-feudal society.'[24] Three categories of people could be ascertained in such land system, viz. the aristocracy, the feudal lords who had revenue free lands and servile dependents to cultivate and work; the servile-population the slaves, serfs and tenants who were absolutely parasite on these landlords and cultivated their lands; and finally, a large number of peasantry holding land directly from the state and paying a rent to it. Of the three categories, majority of the population belonged to the third category, but despite that, they did not form the sole groups. Though there were differences among slaves, serfs and tenants but these differences became hazy and obscure except in the case of domestic slaves. They were all dependent and parasite peasants, working under homogenous umbrellas.

Economy of Assam during the Ahom regime was backward, and use of money was limited and trade among the peasants was largely absent, everything was produced at home. Kaushal is right when he opines that before the advent of the British, Indian economy was in a state of equilibrium, though at a low level. Agriculture, then as now, was a gamble in monsoon.[25]

The villages, in short, are a network in Assam and they are mostly self-sufficient in their economy. Simplicity in the social system and patterns of life is their keynote. The peasant ploughs the land and produce his own food; he builds his house with thatches and bamboos collected from the jungles.[26]

Due to the fertility of the soil and copious rainfall, state could extract surplus and these surplus agricultural commodities were exported from Assam to Bengal, Bhutan, Tibbet and Burma. Thus, the Ahoms kept their trade relations with their neighbouring states. Pemberton in his reports gives a vivid description on the export and import goods from and to Assam. Assam exported cotton, black and long pepper, mustard seeds, fruits like *thaikol* to Bengal in 1809 in Ahom regime.[27] This proves that from long period, Assam was rich in her agri-products and by exercising her trade relations with neighbouring states, she enriched her economy.

Like men, the women of Assam have a distinct place in the economy of the family. They mostly in eastern Assam, take active role in the rearing of crops. They transplant the paddy seedlings and reap the harvest when ripe. It is a pretty sight to see an Assamese girl, a blue mountain under whiffs of vagrant clouds.[28]

However, the people were satisfied with the policy of the state during Ahom period, but that does not mean that they had no grievances at all. Despite that, they were more or less content and happy under the state. The government was more or less concerned for their countrymen and formulated policy for their interest. There was no difference between the rulers and the ruled. Same land and same people feelings gave birth to tolerance and philanthropic attitude among them, in spite of having discrimination and exploitation against one another. But the same people became discontented and ventilated their grievances against the policy of the government in later period. As a result, several peasant uprisings took place in Assam in 19th century. This time, there was difference between the rulers and the ruled. The rulers were outsiders, and the ruled were from the land. Outsiders formulated policy for their own interest, what the native did not like and therefore, opposed it tooth and nail. Ultimately, this gave birth to ignition and confrontation.

The peasant is always in close contact with his land. It is the land which survives him. Historically, for Indian peasant, land is the hope and glory of the rural people. From time immemorial, land continues to be the mainstay of the people and it constitutes not only the structural feature of the Indian countryside but changes in land relations act as the prime mover of social, economic and political transformation as well. It is the land which constitutes the major source of livelihood for the village people. According to one estimate, nearly 3/5 of world population derived their livelihood from agriculture. Most of the peasants do not have their own land and they purchase rights of cultivation and occupancy from others. Land involves an interaction between the land-owner and the actual cultivator. But unfortunately, the dominant castes that have control over major portions of land suppress and exploit the sub-ordinate classes. Oliver Mendelsohn and Marika Vicziany who have discussed the rural land reform with reference to untouchables, argue that the sub-ordinated people have gained nothing out of land reforms.

Due to the decline of indigenous industries, pressure on land augmented resulting the fragmentation of land. Differences in the size of land have created diverse agricultural classes in rural society giving birth to big, small, marginal and landless labourers.[29]

The English East India Company's arrival to India is remarkable in world history from the colonial and commercial point of view. The British colonization of North East India is a fascinating episode who first appeared as traders, and then, gradually took over the reign of administrations and converted it into a colony of Britain. The colonization of North East India in the 19th century was directly influenced by the policy of promotion of the British commerce. The first blood was drawn by annexing Assam which was the largest and the richest in the region.

The British policy towards the trade and markets in North East India and the way they used these markets for economic penetration and colonization, was in no way different from how they colonized the whole of India or established colonies elsewhere in Asia or Africa. They appeared first as traders and next penetrated deep into the mainstay of life and finally, conquered the region in several installments over a period of about hundred years.[30]

The people hoped that with the advent of the British, troubles would end and under a restored native government, peace and prosperity would return to the land. But their hopes were soon belied and the first flush of enthusiasm was logically followed by growing discontent of the people.[31] The people at large in the initial stages welcomed the advent of the British because the latter had expelled the Burmese who had been responsible for reducing Assam to dire straits. Assam had been depopulated to a great extent under the stress of protracted wars and oppression; the peasants had to give-up cultivation, living mainly on wild roots and plants. Famine and pestilence stalked the land.

The enigma of economic backwardness and underdevelopment; issues of rural unrest and violence and of social institutions; and values all are involved in the basic nature of the agrarian question.[32] Daniel Thorner writing on Indian land reform problems in 'the Agrarian Prospect in India' states that the agrarian structure is, after all, not an external framework within which various classes function, but rather it is the sum total of ways in which each group operates in relation to other groups. Notwithstanding this comprehensive definition, he is concerned with only a part of the totality of relations namely those related to the politics of contemporary land reform.[33]

The land reform system under which the cultivator works is of key importance in determining the pace and character of agricultural development. The agrarian structure in the country, despite recent reforms, continues to affect adversely the status of the farmer, as also his capacity to make investments. Further, in an overwhelming number of cases, the size of the unit of cultivation is too far below the minimum required for progressive agriculture.[34]

Baden Powell has contended that the ryotwari village was the original type in India. The ryotwari was first made by Captain Read and Thomas Munro in the districts of Bara Mahal in 1792. Gradually, it was extended to other parts of the province where permanent settlement of the land revenue had not been made or where the permanently settled estates were sold up for inability to pay the fixed revenue. In course of time, it spread to Bombay, Assam and Berar also. Under the ryotwari settlement, every registered holder of land was recognized as its proprietor. He paid revenue directly to the government. He was at liberty to sublet his property or to transfer it by gift, sale or mortgage. He could not be ejected from his land till he paid the revenue. In the long run, the ryotwari settlement created a group of peasants who were sub-ordinate to the proprietor of the land.[35] In ryotwari settlement, each cultivator could hold land as a separate estate under the government and it seemed to have given impetus to the peasantry. The ryotwari settlement included the peasant proprietors who were themselves owners of the land. Desai has made three divisions of the class of peasant proprietors namely upper, lower and middle-class land-owners. With the passage of time, the number of lower classes peasantry increased. A large number of them were reduced to the status of agricultural labourers and paupers.[36]

Inspite of having its merits, the system resulted many evils. Since the Company entered in to agreement with each ryot, the traditional sense of unity that existed among the members of the village community, disappeared. Quite some time, the assessment was thought excessive and this resulted in substantial land going out of cultivation, many ryots abandoning cultivation and fleeing into neighouring areas. Moreover, if a ryot felt that assessment in his case was excessive, he had to deal individually with the state and not through the village community. This naturally reduced his bargaining power and thus, chances of getting his grievance redress were abated.[37] Thomas Munroe said 'it is the system which has always prevailed in the past.' But, the primary consideration to devise a settlement directly with the cultivator was the motive of financial gain to the Company. It resulted in the ryotwari settlement. The primary aims of the ryotwari settlement were the regular collection of revenue and amelioration of the condition of the ryots. The first was realized but the second remained unfulfilled.

A majority of peasants in agricultural India are tenant peasants. Tenancy had its beginning during the colonial period when the British introduced permanent land settlement. Tenants constitute a heterogeneous groups; interestingly enough, some of them are also land-owners. Actually, there are variations among them.[38]

The ryots of Goalpara had been exploited and squeezed by the zamindars and their sub-ordinates. In general sense, they governed over the ryots. On the other hand, there was co-existence of the British imperialism with that of the zamindars' economic relation as a result of which few zamindars also suffered along with the ryots.[39] The British adopted various policies and introduced many reforms. Outer motives of all these were well and good, but their inner motives were only appropriation and exploitation. The most important evil resulting from their rule was the *drain of wealth* which impoverished the country. Probably, between the Plassey and the Waterloo (1757-1815), a sum of 1000 million pounds sterling was transferred from India to English banks.[40]

Land is the gift of God and it is a part of nature. Nobody can distribute water, neither can anybody distribute air. Vinoba Bhave argued that land belongs to God, and therefore, it has to be distributed equally. Nehruji always pronounced that when India will get freedom, land would justifiably be distributed.[41] The British distorted the dreams of the Indians by imposing revenue on land. Sub-ordinate class got nothing out of the land reforms introduced by the British. Most of their reforms and policies were just an eye-wash.

The British imperial rulers of India unleashed far reaching changes in Indian agrarian structure. New land tenures, new land ownership concepts, tenancy changes and heavier state demand for land revenue triggered off far reaching alteration in rural economy and social relationship. So far land revenue and land tenancy are concerned, it can be said despite their discrepancies, by surveying land and settling the revenue, the British slowly and gradually laid the foundation of a modern state in the 19th century.[42] The land revenue was mainly a heritage from the indigenous rule, but the administration of land revenue was a natural growth of the substitution of monetary payment in the place of manual labour. Starting with a fairly detailed knowledge of the practice during the Ahom rule, the Anglo Indian administrators built the present complex of the land revenue administration in Assam.[43]

The British regime introduced a new revenue system by superseding the traditional right of the village community over the village land. For the first time, land ceased to be owned by the community, it became a part of private property. There emerged an intermediary between the tenants and the government. This was a watershed in the history of agrarian system. The government apparatus by initiating an endless process of raising revenue demand created tremors and turbulence in the hearts of the peasants, what they could hardly forget.

Humanitarism underlay many of the reforms introduced by the British in the first half of the 19th century. Practically, it proved futile and meaningless if we go through their policy. The method of collection of land revenue by the officials was rigid and strict. The rates of land revenue during the early British period were much higher than during the pre-British period. In the words of Kaushal, in order to realize the revenues, inhumane methods were used upon the zamindars and the peasants. The zamindars who failed to meet the Company's demands were expropriated, while the peasants were left little else than their families and bodies. The tyranny of Hastings extinguished every sentiment of father, son, brother and husband. Everything visible and edible was seized and sold. Nothing but the bodies remained.[44] Concerning the revenue administration in the Brahmaputra valley, Gait says, 'it was thought inadvisable to make any radical change until the ultimate destiny of the country had been settled.'[45]

II

Soon after the British rule was extended to Assam in 1826, some alterations were made in the land system with a view to suiting the requirements of the colonial rule. Actually, land settlement started in

Lower Assam in 1824-25 prior to the British besiege of Assam in 1826. The government did not change the Mughal land settlement system prevailing in Kamrup and settled all matters relating to revenue with the *choudhuries*. The *choudhuries* could enjoy their privileges till then so long the authority pleased over them. These officials gained some privileges like revenue free lands and *paiks* from the government. In realization of revenues, *choudhuries* were assisted by the *patwaries* and the *thakurias*. The British entrusted the onus of realizing revenues of Raha and Nowgong to Lata Pani Phukan and Aradhan Roy respectively. Thus, the government showed some flexibility, and allowed the old system to continue which meant the rule of the zamindars in Goalpara and those of the *choudhuries* in Kamrup. In Upper Assam, the government introduced the ryotwari settlement almost in a parallel situation with the *choudhuries*.[46]

The condition of Assam province was disappointing when the British took control over her. One of the major concerns of David Scott was to improve her by tapping certain new sources of revenue.[47] After fetching the administration specially the Lower Assam under their control, the prevailing practice of personal service was replaced by the imposition of poll tax, but even this tax was also replaced later on and a regular land revenue was introduced on the basis of the nature and types of the land. The British replaced the native system and introduced a new system based on direct money taxation. Revenue affairs had, under the first seven years of their rule, rather retrograded than improved. In 1832, it was determined to hold the country and arrangements were then made for introducing a taxation of the lands in substitution of the poll tax. Captain Mathie, Rutherford and Bogle were appointed as collectors of Darrang, Nowgong and Kamrup to carry them out.[48]

Land-holdings were divided into four categories; *basti*, *bao-tali*, *farangati* and *rupit*; separate rents were fixed for them and were gradually revised from time to time. The amount in *basti*-land varies in Kamrup from Rs. 3 to Re. 1-8-0 according to the circumstances of the occupants. The *rupit* lands in the same district were originally assessed at one rupee per *pura*, the *bao-tali* at twelve *annas* and the *farangati* at four *annas*. These rates were gradually raised and in 1848, they had reached Re. 1-4-0 per *pura* for *rupit* and one rupee for all other kinds of land, including *basti*.[49]

The land grants made to temples, priests and other charitable purposes during the Ahom regime were made sure either as *lakhiraj* or *nisf-khiraj*. While *debottar*-land grants was made sure as revenue free, *brahmottar* and *dharmottar* lands grants were required to pay half of the revenue rate prevalent at that time. In this manner, the colonial government recognized the *lakhiraj* and *nisfkhiraj* estates and continued as major classes of estates. Thus, the rent free grants were brought under assessment by Scott.[50]

In Assam, there was no dearth of arable land and because of this, the peasants preferred annual leases and were unwilling to tie to a particular plot of land for a fixed period of time. The government declared in 1870 that the right of the periodic lease-holders would be transferable and heritable. Such declaration was made to encourage periodic lease. The annual settlement system was slowly transmuted into decennial leases by the enforcement of the Assam Land and Revenue Regulation in 1886. The rights of tenants under these regulations were fixed for definite period. The decennial lease-holders and those paying revenue directly to the government for the previous ten years were ultimately endorsed as ryots enjoying heritable, permanent and transferable rights of occupancy and use of their lands. However, the existing practice was allowed to continue in the case of annual settlements so that ryots remain satisfied. Thus, the ryotwari system of land revenue administration received a tremendous and colossal boost under the Regulations of 1886. Actually, the peasants considered long term system tedious and opted for annual lease. The settlement policy of the government to cut down the annual lease facilities was looked upon by J.N.Barua as 'deprivation of their rights.' He didnot agree with the repeated assertion of the government about the happiness and improved condition of the peasantry of Assam. Then, came his rebellious assertion, 'I say, the ryots are in no way better off.' Thus, he brought into focus the plight of the ryots.[51] Inspite of its goodness, sometime the annual system also proved defective. Yet, the government effected such settlements. Every year, peasants saw the new masters. The latter exploited them as much as possible during their one year term, as they were uncertain about next term. The condition of the peasantry became worse every time a new settlement was made.[52]

Although the government tried to attract the cultivators towards decennial leases, the system started becoming popular only during the closing part of the 19th century. The main issue involved in such an agrarian situation was the lack of security for cultivators. Even at the beginning of the 20th century, although decennial leases were becoming more popular, the majority of leases were still annual. This unpopularity of decennial leases shows how insecure the Assamese ryots felt under the new revenue system. There was genuine fear of the system, which made them opt for lease and gave them no security of tenure. It also perhaps points to the fact that there were such landholders in Assam who felt economically secure enough to opt for a ten years lease and feel able to pay the government revenue demand on time for the lease years. So, the government, on the one hand, wanted to encourage decennial leases so that they could be sure of the annual revenue to be collected; and they, on the other hand, were not economically strong enough to opt for long term leases.[53]

The Assamese peasants were alien to the transfer and inheritance; and because of this, they were hardly enchanted when the government granted such rights with the long term leases. During the Ahom regime, such rights were not available and that's why, the question of transfer and inheritance of land was not present in the economy of erstwhile Assam.

Alterations in the revenue regulations also fetched a series of changes in the administration of revenue. Alterations, began by the Rules of 1870, were ultimately made sure by the Regulations of 1886. The land was first divided into smaller units called mauzas, and native officials known as *choudhury, patgiri, mauzadar* or *bishaya* realised revenues from landholding ryots. The government appointed them on impermanent basis, and local village accountants called *thakuria, patwari* and *kakati* assisted them. Albeit called by various appellations like *choudhury, patgiri* and *mauzadar* initially, these officers were ultimately designated as *mauzadars.* Only a wealthy and influential person of the concerned *mauza* was employed as *mauzadar* and he was given the onus of realizing and depositing the land revenue demanded from his *mauza* by a contracted and stipulated time. The *mauzadar,* under these circumstances, became powerful in the rural hierarchy.[54] The *mauzadars* were appointed from among the rich and respectable families of every district. Though they had their own tale of woes, they were men of consequence in the society. As commission agents, they had a fair income to lead a comfortable life.[55]

The *mauzadary* system was much popular and well-understood by the people. Although the system was rough and ready, it was cheap and not oppressive. Maxwell, the Commissioner of Assam Valley Division, wrote in the Administrative Report of 1896-97, 'one native gentleman whose ideas are much in advance of his countrymen, was of the opinion that the *mauzadary* system was better suited to the people. He was an inhabitant of the area and was respected by the ryots. He assisted them in times of distress and generally speaking, was their adviser in family disputes.'[56] Revenue bureaucracy was an essential organ of the colonial government and unfortunately, the peasants were utterly at the clemency of them. *Mauzadars* and *choudhuries* were the revenue contractors of the government and extorted more revenue from the ryots and kept substantial portion with them. Their exactions sometime even crossed the limit which resulted expression of ryots anger through other channels. In early 1855, some discontented ryots of Mangaldoi sub-division sent a petition to the Lt. Governor of Bengal complaining against their *mauzdars*. Next year, some Kachari ryots of Kalaigaon and Mangaldoi brought complaint against their *mauzadars*.[57]

The *choudhury* system proved itself as a ban to Assamese peasants. When the peasant failed to pay taxes as demanded by *choudhury*, he was chastised by *choudhury*. As a result, sometimes the remnant of the property of the defaulter tenants was confiscated and at times they had to save their skin by leaving the hearth and home. Such was the plight of the Assamese peasants as a result of the British imposed *choudhury* system.[58]

The *choudhuries* foreseeing the possibility of not being re-elected, launched exactions on all sides sometime five or six times the real amounts of rent collected. These exactions attracted the attention of Robertson and he soon realized that existing disorders in revenue affairs were due to the paucity of European officers; ignorance of the employees on the resources of the country; condition of the people; demands founded on no certain data; irregular and undefined, additional assessments; corrupt practices and intrigues of the *amlah*; embezzlement by all parties and so on. However, he tried to bring transparency in the administration and with this aim in view, settlements were made directly with the ryots and title deeds or *pattas* were issued to them specifying there in the amount of revenue to be paid under signature and seal of the collector.[59]

The *mandal* stood at the lowest rank of the revenue administration and yet he was the pivot of the entire system. His responsibilities were too heavy but he was the lowest paid officer. Land assessment and proposals for settlement were made by the *mandal* who in those days, were appointed by the *mauzadars*. The monthly salary of a *mandal* in 1880-81 was Rs. 6. Little wonder that he supplemented it by illegal exaction from the tenants. Over the *mandals*, there were *kanungoo*, *mauzadar* and *tehsildar*.[60] *Gaonburha* was a respectable man in the village.

The government invested him formally as a government officer, and remunerated him by a remission of land revenue.[61]

The new British Government was eager to appoint Haliram and Jagnaram in administrative services. Haliram was given the charge of land settlement in the districts of Nowgong and Darrang. So efficiently he managed the whole thing that he was given again the charge of settlement in Kamrup.

It remains expressed that the British employed local people in realization of revenue having adequate knowledge on the fields. The British employed those people in their administration who had knowledge on the economic condition of Assam. For instance, they employed Maniram as *sarestadar* and *tehsildar* due to his vast knowledge on the economic condition of Assam. He reorganized the land settlement in Upper Assam and tripled the revenue income from that area. He even prepared a report on the washing of gold in the rivers of Assam.[62]

Naturally, the general character of the land settlement in the plains of Assam was ryotwari except the areas under the permanent settlement. There were no middle men and government dealt directly with the actual ryots and occupants. But despite that, there was some problem on the question of direct contact with the actual tiller as subletting was very common and widespread in *lakhiraj, nisfkhiraj* and in *khiraj* estates when the holdings were very large.

Under the circumstances, tenants formed a major class surviving on land. In fact, tenancy as a form of labour was widespread during the Ahom rule. Many slaves were gradually transformed in to serfs and in the long run, in to tenants-at-will. After the expiry of Ahom rule, large bodies of tenants were found mostly in compact blocks, in the surviving landed estates, paying their rent in one form or other to their landlords.

The *adhi* system was the most widespread and popular form of share-cropping practice. Though variations in the operations of the system were seen from district to district but the essential characteristics remained intact. The Assam District Gazetteers mention five different forms of crop sharing widespread during the closing part of the 19th century in the plains of Assam, viz. *gachch-adhi*, equal division on the standing crop of the fields, each party reaping and transporting its own share; *dal-adhi*, equal division of the harvested bundles, each party threshing and transporting its own share; *boka-adhi,* division of the fields in equal parts, after the tenants had cultivated the land up to the stage of puddling, each party taking charge of its parts thereafter; *chukti-adhi* or *thika-adhi,* the handing over to the landlord of a fixed quantity of grain; and *quti-adhi,* equal division of the threshed grain, each party taking thereafter its own share.

The condition of the tenants during the period was regulated not only by the rent burden under distinct form of *adhi* but also through various religious and customary bond attached to the system. However, to secure fair rent and freedom from arbitrary ejection and fixity of tenure, several legislations were passed during the first half of the 20th century. The Assam Tenancy Act of 1935 was the significant one among them, which recognized three classes of tenants, viz. privileged, occupancy and non-occupancy ryots.

Over and above ryotwari settlement, some parts of Assam were under the permanent settlement which was introduced by Lord Cornwallis in 1793 in Bengal. Before the inclusion of Assam in 1826, the two districts Sylhet and Southern portion of Goalpara were parts of the Bengal presidency. These two districts came under the permanent settlement when it was introduced in Bengal presidency. The settlement known as the zamindari system, continued in these areas when they were brought under the administration of Assam in 1874.[63]

In matters of land settlement and revenue collection, Jenkins adopted reactionary role; and slowly and gradually, he started augmenting the revenue on land. Excluding Goalpara, the incidence of land-revenue from 1832-33 to 1852-53 in the district of the Brahmaputra valley are shown in the following table:

Name of the districts	Years & revenue 1832-33	Years & revenue 1842-43	Years & revenue 1852-53
Kamrup	1,10,181	2,52,991	2,82,304
Darrang	41,506	1,35,453	1,57,795
Nowgong	31,509	1,10,314	1,29,873
Sibsagar		80,843	1,14,463
Lakhimpur		34,729	46,553
Total	**1,83,196**	**6,14,330**	**7,30,988**

Source: A. J. M. Mills' 'Report on the Province of Assam', PP. 66-67.

Thus, a decade after 1832-33, the land revenue in Assam proper amounted to Rs. 6,14,330 in 1842-43 and still a decade after in 1852-53, it amounted to Rs. 7,30,988.[64] The percentage of increased rates were 17,

16.49, 16.82, 41.58 and 33.85 in Kamrup, Darrang, Nowgong, Sibsagar and Lakhimpur from 1842-43 to 1853.

Moreover, the increase in assessment on *rupit* and non-*rupit* land[65] also invited wide spread reaction.

Districts	Years, nature of land assessment *rupit* land (per *purah*)		Years, nature of land and assessment non-*rupit* land (per *purah*)	
	1842-43	1852-53	1842-43	1852-53
Kamrup	1-4	1-8	1-0	1-0
Nowgaon	1-4	1-6	0-4	1-0
Darrang	1-8	1-6	0-12	1-0
Sibsagar	1-4	1-4	0-12	0-14
Lakhimpur	1-0	1-0	0-12	0-12

Source: *H. K. Barpujari's (ed),'The Comprehensive History of Assam (1826-1919)', Vol. V, Appendix-A, Statement-I, P. 19.*

Despite the steady rise in revenue, attempts had been made by the district officers to enhance the rate of assessment. This was considered inexpedient by the Board of Revenue in a newly conquered province. So wishes of the Board of Revenue were respected. In 1852, on the modification of the *tarh,* there occurred a rise in rates in all categories of land.[66]

The burden of revenue became so high that even the members of the royal family also affected by this. The family of the Darrang *raja* failed to pay the revenue even at half rates as fixed earlier and sought permission from the government to resign part of their estates. They tried to impress upon the government their burden of bigness. Hundred of *bighas* of cultivable lands were lying useless and they found it difficult to pay revenue for that land, not really covered by cultivation. Moreover, agricultural produce in their area, they said, did hardly bring them any cash. Bolindranarayan Konwar was in arrear of revenue for the year 1853-54 and 1854-55 to the extent of Rs. 2,451 and declaring himself unable to pay the dues, he offered to transfer to the government more than 5,392 *pooras* of land in liquidation of the revenue amount. The 5,392 *pooras* of land were lying in 27 *mauzas* and of which only 624 *pooras* were under cultivation. Similarly, Suryyanarayan Konwar had 434 *pooras* of land, out of which he resigned 411, and retained only 23 *pooras* paying a *sudder jummah* of Rs. 10-1-9. Amrit Narayan Bahadoor, Rajooram Konwar and Rajnarayan Konwar were also in arrear. They too offered to surrender some portions of their cultivable land. Shortage of labour and low money income from land were the major causes for such situation.[67]

The government heard the agony of the royal families and accepted their complaint. Even the direct descendants of the Ahom kings were also exempted from land revenue and money pension. But such type of agonies and distress suffered by the ryots were not heard by the government which, finally, gave birth to resentments in colonial period. The rise and growth of the *vaishnava satra* was one of the important and significance chapter in relation to the control and ownership of land in colonial Assam. Sri Sankardeva's *vaishnava* reform movement besieged an important place in the Brahmaputra valley by the end of the sixteenth century.

The vaishnavites received substantial grants of land and money for the setting up of *satras* under the patronage of the Ahom kings. These land grants with the *paiks* were rent free and it made the *Gossains* and the *Adhikars* substantial land owners and facilitated the *satras* growth of power and influence. Thus, the *satras* almost became the personal assets of the *Gossains* and the *Adhikars;* and the pattern which started during the Ahom regime, continued even during the colonial period. According to one account, there were 288 *satras* at the turn of the present century and they spread over the entire Brahmaputra valley.

Like the Ahoms, the colonial government also granted *lakhiraj* and in some cases *nisfkhiraj* land to the *satras*. Auniati and Dakshinpat *satras* were granted 2200 and 1200 acres of land respectively by the then British Government. By acquiring rent free land, most of the *satradhikars* exploited the poor ryots by offering them land on share-cropping basis and thus, created a zamindari of their own. Thus, the British Land Settlement System is directly responsible for creating Vaishnavite zamindari class in Assam. All *satras*, of course, were not included in it.[68]

A large number of people were attached to *satras* lands, and they paid regular rent to the *satras*. So as to manage the *satra* lands, therefore, an elaborate structure of revenue administration was utter necessary. It was, finally, evolved by employing several officers and agents in each *satra* to realize rent and thus, the business was managed. The land structure within the *satra* had developed a clear feudal inclination and this inclination was far stronger than in the Ahom monarchical system.[69]

Albeit the relationship between a ryot and *a satradhikar* was that of a tenant-landlord, despite that, the latter hardly acted as an exploitative zamindar due to the absence of forced and coercive power. The ryots had to pay the high revenue rates during the colonial time. Inspite of that, if he defaulted in the payment of rent, he had to forego his rights over his land. But such-type system was not there in the *satra*-system. But it lacks adequate empirical data. Logically, the landlord-tenant relationship is invariably based on dominant sub-ordinate relationship, and some elements of economic exploitation and social oppression are inherent in it. The levels and magnitude of physical coercion and illegal exactions may vary from one system to the other, but to deny and ignore their existence altogether is not easy to comprehend. The *satra* land system was not favourable to the poor tenants but was favourable to the *Gossains* and because of this, they led a comfortable and affluent life in the society.[70]

The colonial government had faced severe financial crisis after the revolt of 1857. The government had to spend Rs.64 crores (40 million pound sterling) in curbing the revolt, and contemplating how to mitigate the crisis by discovering new sources of income and they, finally, discovered it. According to Pemberton, 'looking to the extra-ordinary fertility of the soil, the noble river which flows through the valley from one extremity to the other, the proofs derived from history, of its former affluence, abundant population, and varied products, there can be no doubt that in the course of a very few years, under a more settled government, this province will prove a highly valuable acquisition to the British Government, its revenue already shows progressive improvement and as our communications are renewed with the numerous tribes surrounding it, new channels of commerce will be obtained, that cannot fail to enrich the country and give stimulus to its own agriculture and manufacturing industry.'[71]

There was acute shortage of labour in Assam to run the plantation industries, as almost all were engaged in cultivation. Therefore, to solve the problem of labour, revenue hike on agricultural land was utmost necessary to flush them out of cultivation. According to Guha, planters urged the government to enhance the land revenue rate so that the poor peasants could be flushed-out of their village to work for wages on the plantation.[72] The government sought to wipe out the indigenous and traditional agriculture economy, and wanted establishment in that place of their own economy. They thought that their motive would not fulfil until and unless revenue was hiked. According to the government, the rate of revenue in Assam was ridiculously low, and therefore, hike would not create pressure on the people. Jenkins would not mind even the displacement of local ryots from their lands through the operation of a discriminatory land revenue policy in favour of the white colonists. For such a policy, according to him, would promote the long-run interest of the ryots themselves. He was afraid that if the government assessment upon the natives were generalized and not heavy, they would not be available as tenants cultivators under European superintendence, and therefore, the introduction of commercial agriculture would be inhibited. On the other hand, if the assessment on cultivation was heavy, the ryots would have no alternative other than work for the European capitalist farmers.[73]

Inspite of having enormous fertility of the soil, the peasants of Assam did one crop in a year and spent the entire months without agricultural work. The government thought that the peasants would not spend their time idle if revenue maximized. To the government, this step would break the lethargy of the peasants and make them busy in cultivating the commercial crops.

The resources of the province and the fertility of agricultural land also suited to the Company's policy of revenue maximization. The British interest in India before and after colonization was primarily commercial. They reached India and its prosperous regions for trade; trade led to conquest an empire. Even after conquest, the trade and profit continued to be the key motive of the *Raj*. The actual conqueror was the English East India Company, an enterprising commercial organization. The transfer of authority to the British Crown (1858) hundred years after, did not change the mercantile character of the *Raj*. It aimed at revenue maximization and increasing the wealth of Britain at the cost of India.[74]

Compared to many other provinces of India, scope of taxation was certainly limited in Assam. Some of the important sources of state revenue were not existent here. For example, the revenue derived from salt and supplied to Assam for consumption was not credited to Assam. Custom duties abolished in 1835, had not been revived in the 19th century. In the absence of these two, the government had to depend to a great extent on the land revenue, the rate of which was revised a number of times during the 19th century.[75] Moreover, very lately the capitation and the house taxes were also abolished throughout Assam, and to meet the deficiency of revenue, taxes on *rupit*, *bari*, *baotali* and *farangati* lands were increased.

The assessment of revenue in ryotwari settlement was fixed in the beginning, but the situation was not in tune with this pattern. A steady and rapid increase of revenue was inevitable and order of the day due to the more or less agricultural growth. The principle of periodical settlement left adequate scope for adjusting and maximizing revenues especially with the changing demand of the British Government.

To increase the paying capacity of the ryots, Scott and Jenkins, both encouraged the ryots to grow marketable crops. Jenkins stood opposed to any enhancement in the rate of *rupit* land as that would keep the ryots away from the cultivation of rice crop, the staple food; and in fact, many had already diverted to the production of crops like mustard, the profitability of which had in the meantime gone up several times. In lieu of enhancement of rate in *rupit* land, Jenkins raised the rate of non-*rupit* land in all the districts except Kamrup. In Nowgong and Darrang, it rose to one rupee and two *annas* from fourteen *annas,* and in Sibsagar and Lakhimpur to a rupee from twelve and fourteen *annas* respectively.[76]

Different plans and techniques were made to increase and impose new taxes by different ways. Jenkins planned to increase the rate on *bari* land and tried to convert the waste and jungle land into fruitful fields of different vegetables, like sugarcane, mustard, mulberry, tobacco etc. According to him, people would not hesitate to pay the revenue if such plans are adopted. In 1859, attempts were made to raise the assessments on the plea of equalizing the rate of all the districts with that of Kamrup which was then the highest. They were also motivated by their desire of compelling the ryots by the increased demand to work under the tea-planters who were then facing acute scarcity of labour in their operation. Increased taxation invariably led to agricultural stagnation. Despite this, in 1861, the government acting on the recommendation of Colonel Hopkinson, arbitrarily doubled the rates of land revenue in view of the general progress and prosperity of the province which it argued indicated the increased paying capacity of the ryots. The administration seems to have conveniently overlooked the fact that the wealth generated in the province had little link with the local economy. In the circumstances, the enhanced land revenue was transformed into a virtual rack-rent that impoverished them.[77]

In 1865, Hopkinson renewed proposal into a different form proposing to raise the revenue on land with the object of equalizing the rates in all the districts. The difference in rates, he argued, had encouraged migratory habits of the ryots by driving them away from the areas of heavier taxation to those where assessment was light. He also wanted to raise the rates of household and garden lands since the produce of these lands, viz. betel nut commanded a ready sale on the spot at a higher profit. His proposal received the approval of the Government of Bengal, and consequently rates of *rupit* and non-*rupit* lands increased from 25 to 50 percent in almost all the districts.[78]

The question of raising the assessment of land and also giving the cultivators a permanent, heritable and transferable right in their land was discussed during the period between 1861 and 1867. It was under the Settlement Rules of 1870, the government for the first time, categorically and unequivocally recognized the permanent, transferable and heritable right in *rupit* and *bari* land in private occupation.[79]

The Settlement Rules of 1870 were the first public declaration of the rights in land possessed by the cultivators of the soil. These remained in force till 1887 when Land and Revenue Regulation superceded them. The Land and Revenue Regulation of 1886 did not change the principles of the Settlement Rules of 1870, rather it plugged the loopholes and elaborated the existing rules to meet the changing requirements. Subsequently after cadastral survey, decennial settlement rules were passed in 1883. Under these rules, settlements were to be made only on lands which were to be held permanently.[80]

The land revenue rates on dry and wet crops, both were uniformly and arbitrarily doubled in 1868 throughout Assam. As a result of these enhanced rates which were implemented during 1860-71, the total land revenue demand jumped up from Rs.1,001,773 in 1864-65 to Rs.2,165,157 in 1872-73. In some parts of Assam, people reacted to the new assessment by organizing the *Raij-mels*. The peasants of Nowgong took the path of revolt in 1868-69. In Lakhimpur district, the people protested in a novel way. They surrendered so much of their land to the government that the revised rates, though about double the previous rates in force, yielded an enhancement of only about 26% in the total revenue collection. This was at a time when the acre under foodgrains was failing to increase sufficiently to meet the rising local demand for food. Food prices were higher in Assam than in any part of neighbouring Bengal.

In 1870, the assessment was raised to a uniform rate of one rupee per *bigha* (1/3 acre) for *basti*; ten *annas* for *rupit* and eight *annas* for *faringati*. Between the years 1883 and 1893, a cadastral survey on a scale of 16 inches to the mile was made of the whole area except tracts where cultivation was sparse which were afterwards surveyed by non-professional agency. The assessment was then revised; each class of land was divided in to three sub-classes and new rates were imposed, ranging from Re.1-6-0 to Re.1-2-0 per *bigha* for *basti*; from one rupee to twelve *annas* for *rupit* and from twelve *annas* to nine *annas* for *faringati*.[81]

During the period between 1866 and 1889, the land revenue had more than quadrupled but land under ordinary cultivation had increased by 7% only. The increased land revenue demand had been justified on grounds that there had been a substantial increase in the price of staples and a considerable increase in the wages of labour. There were epidemic diseases, like cholera, small pox and fever in Goalpara, Nowgong, Darrang and Kamrup in 1879-80. Inspite of that, there was neither a fall in land revenue nor contraction of agriculture except Kamrup district. Extension of cultivation and assessment of leasehold grants on the expiry of their revenue free tenure led to the increase inland revenue in Nowgong, Darrang, Sibsagar and Lakhimpur. The term of 20 years of revenue free settlement of land with the former *rajas* of Darrang originated in 1859-60 having expired, the entire land was brought under resettlement. The resettlement records revealed that the ex-*rajas* of Darrang had already resigned 2,512 acres of wasteland to the government, and alienated 3,115 acres of cultivated as well as wastelands to others who again on their part, surrendered 345 acres of wasteland to the government.[82]

Resettlement of Assam proper was made again for ten years in 1893; and the settlement of 1893-94 raised the assessed revenue from 70 to 80 percent and in some cases 100 percent. It was done on the basis of the classification of land and became applicable in the all districts of the Brahmaputra valley except Goalpara.

Districts	1891-92	1892-93	1893-94
Kamrup	9,61,842	9,79,347	13,33,314
Darrang	4,92,709	4,96,682	6,48,820
Nowgong	5,27,736	5,41,144	6,90,980
Sibsagar	8,57,323	8,72,484	12,01,689
Lakhimpur	2,67,127	2,75,853	3,70,124
Total	31,06,737	31,65,510	42,44,927

Source: *Assam Valley Reassessment Report, 1892-93*

The revenue system of the hilly areas of Assam was essentially different from that of the plains in the 19th century. The hilly people were accustomed to shifting cultivation. They seldom cultivated the same land for a period of years and in most cases, moved around the hills in search of new lands. So, collection of land revenue under such circumstances was a difficult proposition and hence, house remained throughout the 19th century, the principal source of taxation of the hill tribes. The Mikirs of the Nowgong district were the first to be assessed but the change proved unproductive. The people in order to avoid taxation, were in the habit of living together under the same roof.

With the consolidation of their authority, the British discovered that land revenue alone was not enough for the growing requirements of the state and therefore, the necessity of exploiting the natural resources for the advantage of their rule had become imperative. Of the miscellaneous revenues, the house tax and the pass tax were the relics of the Ahom system of taxation. The British did not abolish them altogether, rather retained them in certain places in a modified form. Fisheries and the salt wells yielded considerable revenue for the Ahoms. Under the British rule, the former was steadily developed and the latter became an item of secondary importance as a result of the increasing supply of the Bengal salt.[83]

The poll tax introduced by the Burmese was revived and extended to Darrang and Nowgong with the object of equalizing the burden on all classes. In Darrang, it was calculated on the number of mess pots or *charoos* in each house hold from 8 *annas* to Re.1; in Nowgong, it became a capitation tax at Re.1 per head and in Kamrup, *kharikatana* was levied on plough at the rate of Re.1 per plough. Professional tax on the artisans continued to be levied as under the former government. Popular discontentment increased not only for the enhancement of revenue at every resettlement, but for the imposition of new taxes, like stamp-duty and license fee also.

As the prospect of obtaining additional allocations became extremely bleak, the local authorities in Assam then directed their care for tapping new sources of revenue to meet their increasing expenditure. Despite prohibitory orders of the court, stamp-duties were introduced in 1858. Excise duties were levied at the *sadar* stations in Kamrup, Darrang and Nowgong but the same were not extended to tribal areas. Already washing of gold was farmed out and the *jalkar* was offered to the highest bidder. *Gorkhati, bunker* and *khusary* became common.[84]

In land abundant Assam, peasants had enjoyed from time immemorial the traditional right to graze their cattle freely on the village

fields and neighbouring forests. Under the British regime, this right
was gradually encroached upon to bring forth additional revenue to the
exchequer. A grazing fee per head of horned animals was introduced. In
1888, this fee was 8 *annas* per annum per head of buffaloes and 4 *annas*
per head of cows. So, people reacted sharply against this.[85]

The people of Assam were accustomed to chewing areca-nut and
betel vine. The Ahom rulers stressed on maintaining a systematically
planned areca-nut and betel-vine gardens in front of every house.
The *Jayantia* and *Kamrupar Buranji* mention ripe and raw nuts, both
chewn with two different varieties of vines. It is believed that the name
'*Guwahati*' has been derived from the areca-nut and betel vine gardens
abundance here from ancient times onwards.[86]

Anyway, the multiplication of taxes became a matter of concern to
the agricultural ryots. In the district of Nowgong, rumours were afloat
that the governemt was contemplating imposition of taxes on their
houses, gardens and betel leaf cultivations. Although the official sources
dismissed these, the people learnt about the correspondence that was
going on between the *Sadar* Board and the district officials on the
subject. About this time, the introduction of the license tax confirmed
the belief of the villagers, particularly of the tribals of Phulguri that their
paan and betel nut would also be subjected to taxation.

Such type discriminatory colonial trade policy even ignited the Indian
traders also. The servants of the Company carried on free trade all over
their territory, but the Indian traders, on the contrary, had to pay heavy
duties for that. Finally, the colonial government with a view to introduce
free and fair trade, abolished obnoxious inland and custom duties; but
income tax, stamp and ferry funds were levied to meet the increasing
demands of the state. On the advice of James Wilson, income tax was
introduced in 1860, and this was extended in Assam from 1861 onward.

Professional tax on braziers, gold-washers, silk-weavers, fishermen
and the like continued to be levied as under the Ahom Government.
The rates varied from *khel* to *khel*. A gold-washer, for example, paid
rupees five; a brass-worker, the same amount; the makers of oil and the
fishermen, paid rupees three and the weavers of silk, paid rupees two
each.[87]

Opium was an important commercial crop in India in the 19th
century, but the condition of Assam, according to Mills, was not
favourable for production of opium on a large scale due to difficulty
of procuring labour. Bengal was the only source. The use of opium in

Assam was not a thing of the distant past, and according to the view of the Assam Congress Opium Enquiry Committee (1925), it started from the end of the 17th century when Assam came in contact with the Mughals. But it can not be accepted, as it was known even during the times of Sankardeva (1449-1568). Sankardeva's removal of one Surya Sarasvati from the office of the *Bhagavati* for his addiction to opium is a clear example of this. Poppy cultivation in Assam was started during the time of the Ahom king Lakshmi Singha in the 18th century. Poppy grown in Beltola (Guwahati) was a quality product and the royal house had the supply of its quota from there. Gradually, eating opium became not an exceptional, rather not eating opium became an exceptional matter because of its widespread popularity, which, finally, converted the Assamese into an effeminate, weak, indolent and degraded people.

The colonial government of Assam gave more attention on opium as it was the most important source of revenue, next only to land. It was a gold mine for the government not to be lightly surrendered. According to David Scott, in Cachar, the *raja* was not allowed to cultivate opium and the privilege of supplying opium sufficiently for the consumption of the people of Cachar was enjoyed by the British merchants.

Like Cachar, the government wanted to bring this lucrative and coveted business under their control in Assam also. But they approached steadily and gradually with a view to evading reaction of the local people. It was believed that if the cultivation of opium, the most important cash crop grown locally was suppressed, then the problem of shortage of money would become even more actuate. Many cultivators would lose the only source of cash income, while others who were already addicted to opium, would require additional money to buy *abkari* opium.

The sale of opium in Kamrup for the last three years is given below:

Years	Maunds	Seers	Price
1850-51	45	18	18,180
1851-52	57	17	22,970
1852-53	36	16	14,560

Source: A. J. M. Mills' 'Report on the province of Assam', P. 326.

The steady increase in the sale of *abkari* opium and rise of production of local opium clearly indicates that the number of consumers was increasing irrespective of the age and sex. Jenkins was in favour of increasing assessment which would effect prohibition of cultivation in near future and finally, on his recommendation, government prohibited poppy cultivation in April, 1860 through-out the province.

The growing monetization of the economy had induced farmers to grow more poppy for cash, sometimes even at the cost of other crops. However, the government for the fear of losing out a valuable source of revenue, put ban on poppy in April, 1860. With the imposition of ban, the government introduced the system of issuing opium from the government treasury at a high price.[88] Inspite of putting ban on local opium and introduction of *abkari* opium, it cannot be said that there was fall of local opium. It continued but not as previous manner.

The demand of opium was increasing and encouraging in China, and it was met only through the importation of opium from India. Between the cost of production and the price, the government enjoyed a big margin as revenue. Britain was the centre of anti-opium agitation at the international level [89] and the same British put ban on the opium of Assam in 1860. Their ban-intention was not for the welfare of the local people's health. Intention was prohibit local poppy, and introduce foreign poppy; and thus, bring this coveted and lucrative business under their control. Actually, their anti-opium agitation was just like *Ram naam* on devil's lips. The British motive behind the ban was to deter local opium cultivation and import *abkari* opium from Bengal and North India. The planter community recommended to the government to put a ban on the cultivation and sale of opium. To them, suppression would induce the opium eaters to work as labourers in their tea gardens. The British opium policy in Assam like their land revenue, assessment and periodic enhancement policy was dictated more or less by the overall interests of the tea plantation industry under the British finance capital.[90]

Some of the elite and middle classes remained silent when tax was imposed on the opium due to their self interests in tea plantations. The leaders of the Jorhat *Sarbajanik Sabha* also did not demand to stop the opium business fearing loss of revenue and imposition of new tax on them to meet the loss. In addition to that, most of the people did not like opium ban. To them, it cures dysentery and malaria; alleviates pain; gives longevity and livelihood. Dhekial Phukan suggested to the government to discontinue the sale of government opium forthwith and impose heavy tax on the local poppy cultivation. Harbilas Agarwala (1842-1916), an Assamese planter, ran a lucrative opium shop and recommended to the government for the gradual eradication of the evil.[91]

Tea is the only industry that occupies a considerable portion of the economy of the state. The articles more precious than silver and gold grow wild upon its mountains, and the local hill tribes used to call it, '*phinak*' and drink its beverage. Tea shrubs of Assam were planted on an experimental basis in the Botanical garden of Calcutta, but this venture had to be abandoned. The discovery of tea in 1823, coal and petroleum in 1825 in the Brahmaputra valley during the operations against the Burmese inspired the British decision to colonies Assam at the earliest.[92] The strained relation between the British and the Chinese also encouraged the farmers to look for tea plantation in India.[93] But if we believe Trevelyan, there is no denying the fact that Indian tea was within the reach of the mass population of England even in the mid 18th century, and the port of London received these ships.[94]

The area of wastelands in the Assam province was so large that there was no necessary to check the freedom of the ryot to transfer his land. Moreover, Assam abounds in many parts with valuable timber, not of the ornament but the useful order, chiefly adapted for building or for canoes. The main characteristic of the topography of Assam during the British regime was the existence of large tracts of wasteland, and it propelled the rise and growth of the tea industry in Assam.[95]

The first experimental plantation was made by the Company in 1835 in Lakhimpur. The period from 1835 till 1852 has been called the period of experiment in the tea-sector. The growth of tea plantation was largely flourished mainly in the five districts of the Brahmaputra valley and in the districts of Sylhet and Cachar of the Surma valley. The period from 1852 till 1892 has, therefore, rightly been called as the period of foundation of tea plantation.

The discovery of tea and its profitability and potentiality had awakened growing interest of the British capitalists in the cultivation of this plant in the valley from the fifties of the 19th century, and plantation became much more profitable in Indian and international markets. The economy of Upper Assam changed with the plantations from the middle of the 19th century, but Lower Assam retained its traditional character.[96]

The economic resources of the Ahom state, particularly tea, coal and oil mainly guided the British policy. The foothills, along the valley of Brahmaputra were found to be rich in timber, rubber, ivory and other raw materials which could be supplied from Assam. The agricultural land in the valley was highly fertile and it was capable of generating surplus and yielding handsome revenue. These facts impressed the British authority about the commercial prospects in Assam. Therefore, the immediate task of the British authority was to reclaim the land in the plains for the settlement of the cultivators and for the tea plantation.[97] With a view to make their commercial plan, viz. tea plantation successful, they contemplated to utilize the vast tracts of wastelands of Assam in practice and this finally, gave birth to the wasteland rules. Actually, these rules were tools of grabbing the wastelands. Indeed, colonial government in the name of wasteland rules engulfed those lands which were full of forest and natural resources. The planters even usurped the grazing fields and encroached upon the *jhum* rights of the tribal shifting cultivators.

The government brought vast tracts of wastelands under tillage and tired to improve the resource and economy of the people. But they were allergic to the allotment of these lands to the local people and favoured foreign enterprise, skill and capital to serve their motto. The wastelands settlement policy tempted planters to grab more land, than they required or could manage.[98]

To give wastelands to the Europeans and deprive the local people of the same, the govenment, however, framed certain favourable rules of land grants entitled 'Wasteland Grant Rules.' According to Guha, a set of rules were framed 'Wasteland Rules of March 6, 1838' to make these lands available for special cultivation.[99]

As early as September, 1827, David Scott proposed a plan of granting wasteland on the conditions and his successor Robertson also planned the same. But in 1836, Captain Jenkins suggested to the Govenment of Bengal for the introduction of the Gorakhpur rates with some modification for similar grants in Assam. Finally, after several process and surveys, the Govenment of Bengal approved it in August, 1836.

The terms of the wasteland grants were so favourable to the Europeans that a scramble for land took place among the planters. Their intention was not always to plant the whole area with tea, but of acquiring those wastelands which contained valuable materials like timber.[100]

Saikia says that land grants were made at the most liberal rates in Coorg for coffee plantation. The British speculators flocked in, even from Ceylon and Burma; close at their heels came forward the *Kodavas* and all of them took to coffee plantation and their hard work and patience, answered their expectation well. So, this reveals that liberal land grants system of the British was confined not only at one specified regions, rather it scattered various parts of the globe. But noticeable exception is that in Coorg, coffee plantation was done jointly by the *Kodavas* and the British, both but such venture was not seen taken in colonial Assam. The terms of liberal land grants were extremely liberal, no doubt, but its precedent was set by the king Purandar Singha in 1836. On mere request, the *raja* granted to the Assam Tea Company an extensive area near Gabharu hills for cultivation of tea in anticipating that in near future his subjects would be able to reap the benefit of this new enterprise.[101] But his expectation proved failure.

Mills during his visit to Assam in 1853 said, 'in a country like Assam, where there is a super abundance of land and a deficiency of labour, I strongly deprecate the granting of wasteland to natives of the province.' Actually, Mills wanted utilization of these lands and supported grants to the outsiders.

Although no distinction was made between the European and the indigenous, but the Government of Bengal, on the recommendation of the Board of Revenue laid down that no grant should be made of less than 500 acres in extent and unless the grantee satisfied the collector that he possessed the required capital and implements for its utilization. The local entrepreneurs were debarred from applying for these grant as very few had the necessary wealth qualification.[102] In 1856, on the recommendation of Jenkins, the then Commissioner of Assam, the Government of Bengal reduced the limit to 200 acres and in special cases even to 100.

Rules introduced by Lord Cornwallis were too liberal and was objected by the Secretary of the State. Under his direction, the Board of Revenue had to revise some of the provisions which received the approval of the Government of Bengal on 30th August, 1862. Accordingly, grants were to be limited to an area of 3000 acres. The revised rule enabled the speculators to purchase waste lands at a very low rate. Not only the rules were too liberal, but there was also much laxity in their application.[103]

Due to their financial capabilities, the British planters could avail the facilities of the government in opening new tea gardens what the local planters could not dream of such venture and those who could do that, they did that only after retirement with their savings.

Thus, with a view to attract and also to encourage investors to take up land for cultivation of tea and coffee; wasteland grant rules were passed from time to time since 1838. Under these, some land of a lease was held revenue free while others yielded revenue gradually after certain period. Rules were revised in 1854, 1861, 1874 and 1876. Thus, with the help of these tools, viz. the Regulation of Wasteland Rules of 1838, the Old Assam Rules of 1854, the Fee Simple Rules of 1861-62 and the Assam Land and Revenue Regulations Act of 1886, the colonial government wanted to grab the vast tract of wastelands more than one half of the extent of the province covering with deep forests, long grasses and bushes.

The Waste and Settlement Rule created another revenue free estate like the *lakhiraj* estates. But such type of revenue free rule was not framed for the rice cultivation. This type of discriminating rule was incentive to tea plantation, and discouragement to cultivation which invited ignition and irritation among the local people.[104]

Introduced in 1839, tea was firmly established as the most important cash crop by the seventies. The total acreage under tea increased from 2,311 acres in 1841 to around 8000 acres in 1859 and almost 31,350 acres in 1871. In 1872, the total area taken up by the tea planters in the Brahmaputra valley was officially reported to be 3,64,990 acres of which only 27,000 acres were under tea. Up to 1870-71, the British tea planters got settlement of 7 lakh acres of land. But only 56,000 acres of land were under tea cultivation; that is 1/8th of total settled land. In 1881 and 1891, the area under tea cultivation was 710 and 1310 acres; and lands settled with the immigrants were 1400 and 522 acres. According to Atkinson's estimate, plantations covered only 1.01 percent of the cultivated area of British India in 1895.[105]

The colonial government passed several agrarian legislations, viz. Waste Lands Settlement Rules, 1854; Fee Simple Rules, 1862 and the Thirty Years Lease Rules, 1876 to favour the planters. Consequently, by 1896-97, a total of 1,82,366 acres of wastelands on fee simple terms were leased out to the planters at a very low cost of over rupees 5 per acre. According to the census of 1881, the number of plantation households mostly of European individuals and Company share-holders were 35,181

The percentage of increase of land under tea was exceptionally high. The period between 1875-1914 shows an increase by 158.44 percent. In contrast to it, the land utilization under traditional crops was considerably low, which resulted in multifold reaction.[106]

Slavery is an extreme form of inequality, where some individuals are literally owned by others as their property. There are different variants of slavery, and bonded labour is one of them in India. Momai Tamuli Barua, an eminent official of the Ahom period, became bondsman for Rs. 4, prior to his recruitment in to the royal court of Pratap Singha, the Ahom king.

Slavery as a recognized institution might have existed in the kingdom of Pragjyotishpur and Kamrup since ancient times. Slavery still continues to a very considerable extent in Assam, and these poor creatures are bought and sold every day in the market according to their castes. High caste adult sells for about twenty rupees; boys fifteen and girls from eight to twelve. No slaves are allowed to be exported from Assam. But Pemberton, on the contrary, mentions in his report of the exports of slaves from Assam in 1809. According to him, hundreds slaves were exported from Assam to Bengal in 1809 at the Rs. 2000.[107]

Like a bondsman, a *paik* had to render his compulsory manual service and other kinds of duties to the state. But in regard to possession of certain political rights, he was sometime treated as a free citizen. Gait states that this was a most valuable privilege whereby the *paiks* were saved from much of the oppressions. The Ahom rulers organized the peasantry in such a way that the state could obtain the maximum use of its labour force.

The state during the Ahom regime depended for its growth and existence on the peasants, artisans and workers including slaves and servants who formed the body of the labour force. The aristocracy and the nobility for their maintenance, and the peasantry for their own living had to depend on the working classes. Indeed, the peasantry supplied all that was required for the growth and development of the state.

It was one of the laws of the Ahom Government that the land and the subjects were equally the property of the state; and accordingly, not only the houses and the lands, but the cultivators were also assessed.[108]

Pratap Singha engaged Momai Tamuli Barua to arrange and organize the peasantry called *paiks* in certain order. This arrangement of *paiks* into an institutional form came to be known as the *paik* system. Prior to this, one man from every family served the state. Although some families had 4 to 6 working men, there were some which had only one. To do away with this disproportionate demand, Momai Tamuli resettled the old villages by breaking the big families and established new ones and arranged the *paiks* into *khels*, making it compulsory that one member of every *got* of four *paik* was to render service to the state.

The *bhaktas*, who were loyal to Neo-vaishnavite *satras*, were exempted from rendering physical labour in the royal house and they have even been excluded from the *paik* list. Though slave trade was illegal, but it was immensely profitable; and even the Marwaris were also found indulged in this trade.[109]

Some fellows during the Ahom period, borrowed money from the rich peasants and became their slaves or *bandhas* or bondsmen, and remained as such until they could repay the debt. One Baloram Atai of Tapa, a village in erstwhile Kamrup, had mortgaged himself for rupees five and became slave.

At the close of the Ahom period, an estimated 9% of the total populations were slaves and bondsmen. According to the Statistical Report of 1835, the total population of Kamrup district were 1,93,331. Rutherford stated that out of the estimated population, 28,602 were slaves, 24,740 were bondsmen, 70,286 were females and 25,206 were slave girls. As per the advice of David Scott, a census was made of the slaves in Kamrup in 1830, and of the estimated population of 2,71,944 in Kamrup district, about six percent were slaves and three percent were bonded men.

In Assam, there was another kind of labourer known as *'morakiya'* who ploughed owner's land. He was neither a bonded labour nor a freeman. According to Gunabhiram 'he was essentially a free labour.'

Slavery system was prevalent in Goalpara also. Referring to the zamindari system of Goalpara, Guha has mentioned the existing slave system in the district. During the time of Buchanan, there were slaves among the appointed agricultural workers. These slaves, in addition to their entrusted duties in the houses and cultivation fields of the zamindars, helped them against the ryots. The zamindars employed them in violence and subversive activities.[110]

Slavery was an endeavour of solving the problem of labour through exportation and importation at an accelerated rate which was uncivilized and barbaric in the name of civilization. Lord Cornwallis attacked slavery in 1789 in a proclamation. The Bengal Government prevented slave importation by a Regulation in 1811. The Regulation of 1832 laid down that all slaves either the British or the Foreigners should be considered free. The Act of 1843 provided that the civil courts should not take cognizance of claims to slaves, a measure which abolished the right of slavery and ultimately, paved the way for the total eradication of this social evil and it was finally, prohibited by the Penal Code of 1860. In the first half of the 19th century, the British often with the support of enlightened Indian opinion, abolished such institutions, like suttee (1829), female infanticide, human sacrifice and slavery (1833). Though slavery system was abolished formally in 1843, yet it continued as before. Even after getting legal redemption, most of the slaves and their children continued to work for their masters as before.

To abolish the system, had there been no British in Assam, even then too, the system itself would have been wiped out gradually and slowly, as most of them had died already and some deserted the land due to the Burmese invasion of Assam. Even at that time too, they became a misnomer.[111]

The nobility lost its old privileges based on wealth and service of the *paiks,* due to its abolition. Protests against the government's decision of abolition of *paiks* and *khel* system were made by the members of the Ahom ruling class everywhere. They were joined by the Brahmanas and the Mahantas of Kamrup, as they were also affected by this. Maniram Dewan protested the British rule not on behalf of the mass people, but on behalf of the upper classes, as they were hard hit by the abolition of certain feudal privileges, such as slavery and forced labour. He became rebel when his interest received withstands at the British hands in later period.

The abolition of *paik* (1843) almost crippled the old Ahom aristocracy. The Brahmana and the Mahanta land-owners, who had for long depended on slaves and bondsmen for cultivation of their *Devottar, Brahmottar* and *Dharmottar* lands, were also severely affected. The Brahmana slaveholders of Kamrup even held a protest demonstration and submitted to the authorities a bunch of 1000 petitions, seeking permission to retain their slaves and bondsmen.

Due to this abolition, most of the estates of pre-colonial aristocracy became unproductive and were not even in a position to pay the land revenue in the form of money under the colonial system.[112] Like the land-owners of Assam, the land-owners of Sripuram were also the Brahmanas and were ritually prohibited to use the plough and cultivation, and therefore, had to be done by the tenants and agricultural labourers. Normally, the educated members of the Brahmana families when got settled in cities for taking up professional jobs, such as lawyers and doctors; they then leased out their land to the lower castes, allowing thus, the creation of a professional inequality in the society. But, the abolition of *paiks* by the Act V of 1843 by Captain Brodie, the newly appointed Principal Assistant of Sibsagar, irritated the so-called higher castes; and the men of rank found and felt it beneath their dignity to work hand in hand with those who had been till recently their subordinates. The revenue free *khats* were brought under assessment and they were pushed down to the level of ordinary ryots. Those whose ancestors never lived by digging, ploughing or carrying burdens; were now reduced to such degrading employments.[113]

It is true that behind the abolition of *paiks* was the creation and attraction of labourers towards the plantation sector. The Political Agent of Upper Assam urged (June 1, 1836) the necessity of emancipating the unfortunate Assamese and resettling them in the tea districts which would solve the problem of procuring labour from outside.

Tea plantation started in 1840, and labour importation began thirteen years later. Abolition of slavery greatly facilitated the movement of labour. On the south, plantation labourers mostly came from the Harijan castes, where as in Assam, they came from 'clean' castes, Harijans and tribes, such as Mundas and Santhals.

The greater the quantity of land, the greater the labour required. But in land-abundant Assam, the requirement of labour was far from satisfactory. None interested to work under the tea-gardens, due to their limited wants. Moreover, many people were engaged in the houses of the nobilities and the royal families. So, there was shortage of labour. It was further aggravated by some rumours, 'those who go Assam, meet death.' Henceforth, abolition of *paik* was necessary for removing the shortage.

Though, the British talked of the equality by abolishing the *paik* system but their inner motive was altogether different. Employ the labourers as slaves in the gardens were not new for the British. The writings of Dr.Johnson and Horace Walpole are the clear prove to it. They wrote 'it has appeared to us that six and forty thousand of African Negroes are sold every year to our plantation alone! It chills one's blood'.[114] Abolition of the *paik* system was just an eye-wash which manifests the hippocratic characters of the white colonists. They often talked of equality, raised voice against apartheid but these were just on lips.

The exploitation of the tea labourers of Jorhat, Tezpur and Darrang by the planters had been till then kept as a well guarded secret. The tea labourers were kept in sanctuary-type enclosures. In no case, they were allowed to mix with the local people of the neighbouring villages. To the planters, the word *'strike'* was an anathema.

According to Barpujari, the British followed a levelling policy, and slave system narrowed down the gap between high and low. But, this can be accepted partially. The condition of the *coolies* of the tea gardens of Assam was the worst form of serfdom than slavery. The *coolies*, however, were essentially neither slaves nor serfs; they constituted the newly emerged working class of Assam, bound together by a common interest against capital in its colonial form.

Though slaves were there in Assam during the Ahom period, but they were not the worst form; and this might be because of flexibility in casteism and racialism in Assamese society in comparison to the other states of India.

The British judicial system established the principle of equality, but unfortunately, their executives broke the system by inflicting indescribable exactions on the *coolies* and working classes of Assam. What they did in India, just opposite was done outside. They abolished, on one hand, the slave system in Assam and used to kidnap the poor and innocent Chinese labourers, on the other, in order to sell them as slaves in Cuba, Peru, Chile and the Western Coast of the United States. The fate of these Chinese was as tragic as the plight of the ensnared Africans. We can, finally, say that though slavery was abolished formally in 1843, a new form of slavery emerged in tea estates where tea labourers were treated like slaves by their masters.[115]

Migration, according to Mehrotra, is a necessary element of normal population adjustment and equilibrium within a nation or any sub national spatial unit. The immigration into the Brahmaputra valley is classified into five categories of persons: labourers to work in the tea gardens of the valley coming from Bihar, Orissa, Chota Nagpur, North West Provinces, Central Provinces, United Provinces and Madras; farmers settling in the agricultural lands of the valley coming largely from East Bengal; immigrants from Nepal engaged in livestock etc.; traders and artisans and other immigrants such as salary earners, planters, miners, administrators, labourers coming from various parts of India.

Floods, droughts, epidemics and excessive tributes demand, according to Burton Stein, stimulated migration. Cheap and fertile land, attractive earnings and easy matrimony, according to Gunabhiram Barua, also caused migration in Assam.[116] There was scarcity of labour in Assam as local people were loath to work hard due to their limited wants. The planters complained to Lord Curzon, the then Viceroy of India, regarding the labour scarcity, 'the indigenous population had been, wholly insufficient to develop the province.' So, it was found necessary to seek for tea garden *coolies* elsewhere who involved legislation from 1863 to 1901. Moreover, the local people were also not interested to work in the tea gardens. According to Mills, the want of labour in prolific Assam deters speculators from embarking their capital in developing resources.[117]

The large tract of unoccupied areas under deep forests and sparsely populated lands were the main source of attraction for migration into Assam. Srinavasa says that the greater the quantity of land owned by a family, the greater the input of labour required. It is quite natural if we accept his view and apply it in the case of Assam, for her depending on the labour forces from other sources to work in the vast lands. The growing economy demanded an increasing labour supply. The cash crop production needed an immense amount of manpower supply which was lack in Assam.[118]

It was the British who linked the Indian economy with the world economy by introducing the steam powered ships and the building of the Suez Canal (1869). They produced indigo, jute, cotton, tobacco, tea and coffee for consumption abroad; but to produce these goods, they had to rely mainly on the labourers. Srinivasa is right, 'the advent of the plantation marked the beginning of migration of labourers to the two plantation areas; mountainous regions of Assam and Western Ghats. The missionaries were also not lagging behind in this field, as some of them were found encouraging people to migrate to Assam and settle in the wasteland. The completion of the Assam Bengal Railway improved communication network, and facilitated immigration. Moreover, by the end of the 19th century, most of the tribals in Bihar had been evicted from their lands, and had to leave for working in the tea gardens of Assam and the coal fields of Manbhum. The pangs of emigration were portrayed in their literature:

'All partings are painful
I will leave you, my friend.
I shall not be happy
When you go to Assam brother
If you are alive, send letters
If you are dead, come in the dreams.[119]

Sometime despite having facilities, the labourers were still then reluctant to come. In Assam, tea plantations were established in malarious and lightly populated areas where labourers declined to come. The rumours, those who had gone to Assam, none had returned and all had died, again aggravated the labour crisis in Assam. In addition to that, the unfavourable climate, *kala-zar*, lack of medical treatment, insufficient food and many other factors helped in increasing the labour crisis, as many immigrant labour deserted due to the fear-psychosis of mortality.[120]

H.L.Johnson, the Commissioner of Assam, adopted some measures in May, 1885 to encourage immigration. The fares of trains and ships were decreased and even revenue free land was given. He said, 'I have now authority under Rule 35, Section-2 of the Settlement Rules, to allow a revenue free term of three years to encourage immigration.'[121]

Heavy burden of revenue and taxes; and thickly population density compelled peasants to migrate from one district to another. The Kachari people from Kamrup and Mangaldoi subdivision migrated to the tea districts due to revenue hike and epidemic havoc. With a view to discourage this habits, Hopkinson proposed the rates of revenue equal in all the districts and even got the approval of the Government of Bengal.[122]

Immigration was, mainly, due to the growth of tea plantation and the available cultivable land. Thus, so far the growth of population of the Brahmaputra valley as a whole during 1881 to 1931 is concerned, it was environmental and medical factors combined with economic forces that generated declining movement in death rates and increasing movement in immigration, rather than the biological factors which are generally responsible for the rapid growth of population.

The number of deaths and desertions during the period of the Civil Wars and the Burmese invasions of Assam was enormous, as is evident from the fact that in 1826, the population stood at 8,30,000. The administrative confusion; oppression and extortion in the early days of the Company's rule reduced the number, according to Pemberton, to less than seven district. The population of Assam proper including Goalpara exceeded 12 lakhs in 1853 and this rose to about 15 lakhs in 1872. This increase was due to the influx of outsiders, imported labourers particularly to meet the growing demands. Of 18 lakhs in 1881, nearly 3 lakhs were immigrants and their number reached over 6 lakhs in 1901.

    1826—8.3 lakhs
    1853—12 lakhs
    1872—15 lakhs
    1881—18 lakhs

Source: H. K. Barpujari's (eds), 'Political History of Assam', PP. 59-60.

Due to the rapid growth of population in Assam, density of population also began to augment spontaneously.

Density of population per sq. mile (in the Brahmaputra valley):

District	1872	1881	1891
Kamrup	146	167	164
Darrang	69	80	90
Nowgong	68	82	90
Sibsagar	64	79	96
Lakhimpur	27	40	56
Goalpara	98	113	115

Source: A. Guha's 'Planter Raj to Swaraj', Appendix-3, P. 279

According to the Census of Assam (1931), Nowgong was the district where there was the greatest concentration of immigrants from East Bengal. These immigrants occupied large areas of unsettled wasteland.[123]

The area under cultivation, the nature of the crops grown and the extent of the livestock may be accepted as the best standards of agricultural prosperity. But these elements were found absent in colonial agricultural sector of Assam. Despite that, agricultural prosperity flourished in Assam due to the availability and fertility of the soil.

The Ahoms constructed more roads, embankments, bunds, canals and bridges in and around their capital. About 90% of the roads in old Sibsagar district were built by the Ahoms. This proves that they did something more for the welfare of the peasants and the masses. But the British only got them repaired, and that too restricted in limited numbers.

For the improvement of agriculture, even Muhammad Bin Tughluq in medieval period (14th century) opened a *'Diwan-i-kohi'* in India.[124] But the so called modern men with modern outlook, hardly did such steps even outside of Assam. The British neither set up Agriculture Technology Development Centre nor set up Agriculture Information Centre to bring revolutionary change in agricultural sector. Agriculture is regarded as the life-blood of peasants. Behind the crops, lies the peasants' drop. Peasants' drop means peasants' bloods and their hard labour. The colonial government sucked the blood of peasants, and squeezed them like lemons through the maximization of land revenue and others like that.

Major Jenkins, the then Commissioner of Assam, realized that the development of a province by and large depended on the improvement of communication; and wanted, therefore, to set apart a certain percentage of revenue for repair and construction of roads. For the protection of cultivation, he emphasized the need for gradual restoration of the old causeways which were as essential as embankments. But it is doubtful how sincerely he spent the revenue for the protection and development of cultivation.

In spite of the systematic revenue maximization, the government did nothing to improve the condition of agriculture. Unfortunately in Assam, industrial growth and development had no links with the agricultural sector. Foreign Government cared more for revenue than for the material improvement of the people. They were interested in a highly bureaucratic unaccountable administration and in the exploitation of the vast natural resources of the conquered province.[125]

Anandaram Barua, the harbinger of modern age of Assam, suggested to Mills in 1853 for the all round development of agriculture. To improve the peasantry, he stressed the need of production of varied and marketable crops by improved methods of cultivation. He wanted the government to take the lead in bringing agricultural experts from abroad to teach the people regarding the means connected with agriculture. He also wanted the government to furnish modern technology to the cultivators and advocated the importation of foreign technical knowhow and pleaded for the setting up of a number of technical schools to teach the students to construct implements of agriculture and other works of utility. But all became cry in the wilderness, as the authority showed little interest on it. Among other things, he also pointed out that the implements of agriculture were the 'rudest' and the animals used in the plough were the 'feeblest' and manuring of fields were 'ill understood'; and asked the authority to introduce new modern technology by replacing these drawbaks. But the authorities showed little interest to his suggestions.

Some of the elites of Assam province tried their best to bring agricultural change through their writings; and thereby, attempted to change the way of life of the peasants. The book entitled 'Krishi Darpan,' written by Kefayat Ullah, sadar munsiff of Guwahati in 1853, was mainly written for the cultivators of Assam. The book gave instructions on tilling lands, selection of seeds and discussed the utility of crops. The monthly journal 'Orunodoi' in 1854 appealed to the people of Assam to make use of the book.[126] But the efforts, finally, ended in smoke.

It would be biased and partial, if we do not mention the name of Dr. Voelcker. Like some native, some foreigners also made recommendation for the improvement of agriculture. Dr. Voelcker,

Consulting Chemist to the Royal Agricultural Society exchanged views with the delegates and experts in two conferences held at Simla in 1890 and 1893. The report which he, finally, submitted extended to all matters affecting agricultural improvement: the character of the soil and the manure suited to them; the diseases of cattles, plants and their causes and the means by which they may be prevented; minimized the improvement of fuel and fodder supplies; the reclamation of the wasteland economic products; improvement of old and introduction of new staples and agricultural implements; and possible reform in the methods and practices of cultivation.

For the bad agricultural and economic condition of the peasants, they themselves were also responsible. They did not take little interest in raising non-food crops in an organized way and showed indifference in sericulture and horticulture sector. Active interest and participation; and land used for different kinds of farming could have brought development in their economy. According to Bhalla, the use of land for orchards, dairy, goats, poultry, fishery and bee keeping was not extensive and small even today.[127] But according to Barpujari, lack of strong embankments and device for the protection of land from the frequent ravages of floods, primitive mode of agriculture, feeblest animals prevented the ryots from raising more than one crop throughout the year.

Seed is a critical and basic input for attaining sustained growth in agricultural production. So, the use of high yielding varieties and their timely and regular replacement are important for maintaining yield levels of crops. But the peasants of Assam were neither acquainted with this, nor did the government take effective measures for it. To avail the services, namely credit, marketing services, services relating to seeds, fertilizer, agricultural implements; there was lack of co-operative office. Even the white colonists also remained silence to them. According to Bhalla, this service is not very encouraging even today.[128] There was not much change in the set of agricultural implements when the British occupied this land in the early part of the 19th century. The mode of cultivation continued to be primitive, and the implements, the ryots used, were of the archaic type. According to Barpujari, the apparatus and process of agriculture throughout the regions, hills and plains, both remain till date almost the same except that chemical fertilizers and power tillers have come to be used in a very limited way in some rice-fields.[129]

Green Revolution coupled with the introduction of new technology changed the mode of production in agriculture resulting the emergence of capitalism in agriculture.[130] But in Assam, such change was hardly seen due to the primitive mode of agricultural tools. Bullock was used for ploughing in Assam and other states of India during the colonial period. But unfortunately, while the peasants used diesel and electricity power for ploughing in the west, the same was not applied in the field of cultivation of Assam and other Indian states. Even today, while agriculturally advanced states use more of diesel or electricity for most operations, the poorer states are still relying on bullock power. Like ploughing, animal power was used in Assam in harvesting and threshing also. The people were unaware of the use of power and government's steps were also not found satisfactory in this field.

Except to some extent in plantation industries, the application of modern technology in cultivation sector was far from satisfactory where there had vast prospect of fetching revolutionary change in that sector. Ignorance and indifference of the people also equally responsible for that. Despite repeated request, the authority showed little interest in that field. Even today, according to Situation Assessment Survey (SAS), undertaken in 2003, nearly 60% farmers do not access any information on modern technology from any source. According to SAS of 2003, the percentage of farmer households accessing information through radio was 28.9, extension worker 5.9, TV 9.3, Newspaper 10.2, input dealer 8, other progressive farmers 15.9 and any source 46.1.[131] To improve the quality of agriculture, there was lack of information centre in Assam. If such centers were there in Assam at that time, the then peasants could have accessed some suggestions and recommendation, and developed their economy. Like today, there was no Agriculture Technology Development and Information Centre in colonial Assam. As a result, prospect of high yielding became hazy but despite that, peasants got no respite from revenue burden which gave birth to disdain in the minds of the peasants.

Water is to land what food is to human body. The part played by irrigation in Indian agriculture is all the greater due to the uncertainty, unequal distribution as well as the insufficient rainfall. In large parts of the country, rainfall is the only source of water supply and its failure causes almost famine like condition.[132] The actual success of agriculture in India largely depends on nature. Cultivation depends on climate and if there are irregularities in the climatic rhythm, the programme of cultivation is upset. The greatest single climatic factor which dominates Indian agriculture is the monsoon. It rains sometimes, when the peasant needs sunshine and it shines sometimes, when he needs rain. Due to the uncertainty of monsoon, the peasant must expect upon occasion to see much of his year's work wiped out by a cloudburst, hail storm or a plague of grass-hoppers.[133]

The positive and encouraging results from the improved West Jamuna Canal (1820) and the opening of Eastern Jamuna were not unknown to Anandaram Dhekial Phukan. Again, the Grand Upper Anicut (1844) under the Cauvery Delta Scheme, the Dowlesh Waran and the Madduru Anicuts (1848) under the Godavari Delta Scheme were already completed by that time, and the construction of the Ganga Canal and the Krishna Delta Irrigation Poject works was then in progress.

Large scale irrigation and water supply could have changed the pattern of agriculture in the state and brought green revolution in the agriculture sector. But, the government did nothing to provide such type of irrigation facilities to the peasants. Scarcity of water, thus, remained as an impediment of agriculture in the state for centuries.

Canal-irrigated lands give much higher yields than un-irrigated lands. The yields of irrigated and un-irrigated land in the Punjab (1896-97) bear the testimony to it.[134]

Crops	Irrigated (kg per hectare)	Non-irrigated (kg per hectare)
Rice	1,308	298
Wheat	1,028	645
Barley	667	630
Jawar	661	419
Bajra	661	409
Maize	1,359	749
Gram	846	585
Sugarcane	1,851	1,078
Cotton	112	64

Source: Irfan Habib's 'A People's history of India—Indian economy 1858-1914'

By initiating such type of canal-irrigation system, the colonial government could have increased the incidence of crops in Assam also. But, they cared for only revenue maximization, not for the agricultural improvement of the state. Today, farmers irrigate their lands from various sources, viz. tube-wells, wells, canals, river spring during *khariff* and *rabi* season. But unfortunately, the peasants of Assam during that time depended on rain and river for irrigation. Even today, it remains unchanged to some extent.

Forests are a handmaid to agriculture and it influence on climate, rainfall, water supply, flood control, soil erosion, fertility of the soil and direction of winds.[135] The colonial government hardly planted and extended the areas of forest lands. They rather reserved and engulfed forests lands in the name of wastelands, and destroyed and exported them to their native land. Large scale destruction of forest lands invited deforestation followed by some evils, viz. drought, floods and soil erosion resulting bad effects on agriculture.

In the fertile and land abundant Assam, the peasants were least interested towards fertilizer and manure. But that does not mean that they did not know of its use. Use of manure was known to them, but they made limited use of it. Generally, sugarcane was manured. In Nowgong, the growers used to manure tobacoo. With no scarcity of cultivable land, the peasants did nothing to increase the productivity of the land. Though area under cultivation was increasing in all the districts of the valley, the average productivity stagnated day by day. As a result, there could have been no improvement of the peasants'lot. They used to produce the same crop from the same land annually and were not accustomed to rotation of crops. Measures for the improvements of the soil with the help of chemical fertilizers, modern implements and seeds were not used.

The cultivators had no any special efforts except in the protection of the crops from wild animals and other.[136] To get rid of the exactions of the insects, the farmers of South-West Kamrup of that period, probably, planted *jarmoni* and the skin of *sumathira* in their crop-fields. Moreover, leeches of several varieties abound in all parts of Assam, and every bush and blade of grass is frequented by them, particularly during the rainy season. The peasants at that time had to bear the bite of leeches, especially, at the time of ploughing, harvesting and threshing which was a natural and thrilling picturesque of that time. The people, probably, to get rid of them, rubbed either salt or cucumber and its leaves which had acted as anti-leeches. This practice to some extent still prevails in South West Kamrup. To evade attack of the insects, like caterpillars, larva, grass-hopper, locusts, crickets and others; the peasants, usually planted either *jarmoni* or kept dead and dry frogs in the crop-fields. Fire was caught at night to disperse and kill the insects. Even today, some peasants catch fire on tyres at night to kill the insects.

The matter of regret is that when the entire Europe was flooded with goods due to the emergence of green revolution in agriculture because of the application of modern technology, the same people showed their apathy in that field, specially, in their colonial lands. Being basically traders, their main intention was to take from, not take back for that.

Today, Situation Assessment Survey of the Farmers (SASF-2003) brings out the fact that the proportion of farmers using pesticides during *rabi* season was the highest in West Bengal (65%) followed by Punjab, Assam and Haryana. The use of chemical pesticides and other agro-chemicals are getting reduced being banned globally, because of their toxic effects on human beings and live-stock, residual toxicity, environment problems, pest outbreaks and drastic effects on beneficial insects. The scientists are trying today to develop a holistic system of tackling pests to make it more eco-friendly, economically viable and socially acceptable for the farmers. Use of bio-control agents and bio-pesticides are increasing gaining acceptance with farmers and therefore, Integrated Management Practices have been adopted since 1985 to tackle the pests and diseases of major crops.[137] When IMP have been adopted today to tackle the pests and diseases of crops, our ancestors not using chemical fertilizers and pesticides emancipated the natural environment from being contaminated. Indeed, they were the harbinger and sentinel of nature, in true sense of the term.

The land reforms measures made the government super power in agricultural relations, and they paved little attention to landlords, jagirdars, zamindars and peasants. The government gave no opportunity to landlords and others to take any measures to provide technology and improved agricultural input to farming. Foreign Government of India did not implement radical land reforms due to some political reasons. But some social scientists try to explain the agricultural problem of India as an offshoot of population, pressure on land and retrograde social institutions, like caste and joint-family system. The peasantry also lacked capital, required for scientific farming.

It is said that humanitarianism underlaid many of the reforms introduced by the British in the first half of the 19th century.[138] It can be accepted to some extent as they brought revolutionary changes in Indian society by eliminating some social injustice and evils. On the contrary, their land reforms measures did little benefit to the Indian peasants. They sucked and squeezed the bloods of the Indian peasants through their land reform measures, and finally, constructed graveyard for them. Indeed, land reforms and revenue administration enriched and empowered colonists; and impoverished and pauperized the indigenous.

The Ahoms encouraged peasants for cultivation and therefore, new lands were given to them either revenue free or for a lump sum of produce as revenue. But such venture was found to be rarely taken by the British. The land reforms and revenue administration of the British was not encouraging for the Indians. Their land reforms made them superpower in agricultural sector. They gave no scope to land-owners and peasants to develop agricultural technology through which they could have developed their fortune.[139] Actually, the government did not want drastic change in agriculture. Development of agriculture in Assam would develop the economy of the local people, what they did not want. They wanted local people to become economically dependent and parasite on them.

Gandhiji very rightly observed that if villages live, who can perish India and if villages perish, who can save India.[140] Indian villagers are mostly cultivators and their mainstay is agriculture. The British were well known to the fact that to cripple the Indian economy, attack on agriculture would be the proper. With this aim and motive in view, they most probably sought to harm the traditional agriculture system of Assam. The revolts of Phulaguri, Patharughat, Lachima and Rangia were the best examples of this. They never wanted to see rich and prosperous peasants in Assam, and because of that, did not introduce any modern method of technology in Assam what was available in England at that time. Even some of the Commissioners of Assam also did not encourage the cultivators to cultivate traditional crops. Jenkins encouraged the cultivators to cultivate such crops which were easily marketable. Motive behind this encouragement was to increase the paying capacity of the ryots.[141] Probably, they sought to increase the paying capacity of the ryots not because of improving the economy of the local cultivators, but because of the collection of more revenue from them. They liked to squeeze and suck the locals through revenue and tax augmentation. They never sought their material improvement.

The lease of mauzadar was of short duration and his office was insecure.[142] Probably, the government did not introduce long lease duration and secured office for the mauzadar thinking it would strengthen his position in the locality, and bring rejuvenation in agriculture. But it is also true that some of the mauzdars inflicted indescribable exactions on the peasants of Assam.

It was a matter of great concern for the peasants of Assam that they did not get any return from their government. The revenues collected from the peasants were not spent for their development, and it became transparent in1888-89 when a local board grant was needed for the renovation of the Janji bund to protect thousands of acres of paddy land from inundation. The local taxes collected from the rice cultivators were spent in building the roads and bridges, mainly convenient for tea gardens. Both public and private funds were spent for the tea cultivation. They gave every encouragement to the colonial planters, and even granted leases on very favourable terms for the cultivation of new staples. They prepared wasteland rules for their people's interest. Funds were rarely spent for the cultivation of rice, mustard oil etc. and thus, local crops were totally neglected. Owing to such type of parochial nature, local cultivators did not like the colonial bureaucrats and held them responsible for their wretched condition. Behind the hike of revenue and tax, they suspected the hands of the bureaucrats and therefore, expressed their anguish in the revolts of 1861 and 1893-94.

The British developed communication network for profitable exploitation of the region. The tea producing districts had a better communication system than the non-tea producing districts of colonial Assam.[143] This is a clear example of deprivation and there are many examples of such deprivation.

Sir Henry Cotton, the then Chief Commissioner of Assam (1896-1902) encouraged the planters to take up lands for ordinary cultivation.[144] It proves that the government in addition to plantation, encouraged their men in cultivation also. But local people were neither encouraged in plantation, nor in cultivation.

Throughout the 19th century, the government had been primarily guided by financial consideration; priority was always on quicker and larger collection of revenue rather than on increased production and efficient distribution. Complete protection of the peasants from the oppression had been a mere dream in Assam under the British. Instead of giving protection, the government even incited the planters against the cultivators. Planters' disdain and anguish towards the local cultivators began to augment in such manner that they even disrupted inter-village communications by fencing in portions of existing public roads and denying the right of way to villagers.[145]

Greater concentration on plantation, ultimately, brought anathema in agriculture resulting shortage of food. At the time of shortage of food, the entire population of tea gardens was fed on imported rice.[146]

Early records show that the Ahom rulers in order to extend cultivation, got built embankments to prevent frequent flood raids from the Brahmaputra and her innumerable tributaries. Some natural and human factors also sometime handicapped the agricultural extension, but the Ahom rulers overcame these problems by fully utilizing the existing manpower and advanced technology.[147]

Like the Ahom period, the natural calamities, like flood, fire, earthquake, drought and cattle disease aggravated the situation of Assam in colonial period also. Locusts and white ants did not lag behind in their destructive operations. The measures of the government to tackle these were not satisfactory. The government instead of adopting some relief measure to protect the victims, they were found busy in collecting and maximizing the revenue.

Floods of varying intensity was almost an annual occurrence in Assam. Due to the floods, there was fall of harvest. No attempt was made to raise embankments or devise means for the protection of the land from ravages of the floods. There was growing demand for such protective measures.[148]

Like the floods havoc, there was locust havoc in Assam during the first half and even the second half of the 19th century. There was large scale destruction of harvests because of appearance of locusts in the district of Nowgong in 1822, resulting scarcity of food. The ravage was not confined to the crops alone. The locusts ate up the leaves of all fruits and other trees. A second blight was noticed in 1840. The third occurred in 1858 and this time, the ravage of locusts was aggravated by the appearance of other insects.[149] Though the officials of the government took note of the damage of crops caused by locusts, but the steps taken by them were not satisfactory.

Assam was not the only state squeezed by the British during the time of famine and natural calamities. In the year 1770, there was a great famine in Burdwan (Bengal). The revenue statistics for Burdwan shows that this rich district was so optimally squeezed till the time of famine that there was no scope for revenue maximization. In the year of famine, revenue raised from Burdwan was Rs.40,57,432.[150] The habit of collection of tax and revenue was in their bloods and veins, and it continued unto their death. Question of humanity was secondary;

revenue was their primary and principal consideration. According to Srinivasa, humanitarianism underlaid many of the reforms introduced by the British in the first half of the 19th century. Humanitarianism resulted in many administrative measures to fight famine, control epidemics etc.[151] The British Government brought some radical change in our society by eliminating social evils from the society through reforms. But in such measures, they were helped by Raja Rammohan Ray, Vidyasagar, Ranade and others. But, what policy they did adopt towards agriculture, that hardly benefited the Indians. Their role in fighting natural calamities, like famine, drought, floods etc., revealed their hippocratic nature. They sometime constituted some committee and sometime conducted some investigations. But all of them were just eye-wash. The eyes of so-called humanitarian people were only on the wealth and revenue of India; not on the famine, drought and the floods of her people.

The people of Assam produced crops only for their annual need. Henceforth, there was scarcely surplus for sale or for bad days, like drought, floods etc.[152] So, their condition became deplorable when crops damaged due to floods or drought. Moreover, to compensate their loss, there was no crop insurance system. The colonial government was also not interested for giving compensation for the damaged caused by natural calamities.

For their miserable and deplorable condition, they themselves were also responsible. Even today, the extent of crop insurance is very limited. According to the 'Situation Assessment Survey of the Farmers' undertaken at the all India level by the 'National Sample Survey Organization of the Ministry of Statistics and Plan Implementation, Government of India' during 2003, only 4% of farmer households reported ever having insured their crops. Among those who had never insured their crops were found to be unaware of the practice of crops insurance.[153]

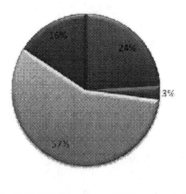

Source: G. S. Bhalla's 'Condition of Indian Peasantry', PP. 6-7.

Due to the drought and floods, many crop-fields damaged, and it gave birth to scarcity of foods. Due to the fall of harvest, the prices of foodgrains rose. Sometime, foodgrains were not found even at high cost. A.D.Phukan described the year 1851 in this manner, 'people in some parts of Darrang and Kamrup actually obliged to dispose of their children and to part with their valuable ornaments and utensils for a few seers of rice due to famine.'[154]

The prices of foodgrains were rising and many starvation deaths were reported from Nowgong in the bad season of 1896. On October 16 of that year, troops had to be called out there to suppress a riotous outburst against the *banias* who had cornered the grain market. Conditions were further worsened by the great earthquake of 1897, that caused many deaths and havoc over many hundreds of acres of farm land.[155]

III

During the Ahom period, Assam had good trade and commercial relation with her neighbouring states, viz. Tibbet, Bhutan, Burma and Bengal. The treaty with the Ahom king Gaurinath Singha facilitated free intercourse between the subjects in Bengal and Assam, permitted the merchants to proceed anywhere in Assam in boats loaded with merchandise and removed all earlier restrictions. Actually, this treaty opened the gate of trade. In Ahom period, Assam had trade relations with Bengal. There was export and import between the two states. Assam exported to Bengal stick lac, *muga silk*, *muga* cloth, *munjeet* (Indian madder), black pepper, cotton, iv ry, bell-metal vessels, mustard seed, iron hoes, slaves, *thaikol* fruits etc. In 1808 and 1809, when the country was still suffering from the effect of long internal dissension and its inhabitants were living in a most unsettled and precarious state of society, the exports and imports to and from Bengal amounted to Rs.3,59,200.[156]

Though Assam had trade relations with her neighbours, but the fact is that the economy of Assam during the Ahom regime was backward, and the use of money was limited and trade among the peasantry was largely absent, everything was produced at home. Monetization came very late in the economy of Assam. Money, therefore, became hardly collected at the hands of the peasants. Cultivation and production of money in Assam was very limited till the second half of the 18th century.[157]

In 1809, trade between Bhutan and Assam was said to amount to two lakh of rupees per annum, even when the latter country was in a most unsettled state. The exports from Assam were lac, madder, silk, *erendi* silk and dried fish. The Bhutias imported woolen cloths, gold dust, salt, musk, horses, the celebrated Tibbet *chowries* and the Chinese silk. As the state of affairs in Assam became more distracted, this trade necessarily declined but under all these disadvantages, the Khumpa Bhutias or Lassa merchants just prior to the Burmese invasion, brought down gold which alone amounted to upwards of 70,000 rupees. But so severely had the trade suffered from the occupation of the country by the Burmese that in 1833, two Bhutia merchants only came down from the hills when Lt.Rutherford was the in-charge of the purgunnah of Darrang.[158]

The British were attracted to the north east not only by the possibility of extracting the raw materials and marketing the English goods in the region, but also by the prospects of trade with China, Burma and Tibbet.[159] Basically being business-minded, the British understood that the future economy of a country depended on road and communication. That's why, they laid more importance on it so as to boost their trade and economy. Of course, it brought reward for them. Jenkins and Fisher discovered the route, and it opened the lines of communication facilitating the merchants to enter with varied goods. Raw materials and forest resources sounded the economy which helped them in establishing a sound and stable government in Assam.[160]

When the British came to Assam, at that time the availability of cash was limited in day to day's transactions, and it was difficult for the peasants to go to the market to seek relief. The Assamese peasants of late came into contact with the trade economy. Of course, they were not the only peasants who came of late with it. Entire Indian picture was more or less the same. The Patidar of Gujarat are a peasant caste who took to trade and commerce only during the closing decades of the 19th century.[161]

In course of time, the resources, manufactures and the trade in North East India passed into the complete control of the British *raj*. The trade was, ultimately, used as an instrument of colonial control and governance. It was so vital to the life and existence of the people in the region that the government could always dictate its own terms, and suppress the anti-British plots and revolts.

So long there was native government in Assam, fortune and prosperity went hand to hand. But arrival of the British, shattered it completely to the ground. The hills-plains cordial relations, hitherto maintaining since the time of the Ahoms, was disturbed by the British. Though the colonial government at the initial stage of their rule, tried to maintain unity between the hills and the plains, but later they changed their policy due to longer political considerations of trade and defence.[162]

The people of Assam were unaware of the term 'market economy.' The arrival of the British let them to know of it. They asked people to grow crops for commercial purpose which would give them money, and sound their economy. David Scott created taste among the Assamese for commodities not locally available, and gradually, *hats* and markets were established in and around the *sadar* station where traders from Dacca and Calcutta arrived there with loads of foreign goods. They collected local produce in exchange of foreign goods. The growth of tea, coal and oil industries had stimulated the interest in cash crops. This together with the introduction of *abkari* opium and the liberal issue of licenses for liquor shops led to an increasing demand of money in the new economy. The money economy, gradually, out-weighed the barter system. However, the limited flow of currency was a serious check on the capital formation.[163]

The introduction of money as the medium of exchange without substantial increase in the existing currency inevitably fell crushingly on the ryots, for whom there was no alternative but to leave their hearths and home to find shelter even in the adjoining hills. People not only in the hilly regions, but in the plains also felt it difficult to pay tax and revenue in cash. Moreover, there were no markets in close proximity to sale their produced goods, and therefore, the common people were harassed and fed up with the tax and revenue collection policy of the British, as they were not acquainted with this new system. The rural peasants, especially, of north Kamrup and Mangaldoi faced problem in adjusting with the new market economy, as they got less opportunity to sell their produce in cash whenever necessary and because of this problem, they could not pay their revenue to the mauzadars in time. Same problem developed in the payment of revenue by the mauzadars to the government.[164]

The term 'commercialization of agriculture,' according to Habib, is used to describe the extension of trade and money relations in India's countryside. The commercialization of agriculture refers to the process of production of crops for market to be sold for cash, rather than for family use or subsistence which dominated Indian agriculture from times immemorial until the arrival of the British in India. The process commenced sometime in the beginning of the 19th century and gained momentum in and after the middle.

The commercialization of agriculture had progressed mostly in those tracts where the crops were largely grown for export. It brought transformation in agriculture and thus, agriculture became capitalistic. Need for cash; activities of the new class of commercial middlemen; village market linked with world market; agricultural policy of the government; development of roads and railways; impact of the American Civil War and opening up of the Suez Canal (1869): all these led to the emergence of commercialization of agriculture in India.[165] Due to the commercialization of Indian agriculture, the income of the agriculturists increased; self-sufficiency of village disappeared; new crops took the place of traditional crops and the market of Indian agricultural crops widened. Anyway, commercialization of agriculture affected the balance of village economy.

For the vast majority of poorer peasants, commercialization was often a forced process, as money was needed to meet the growing demand of revenue in cash. The peasants of Coimbatore once told a British collector that they were growing cotton simply, because they could not take it; the grain they might have cultivated had it been consumed by them. They went half-fed because the least remained with them had to meet revenue demands.[166]

Rural indebtedness is an evil which has accumulated over very many years in the past, and passed from generation to generation. Sir

M.L.Darling once said that it has long been recognized that indebtedness is no new thing in India. What really new was the significance it acquired after the establishment of British rule. Darling was of the view that extravagance and improvidence of the agriculturist was responsible for his debt. The views of the Deccan Riots Commission (1875) were that undue importance has been given to the expenditure on marriage and other festivals, but it rarely appears as the nucleus of his indebtedness. It would not be true to say that the money-lender and the method of his business were mainly responsible for the indebtedness and poverty of the agriculturist. Indebtedness has not been so much the result of poverty, but a cause of poverty. The poverty was more the cause than the effect of indebtedness.

A society steeped in debt is, necessarily, a social volcano. Discontent between classes is bound to arise and smoldering discontent is always dangerous. The exploitation of the peasantry at the hands of the money-lender shattered the traditional peace and harmony of village life, and created in its place tension, anger and a smoldering feeling of revenge.[167]

An important consequence of the growing demand of money in the new economy was the growing indebtedness of the peasants which drew swarms of money-lenders and middlemen in to Assam province. The *keya* and the *mahajan* assumed a prominent place in the economy of the region.

Without adequate monetization of the economy, the British demand to pay revenue in cash caused problem for the Assamese peasants. The Marwari shopkeepers found this situation ripe for lending money, and thus, multiplied the earning rate. They came forward to advance loans to the peasants to enable them to pay the revenue. This loan was advanced at an interest rate of one *anna* per rupee in a month, in other words 75%.

The market of the peasant economy had been completely in the grip of the Marwaris since the advent of the British. The peasants used to receive cash advances from the Marwari traders as against pledged crops and mortgage.[168] Out of 9,801 professional money-lenders in Assam as per the Census Report of 1891, only 1793 were in the Brahmaputra valley (1,211 were in Kamrup alone); the rest were in the Surma valley.[169] Loanees had to mortgage movable and immovable property, such as land, land documents, ornaments, utensils and others. Cases were not rare when peasant loanees failed to redeem the mortgage, and lost their mortgaged property forever. As the peasants could not pay so much of taxes, their arrears went on ever increasing and there by, paved the way for rapid growth of indebtedness and pauperization. It is obvious that non-realization of taxes forced the ryots to sell his or her lands at a very cheap rate. Even household utensils were not spared for. Marriage, purchase of cattle and rituals also forced the ryots to run to take loan from *mahajans* and others.

Massive fiscal pressure due to the maximization of land revenue led to increasing indebtedness in the villages caused peasants' flight. The peasants' flight due to revenue hike and indebtedness is not new. To get ride of the exactions of the *bhog-patis*, many peasants abandoned their villages, as described by Varahmihir in the 6th century. As oppression of the jagirdars on the peasants for the collection of revenue increased, the number of absconding peasants grew resulting decline of agriculture.[170]

Regarding the incidence of indebtedness in different states of India, Situation Assessment Survey undertook a survey in 2003. According to Bhalla, the established number of indebted farmer households is 4,536 and indebted farmer households is 18.10% in Assam. But regarding the incidence of indebtedness in colonial Assam, he is silent. The SAS data on indebtedness brings out that at all India level, 60.4% of rural households were farmer households and 48.6% of these were indebted. But states with very low incidence of indebtedness were: Meghalaya, Arunachal and Uttarakhand.[171]

Decline of the nobility was followed by the decline of the old crafts. The decline of the crafts was neither sudden nor totally unexpected. The commercial treaty of 1793, between the Ahom king Gaurinath Singha and the East India Company gave the first blow on the traditional crafts of Assam.[172] The ideological make-up of the British Government led them to believe, notwithstanding the fact that India was now to serve the ends of the industrial revolution, that the new India could be created as an image of England.[173]

The British Government resorted to the policy of *laissez-faire* in order to flood the Indian markets with machine made commodities of England. In pursuance of this policy, the government imposed nominal import duties on British goods and boosted the export of raw materials to England. Thus, their discriminatory commercial and industrial policy helped them lot.

Like the Indian, the Chinese handicrafts also met decline after the arrival of the colonial government. For example, the new tariff system encouraged the foreigners to import foreign goods in China leading to a serious damage to the nascent industries of China.[174]

The indigenous industries of Assam were neglected to make way for new enterprises which were European in capital and management. Consequently, a situation developed leading to the disruption of the traditional economy of Assam. European goods were popularized in Assam and the introduction of the finished goods reduced the demand of the local products. The imported salt, for example, resulted in the depreciation of the Tibbetan salt. The Tibbetan pony also lost its demand in Assam since the roads and other means of transport emerged in the scene. The mill-made cloths and woolens pushed the indigenous handloom products out of market. The introduction of synthetic rubber displaced the Indian-rubber while the indiscriminate trapping of the rubber forest caused the natural end of the rubber trade. Similarly, the Wildlife Protection Policy reduced the prospect of elephant trade. In the changed situation, the demand for the local products declined drastically and this reduced their purchasing power.

The businessmen from outside the region not only imported goods for marketing locally, but they even specialized in manufacturing the items of local market. Some local people were employed by the outsiders to manufacture local implements and emphasis was given on such implements which had liking in the locality. A number of indigenous industries particularly spinning and weaving of cotton and silk continued to exist and met domestic requirements, but qualities being comparatively poor, they could hardly compete with cheaper and better varieties imported from abroad. Likewise, the increasing import of brass, copper and iron wares hit the local artisans hard and as a result, the gold washers took to agriculture when they found their time-honoured pursuits less economic.[175]

Export of raw materials from India; investment of British capital in the industries of India; mercantilism and restrictions on import from India; the nature of demand from new educated classes; import of factories goods from England; free trade policy and other policies of government and organizational weakness of the Indian handicrafts led to the decline of cottage industries of Assam. The decline started in the beginning of the 19th century, and got accelerated after1850.

Throughout the British rule, India was mercilessly impoverished. Her famous manufactures were ruined and poor artisans and craftsmen driven to make out a living from primitive agriculture.[176] The cottage industry in India had, in the past, acted as a safety valve for those who depended on agriculture because it gave a second source of income to the farmer. Its decline deprived the farmer of his subsidiary occupation, thereby, considerably reducing his income and compelling him to take recourse to borrowing.

The British did nothing to absorb the people who were driven out from their old crafts, and these displaced people created pressure on the agricultural land. The pressure of population on agriculture led to the inevitable sub-division and fragmentation of the peasants' holdings. The growth of population hastened this process. The fragmentation of lands resulted in the limitless growth of uneconomic holdings leading to the birth of poverty. The decline of village industries not only threw vast numbers of men from agriculture, but also created large numbers of landless rural labourers.[177]

The surplus revenue was spent for buying goods for export to England. This marked the beginning of the drain of wealth. Dadabhai Naoroji was of the opinion that large sums of money were privately sent by the opulent servants of the British East India Company. These remittances amounted to 2 million pounds a year. The drain was just like one-way traffic as India got nothing in return for the drain of her wealth. With the passage of time, the process of drain assumed large proportions. R.C.Dutta has estimated that the annual drain which was 31/2 million pounds in 1857, rose to 17 million pounds by 1901-02.[178]

Initially, in the wake of turmoil and disturbances, the long and continued wars, repeated acts of oppression, famine and pestilence; the transition to the British rule in Assam was received with much enthusiasm, hopes and assurances. But these hopes and assurances were, however, belied as soon as the colonial rulers introduced substantial changes in agrarian class relations. The introduction of new agrarian system did not generate any structural development, rather expedited the process of pauperization and rapid stagnation. The horrible result of such policies appeared within two or three decades since its inception. Krishna Sarma strongly criticized the agrarian policy of the colonial government by depicting the deplorable condition of the farmers.[179]

The conduct of the Cadastral Survey was so erroneous that these were always confronted with numerous objections. The measurements of the fields of each mauza were not carefully and systematically tested, as Mills reported in 1853. Objections of the peasants were hardly discussed and less examined; moreover, surveys were not free from errors.[180]

The Ahom period was the halcyon days for the peasants of Assam, as they had to pay less revenue during that time compared to that of the colonial period. The rent realization mode was modified from personal to territorial basis. Historically, for India's peasant, land is the hope and glory of the rural people. By augmenting the incidence of revenue, the alien government wounded the feelings of the peasants which ultimately found manifestation in criminal offences.

The revenue policy of the government dissatisfied the people of Assam. In addition to the arbitrary and unjust settlement, classification of land was neither scientific nor based on actual productivity of the soil. Formerly, the ryots were the owners of the land. Now, they could be ejected from their land on the breach of any of the conditions of lease. They, formerly, could transfer their land, now required permission. Former single *patta* had been multiplied during the British regime for which the farmers had to bear extra-stump duty.[181]

The government classified and increased the rate of revenue on land at a time when productivity was considerably declining. Even the rate of revenue was not reduced at the time of fell of prices of paddy. With every assessment and survey, the alien rulers used to augment the rate of revenue without caring for low productivity and yielding. The government demand went on accumulating huge arrears; vast areas of land were thrown out of cultivation and ryots were exposed to the rapacity of the revenue officers whose extortion had then become proverbial.

The nature of British exactions was manifested in the growing pauperization of India. Consequently, tenants suffered lot under the exactions of landlords, mauzadars and choudhuries who were fully guarded by the machinery of the state. Moreover, the arbitrary confiscation of huge produce of the peasants was the root of all major social conflicts involving the peasants.[182] Prohibitory order of poppy cultivation in 1860-61, shattered the domestic economy of the tribal people of Nowgong. Opium policy, ever increasing land revenue and the tea plantation industry were the three major sources of colonial exploitation in Assam during the British regime.

Imposition of new taxes, like stump duty, license fee for collecting forest products, grazing fee for grazing cattle invited widespread discontent against the alien government.[183]

The colonial government in the name of wasteland rules engulfed those lands which were full of forest. They exported valuable woods to England, and thus, continued their holocaust of forest destruction inviting catastrophe to agriculture, viz. droughts, soil-erosion and floods etc. These rules were made to boost plantation sector in Assam, local cultivators got nothing from these.[184]

The government encouraged migration to remove the shortage of labour in their plantation industries. These migratory people first came in small numbers, but later on in large proportion including their children and families which found manifestation in the growing population pressure on the land.

By abolishing the *paik*-system in Assam, the British did a yeoman service to the people of Assam. But they did it only for their own interest. High classes, like aristocrats and nobilities, member of royal families did not like its abolition as it degraded their so-called social status hitherto enjoyed in the society.

The British sucked and squeezed the blood of the masses by the systematic maximization of revenue. It was like one way traffic, nothing was done in return to ameliorate the condition of agriculture. The government did not provide the people with better facility and improved means of cultivating their lands. Even their measures to prevent natural calamities, like drought, floods etc. were not satisfactory. The British, like Nero of Rome, were busy in revenue collection and revenue maximization when people were hammered by frequent floods and droughts.

The British introduced money economy just to meet their revenue demand. The peasantry, traditionally, unaccustomed to any kind of money taxation and now constantly in dread of the enhancement of land revenue and imposition of new taxes kept up the smoldering fire of protest and hatred against the *raj*.[185] For most of the peasants, commercialization of agriculture and development of money economy was just like an anathema. They did not like this system and rather sought to back to their former system, viz. barter system and self-sufficient village economy. Lack of adequate currency and payment of revenue in cash created another problem for them. The money-lenders, finally, came to their rescue and thus, they fell in their cobwebs. They had to lose their agricultural lands, households properties and even the ornaments and utensils at the hands of the money-lenders, especially, at the hands of the *keyas*. Thus, the incidence of rural-indebtedness continued to mount and ultimately, it engulfed the entire regions. There was no hope of respite from this.

Exploitation and extirpation continued in unabated manner. The local people had to sell their raw materials to the agents of the government at a very cheap rate which had been exported to England and been imported again to Assam as finished goods. These finished goods manufactured in England flooded the markets of Assam and due to the better quality and cheap price, the British products sounded the death bell of the local products resulting the decline of the indigenous industries of Assam. Decline of indigenous industries put additional pressure on agricultural lands. Due to the policy of the British, some became labourers and some became slaves in the land.

Anyway, the economic condition of almost all sections of the peasantry under such conditions started deteriorating deeply during the second half of the 19th century, resulting widespread discontent and irritation among them which was, finally, manifested in the outbreaks of Assam that the state had to witness during that period.[186]

Notes & References

1. *cf* Doshi, S.L.& Jain, P.C.   :   *Rural sociology*, Rawat Publications, Jaipur and New Delhi, Reprinted, 2006, PP. 115-116.

2. Karna, M.N.   :   *Agrarian structure and land reforms in Assam*, Regency Publications, New Delhi, 2004. P. 18.

3. Barua, Hem   :   *The red river and the blue hill*, Lawyers Book Stall, Gauhati, Assam, Revised, 1962, P. 78.

4. Nath, J.G.   :   *Agrarian structure of medieval Assam*, Concept Publishing Company, New Delhi, 2002, P. 60.

5. Hamilton, F.B.   :   *An Account of Assam*, S. K. Bhuyan (ed), Guwahati, 1963, P. 26.

6. Nath   :   *op. cit.*, PP. 63-64.

7. M'Cosh, John   :   *Topography of Assam*, Logos Press, New Delhi, Second Reprint, 2000, P. 29.

8. Lekharu, U.C.   :   *Katha Guru Charit*, Nalbari, 15th edn, 1987, PP. 11f, 38.

9. Barua   :   *op. cit.*, P. 86.

10. Gait, S.E.   :   *A History of Assam*, L. B. S. Publications, Guwahati, Assam, 1984, P. 267.

11. Barua, Gunabhiram   :   *Assam Buranji*, Guwahati, Reprint, 1972, P. 187.

12. Allen, B.C. Gait, E.A. Allen, C.G.H. Howard, H.F.   :   *Gazetteer of Bengal and NEI*, Mittal Publications, New Dehli, 2001, P. 63.

13. Hunter, W.W.   :   *A Statiscal Account of Assam, Vol. I*, PP. 369f.

14. Bhuyan, S.K.   :   *Studies in the History of Assam*, Guwahati, 1965, P. 147.

15. Mills, A.J.M.   :   *Report on the province of Assam*, Publication Board of Assam, Guwahati, Second Edition, 1984, P. 2.

    Nath   :   *op. cit.*, P. 92.

16. Barua, Gunabhiram : *Assam Bandhu* (periodicals), N.Saikia (Compiled & edited), Guwahati, 1984, P. 74.

17. Bhuyan, S.K. (ed) : *Deodhai Asam Buranji*, Guwahati, Reprint, 1962, P. 84.

Barbarua, Srinath Duara : *Tungkhungia Buranji*, S. K. Bhuyan (ed), Guwahati, Second Edition, 1964, P. iii.

Barua, Raisahib G.C. : *Ahom Buranji*, Guwahati, Reprint, 1985, P. 126.

(trans & edited)
Nath : *op. cit.*, P. 167.

18. Goswami, P.C. : *The Economic Development of Assam*, Asia Publishing House, Bombay, 1963, Appendix-II, PP. 280-281.

19. Karna : *op. cit.*, PP. 19-20.
Nath : *op. cit.*, P. iii.

20. Guha, A : *Planter Raj to Swaraj* (1826-1947), Tulika Books, New Delhi, 2006, P. 40.

21. Nath : *op. cit.*, P. 102.

22. Roychoudhury, Anil : 'Socio-Economic Aspect of Neo-Vaishnavite Satras—A Survey' in S. Barman's (et al), *Oitihya aru Itihas,* Journal Emporium, Nalbari, Assam, 2005, P. 35.

23. Mills : *op. cit.*, P. 2.
Gait : *op.cit.*, P. 239.

24. Guha, A : *Assamese Peasant Society in the late 19th century; Structure and Trend,* Centre for Studies in Social Sciences, Calcutta, Aug. 1979, P. 2.

25. Kaushal, G. : *Economic History of India* (1757-1966), Kalyani Publishers, New Delhi, Reprint, 1991, P. 1.

26. Barua, Hem : *op. cit.*, P. 87.

27. Pemberton, Capt.R.B. : *Report on the Eastern Frontier of British India,* Department of Historical and Antiquarian Studies in Assam (DHASA), Gauhati, 1966, PP. 82-83.

28. Barua, Hem : *op. cit.*, PP. 87-88.
29. *cf* Doshi & Jain : *op. cit.*, PP. 105, 117-118, 127, 173, 175
30. Bhattacharjee, J.B. : *Trade and Colony—The British Colonization of NEI*, NEIHA, Shillong, 2000, Prologue, PP. 1, 47, 82.
31. Barooah, D.P. : *Aspects of the History of Assam*, Darbari Prakashan, Kolkata, 2002, PP. 28-29.
32. Karna : *op. cit.*, P. 1.
33. *cf* Stein, Burton : *Peasant—State and Society in medieval South-India*, Oxford University Press, New Delhi, 1999, P. 14.
34. Agarwal, A.N. : *Indian Agriculture*, Vani Educational Books, New Delhi, 1980, P. 370.
35. Kaushal : *op. cit.*, P. 103.
    Doshi & Jain : *op. cit.*, P. 140.
36. Saikia, R. : *Social and Economic History of Assam* (1853-1921), Manohar, New Delhi, 2001, P. 93.
    cf Doshi & Jain *op. cit.*, P. 131.
37. Desai, S.S.M. : *Economic History of India*, Himalaya Publishing House, Bombay, July, 1990, P. 45.
38. Doshi & Jain : *op. cit.*, P. 133.
39. Barman, Santo : 'Socio Economic condition of Goalpara district during Zamindari regime-An apraisal' in S. Barman's (et al), *op. cit.*, P. 270.
40. Digby, William : *Prosperous British India*, Sagar Publication, New Delhi, 1969, P. 33.
41. Doshi & Jain : *op. cit.*, PP. 137-138.
42. Srinivasa, M.N. : *Social Change in Modern India*, Orient Longman Ltd. Delhi, 1995, P. 49.
43. Bose, M.L. : *Development of Administration in Assam*, Concept Publishing Company, New Delhi, 1985, P. 71.
44. Kaushal : *op. cit.*, P. 97.

45. Gait : *op. cit.*, P. 293.
46. Mills : *op. cit.*, PP. 3,19.
    Saikia : *op. cit.*, P. 161.
47. Goswami, S.D. : 'Revenue Reorganization of Assam under David Scott', *NEIHA-I*, 1980, P. 153.
48. Mills : *op. cit.*, P. 4.
49. Gait : *op. cit.*, P. 295.
    Karna : *op. cit.*, P. 21.
50. Barpujari, H.K.(eds) : *Political History of Assam, Vol. I (1826-1919)*, Publication Board of Assam, Guwahati, Second edn., 1999, PP. 8-12.
51. Saikia : *op. cit.*, P. 116.
52. Chopra, P.N. : *A Social, Cultural and Economic*
    Puri, B.N. & Das, : *History of India, Vol. III*, Macmillan
    M.N. India Ltd., Madras, 1990, P. 176.
53. Sarma, Manorama : *Social and Economic Change in Assam: Middle Class Hegemony*, Ajanta Publication, New Delhi, 1990, P. 59.
54. Karna : *op. cit.*, PP. 22,28.
55. Saikia : *op. cit.*, P. 93.
56. : *Report on the Administration of Revenue in Assam, 1880-'81*, Part-II, Para-2 (1874-1905, 1912-22)
    Bose : *op. cit.*, P. 68.
57. Sarma, Manorama : *op. cit.*, P. 63.
    Saikia : *op. cit.*, PP. 105-106.
58. Barooah, D.P. : *op. cit.*, PP. 39-40.
59. Barpujari (eds) : *op. cit.*, PP. 14, 30-31.
60. Saikia : *op. cit.*, P. 93.
    Hunter, W.W. : *The Imperial Gazetteer of India, Vol. IV & VI*, Calcutta, 1879, P. 50.
    Bose : *op. cit.*, P. 69.
61. : *Report on the Administration of Revenue in Assam, 1880-81*, Para-25, (1874-1905, 1912-22)
    Bose : *op. cit.*, P. 70.

62. Guha, A. : 'A peep through 19th century Assam-Maniram Dewan' in S. Barman's (et. al), *op. cit.*, PP. 349, 354.

63. Karna : *op. cit.*, PP. 23-25.

64. Mills : *op. cit.*, PP. 66-67.

65. Barpujari, H.K.(ed) : *The Comprehensive History of Assam (1826-1919)Vol. V*, Publication Board of Assam, Guwahati, 2004, Appendix-A, Statement-1, P. 19.

66. Barpujari (eds) : *Political History of Assam, Vol. I*, P. 51.

67. Saikia : *op. cit.*, PP. 33-34, 37.

68. Saikia, Anand : 'The British Land Revenue Policy in Assam: Its impact upon peasantry' in J.B.'s (ed), *Studies in the Economic History of NE India*, NEHU Publications, Shillong, 1986, P. 103.

69. Sarma, Manorama : *op. cit.*, P. 126.

70. Karna : *op. cit.*, P. 30.

71. Pemberton : *op. cit.*, P. 76.

72. Hussain, M : *The Assam Movement Class, Ideology and Identity*, Manak publication in association with Haranand Publications, New Delhi, First edn, 1993, P. 42.

73. Goswami, P. : 'Colonial penetration and the emergence of Nationalism in Assam' in A. Bhuyan's (ed), *Nationalist Upsurge in Assam,* Govt. of Assam, Dispur, Guwahati, 2000, P. 17.

74. Bhattacharjee, J.B. : *op. cit.*, PP. 2, 54.

75. Goswami, S.D. : 'The British Taxation Policy in Assam' in J. B.'s (ed), *op. cit.*, P. 91.

76. Barpujari (eds) : *Political History of Assam, Vol. I*, P. 51.
    Barpujari(ed) : *The Comprehensive History of Assam, Vol. V*, Appendix-A, Statement-II, P. 20.
    : *Assam Secretariat Revenue Proceedings-A*, Sept. 1890, Nos.9-14, Hopkinson, 14th June, 1865.

77. Goswami, P : 'Colonial penetration . . . .' in A. Bhuyan's (ed), *op. cit.*, P. 17.

Barpujari (eds) : *Pol. Hist. of Assam, Vol. I.* P. 51.

Guha, A : *Planter Raj to Swaraj,* P. 7.

78. Barpurjari (eds) : *Pol. Hist. of Assam, Vol. I,* PP. 94-95.

Barpurjari (ed) : *The Comprehensive . . . . . . .Vol. V,* Appendix-B, Statement-I, P. 35.

: *Assam Secretariat Revenue Proceedings-A*, Sept. 1890, Nos.9-14, *Revenue and Agricultural Department proceedings,* March, 1893, No.3.

79. *Guha* : *op.cit.,* p. 3.

: *The Assam Land Revenue Manual, Vol. I,* Calcutta, 1896, Reprinted, 1965, Shillong, P. iv.

80. : *Assam Valley Re-assessment Report,* 1892-93.

Bose : *op. cit.,* P. 59.

81. Guha : *op. cit.,* P. 8.

Gait : *op. cit.* P. 343.

Barpujari (ed) : *The Comprehensive . . . . . . .Vol. V,* Appendix-B, Statement-II, P. 36.

: *Assam Secretariat Revenue Proceedings-A,* Sept. 1890, Nos. 9-14;

: *Revenue and Agriculture Department Proceedings,* March, 1893, No. 30.

82. Goswami, P. : 'Opening up of Nambor forest for Settlement-A missed opportunity', *NEIHA-XXIII,* 2002, P. 119.

: *Report on the Administration of Land Revenue,* 1879-80, Shillong, 1881.

Saikia : *op. cit.,* PP. 86-87.

83. Barpurjari (eds) : *Pol. Hist. of Assam, Vol. I,* PP. 96-97.

Bose : *op. cit.,* P. 59.

Goswami, S.D. : 'Revenue Settlement in the Hill districts of Assam: A studies of the House tax' in J.B.'s (ed), *op. cit.,* PP. 106-107.

	Goswami, S.D.	:	'The British taxation policy in Assam' in J.B.s (ed), *op. cit.*, PP. 91, 94.
84.	Barpujari (ed)	:	*The Comprehensive . . . . . Vol. V*, P. 7.
	M'cosh	:	*op. cit.*, PP. 122-123.
	Dutta, K.N.	:	*Landmarks of the Freedom Movement in Assam*, Gauhati, 1958, P. 25.
	Mills	:	*op. cit.*, PP. 20, 24, 323.
	Barpujari (eds)	:	*Pol. Hist. of Assam, Vol. I*, P. 88.
85.	Guha	:	*Planter Raj to Swaraj*, PP. 74-75.
86.	Nath	:	*op. cit.*, PP. 76-77.
	Bhuyan, S.K.(ed)	:	*Jayantia Buranji*, Gauhati, Second edn, 1964, PP. 98f
	Bhuyan, S.K.(ed)	:	*Kamrupar Buranji*, Gauhati, Second edn, 1958, P. 86.
	Sarma, S.N.	:	*A Socio Economic and Cultural History of Medieval Assam (1200-1800 AD)*, Gauhati, 1989, P. 75.
87.	Barpujari (eds)	:	*Pol. Hist. of Assam, Vol. I.* PP. 89-90.
	Chopra, Puri & Das	:	*op. cit.*, P. 166.
	Goswami, S.D.	:	'British taxation . . . .' in J.B.'s (ed), *op. cit.*, PP. 94-95.
	Goswami, S.D.	:	'Revenue Reorganization of Assam under David Scott', *NEIHA-I*, 1980, PP. 150-151.
88.	M'Cosh	:	*op. cit.*, P. 30.
	Saikia	:	*op. cit.*, PP. 213-215.
	Mills	:	*op. cit.*, PP. 110, 326.
	Guha	:	*Planter Raj to Swaraj*, P. 45.
	Bhattacharjee, J.B.	:	*op. cit.*, P. 37.
	Goswami, P.	:	'Colonial penetration . . . .' in A. Bhuyann's (ed), *op. cit.*, P. 18.
	Kalita, R.C.	:	'British exploitation in Assam: The opium policy and revenue (1850-1894)', *NEIHA-XII*, 1991, P. 344.
89.	Singh, A.K.	:	*History of Far East in modern times*, Surjeet Publications, New Delhi, P. 9.
	Chopra, Puri & Das	:	*op. cit.*, P. 188.
	Saikia, R.	:	*op. cit.*, P. 217.

90. Goswami, P. : 'Colonial penetration . . . .'
in A. Bhuyan's (ed), *op. cit.,* P. 18.

    Guha : *Planter Raj to Swaraj*, P. 8.

    Kalita, R.C. : 'Opium prohibition and Rai Bahadur J.N. Barua', *NEIHA-XVI*, 1995, P. 186.

    Kalita, R.C. : 'British exploitation in Assam', *NEIHA-XII*, 1991, P. 343.

    Chopra, Puri & Das : *op. cit.,* P. 183.

91. Saikia : *op. cit.,* P. 218.

    Guha : *op. cit.,* PP. 18, 46, 71.

    Chaudhury, Prasenjit : 'Hero-worshipping and intellectual disease; Assam in the 19th century and an aspect on the study of leftist history' in S. Barman's (et al), *op. cit.,* P. 68.

92. Barua, Hem : *op. cit.,* PP. 78, 82.

    Bhattacharjee : *op. cit.,* P. 49.

93. Barpujari, H.K. : *Assam in the days of the Company*, NEHU Publications, Shillong, 1996, P. 241.

94. Trevelyan, G.M. : *English Social History*, Orient Longman Ltd., Mumbai, Indian Reprint, 2001, P. 388.

95. Allen, Gait, Allen & Howard : *op. cit.,* P. 105.

    M'cosh : *op. cit.* P. 36.

    Hilaly, Sarah : 'Railways in Assam and immigration of peasants in the colonial period', *NEIHA-XXII*, 2001, P. 225.

96. Saha, Subhash : 'Capital labour relations: A study of tea plantation in Assam (1835-1926)' in J.B.'s (ed), *op. cit.,* P. 331.

    Goswami, H. : *Population trends in the Brahmaputra valley*, Mittal Publications, New Delhi, 1985, P. 90.

    Bhattacharjee, J.B. : 'The Eastern Himalayan trade of Assam in the colonial period' in J.B.'s (ed), *op. cit.,* P. 202.

Dasgupta, Keya : (1) 'Industrialization in the Brahmaputra valley (1881-1921)' in J.B.'s (ed), *op. cit.*, P. 292.

: (2) 'Coming of tea in the Brahmaputra valley: Changes in pattern of trade' in J.B.'s (ed), *op. cit.*, P. 264.

97. Bhattacharjee : *op. cit.*, P. 49.
98. Barpujari (eds) : *Pol. His. of Assam, Vol. I*, P. 52.
    Guha : *Planter Raj to Swaraj*, PP. 11-12.
99. *Ibid.* : P. 10.
100. Barpujari (ed) : *The Comprehensive* . . . . *Vol. V*, PP. 37-39.

    Goswami, P : 'Colonial penetration . . . .' in A. Bhuyan's (ed), *op. cit.*, P. 15.

101. *cf* Saikia, R : *op. cit.*, PP. 181, 184.
102. Mills : *op. cit.*, P. 16.
     Barpujari (eds) : *Pol. Hist. of Assam, Vol. I*, PP. 52-53.
103. Barpujari (ed) : *The Comprehensive* . . . . *Vol. V*, PP. 42-43.

104. Saikia, R. : *op. cit*, P. 228.
     Bose : *op. cit.*, PP. 60-61.
     : The Assam Land Revenue Manual Vol. I

     Saha, Subhash : *Grass root nationalism–a study of mass resistance in the district of Darrang and Nowgong of Assam, 1937-1947*, NEHU, Shillong, 1989.

     Karna : *op. cit.*, PP. 25-26.
105. Goswami, P : 'Colonial penetration . . . .' in A Bhuyan's (ed), *op. cit.*, P. 15.

     Saikia, Anand : 'The British land revenue policy in Assam' in J.B.'s (ed), *op. cit.*, PP. 103-104.

     Goswami, H : *op. cit.*, P. 112.
     cf Habib, Irfan : *A people's history of India—Indian economy, 1858-1914*, Tulika books, New Delhi, 2007.

106. Saha : *op. cit.*

107. Doshi & Jain : *op. cit.,* P. 152.

Bhuyan, S.K. : *Lachit Borphukan and his times,* Guwahati, 1947, P. 17.

: *Journal of Historical Research,* Dibrugarh University.

M'cosh : *op. cit.,* PP. 26-27.

Pemberton : *op. cit.,* PP. 82-83.

108. Gait : *op. cit.,* P. 239.

Nath : *op. cit.,* P. 118.

M'Cosh : *op. cit.,* PP. 119-120.

109. Lekharu, U.C. (ed) : *Katha Guru Charit,* Nalbari, 15th edition, 1987, PP. 101, 469-470.

Nath : *op. cit.,* PP. 128-129.

Sarma, N : The rise and growth of the peasant movement in Kamrup district the period between 1826-1900, G.U., Guwahati, 2003, PP. 48-49.

Nath : *op. cit.,* P. 93

RoyChoudhury : *op. cit.* in S. Barman's (et al) *op. cit.,* P. 35.

Bhattacharjee : *op. cit.,* P. 87.

Nag, Sajal : 'Economic roots of the regional capitalist class—a study of the primitive accumulation of the Marwari community in colonial Assam' in J.B.'s (ed), *op. cit.,* P. 352.

110. *cf* Nath : *op. cit.,* PP. 128-130. *cf*

Sarma, N : *op. cit.,* PP. 48-49.

Guha, A : 'Land rights and social classes in medieval Assam' in *Indian Economic and Social History Review* (IESHR), Sept. 1966, P. 56.

cf Guha, A : *Jamidarkalin Goalpara jilar artha— samajik awastha ek oitihasik dristipat,* Natun Sahitya Parishad, Guwahati, 2000, P. 47.

111. Hussain, Haidar : 'Daas-Prathar Nirlajja Parisangkha' in *Sambhar,* Guwahati, March 22, 2009, P. 16.

Srinivasa	:	*op. cit.,* P. 50.
Sarma, N	:	*op. cit.,* P. 49.
Barpujari (eds)	:	*Pol. Hist. of Assam,* Vol. I, P. 16.
112. Barooah, D.P.	:	*op. cit.,* P. 28.
Saikia, R	:	*op. cit.,* P. 39.
Guha, A	:	'A peep . . . . Maniram Dewan' in S. Barman's (et al), *op. cit.,* P. 354.
Barooah, D.P.	:	'The rebellion of 1857 and its impact on Assam' in A. Bhuyan's (ed), *op. cit.* P. 46.
Guha	:	*Planter Raj to Swaraj,* P. 9.
Hussain	:	*op. cit.,* PP. 39-40.
113. Doshi & Jain	:	*op. cit.,* P. 152.
Barpujari (eds)	:	*Pol. Hist. of Assam,* Vol. I, PP. 63-64.
114. Sarkar, Sumit	:	*Modern India, 1885-1947,* Macmillan, New Delhi, 1983, PP. 30-31.
Barpurjari (ed)	:	*The Comprehensive . . . . Vol. V,* P. 216.
Srinivasa	:	*op. cit.,* PP. 40-41, 63.
Trevelyan	:	*op. cit.,* P. 389.
115. Bhuyan, A	:	'The Non-co-operation stir in Assam' in A. Bhuyan's (ed), *op. cit.* PP. 159-160.
Dutta, Ajit Kr.	:	'The background of national awakening in Upper Assam' in A. Bhuyan's (ed), *op. cit.* P. 70.
Guha	:	*Planter Raj to Swaraj,* P. 37.
Bora, Dr.Dhrubajyoti	:	'Caste system in history: role of caste in Assam' in S. Barman's (et al), *op. cit.* P. 104.
Srinivasa	:	*op. cit.,* P. 51.
Singh, A.K.	:	*op. cit.,* P. 15.
Hussain	:	*op. cit.,* P. 44.
116. *cf* Goswami, H	:	*op. cit.,* PP. 88,90.
cf Srinivasa	:	*op. cit.,* PP. 41-42.
cf Guha	:	*Planter Raj to Swaraj,* P. 55.
117. Barpujari (eds)	:	*Pol Hist. of Assam,* Vol. I, P. 56.
Goswami, H	:	*op. cit.,* PP. 90-91.

Gait : *op. cit.*, PP. 360-361.

Mahanta, Arpana : 'Planter Raj to Swaraj—an observation' in S. Barman's (et al), *op. cit.*, P. 263.

Mills : *op. cit.*, P. 30.

118. Saha : *op. cit.*

Srinivasa : *op. cit.*, PP. 40-41.

Nag, Sajal : 'Religion and ethnicity in class formation: aspect of peasants class composition in colonial Assam in the context of communalism', *NEIHA-V*, 1984, P. 160.

119. Srinivasa : *op. cit.*, P. 63.

Saha : 'Capital labour relations: a study of tea plantation in Assam (1835-1926)' in J.B.'s (ed), *op. cit.*, P. 331.

Barman, S : 'Christian missionaries and the 19th century Santhals migration to Assam', in *NEIHA-XXVIII*, 2007, P. 353.

Hilaly, S : 'Railways in Assam and immigration of peasants in the colonial period', *NEIHA-XXII*, 2001, P. 227.

Das, Pramodanand : 'Tribal peasantry in Bihar: a structural analysis' in V. K. Thakur and A. Aounshuman's (eds), *Peasants in Indian History-I*, Janaki Prakashan, Patna, Delhi, 1996, PP. 502-503.

120. Habib : *A People's history* . . . . .

Goswami, H : *op. cit.*, P. 94.

121. Gohain, H.(eds) : *Pratishruti aru Phalashruti*, Banalata, Second edn, Dec, 2007, P. 18.

122. Saikia, R. : *op. cit.*, P. 109.

Guha : *Planter Raj to Swaraj*, PP. 31-32.

Borpujari (eds) : *Political History of Assam, Vol. I*, PP. 94-95.

123. Goswami, H. : *op. cit.*, P. 176.

Barpujari (eds) : *Political History of Assam*, PP. 59-60.

Sarma, Manorama	:	'Class formation in Assam: The agrarian sector (1911-1947)' *NEIHA-XII*, 1991, P. 379.
Guha	:	*Planter Raj to Swaraj*, Appendix-3, P. 279.
124. Saikia, R	:	*op. cit.*, P. 94.
Gadgil, D.R.	:	*The industrial evolution of India*, Delhi, 1982, P. 66.
	:	*Gazetteer of India*, Assam State, Sibsagar district, Govt. of Assam, P. 227.
Dutta, Ajit Kr.	:	'The background of national . . . . .' in A. Bhuyan's (ed), *op. cit.*, P. 70.
Srivastava, A.L.	:	*The Sultanate of Delhi (1206-1526)*, Agarwala & Company, Agra, 1971, PP. 189-190.
Barpujari (ed)	:	*The Comprehensive history of Assam (1826-1919), Vol. IV*, Publication Board of Assam, Guwahati, 2004, PP. 292-293.
Goswami, P.	:	'Colonial penetration . . . .' in J.B.'s (ed), *op. cit.*, P. 18.
125. Dutta, Anuradha	:	'Aspects of growth and development of nationalism in Assam in the 19th century' in A. Bhuyan's (ed), *op. cit.*, P. 60.
Barooah, D.P.	:	'The rebellion of 1857 . . . .' in A. Bhuyan's (ed), *op. cit.*, P. 41.
126. Barpujari (eds)	:	*Political History of Assam*, Vol. I, PP. 121-122.
Mills	:	*op. cit.*, Appendix (J), P. XXXIX.
Saikia, R.	:	*op. cit.* PP. 81-82, 113.
127. Barpujari (ed)	:	*The Comprehensive . . . . Vol. V*, P. 65.
Bhalla, G.S.	:	*Condition of Indian Peasantry*, National Book Trust India, New Delhi, First edn, 2006. P. 17.
Saikia	:	*op. cit.*, PP. 72, 82, 104.
128. Barpujari (ed)	:	*The Comprehensive . . . . Vol. V*. PP. 7, 19, 63.

129. Nath : *op. cit.*, P. 68.
     Barpujari (eds) : *Political History of Assam, Vol. I*, P. 58.
     Nath : *op. cit.*, P. 69.
130. Doshi & Jain : *op. cit.*, PP. 174-175.
     Saikia : *op. cit.*, P. 81.
131. Bhalla : *op. cit.*, PP. 24, 32-33.
132. Ram, N. (editor in : *The Hindu Survey of Indian*
     chief)   *Agriculture*, M/S Kasturi & Sons Ltd.,
                Chennai, 2008.

     Kaushal : *op. cit.*, P. 168.
133. Chopra, Puri & Das : *op. cit.*, P. 149.
     Doshi & Jain : *op. cit.*, P. 105.
134. Saikia : *op. cit.*, PP. 83, 104.
     Habib : *op. cit.*
135. Desai : *op. cit.*, P. 70.
136. Saikia : *op. cit.*, P. 96.
     Sarma, N. : *op. cit.*, P. 150.
137. M'cosh : *op. cit.*, P. 51.
     Bhalla : *op. cit.*, P. 13.
     David, Dr.B.Vasantharaj : 'Integrated management of pests and
                diseases' in *the Hindu Survey of Indian
                Agriculture*, 2008, P. 118.

138. Doshi & Jain : *op. cit.*, PP. 120-121.
     Srinivasa : *op. cit.*, P. 51.
139. Nath : *op. cit.*, P. 61.
     Doshi & Jain : *op. cit.*, P. 121.
140. *Ibid.* : *op. cit.*, P. 114.
141. Barpujari (eds) : *Political History of Assam*, PP. 51-52.
142. Mills : *op. cit.*, P. 8.
143. Guha : *Planter Raj to Swaraj*, P. 27.
     Mahanta, Arpana : *op. cit.*, in S. Barman's (et al), *op. cit.*
                P. 262.

     Saikia : *op. cit.*, P. 230.
     Hussain : *op. cit.*, PP. 44-45.
144. Guha : *Planter* . . . . P. 34.
145. Goswami, S.D. : 'The British Taxation Policy in
                Assam' in J.B.'s (ed), *op. cit.*, P. 95.
     Guha : *Planter* . . . . . P. 12.
146. Saikia : *op. cit.*, P. 228.

147. Nath	:	*op. cit.*, PP. 60-61.
Bhuyan, S.K. (ed)	:	*Satsari Asam Buranji*, Gauhati, Second edn, 1964, P. 76.
Saikia	:	*op. cit.*, PP. 103, 226.
148. *Ibid.*	:	*op. cit.*, P. 101.
Barpujari (ed)	:	*The Comprehensive . . . . Vol. V*, P. 63.
149. Saikia	:	*op. cit.*, P. 103.
150. Sen, Ranjit	:	'General pattern of revenue maximization in Bengal (including Lower Assam) in the 18th century' in J.B.'s (ed), *op. cit.*, PP. 116-117.
151. Srinivasa	:	*op. cit.*, PP. 51-52.
152. Barpujari (eds)	:	*Political History of Assam*, PP. 58-59.
153. Bhalla	:	*op. cit.*, PP. 6-7.
154. Barpujari (ed)	:	*The Comprehensive . . . . .Vol. V*, P. 63.
155. Guha	:	*Planter . . . .* P. 30.
156. Bhattacharjee	:	*op. cit.*, PP. 41-42.
Pemberton	:	*op. cit.*, PP. 82-83.
157. Barpujari (ed)	:	*The Comprehensive History of Assam, Vol. II*, Publication Board of Assam, Gauhati, First edn, 1992, P. 19.
158. Pemberton	:	*op. cit.*, PP. 83-84.
159. Bhattacharjee	:	*op. cit.*, P. 83.
160. Pemberton	:	*op. cit.*, P. 76.
161. Srinivasa	:	*op. cit.*, PP. 71-72.
162. Bhattacharjee	:	*op. cit.*, P. 89.
Kalita, B.C.	:	'Administrative Units of NEI-A Geographical Note' in the '*North Eastern Geographer*' Vol. XII, Nos. 1 & 2, 1980, P. 53.
163. Barpujari (eds)	:	*Political History of Assam*, PP. 56-57.
Goswami, P.	:	'Colonial penetration . . . .' in A. Bhuyan's (ed), *op. cit.*, P. 21.
Bhattacharjee	:	*op. cit.*, P. 90.
164. Barpujari (eds)	:	*Political History of Assam, Vol. I*, P. 15.
Guha	:	*Planter . . . .* P. 7.
Mahanta, Arpana	:	'Op. cit' in S. Barman's (et al), *op. cit.*, P. 263

Goswami, P.   :   'Colonial penetration . . . .'
in A. Bhuyan's (ed), *op. cit.*, P. 16.

Saikia   :   *op. cit.*, P. 106.

165. Habib   :   *op. cit.*,

Desai   :   *op. cit.*, PP. 62-64.

166. Desai   :   *op. cit.*, PP. 64-65.

Sarkar   :   *op. cit.*, P. 32.

167. Agarwal   :   *op. cit.*, P. 209.

cf Kaushal   :   *op. cit.*, PP. 177, 179-180, 183.

168. Ghosh, Lipi   :   'Indebtedness in Peasants Sector: A
study of Assam proper in late 19th
century' in J.B.'s (ed), *op. cit.*, P. 339.

Goswami, P.   :   'Colonial penetration . . . .' in
A. Bhuyan's (ed), *op. cit.,* P. 21.

Nag, Sajal   :   'Economic roots of the regional
capitalist class in colonial Assam' in
J.B.'s (ed), *op. cit.*, P. 353.

Guha   :   *Planter* . . . . P. 40.

169. *Ibid.*   :   P. 39.

170. Saikia   :   *op. cit.*, P. 117.

Saha   :   *op. cit.*

Sarma, R.S.   :   *Indian Feudalism, c. AD—300-1200,*
Macmillan India Ltd., Madras,
Reprinted, 1996, P. 267.

Rana, R.P.   :   'Was there agrarian crisis in Mughal
North India?' in *Social Scientist, Vol.
XXXIV*, Prabhat Patnaik (ed), Tulika,
New Delhi, Nov-Dec, 2006, P. 23.

171. Bhalls   :   *op. cit.*, PP. 43-44

172. Saikia   :   *op. cit.*, P. 226.

173.   :   Josh, Bhagwan & Joshi,

Shashi   :   *Struggle for hegemony in India
(1920-47)*, Sage Publications, New
Delhi, P. 28.

174. Singh   :   *op. cit.*, P. 19.

175. Goswami, P   :   'Colonial penetration . . . .' in
A. Bhuyan's (ed), *op. cit.,* P. 13.

Bhattacharjee   :   *op. cit.*, PP. 87-89

Barpujari (eds)   :   *Political History of Assam*, P. 59.

176. Desai	:	*op. cit.*, PP. 32-34.
Kaushal	:	*op. cit.*, P. 8.
177. *Ibid.*	:	*op. cit.*, P. 180.
Goswami, P.	:	'Colonial penetration . . . .' in A. Bhuyan's (ed), *op. cit.*, P. 16.
Chopra, Puri & Das	:	*op. cit.*, P. 183.
178. Keswani, K.B.	:	*Modern India (1819-1964)*, Himalaya Publishing House, New Delhi, First Edition, 1990, PP. 245-246.
179.	:	*Krishna Sarmar Diary*, Assam Publication Board, Guwahati, 1972, P. 249.
180. Gait	:	*op. cit.*, P. 343.
181. Barooah, D.P.	:	'Op. cit' in A. Bhuyan's (ed), *op. cit.*, P. 41.
Barpujari (eds)	:	*Pol. Hist. of Assam, Vol. I*, PP. 99-100.
182. Goswami, S.D.	:	'British taxation policy in Assam' in J.B.'s (ed), *op. cit.*, P. 95.
Bhattacharjee	:	*op. cit.*, PP. 2-3.
Habib	:	*Essays in Indian History—towards a Marxist perception*, Tulika Books, New Delhi, 2001, PP. 154-155.
183. Kalita, R.C.	:	'British exploitation in Assam: the opium policy and revenue (1850-1894)', *NEIHA-XII.*, 1991, P. 343.
Dutta, K.N.	:	*Landmarks of the freedom movement in Assam*, 18 Guwahati, 1958, P. 25.
184. Guha	:	*Planter* . . . . P. 12.
185. *Ibid.*	:	P.21.
186. Karna	:	*op. cit.*, P.31.

CHAPTER – FOUR

MIDDLE ALIAS ELITE GROUP: CENTRIFUGAL AND CENTRIPETAL ROLE

Everywhere in the world, the middle class people played a major role in the movements. The controversy still persists pertaining to the exact connotation of the term 'middle class.' Hence, the question arises who the middle class people are. Generally, the middle class people are those who are neither rich nor poor. They may be divided into two groups: the lower and the upper middle class. The position of middle class is in between the higher and the lower class. This middle class emerged out of development of economic disparity in the society.

The middle class people are found almost all the countries of the world. They play an important role in the construction and destruction of a nation. The rich becomes richer and the poor becomes poorer, but the middle class people have been adversely affected. That is why, there is too much criticism against the government. The middle class people make the intelligentsia of a nation. They regularly read newspapers and form opinions in the light of day-to-day's achievements and failure of the government, and mould the public opinion.

The people below the middle class criticize them out of jealousy; the people above the middle class criticize them because they are afraid of them. Besides this, they criticize one another on account of envy and emulation. The middle class people always face a conflict between their vain show and empty pockets with the result that they are snobs in majority. Karl Marx says that the middle class people are the unhappiest creatures in the society. They try their best to become rich and remain worried. The people below and above them oppose them tooth and nail. In consequence, there is a constant struggle in the society. In the long run, this develops into a social problem.[1]

The middle class people are always considered the most useful group in any society; and a country's welfare depends to a large extent on this class. If there is ever to be a social or any other movement, it is by this class.

The middle class is, essentially, an urban concept which originally developed in Europe with the break-up of feudalism followed by the emergence of commercial and industrial bourgeois in the newly developed towns and cities. It emerged in the west, basically, as a result of economic and technical changes. In India, on the contrary, they emerged most in consequence of the changes in the system of law and public administration.[2]

II

The 19th century is wonder for entire India as a new wave of change penetrated in the eco-political and socio-cultural field of India. The direct rule of the imperialist British gave birth to a middle class in India. This elite middle class, imbibed by the spirit of western thought and ideology, began to criticize the feudalistic and traditional system of India; and with the association of the ruling class, they gave birth to renaissance and reformation movement in their society. In Bengal, this movement was led by the zamindars and officials of the East India Company. Under the aegis of Raja Rammohan Roy, Debendra Nath Tagore, Dwaraka Nath Tagore, K.C. Sen, Swami Vivekanand and Henry Derozio, this renaissance and reformation movement received tremendous impetus in Bengal. In Bombay, rich and wealthy class; and in Madras, the business class took the leadership of these movements.

Slowly and gradually, the English education expanded and as a result, a new bourgeois class comprising of engineers, doctors, lawyers and businessmen emerged in the Indian scene who fetched messages of new age to their society. This newly emerged middle class, totally depended for their change and development on the colonial government, expressed their allegiance to the government. Indeed, the Indian middle class prior to 1919, showed their allegiance to the governmnet, as their economic life was entirely depended on the government. The newly emerged middle class understood that they were unable to throw off the yoke of British rule, and therefore, accepted their rule and demanded certain facilities from them. The Landlord Association of 1837, the Bengal British Society of 1843, the British Indian Association of 1851, the Indian Association of 1875 and the Indian National Congress of 1885 were some of the middle class organizations; and these organizations confirmed their aims and objects through prayer and petitions. Ram Mohan Roy, the father of Indian renaissance was a true supporter of British imperialism. He and his contemporaries even welcomed the British rule. Ishwar Chandra Vidyasagar, an eminent social reformer of 19th century also supported the British rule and sincerely believed that the British would bring peace and prosperity to the country and under their shade, reform of the society would be possible. Ram Mohan and his contemporaries noticed the superstitions and prejudices that prevailed in their society and condemned them tooth and nail. But surprisingly, they rarely criticized the exploitation and appropriation policy perpetrated by the white government on the masses. To reform the society, was their primary concern and country's liberation, on the contrary, was secondary one.[3]

The Indian middle class could not become independent due to their loyalty and slavish mentality towards the colonial government. Lock and key to the trade and commerce was at the hands of the government; and the capitalist and newly emerged class carried on their business under them by keeping good relation with them.

Towards the close of the 19th century, industry and commerce developed by the British capital gave birth to a bourgeois class in India. This bourgeois class was independent in wealth and money. But the problem was that despite having capital, this indigenous capitalist class could not compete equally with the white capitalists due to their bias trade policy, which, finally, forced them to support the independence movement against the Government of India.

The British administration scared of introducing higher education in India, but for their administrative interest, they contemplated for the introduction of primary education. The landlords were dead-against of imparting primary education to the lower classes, as this would end their exploitation and supremacy over them. So, they tried their level best to dash the noble attempt of the government to the ground. They favoured illuminating the higher classes than the lower classes, and even took step for that. Vidyasagar was not dead against of the primary education like the landlords. But his class weakness was detected when he set framed certain rules that women education should be kept restricted to the rich and the higher caste Hindu families only.[4]

The Indian nationalism was not the outcome of anti-imperialist struggle and because of this; the middle class had no relation with the peasant class. The middle class witnessed the distress, ups and downs of the peasant classes; but despite that, they did not come to their rescue. Due to their allegiance to the government, the Indian National Congress, comprising of the bourgeois class from the very beginning, had no relation with the peasant class. Prior to 1919, the nationalistic movement began in India was not transmuted to the war of independence. Free participation of the peasants and the labour class made the independence movement dynamic, strong and alive. The Congress did away with their parochial and conservative character by freely allowing the lower class to become its member, and made, thus, the independent movement strong.[5]

Assam came under the colonial yoke just after the occupation of other provinces of India. As a lately developed and emerging class, the influence of all India middle class, especially the Bengalee middle class, was clear on the Assamese middle class. According to Guha, three types of influence are clear on the newly developed Assamese middle class: the spread of British administration and its associate infra-structure; the cultural activities of the Christian missionaries, particularly the American Baptists and the direct and indirect impact of the Bengal renaissance.[6]

III

The industrial revolution of England in the 18th century brought some socio-economic and political changes which gave birth to a new middle class in England. But their taste, mentality and outlook were totally different from the middle class of pre-industrial revolution era. But in India, a westernized intelligentsia had emerged among the Indians by the sixties of the 19th century and they become the torchbearers of new modern India.[7]

The middle class existed in Bengal even towards the close of the 18th century. On the consolidation of the British rule, the growing demand for administrative and professional skill created the urban middle class educated on western lines possessed of professional qualifications.[8]

Up to 1860's, the number of middle class was small in Assam. This class emerged as a class by the close of the 19th century and began to make its influence in the social life of Assam. Although the middle class is an urban and modern concept in Assam, they had their moorings in the rural areas. Even in Bengal, many of the *bhadralok* classes in the past wanted to live and die with their kith and kins in the villages. Towns and cities attracted them a little later. The Assamese middle class like the moderates was the product of the colonial age and their appearance as a class was primarily an urban phenomenon.

Anil Seal and John Broomfield termed the English educated as 'elite' and there were more tendencies among the high-caste Indians to include themselves under the banner of this group. According to Sarkar, the very use of the term 'elite' is dubious as the genuine and exclusive elite in colonial India consisted of the whites.[9] If we accept Sarkar, then Indian elite is not genuine elite.

The trading and commercial classes in Kamrup and Goalpara with direct contact with the European traders in the last quarter of the 18th century, the land revenue system in the district of Goalpara, the Mughal land revenue system introduced in Kamrup and the material foundation laid by the British rule in Assam accelerated the pace of development of these segments of middle class, on one hand and contributed towards the creation of this class in other parts of Assam as a distinct social entity, on the other. Among the factors responsible for the rise, growth and development of the Assamese middle class were: the increasing trade and commerce, the paraphernalia of a bureaucratic administration and courts, a new system of education based on western ideals of civil liberty, social ethics, legal procedure, notions of state and political theories and organizations, the creation of private property inland in absolute terms with the right of transfer, sale and mortgage and the introduction of the institutional devices for the collection of land revenue and the opening up of modern system of roads and communication, the railways and the tea industry.[10]

The social roots of the Assamese middle class can be traced back to the mauzadars and the *vaishnava satras* of Assam. Dutta Dev Goswami (1818-1904), Hem Chandra Goswami (1872-1928), Pitambar Dev Goswami (1885-1962) hailed from three *satras* of upper Assam; and Abdul Majid (1867-1924), Ghanashyam Barua (1867-1923) and P.N.G.

Barua (1871-1946) hailed from the mauzadars families contributed lots towards the emergence of early educated elite and middle class in Assam.

Like the Indian middle class of the 19th century, the newly emerged Assamese middle class also expressed their deep loyalty to the colonial government and wanted change and development of Assam under their tutelage. The allegiance they showed to colonial government gave birth in their mind a colonial outlook and with such outlook, they judged their society and literature. This clearly safe-guarded their class-interest rather than the collective interest of Assam.

The Assamese middle class was the compound product of colonial bureaucracy, English education and tea industry. Though the three components played mutually supportive role, the social formation of the class was flexible and it was capable of absorbing newer elements.[11]

Though the Assamese middle class was not a ruling class during the colonial period, it was able to maintain dominance over the Assamese society. Along with the middle class, another two classes emerged in the society. New industrial and commercial enterprises created new conditions and generated a new class of big businessmen and industrialists or planters who swelled the bourgeois rank. A class of labourers who were completely dependent on wages for their subsistence-a phenomenon entirely new in the history of the region, emerged in the economy of the province.[12]

Redundance to say that a great wave of change came in the socio-economic aspect of Assam just after the arrival of the British East India Company. Money economy was introduced in place of feudal economy based on *paik* system. Slowly and gradually, western system of education engulfed the old system of education. As a result, a new Assamese middle class emerged on the debris of old social system. The birth and development of Assamese middle class is the output of British rule. The capitalist economy and education culture carried by the British gave birth to the Assamese middle class. The newly emerged middle class was comprised of two classes; one comprising of mouzadars, *gaonburhas, mandals, satradhikars,* Brahmins intellectuals who resided at villages. This class welcomed and co-existed with the new social system, but did not want to cut off their relation with the feudal social system. They scared of losing their social status if the feudal system was eschewed. But, the British dashed their so-called social status, dynastic splendor, arrogance to the ground. The other was comprised of magistrates, *munshifs,* clerks, doctors, lawyers, engineers, police inspectors who resided at towns.

Undoubtedly, the middle class of towns were more radical than that of the villages. Western education, culture and rationalism made the minds of the middle class of towns more progressive, liberal and dynamic. But the fact is that despite having progressive and dynamic minds, this section still then stuck to the feudalistic culture of their ancestor. Therefore, the nature and character of this radical middle class of the towns also became half-feudalistic. As a result, confrontation between the old and new thought became clear and discernible in their mental world. For instance, Haliram Dhekial Phukan, A.D.Phukan, Gunabhiram Barua, K.K.Bhattacharjee and some other western educated Assamese of the 19th century advocated the education and rights of the women and introduced themselves as the radical. Some even criticized the *Bihu* song and *Bihu* dance by becoming the blind followers of western education. Ratneswar Mahanta who represented the feudal and male class by advocating against the rights and education of the women, same Mahanta again tried to introduce himself as a radical by shrinking his nose with disdain terming the *Bihu* songs as the shameless songs. These were some of the self-contradictory and weakness of the Assamese middle class of the 19th century.[13]

The Assamese middle class did not rise as a result of a single historical event and had passed through four stages of development[14]: the period of gestation from the latter half of the 18th to about 1820.; rise and growth from 1820 to 1850.; further growth from 1850 to 1880 and again further development of expansion from 1880 to 1947.

The middle class of Assam is the outcome of the colonial era, but the way it emerged in the province is unlike in the other provinces of India. In the process of colonization, a dependent colonial middle class was automatically and integrally created, though sick and deformed from its very birth and inception. It was, therefore, incapable of growing into a mature bourgeois class and leading the mass struggles with courage and conviction against imperialism. In other words, colonial capitalist development was a distorted development.[15]

The middle class of Assam, though an outcome of the colonial regime, had their inspirations from their neighbouring Bengal. Under the colonial shade, a new Calcutta-oriented Assamese middle class developed slowly in the late 19th century located in colonial hinterland. This tiny middle class was mainly comprised of high castes, like Brahmins, Kayasthas, Ganakas, Kalitas, Gosains, Mahantas and few Assamese muslims. The colonial situation imposed on the Assamese middle class a stiff competition from the migrant Bengalee middle class in Assam. Unfortunately, the colonial government was not interested in educating the Assamese which delayed the process of class formation in Assam. They served their administrative purpose by importing Bengalee *baboos* from Bengal. The Assamese middle class, under such circumstances, had to play a collaborative role with the colonial rulers to keep pace. However, with the emergence of a national movement for independence, and the growing popularity of the Congress and the consolidation of Assamese middle class in the 20th century; a large section of this class could gradually overcome this. The merger of the Assam Association with the Indian National Congress, the Assamese middle class gradually abandoned its collaborative politics with colonialism.[16]

The Assamese middle class accepted colonial bondage unconditionally and therefore, sought their development under the aegis of colonial government. Like the Bengali middle class, Assamese middle class also expressed their allegiance to the colonial government. The feudalistic gesture still then stuck at their behaviour and contemplation. Many Assamese bureaucrats under the colonial government involved in corruption in addition to the exploitation of their own people. With the establishment of some organizations, viz. Jorhat *Sarbajanik Sabha* and Assam Association; some middle class, like J.N.Barua, M.C.Barua, D.C.Barua and others came forward to safeguard the class interest of middle class. In matters of religion, there was division among the middle class. None came to reform their society out of their religious boundary. The Assamese middle class was not self dependent in the field of trade and commerce, and had to rely, therefore, on the British for capital. On question of women education, there was division of thought and action among the Assamese middle class. Haliram, Anandaram, Gunabhiram and Lakshminath, all raised voice on behalf of women education. On the contrary, Lambodar Bora, Bolinarayan Bora and Ratneswar Mahanta opposed it tooth and nail. Regarding the extension of support to the peasant movements of Assam, there was also division among them. The elite and middle class did not come to take the leadership of these movements scaring of losing their jobs and sympathy from the government. Same role they did play when the European planters harassed and exploited the tea labourers of Assam. On the question of extension and introduction of higher education in Assam, lots of debates cropped-up among the Assamese middle class. Some favoured higher education where as some others favoured primary education in the land.

Finally, unlike the all India middle class, the birth of nationalism in Assam under the middle class leadership was not the outcome of anti-British uprising.[17]

IV

Occupation of Assam by the British in 1826 ended the six hundred years of ascendancy of Ahom monarchy and began in that place, the modern age in Assam. The British rule carried with it the message of new age, on one hand and new and developed means of exploitation by the imperialistic class upon the Assamese, on the other. The people of Assam welcomed the British rule and hoped that the new government would end the anarchy and disorder from the province. But the members of the royal and aristocratic families did not accept the alien rule easily. Gomdhar Konwar and Piyali Phukan adopted armed-path to annihilate the British imperialism for the restoration of monarchy, but their efforts, finally, ended in smoke. Slowly and gradually, a new class emerged in Assam at a time while confrontation between the alien government and the aristocratic class went on. This new class, instead of criticizing the British rule, praised their rule and surprisingly even did away with the demand of freedom. The colonial apparatus in India created a market for the employment of English educated Indians in the various administrative departments.[18] Probably, because of this, the elite class did not oppose colonialism initially. According to Srinivas, the new elite had two faces. One face turned towards their own society, while the others turned towards the west.[19] According to him, westernization is a fundamental process and the fact is that the Indian elite took up the great task of modernizing their own society. In Assam also, we find some sections who had their inclination towards the European style and system; and some, on the contrary, showed their weakness towards their own society and culture. The Assamese middle class reconciled with the British rule and they formed an organization 'Assam Association.' As it was partly a political organization, so the government officer kept aloof from this. The Assamese middle class did not take part in any political movement against the British imperialism; on the contrary, they selected the flag of language to unite the entire people.

The Assamese middle class, in addition to showing their allegiance to the British rule, they even started to imitate them also. Some of the

English educated youths even considered their local good goods as bad and foreign bad goods as good. To them, all European goods were good and all local goods were bad. The educated youths even started to imitate the English in dresses and costumes. To them, these are the symbol of development of civilization. Traditional dresses, to them, created problem on their lips in speaking English. This section sank into the laps of western thought and lost, thus, their indigenous heritage. It seemed that their relations and attachments were only with the English costumes and menu, English temperament, English caps and steps, English traditions and customs.[20] George Bernard Shaw termed the Greek scholars as the privileged men. To him, few of them knew the Greek and most of them knew nothing. Similarly, some of the middle class of Assam in 19th century neither had command on the English, nor had the overall knowledge on any subjects. Despite that, they tried to show them as scholars and intellectual class. In the words of Gunabhiram Barua, he is fool who can and he is wise who cannot 'Narai adhyapak aru Ramai pandit'.[21]

The attitude of the Assamese middle class of the 19th century towards the British imperialism can be discussed as under:

Haliram Dhekial Phukan: In addition to becoming the chief associate of David Scott in matters of the land settlement, he also became the seristadar of lower Assam and assistant magistrate of Guwahati and thus, introduced himself as one of the faithful officials of the colonial government. Being enchanted, he praised the British rule in his work 'Assam buranji' saying that the people of the province would become more civilised if the British rule continued.

M.R.Dewan: He was a prominent and influential leader of then Assam who expressed loyalty towards the British prior to 1857. He helped the government from all corners starting from collecting revenue mercilessly from the people to the curbing of the revolts. Instead of helping Piyali Phukan against the government, he rather helped the government. Enchanted with the British rule, he even prayed to the Almighty to give long-life to the British rule. Undoubtedly, his help to the government revealed his parochial self interest. But his sweet relation with the British began to turn towards bitterness when the British started to consider him as their business rival. Ultimately, such a situation developed when he had no other option left than to oppose the British. It is obvious that had his personal interest not been received withstand at the hands of the British, probably, he would not have gone against the British.

Harkanta Sarma Majinder Barua: Majindar Barua was an outstanding and magnificent personality of then Assamese society. First as *seristadar* and next as *sadaramin,* he became able to extract praise from the British Government. He did not co-operate with those people of Assam who opposed the British rule. He even abandoned Maniran at a time when the latter became enemy of the British and asked people to boycott him. The government became satisfied at his allegiance and was bestowed with various presents.

Jaduram Duttabaruah: The first Assamese dictionary writer Jaduram was also an obedient British employee. He was given the post 'sadaramin' by the British. He became highly satisfied with the British rule and never tolerated its opposition. For example, when trial of Gomdhar went on at panchayat, he alongwith Maniram, Madhavram Borgohain and others gave verdict against Gomdhar.[22]

Jagnaram Khargharia Phukan: Khargharia Phukan, the brother of Haliram Dhekial Phukan was the high official of the British administration. He became the police superintendent in the beginning and the *sadaramin* later on. At each and every moment, he had his British gesture and style. He sat and ate together with the British and expressed loyalty to the British. He was more enthusiastic about the development of the English and the Bengali language, rather than the Assamese language. For example, when some elites of Gauhati took initiative for setting up of the Bengali and English schools, he assisted them even financially. Thus, he expressed his hatred and disdain towards the Assamese culture and language.

A.D.Phukan: Anandaram is recognised as the father of Assamese nationalism and the harbinger of the new age. He sought development of Assam under the shade of the British and believed that modernization of Assam possible only under the British. He dreamt of building a beautiful Assam under their rule. Surprisingly, he did not want freedom from the British. Being a high official, he expressed his disdain to them who opposed the British rule. He promised to the government that the Assamese would not resort to the path of revolution against them. Anandaram had an unflinching faith in the British rule and his practical insight was that there could be no better substitute than their rule. He was certainly not a revolutionary like Maniram, but that does not mean that he was a less patriotic.

Gunabhiram Barua: He was an obedient official of the British Government and in 1887, he was given the title of 'Raibahadur.' Due to having deep faith and love, he unconditionally supported and praised the British rule. He saw all round development of Assam under the British and thanked God for their rule in Assam. The Assam, he said, got lot from the British but the British in return, whatever exported from Assam, that was their due.[23]

Dinanath Bezbarua: He had his deep faith and love towards the British rule. He was a *seristadar* under the British Government and expressed his loyalty and sincerity to them. His son Lakshminath wrote about his father that he did not support any work that went against the British rule and advised people to accept their rule.

Radhanath Changkakati and Bolinarayan Bora: Radhanath, the founder secretary of '*Times of Assam*' and Bolinarayan, the editor of '*Mou*', both were loyal to the British. Radhanath through his paper expressed allegiance to the government. Bolinarayan wrote in '*Mou*' that lots of progress India achieved under the British and the British queen. He wrote that the English rule was necessary for long for the welfare and betterment of the Indians and India. Bora possessed a deep understanding of the basic malady of Assamese society. But instead of removing these maladies from Assamese society, he put his energies in cultivating the English ways of life.[24]

Hemchandra Barua: He also exhibited his allegiance and loyalty towards the British Government and paved attention in the cultivation of Assamese language and literature.

M.C.Barua and J.N.Barua: M.C.Barua, J.N.Barua, Gobinda Bezbarua, Ganga Gobinda Phukan they all accepted the British rule unconditionally and sought progress of the province under their shade. Barua and Barua submitted a petition before Northbrook, the then Viceroy of India in 1872 on behalf of '*Asomiya Sahitya Sabha*' and revealed their allegiance and loyalty to the British rule. They could not give up their affection towards the British rule. Ganga Gobinda Phukan, Gobinda Bezbarua and J.N.Barua criticized the revenue hike through 'Assam Association' and 'Jorhat *Sarbajanik Sabha*'. Though they protested on behalf of the peasants but did not stretch-out their hand to root-out the British imperialism.

Lord Curzon, the then Viceroy of India came to Assam in March, 1900 and he was welcomed by the Assamese middle class. In his address, J.N.Barua even expressed his loyalty to the British Government on behalf of the people of the province. To retain the memory of Lord Curzon, 'Curzon Hall' was built on the west direction of the *Dighalipukhuri* of Guwahati.

Lakshminath Bezbarua: The representatives of '*Jonaki* age,' they accepted the bondage of alien rule and tried their level best for the amelioration of language and culture of Assam. Of them, the name of L.N.Bezbarua who was the pioneer of the middle class of the *Jonaki* age, deserves special mention. Though he expressed liberal view towards the alien rule, sometime he also criticized their imperialistic design. Nevertheless, he never wished the sunset of their rule from India and always kept himself away from the independence movement. Absence of anti-imperialism found manifestation in his writings as he had his deep inclination towards their rule.

Harbilas Agarwala: He also expressed his deep loyalty towards the British in the early part of their rule. Basically being a businessman, he kept good relation with the government. He had his deep love towards Assam but despite that, he kept his relation with his original home land Rajasthan. Instead of employing local masons and carpenters in building his houses, he brought them all from Rajasthan. Probably, he had his doubts towards the skill of the local artisans and labourers. In the question of opium, he did not take strong stand against its prohibition, rather favoured its slow and gradual eradication. He had several businesses, like timber, rice, rubber and banking and had sixty shops in entire Assam. He had a tea garden at Tamolbari. But, bad eyes of the British fell on his garden also. His saw-mill opened at Tezpur had to shut down due to the conspiracy of the British. While many of the tea labourers after the expiry of their term had left their garden jobs due to the indescribable and inhuman exactions of the British planters, some of them worked in the saw-mills of Harbilas. Ultimately, this invited wrath of the British and gave birth to conflicts between the planters and the manager of Harbilas.

Pandit Dhireshwaracharyya: Edward VII, the king of England died and George V ascended on the throne of England in 1901. Regarding the two events, he composed two verses. One was expression of condolence and another was expression of joy. Same year when Lord Curzon, the Viceroy of India came to Assam in 1901, he greeted him with Sanskrit language and thus, proved his scholarly excellence in Sanskrit. Due to his allegiance showed to the alien government, he was bestowed with the title '*mahamahopadhyai*' by the government.[25]

Hemchandra Goswami and P.N.Gohainbaruah: Goswami and Gohainbaruah, both were the pioneers of *Jonaki* age of Assamese literature. Both of them were loyal officials of the British Government.

L.N.Bezbarua was loyal to the British rule but some time he criticized their rule. But Goswami and Gohainbaruah, they neither participated in the war of independence, nor pointed to the government of their shortcomings. When Bengali language was introduced in Assam for the interest of administration, he instead of criticizing the British, criticized the Bengali bureaucrats and held them responsible for that. Being overjoyed and enchanted, Gohainbaruah unhesitatingly praised the British rule. He said that unlike the pre-British rule, there was no want during the British rule and there was, according to him, no sound ground to express dissatisfaction under their rule.

C.K.Agarwala and A.C.Agarwala: C.K.Agarwala, unconditionally, accepted the bondage of the alien rule. A.C.Agarwala rendering his duty in police department, embraced the British rule with supreme joy. He expressed his royal allegiance even through his poetry. The government, being pleased with him, honoured him as 'Raisahib' in 1916 and 'Raibahdur' in 1921.

Uttam Chandra Baruah: Supplying boats and labourers to the British in 1911 in their Arab expedition, U.C.Baruah, the first *Choudhury* of Borbhag *purgunnah*, introduced himself as a faithful and obedient servant to the British Government.[26]

Kamalakanta Bhattacharjee and Ratneswar Mahanta: Among the government employed Assamese middle class of the 19th century, the name of K.K.Bhattacharjee and R.Mahanta are especially significant. Mahanta by terming the revolt of Piyali Phukan as 'seditious' tried to convince his allegiance to the British. K.K.Bhattacharjee who ended his life for the development of his people and land, and alerted and awakened the people, bowed down to the British imperialism with honour and respect. He believed in the British rule and thought of his natives' welfare and progress under their rule. He even said that the British were fit to rule the country and people should remain satisfied with their rule and imitate them. He even appealed to his countrymen that they should not ask the British to quit the land as their quit would not be good for the land. He in the 80's and 90's of the 19th century, did not want the British to leave Assam or India, rather welcomed Albert Victor, the British prince at Calcutta writing a poem *'Prince Albert Victor adarani.'*[27]

Finally, we have found that the Assamese middle class, instead of taking anti-British attitude, considered the British imperialism as blessings. It is to be noted that not only the middle class of Assam but the middle classes of other states of India also expressed their allegiance and support to the British imperialism. Right from Raja Ram Mohan Roy to Bankim Chandra Chatterjee, Michal Madhusudan Dutta, Ishwar Chandra Vidyasagar, Dinabandhu Mitra and others harbingers of Indian renaissance wished stability and permanency of the British imperialism. They thought that their onus was to point out the loopholes of the British rule giving them opportunity to get reformed. Reminding and remembering the heterogeneous good heritage of India, the middle class, like R.N.Tagore believed that the British would also submerged one day with the Indian society, like the Huns, Pathans and the Mughals. But it is also true that a nation culturally and educationally rich would never want to assimilate and mingle with a nation that culturally and intellectually poor, rather they would try to impose their culture and education on others and it is a main characteristic of an imperialist class. Culturally and educationally developed British did not come with the mission and vision of getting them assimilated with the Indians, rather got assimilated the Indians with their culture and education. Why the Indian middle class could not feel the exploitative nature of the British that marked the intellectual poorness of the middle class!

Prior to 1920, allegiance towards the British imperialism was the characteristic features of the Indian middle class. They sought and wished development of their land sheltering under the British umbrella. To work under and praise their rule, lead a peaceful and comfortable life were the objects of the Assamese middle class. They spent less time to think of the exploited masses of the province, and the shrewd and astute British liked this. Loyalty and allegiance that the Assamese middle class had towards the British, brought a negative influence on the society and because of this, anti-British uprising instead of accelerating, halted in Assam.

Nevertheless, we can say that the middle class contributed lot in the field of language and culture of India. They expressed their loyalty and allegiance not only to the colonial government but also to the European scholars who helped them to know of their past. European scholars translated the Sanskrit books of Indian scholars in English which benefited the Indian middle class and the elite to know of their own past and the people. Getting the taste of rich thought of their great Sanskrit scholars' writings through English books is a great discovery for intellectuals who discovered real India.[28]

V

The lion's share of the income of the government came from the middle class people. The rich can pay taxes easily because they are industrialists, manufacturers, businessmen and highly placed officials. Sometime they evade tax and befool the government and cause financial loss to the nation. The middle class people are the real consumers. When the government imposes new taxes upon different commodities, the poor are less affected as their standard of living is low and wants are few. Therefore, the middle class people are badly hit.

In Assam, when the government was contemplating to prohibit the opium, the fear of other taxes was there all the time in the minds of the people of the middle class society.[29] In 1860 on the advice of James Wilson, income tax was introduced and this was extended in the following year 1861 to the province of Assam. The middle class consisting of small land owners, government servants, mauzadars, traders and merchants all were affected by recent taxes on income.[30]

The British motive behind the imposition of income tax was to make their economy sound and powerful. But other motives were to bend the backbone of the middle class so that they cannot lead the peasants and the masses, and then the government would come to lend money to them for cultivation. Anyway, the colonial apparatus sought to cripple the indigenous and traditional agricultural economy of Assam and thereby, make the local people totally parasite on them.

About the economic and political condition of Assam, most of the Assamese middle class were not found to be serious. Those who were found to be serious, their role were also not satisfactory. Their grievance was confined in the papers only. For example, a letter entitled 'Distress in Assam' was written by an inhabitant of Guwahati, published in the 'Samachar Darpan' where he had given a vivid description of erstwhile British occupied Assam. It was mentioned that the people of Assam had to pay less revenue during the Ahom period than they had to pay during the time of the British.[31]

In the 19th century, many problems engulfed Assam. Some of them, mainly the revenue hike was highlighted by A.Dhekial Phukan. Regarding the hike of revenue, he wrote to Mills, 'the present rate of taxation, however, has far exceeded that limit and the assessment on some of the poorest classes of *roopit* lands is nearly equal in value to one half of their produce. In illustration to this fact, we would beg to point out that a *poorah* of high *roopit* land yielding twenty or fifteen maunds of rice valued at from Rs.2 to 3 is loaded with a tax of one rupee and four *annas*! Unless, therefore, the government provides the people with better and improved means of cultivating their lands and increase of assessment will inevitably lead to an increase of the unhappiness of the people.[32] Revenue hike was one kind of exploitation but Phukan did not accept it. To him, the British came to Assam not for exploitation but for the development of the region. It is because of this, he neither participated nor supported the anti-British uprisings. Indeed, his concept of development of Assam was based on theoretical contemplation, nothing else than that.

The British administration hiked the rate of revenue double in 1868 and the peasants of Nowgong reacted sharply against it. Gunabhiram, on the other hand, supported the hike and said that the prospect of development of Assam was high as a result of revenue hike. But he had his apprehension in mind that if the revenue hike affected the priestly class as well as the gentry whose caste rules and family traditions compelled them to engage in other pursuits of life, they would be obliged to use hired labour to till their lands.[33]

There were anomalies in the revenue system of colonial period. The anomalies in the revenue system had been described by a correspondent of the '*Indian Nation*'. The paper described that formerly the ryots of Assam were the proprietors of their land and if they made any default to pay revenue, their land was sold at auction, the surplus being paid to them after deducting arrear costs. But during the colonial regime, they were neither landholders, settlement holders nor tenants-at-will liable to be ejected or to have their lease cancelled on breach of any of the conditions of lease.[34] The paper described how the colonial government exploited and harassed the peasants through the revenue hike and ejection. Thus, the paper became successful in bringing the local issues to the national level.

The middle class who were working under the colonial government did not criticize the land revenue policy scaring losing of their jobs. Moreover, they had fear in mind that if they opposed revenue-hike, the government would then impose tax on them to meet their loss. Those middle class who attempted to raise voice against the hike of revenue, they had been silenced by giving them lucrative and covetous posts. Ultimately, the peasants got no respite from the exactions of the revenue and revenue officials.

VI

Smoking and taking of opium were the blackest chapters in the history of India. In Assam, most of the smokers and takers were the local Assamese people. The Opium Enquiry Committee and the leaders of the Congress brought into focus the disastrous effects of opium in Assam. The influence of opium was so bad that some even gave false evidence in exchange of opium. The excessive use of opium had converted the Assamese into effeminate, weak, indolent and degraded people. Though, highly consumption of opium by the local people was a burning problem, yet the anti-opium agitation took time to gather momentum. The dependent educated middle class, with their vested interest in tea plantation and in the bureaucratic distributive system, appears to have been not fit for the step. Despite that, the question of opium was raised and mooted in right earnest by some of the influencial members of the community. But due to the conflicting and contradictory views of the members, the Royal Commission ended in nothing, but it roused public consciousness which led to the emergence of 'kani nibarani sabha' in several districts to combat the opium evil.[35]

That the opium is injurious to health, that was known to the colonial government very well. But they saw bright business prospect of it and therefore, determined to bring this lucrative business to their hand by banning local opium cultivation in 1860-61. The government became able to earn more profit by introducing their *abkari* opium. From 1873 to 1893, the colonial government of Assam sold a total of 31,392 maunds of opium and realized a net price of Rs.3,14,55,576 and a license fee of Rs.47,60,657 from the opium sellers. In this way, they exploited the people of Assam in terms of opium revenue itself to the tune of Rs.3,62,16,233.[36]

On the question of opium ban, the middle class was divided in to three groups. One section did not want its ban as they had their narrow vested interest on it. They guessed that its banning would lead the government to a huge loss of revenue and then the government would impose tax on them to meet their loss. According to Kalita, the fear of other taxes being raised in the event of the suppression of opium was there all the time in the minds of the people of the middle class society.[37] In 1860-61, when opium was banned, discontent started against the order. Merchants and local traders suffered lot due to this ban as they had to shut-down their shops. Again, some sections were in favour of the opium ban. These sections were deeply concerned of its destructive affects on their people and society. There were still others who neither supported nor opposed its ban. They totally remained neutral on this core issue. They scared if they opposed it, the government would then impose other taxes on them to meet their loss and might even lose their jobs also. Local people would disdain them if they supported the ban. So, they thought it better to remain neutral and indifferent towards it.

More or less, the middle class of Assam in colonial period were concerned on the question of opium. However, the role of the middle class of Assam in the 19th century can be evaluated in the following manner:

J.N.Barua: J.N. Barua played a very negative role with regard to the prohibition of opium in Assam. His role in this regard was most detrimental so far as the interest of the Assamese people were concerned. His enlightenment and public service served the British interest best and a little of the Assamese tea planting class. As in the case of other middle class men of his period, with little exception, he could not rise above his own class interest and could do nothing for the amelioration of a public vice which had attained the magnitude of a national vice even before his birth. He expressed his opinion against the suppression of the consumption of the opium by the people of Assam with a striking clarity of purpose and without any hypocrisy and did not maintain a double-standard in this regard. Barua gave evidence before the Royal Commission on opium in Calcutta on 28th Dec, 1893 and told the Commission that opium was necessary in a jungly and malarious province like Assam. The use of opium had been prevalent from time immemorial. During the regime of the native government in Assam, a large number of people of all classes indulged in opium. Opium was highly useful in alleviating pain and in removing disorders of the stomach and was also a prevention of fever to some extent. He held the existing policy of the government on opium to be the best and said that the people of Assam would consider that the government would not be justified in adopting any change in the policy hitherto pursued.[38]

Hemchandra Barua: Hemchandra was the lone-crusader against the use of opium. He was called by the Indian Opium Commission but could not attend the Commission due to physical ground. But a copy of English translation of 'kaniyar kirtan' (Opium eaters' earol) was sent to a member of the Commission. Kaniyar kirtan was perhaps the first manifesto in the world. Referring to the dreadful effects of opium eating, he in his *'kaniyar kirtan'* writes, k*epa kani bihor ses kaniar nai gynar les hai hai ki ghor kles kaniai khale Asom des*[39]

Thus, he exposed the evils of the opium eating and ridiculed the vices of the Assamese society. He lamented that there was hardly any other more deadly poison than opium and it was the root to the ruin of Assam.

In a note dispatched to Indian Opium Commission, it was said that addiction to opium by the Assamese was a natural instinct and his suggestion was clear, 'sale of opium by the government should not, I think, be prohibited for non-medical purposes.' Hemchandra wanted to save the Assamese society from the influence of opium. But after meticulous study, it is found that he was not at all bother of the bad habits of opium eating among the lower classes.

A.D.Phukan: Regarding the opium policy of the government, Phukan commented in this manner, 'the tree will go so long as the root is not destroyed. The source must be completely exhausted and the introduction of fresh supplies (from) out of the country carefully be suppressed'. To eradicate the evil, he suggested to Mills the total stoppage of government opium and restriction of the cultivation of poppy subjecting it to heavier taxation.[40]

The influence of opium was so bad that some even gave false evidence in exchange of opium. Opium and prostitution was well known to the people of Assam and it engulfed the entire society. A.D.Phukan expressed his deep concern and disdain on it and dreamt of a noble dream and prayed God for the betterment of Assam. 'When none will give false evidence for two *tolas* of opium and will rather throw aside lacs of rupees; in such cases, prostitution, opium and wine will be unknown in the country. That time, O God, the Almighty Father, bring about in no time.'[41]

L.N.Bezbaruah: Bezbarua paid no heed to the opium debate which was going on in the 19th century. He never associated himself with the anti-opium campaign in the state.

Gunabhiram Barua: One significant issue that confronted the middle class was the addiction of the Assamese to opium. Gunabhiram said that opium came as a destroyer of disease and finally, it turned out to be the root of diseases.[42] He spoke out against the abuse of opium in the Provincial Legislative Council and exposed the hollowness of the government policy on opium. Appearing before the Royal Commission on opium in 1891, he demanded its total abolition since the opium eaters themselves felt the term *'kania'* was a byword of reproach.

P.N.G.Barua: Among the leading members of the Assamese community, only P.N.G. Barua continued to give vent to his indignation and never betrayed his consistent opposition to the use of opium under any pretext.[43] On 10th April, 1913 in the Provincial Legislative Council, he said in his maiden speech 'if the British really sought to reduce opium consumption, then why they sought again to introduce *abkari* opium? Actually, by this step, they wanted to root out the local poppy cultivation and thereby, wanted introduction of *abkari* opium as they saw it more lucrative.

Harbilas Agarwala: He ran an opium shop, on one hand and recommended to the government a policy of gradual eradication of the evil, on the other. This revealed his double standard nature.

M.C.Bordoloi: Bordoloi, an Extra Assistant Commissioner, never found fault with any government policy. On 29th December, 1893, he said before the Royal Commission on opium, 'in my humble opinion, I think that opium is one of the choicest gifts of Heaven which God has . . . . for the relief of suffering humanity as far as the ignorant people of my country are concerned.'

M.R.Dewan: Dewan depicted a bad picture of Assamese society during the Burmese rule due to his people's addiction to opium. To him, the withdrawal of old penalties against the opium eaters was mainly responsible for this. The Burmese were responsible for creating such a bad environment in Assam. The British would have seen possibly opium free Assam if the old penalties against the opium eaters were not withdrawn. To Maniram, the continued sale of *abkari* opium by the government had made the people unfit for agriculture. He, in his petition to Mills, condemned the introduction of government opium as people were becoming unfit for agricultural pursuits but he took a realistic view when he recommended a policy of gradual eradication of poppy cultivation.

P.Chaliha: Chaliha spoke out against the abuse of opium in the Provincial Legislative Council. He even resigned his seat in 1919 and thus, exposed the hollowness of the government policy on opium.

C.K.Agarwala: Agarwala was silent on the issue of opium. His father Harbilas owned an opium shop and probably because of this, he was silent on this burning and detrimental issue. This interest of Agarwala manifested his parochial character.

M.C.Barua, Bolinarayan Bora and H.Ch.Goswami: Barua, Bora and Goswami, they never troubled themselves with the thought of opium.[44]

R.N.Changkakati: Changkakati, the editor of the '*Time of Assam*' urged the Royal Commission on opium to prohibit the drug altogether making up the loss of revenue.

J.N.Barua: He expressed his opinion in favour of the suppression of the opium evils. He said to the Royal Commission on Opium that opium was not a preventive to malaria and it was never prescribed either as a preventive or a remedy. In his words, 'it is never considered to be a protective against malaria. I belong to Kamrup. I was born there. A bad type of malaria known as *kala-azar*, has been raging there for about ten years and in these ten years, I have never known a man who took opium as a remedy for that type of fever. I have never heard even that opium is prescribed as a remedy for malaria.' He said that the educated Assamese people wanted the prohibition of opium and he also supported them.[45]

Lalit Mohan Lahiri: Lahiri of Nadia of West Bengal who had spent about 9 years in Assam by 1893, said that opium was considered as a good preventive of and a remedy for malarious fever was certainly new to him. He never heard of opium being prescribed by doctors either as a preventive or as a remedy. He, on the otherhand, said that the habitual opium eaters and smokers had largely and easily fallen victims to such fever.[46]

J.Nehru was dead-against the opium and its use. According to him, probably, it could have been stamped out almost completely, if the government had pursued a more rigorous policy during the past dozen years or more.[47]

VII

The introduction of English education created an enlightened middle class who took initiative in the formation of regional organizations, for socio-economic and cultural development of the province and heralded an era of reawakening.48 In the second half of the 19th century, there also emerged several associations and organizations mostly of cultural and literary character, which provided meeting places for exchange of views. Priyalal Baruah gave birth to '*Assam desh hitaishini sabha*' in Sibsagar in 1885, Anandaram and Gunabhiram '*Gyan pradayini sabha*' in Nowgong in 1857, Ganga Gobinda Phukan '*Asamiya sahitya sabha*' and 'Upper Assam Association' in Calcutta and Sibsagar in 1872 and 1880 respectively. '*Asamiya bhasa unnati sadhini sabha*' was also the product of this period.[49] In 19th century, what we find most of these organizations were led by the planters and the landlords classes as they were the influential and powerful persons in the society. Actually, land conferred them 'power and prestige'[50] in the society and facilitated upward mobility.

Jorhat *Sarbajanik Sabha* was formed, most probably, just some time before the promulgation of the 'Assam Land and Revenue Regulation of 1886.' In 1884, this was given shape with the object of representing the wishes and aspirations of the people of Assam, explaining to the people the objects and policies of the government and generally, ameliorating the condition of the people. The *sabha* criticized the land revenue policy and exposed the cause of the Assamese ryots. The *sabha* took up a number of issues for the socio-economic development of the province and for the protection of the rights and interests of the people. In 1886, it deplored the introduction of 'The Assam Land and Revenue Regulations' without consulting the people. In 1892, the *sabha* expressed its solidarity with the ryots who agitated against the enhancement of land revenue.

J.N.Barua played a positive role in the organization of a public *sabha* at Jorhat against the 'Land and Revenue Regulations of 1886,' where about 10,000 people gathered. The members of the *sabha* expressed their deep concern in the wake of the appointment of the Royal Commission on Opium by the British Home Government in 1893 for the fear of imposition of tax on them. They, actually, wanted gradual abolition of opium business. As against the suppression and prohibition of opium, their arguments were: opium had useful medicinal value; fall in excise revenue would lead to an increased taxation; opium use was not barred by any religious principle.

The *sabha* expressed its deep concern that if opium be prohibited altogether, the people would be quite unwilling to bear any further taxation.[51] Therefore, the members, finally, adopted a resolution and in 1893, submitted a memorandum to the Royal Commission on Opium recommending the gradual abolition of opium, as sudden abolition would be disastrous to those who were already addicted to it.

The *sabha,* on the question of lease term, favoured the grant of long term leases with the right of sub-letting the land and expressed concern that short term leases had failed to improve the condition of the ryots or extend cultivation. Like the *sarbajanik sabha* of Jorhat, there was also the same *sabha* in Pune. In Maharastra in 1896-97, 'Poona *Sarbajanik Sahba*' which had been recently captured by B.G.Tilak, sent out agents into the countryside 'to encourage peasants to resist payment of revenue in a period of famine.' After the famine of 1899-1900, no-revenue campaign allegedly led by rich peasants and money-lenders were reported from Surat, Nasik, Kheda and Ahmedabad, though the Poona *Sarbajanik Sabha* had by then become quite inactive.[52]

Tezpur Ryot *Sabha* was a broad based common platform of the ryots. Organized chiefly to protest against the enhancement of land revenue, Tezpur Ryot *Sabha* had a wide-base in the villages. It collected small subscriptions from hundreds of peasants and in 1887, built the Tezpur Town Hall, the first of its kind in Assam.

By 1886, the Shillong Association, the Nowgong Ryot *Sabha* and the Upper Assam Association came into being to represent popular grievances and protest against any enhancement or fresh imposition of taxes. The new elite made a united front with the proprietary peasants against the rulers on all common issues.

Opium attracted the attention of the *Brahmos* also. The *Brahmos* pointed out the devastating and degrading effects of opium and pleaded for its total eradication. They declined to concede the government stand to continue with it on ground of loss of revenue. Ram Durlabha Majumdar, an advocate of Nowgong pleaded with the Royal Commission on Opium to stop opium trade on the ground that the lower classes had suffered lot by it.[53]

From 1886 to 1892, the members of different associations and ryot *sabhas* from the Brahmaputra valley took part in the sessions of the Indian National Congress held at Calcutta, Madras, Allahabad, Bombay and Nagpur and placed their demand to the government. S.N.Bora represented Nowgong Ryot Association at Calcutta in 1886 and Lakshmi Kanta Barkakati represented Tezpur Ryot *Sabha* at Madras in 1887. From Nowgong Ryot Association, Ghanashyam Barua took part at Allahabad session in 1888 and Haridas Roy from Dibrugarh took part at Bombay session in 1889. But their participation failed to fetch fruits and therefore, all became futile. That's why, in the years 1893 and 1894, these associations and *sabhas* did not take part in the further sessions of Indian National Congress and extended their support to the ongoing peasant-uprisings of Assam, 1893-94. Though the question of opium was discussed and debated in right earnest by the leading members of various organizations, despite that, it could not be rooted out altogether. Several decades after in 1921, leaders of the Assam Association strengthened the movement against opium at the time of Gandhiji's visit to Assam, and it became an integral part of the Non-Co-Operation movement in Assam.

Though the consumption rate decreased, still then, the rate and incidence of consumption of opium in Assam was much higher than the medical requirements of the League of Nations. In the World Conference on Opium in Geneva in 1924, the All India Congress Committee asked C.F.Andrews to undertake an enquiry in Assam and this led to the existence of the Assam Congress Opium Enquiry Committee. The report of the Enquiry Committee was published in September, 1925. The report revealed that the opium consumption of Assam had exceeded the medical requirements of the League of Nations.[54]

VIII

The so-called elite and educated, shrewd and intellectuals in a society are called the middle class. In each and every movement, they are guided by some vested interest. Division starts among them while their interest and intention receive withstand. In the colonial regime, the so called middle class and the rural elite sections of Assam were divided on the questions of some issues, viz. revenue, opium, plantation, abolition of *paik*, migration, the peasant uprisings and others. The divided sections may be termed as the imperialists, patriotic or nationalists and semi-imperialists and semi-patriotic.

On the question of plantation, the imperialist section of the Assamese middle class gave their whole hearted support to the alien government due to their own vested interest. Planters, businessmen, traders, merchants, magistrates and government servants were within this group. Hemdhar Barua, Ganga Gobinda Phukan, Dinanath Bezbarua, Narayan Bezbarua, Kaliprasad Chaliha, Radha Nath Neog, Ghanashyam Barua, Gunindra Nath Barua, Guru Prasad Kakati, A.Dhekial Phukan, Gunabhiram Barua, P.N.G.Baruah, B.N.Bora, Sheikh Shahnur Ali, Harbilas Agarwala, J.N.Barua, Radhanath Changkakati, Bistu Ram Barua, Bishnu Ram Dutta Barua all supported the government due to their own interest. They accepted the British rule as the blessings of God. They also, like the European planters, ran tea gardens at Banamali, Barting, Chenimara, Chinglou, Daloujan, Besabari, Gosaibari, Naharani, Thengalbari, Roroia, Letekujan, Madhpur, Matijan, Singhaduar, Rajabari, Lahowal, Narajan, Tamolbari and Tipamia. When the colonial government engulfed forest and naturally enriched land in the name of wasteland rules, these sections supported the government as this rule benefited them also.

Actually, the government reserved such land in the name of wasteland for their plantation industry. The tea industry created a stable middle class in Assam, especially, in Upper Assam. Without tea industry, a stable middle class would not have come into existence in Upper Assam.[55] But they had to face some problems, like the shortage of labours as most of them were engaged in traditional crops. To flush out the local labourers (*paiks*) from the traditional crops, they abolished the *paik* system in the name of emancipation of the *paiks*. But, that was just an eye wash. The middle class of Assam, specially, the imperialist section did not raise voice against it because they were also in need of labours in their tea gardens. Even the abolition of the *paik* system also could not solve the labour problem as the local labourers were not interested to work in the tea gardens. Finally, the government had to import labourers from outside the province. Most of the labourers, whether outside from the state or the local, were not interested to work in the tea gardens due to certain reasons, viz. unhealthy environments, deadly diseases, exactions and exploitation of the tea-planters.

But surprisingly, the middle class of Assam did not mention the exactions of the European planters on the coolies of Assam. They rather showed their decisive apathy towards the British planters' indescribable exactions on the coolies of the garden and finally, became their supporters.[56]

Bolinarayan Bora was the blind follower of the British rule and he in his '*mau*', tried to draw up some lists of benefits that the coolies derived from their masters (planters). The role of '*mau*' was praised by the British mouthpiece 'Englishman,' But, some of the middle class like L.N. Bezbarua did not support the view of '*mau*.' Bezbarua rather lauded the role played by the Bengalee press. The editor of '*mau*' was more conservative and pro-British bent of mind.[57]

The greatest social evil in Assam in the 19th century was the pitiable condition of the indentured tea-garden coolies, the 'beasts of menagerie' in Fuller's words, which attracted the attention of the Bengalese of Bengal, but not the Assamese and the Bengalese of Assam. None dared to defend the causes of the coolies in Assam except L.N.Bezbarua and 'an unknown gentleman' from the target of lash and lust of the European planters, the lords of the wilderness.[58] Instead of criticizing and condemning the exactions on the coolies, M.C.Barua even expressed happiness and opined 'it is superfluous for me to state here that, were it not for the tea industry, Assam would not have been what she is today.'

The planting community have the pioneers of progress and enlighten in Assam.[59] Barua was right, no doubt, but it would have been better had he or they condemned the atrocities of the planters on the coolies. But the halcyon days of the imperialist sections were about to set in when they began to understand the real motives of the colonial government. The wasteland rules and other tea-related benefits, all went in favour of the European planters. They got nothing from it and started to express their disdain and anguish against the government. Sometime even under colonial pressure and conspiracy, they had to sell their gardens to the European planters. Indeed, European never wanted local planters as their rivals in this lucrative and covetous business. In one words, they sought monopoly in the field of tea-sector by kicking-out the Assamese tea planters. The position of the Assamese tea planters was that of a 'Liliput surrounded by the British Gulivers' from all sides. Nevertheless, the Assamese tea planters were significantly the first group of Assamese capitalists though they were very weak and insignificant compared to their British counterparts. They obviously became a collaborator class under the colonial constraints.[60]

The relation between the European tea planters and the local tea planters began to deteriorate day by day. What privileges were granted to the British planters by the government in matters of rebate in land revenue and fee simple grants; same were denied to the local planters. For example, the government declined to give privileges to Maniram Dewan but he took up the challenge which led his relation with the government estranged. Thus, finally he had to earn the resentment of the alien government.

The patriotic or nationalist sections of the middle class raised their voice for the sake of their motherland. At each and every issue where people's interests were there, they instantly reacted on behalf of them. On the question of plantation, abolition of *paik*-system and migration; they reacted sharply. This section understood the real motives of the government. The British came to Assam to dismantle the traditional crop-system and to introduce, in that place, plantation industry in the province. They also criticized the wasteland rule of the alien government. They opposed Mills when he strongly deprecated the granting of wasteland to the natives in 1853. Moreover, to the patriotic section, abolition of *paik*-system in the name of emancipating them from the yoke of the aristocrats and nobility was just an eye-wash. Their motive behind this abolition was to create some labour class and attract them towards tea gardens, on one hand and ruin and dismantle traditional agriculture, on the other. But, abolition of the *paik* could not solve their problems as the local people were not interested to work in their gardens. The government then resorted to other means. They began to encourage migration from other states to Assam. Due to abundance of land, there was no protest against this at the early stage but when it started to change the demographic and population pattern of the land, they then began to shout against it tooth and nail. Kamala Kanta Bhattacharjee in his poetry collection entitled '*Chintanol*' (burning thought, published in 1890 in Calcutta) regretted through his poem '*Udogoni*' (inspiration) that the immigrants who had settled in Assam were intelligent and wicked and become the virtual overlord of Assam exploiting Assamese resources. He appealed to the Assamese to shed-off their lethargy and take lessons from the humiliation they were being subjected to. He through his poetry '*Udogoni*', '*Purnimar ratiloi chai*' (looking at the full-moon night), '*Ei no Assam, nohoi ne smashan*' (is this Assam, not a graveyard), '*Jatiya gourav*' (national pride), '*Marishali endhar nisha*' (the dark midnight), '*Bhiksha*' (alms), raised voice against exploitation and wanted to awaken his countrymen from slumber. His purpose was to make people conscious of their real plights and duties.[61] Like Kamalakanta, Krishnakanta Bhattacharyya and L.N.Bezbarua were also patriotic middle class of Assam. C.K.Agarwala also contributed lot through his two papers '*Jonaki*' and '*Asamiya*.' But his activities reflected his dual character: inhuman and capitalists.

Migration created problem for the educated middle class of Assam as they had to compete with the Bengalee educated middle class in the field of government jobs, and this gave the British an opportunity in creating fear in the minds of the Assamese middle class. Moreover, increasing population created pressure on the agricultural land and also altered the demographic pattern of the province which found manifestation at the resentment of the middle class towards the close of the 19th century.

The semi-imperialist and semi-patriotic sections of the middle class were just like the bats, neither birds nor animals. They neither wanted to incur enmity from the colonial government nor from their own society and thus, enjoyed privileges from both wings. On the question of plantation, abolition of *paik* and migration; they kept their mouth shut. To give support to plantation, abolition of *paik* and migration would invite problem from their society; and to oppose those would from the alien government. After contemplation, this section thought it better to remain neutral. This section can also be termed as weak, feeble, intellectual, astute and shrewd class in the society. Astute, shrewd and crafty in the sense that they maintained good relation and kept away from incurring enmity from the government and the people of their society; weak and feeble in the sense that they lacked courage to face the government and their society. Actually, this section was indifferent towards their own society as well as towards the ruling class. Moreover, they probably had to face opposition from the leaders of orthodox opinion as the latter had the power to fine and excommunicate temporarily or permanently. Excommunication was a serious matter as no member would have social intercourse including marriage, with the excommunicated person and his family. Until they increased substantially in numbers, they were subjected to harassment at the hands of the orthodox.[62]

IX

Several peasant uprisings took place in colonial Assam in 19th century against the exploitation and revenue hike of the colonial government. The revolts of Phulaguri (1861), Patharughat, Rangia and Lachima (1893-94) were the most prominent in the history of Assam. Surprisingly, the middle class of Assam neither supported nor participated in the uprisings collectively. But, some sections of them stretched-out their helping hands to the colonial government. Most of them found less time to think of the distress and agonies of the poor peasants. They wore colorful spectacles and saw all things colorful. Wealth, prosperity flourished their life and guessed the same in the life of the poor peasants also. They even never felt hesitation to pass-out comments that the peasants of Assam were happy and peaceful under the British. Some of the middle class truly and sincerely supported the peasants in their uprisings and some others, on the contrary, surprisingly maintained neutrality and indifference. Still, there were others who maintained dubious and double-standard role in the uprisings. But all sections, undoubtedly, had their vested interests. Abolition of *khat* system caused pain and hurt the prestige and standard of living of the higher classes. They had to work hand in hand with those who had been their sub-ordinates. The *khats* which they held rent free were now assessed. Abolition of slavery (1843) made their position like ordinary ryots. They had to lose their former privileges and had to sell or mortgage their property to meet the rising demand of the government. They held the government responsible for their pitiable condition and extended support to the peasants in their revolts against the administration. The middle class who were kicked-out of the employment by the British, they also joined in the revolt against the British. Moreover, the government encouraged tea-cultivation and prepared certain favourable rules in favour of the European planters. The local planters expressed their concern and disdain against these rules, as such rules went against their interest. So, they also gave their support to the peasants.

When some of the middle class exploited and harassed the peasants for the interest of their own and the government, some even raised their voice for the betterment of the poor peasants. Madhab Chandra Bordoloi, the Extra Assistant Commissioner and Sub-Divisional Officer of Barpeta at the time of the peasant movement of 1893-94 was the prime mover of the governmental oppression in and around Sarthebari, Bajali and Lachima.[63] He inflicted indescribable atrocities on the peasants of that regions. Rebel peasants were fastened with the plough and dragged like animals. Hem Chandra Goswami even presided over the atrocities and torture on the peasants of Boko and Chaygaon.[64] Bhabani Chandra Bhattacharjee was the tahsildar of Patharughat during the time of the revolt of 1893-94 and was instrumental in organizing governmental offensive against the peasantry in and around his tahsil. Radhanath Barua held the tahsils of Rangia and Tamulpur and became the symbol of terror to the people in both the tahsils. He earned bad name for his oppression of the peasantry.[65]

Ganga Gobinda Phukan and Gobinda Bezbarua criticized the revenue hike through 'the Assam Association', 'Land and Jungle Rule' and 'Jorhat *Sarbajanik Sabha*'. Though they protested it for the interest of the peasants, but did not stretch-out their helping hand against the government.

A.D.Phukan was more concerned of the agriculture and the peasants of Assam. He submitted memorandum to Mills in 1853, where he detailed the drawbacks of the prevailing system of agriculture and appealed, therefore, to improve the agriculture system for the betterment of the Assamese peasants. He expressed his sorrowness and concern for not adopting slightest step for improving agricultural prospect by the government. He thought some irrigation and embankments projects for Assam like some of the contemporary states of India and suggested government for its implementation, but no response evoked from the government. Phukan stated in his memorandum to Mills on the 24th July, 1853, 'an enhancement of the rates under the present circumstances of the province without any marked improvement in agriculture and commerce, would be overburdened to the people with taxes which they could but ill . . . . to bear'.[66]

J.N.Barua was also more concerned of the peasants and criticized the long term leases of land and favoured the annual lease. The settlement policy of the government to cut down the annual lease facilities was looked upon by him as 'deprivation of their rights.' He did not agree with the repeated assertion of the government about the happiness and improved condition of the peasantry of Assam. He said that the ryots were in no way better off. Kefayat Ullah, a *sadar munsiff* of Guwahati, was more concerned of the benefits of the Assamese cultivators. He even wrote a book entitled '*Krishi Darpan*' in 1853 for the cultivators of Assam.[67] Maniram Dewan was also concerned of some of the evils of Assam. Amongst the evils, he referred to the government, were the introduction of government opium, the destruction of indigenous artisans, the neglect of the study of the *satras*, appointment of Marwaris and Bengalees as mauzadars. Had the government heard of Maniram, probably, the revolts of 1861 and 1893-94 could have been averted.

The peasants' issue entered even in the Imperial Legislature of England. Dr.R.B.Ghosh put as many as eight questions on the '*Assam riots*' at the meeting of the Imperial Legislature on the 29th March, 1897. But government's reply was far from satisfactory. The repressive measures of the government to suppress the popular movement tarnished their fair name.[68]

There were some middle class who did not view with any favour the outbreak of the peasant movement. Nidhi Libai Farowel, an Assamese convert to Christianity and a middle class, spoke ills of the Phulaguri peasant movement of 1861. In his article captioned '*Nagaya drohi lokar charitra barnan*' published in '*Orunodai*,' he ridiculed the leaders and peasants who organized and led the movement against the government and said, 'these were fools and self seekers.' Gunabhiram instead of criticizing the revenue hike in 1868, supported it. He wrote the happenings at Phulaguri of 1861 in 1875 and said that the punishment meted out to the people was commensurate with their crimes and as per law was justified. Balinarayan Bora was not at all concerned of the peasants and he termed the Ryot *sabha* in his article in '*Mau*' 'if one fox howls, others in the group follow suit.'[69]

In 1886, the Jorhat *Sarbajanik Sabha* deplored the introduction of the Assam Land and Revenue Regulations without consulting the people. In 1892, the *sahba* expressed its solidarity with the ryots who agitated against the enhancement of land revenue. For the improvement and betterment of the ryots, the *sabha* favoured the long term lease as the short term leases had failed to improve the condition of the ryots. The *sabha* also favoured gradual abolition of poppy cultivation. According to the *sabha*, if poppy cultivation stopped immediately, then government would increase revenue on other land and its affect would, ultimately, fall on the peasants.

Press highlighted the grievances of the peasants of Assam before the Indian public. A middle class from Guwahati wrote a letter entitled 'Distress in Assam' in '*Samachar darpan*' and the letter mentioned that the people had to pay more revenue in colonial period than the Ahom period.[70] In 1867, the '*Somprakash*' protested against the frequent reassessment which compelled the *ryots* to migrate to areas where revenue was lower making difficult thereby for the mauzadars for the collection of revenue.[71] '*Jonaki*' the literary journal of '*Asamiya bhasa unnati sadhani sabha*,' Calcutta did not carry in any of its issues any sort of writings on the contemporary peasant movements of Assam. This was because none of the Assamese middle class had any compassion towards the cause of the peasantry. But, the Bengalee middle class on the contrary, played a laudable role towards the cause of the peasantry. Dinabandhu Mitra's drama '*Nildarpan*' (1860) was a better example of it.[72] The members of the Indian National Congress from Assam took part several sessions and placed their demands, but all their efforts ended in smoke. So, they did not take part in the sessions of 1893-94, and decided to give whole hearted support to the peasants in their revolts of 1893-94.[73]

Almost all the movements from below, leadership was ostensibly provided by the 'elite' elements. Probably, some of the higher castes gave up their Sanskritic value and had interacted with the lower classes. These sections stretched-out their helping hand to the movements of the lower classes. The elites were never out of sympathy with the cultivators, and the cultivators also in turn never doubted their sincerity. The middle class even helped the lower class and the peasants in their upward mobility, and were not jealous of their upward mobility.

The nationalist and imperialist historians defy the role of the peasants in their movements against the British. They rather emphasized to study it through their own eyes and leadership.

Prior to 1857, peasants took the leadership of the resentment against the dominant classes. But after 1857, the leadership changed and elite took the leadership of that.[74]

The challenge of the British rule produced in the minds of these elite Indians an urge to free themselves from all shackles of imperialism, and for the first time, they learnt the art of mass mobilization for a movement of a new type.[75]

Some sections of the Assamese middle class being influenced by westernization tried to change their societies and gave their helping hands to the peasants in their exploitation by the alien government. Moreover, the Assamese middle class emanating largely from landlord class and marginally from upper strata of the peasantry made common cause with the peasantry, and helped them keeping alive their new born spirit of militancy.[76]

With the emergence of the Assamese middle class as a dominant class in Assamese society, the peasantry lost its earlier leadership and began to accept the leadership of this class who not only changed the leadership of the peasant movement but also changed the nature of the movement.77 Kalita while studying the peasant movements of Assam as well as the socio-economic roots of the Assamese middle class of the 19th century, is of the opinion that the middle class of Assam or its members did not take part in or lead the peasant movements at any stage against the British Government in Assam. The peasants launched and led their movements against the government without elite and middle class leadership.[78]

Generally, the Brahmanas, Mahantas, the Gosains and the Dolois were the landowners in the villages of Assam. They did not plough their land and therefore, had got their land ploughed and cultivated by lower class agricultural labourers and tenants. Moreover, they were not at all concerned of the problem of the lower classes. When revenue hike brought down anathema in the life of the ordinary peasants, these higher class sections were not at all concerned of that hike, as it did not affect them severely because of their capacity to bear that to some extent. Therefore, the peasants themselves had to gird waistbands on their loins for their destiny. The first and the basic characteristic of the new elite was that they were indifferent towards their own societies.[79]

The peasants had no any planned and long-termed scheme at their hands. Probably because of this, the elite and the middle class did not come to take the leadership of the uprisings of 19th century. In addition to that, they scared of going against the government, lest they might lose their jobs and sympathy from them. Anyway, the middle class failed to usher a deep and standing impact on the mass people of Assam, and did not make common cause with the peasant movements of the 19th century.

According to Kalita, middle class participation in the peasant movements of Assam in the 19th century is a sheer myth. The Assamese middle class was not so much progressive at that distant date as to lead them to participate in the peasant movements. The emergence of the middle class in Assam was the result of direct government patronage, and their interests were also inextricably linked up with the British administration. The Assamese middle class was a social buttress of the colonial government right up to 1920. Therefore, the participation and leadership of the middle class in the peasant movements of Assam was historically impossible. According to him, the *Raij mels* assumed the leadership in 1861 and 1893-94.[80]

But according to Sarkar, the no-revenue movements between 1885 and 1905 were characterized by the 'leadership of local notables.' To him, the movements of Assam in 1893-94 was led by the rural elite. The uprising of Maharashtra in 1879 was led by Vasudeo Balvant Padke, an English educated Chitpavan brahmin who seems to have been influenced by Ranade's lectures on drain of wealth. The three principal leaders of Pabna agrarian league were: the petty landholder Ishan Chandra Roy, the village headman Shambhu Pal and the muslim *jotedar* Khoodi Mollah. The Deccan riots of 1875 were an example of 'a type of rural protest' deriving its leadership and much of its supports from relatively better off sections of the peasantry.

In Maharashtra in 1896-97, 'the Poona *Sarbajanik Sabha*' which had been recently captured by B.G.Tilak, sent out agents into the country side to encourage peasants to resist payment of revenue in a period of famine. After the famine of 1899-1900, no revenue campaigns were allegedly led by rich peasants and money-lenders, who were reported from Surat, Kheda, Nasik and Ahmedabad. The better example of emergence of leadership 'from below' is that of Birsa Munda, the son of a share-cropper who received his education from missionaries.[81] In the Tebhaga movement of Bengal (1946-47), the leadership was taken by the upper caste communist party and the *Kisan sabha,* which came either from the urban middle class or from the well-to-do-rural families.[82]

The revolts of the peasants of Mewar were organised by Sitaram Das, a *sadhu* in 1913 and Maniklal Verma and Vijay Singh Pathik from 1916 onwards. In Marwar, no revenue movement was led by Jai Narayan Vyas. The Bhils were organized by Motilal Tejawat, a spice merchant from Udaipur who claimed to be the emissary of Gandhiji. Darbhanga Peasant revolt of 1919-20 was led by Swami Vidyanand, the son of a prosperous occupancy tenant who was inspired by Gandhiji's Champaran Campaign.[83] In the Indigo revolt (blue mutiny-1859) of Bengal, the organizers came from zamindari-based intellectuals, money-lenders, substantial peasants, headman of villages, Calcutta-educated attorneys and journalists and missionaries. The patidars and brahmins and intelligentsia took the leadership of the peasant movements of Bordoli and Kheda (Gujarat). Rich peasants, local money-lenders, school teachers and members of urban intelligentsia provided leadership in Champaran besides Gandhiji.[84]

Notes and References

1. Banerjee, Prof. B. & Singh, K. : 'Middle Class people and rising prices' in *Competitive Essays,* Prakashan Kendra, Lucknow, 1997, PP. 21-22.

2. Barpujari, H.K. (ed) : *The Comprehensive History of Assam, Vol. V,* Publication Board of Assam, Guwahati, 2004, P. 363.

3. Borkataki, S. : *Asomiya Madhyashreni,* Navajeevan Prakash, Gwuahati, 2000, PP. 17-18, 20.

4. *Ibid.* : P. 24.

5. *Ibid.* : P. 25.

6. Guha, A. : *Medieval and Early Colonial Assam,* K. P. Bagchi and Co., Calcutta, New Delhi, 1991, P. 213.

7. Srinivasa, M.N. : *Social Change in Modern India,* Orient Longman Ltd., New Delhi, 1995, P. 78.

8. Barpujari (ed) : *op. cit.,* P. 363.

9. Sarkar, S. : *Modern India* (1885-1947), Mac Millan, Delhi, Reprinted, 2008, PP. 66-67.

10. Kalita, R.C. : 'The 19th century peasant movement and the Assamese middle classes', *NEIHA-XV,* 1994, PP. 200-201.

11. Saikia, R.   : *Social and Economic History of Assam* (1853-1921), Manohar, New Delhi, 2001, PP. 160, 163-164.

12. Bose, M.L.   : *Social History of Assam*, Concept Publishing Company, New Delhi, 2003, PP. 76-77.

13. Borkataki   : *op. cit.*, PP. 28-29.

14. Kalita   : *op. cit.,* PP. 200-201.

15. Guha, A.   : 'Saga of the Assamese middle class (1826-1921)-a review article,' *NEIHA-XXIII*, 2002, P. 20.

16. Hussain, M.   : *The Assam movement–class, ideology and identity*, Manak Publications Pvt. Ltd. in association with HarAnand Publications, New Delhi, 1993, PP. 49-51.

17. Borkataki   : *op. cit.*, P. 31.

18. Josh, Prof. B.& : *Struggle for Hegemony in India* (1920-1947), Sage
    Joshi, Shashi   Publication, New Delhi, P. 28.

19. Srinivasa   : *op. cit.,* PP. 81,95.

20. Bhuyan, J.N.   : 'Assam Bandhu aru Asamor Samasamayikata' in J. N. Bhuyan's *Unavimsa Satika: Shristi Aru Chetana*, Lawyers Book Stall, Guwahati, 1998, P. 71.

21. Bhuyan, J.N.   : 'Gunabhiram Baruar Kathin Sabdar Rahasya Byakhya' in J. N. Bhuyan's *op. cit.*, P. 93.

22. Borkataki   : *op. cit.*, PP. 34-35.

23. Choudhury, P.   : 'Bir Bandana Aru Bouddhik Byadhi—Ounoish Satikar Asom Aru Baopanthi Itihash Sarsar Ati Dis' in S. Barman's, (et al), *Oitihya aru Itihash*, Journal Emporium, Nalbari, Assam, 2005, PP. 52-53.

24. Guha, A.   : *Planter Raj to Swaraj* (1826-1947), Tulika Books, New Delhi, 2006, P. 51.

25. Borkataki   : *op. cit.*, P. 39.

26. *Ibid.*   : P. 41.

27. Sarma, G.P.   : 'The Assamese Literature and the Nationalist Upsurge' in A. Bhuyan's (ed), *Nationalist Upsurge in Assam*, Govt. of Assam, Guwahati, 2000, P. 346.

28. Saikia   : *op. cit.*, P. 175.

29. Kalia, R.C.   : 'Opium Prohibition and Rai J. N. Barua Bahadur', *NEIHA-XVI*, 1995, PP. 188-189.

30. Dutta, Ajit   : 'The background of national awakening in upper Assam' in
    Kumar   A. Bhuyan's (ed), *op. cit.,* P. 67.

31. Majumdar, Paramananda : 'Samachar Darpanat Asamar Katha' in S. Barman's (et al), *op. cit.,* P. 145.
32. Mills, A.J.M. : *Report on the Province of Assam,* publication Board of Assam, Guwahati, Second edition, 1984, P. 102.
33. Barpujari (ed) : *The Comprehensive .... Vol. V.,* P. 28.
    Choudhury : 'Bir Bandana . . . .' in S. Barman's (et al), *op.cit.,* P. 54.
    Guha, A. : *Asamor Itihash Adhyayan aru Rasana,* 1979, PP. 8-9.
    Barua, Gunabhiram : *Asam Buranji,* Guwahati, Reprint, 1972, P. 171.
34. Barpujari (eds) : *Political History of Assam, Vol. I,* 1826-1919, Publication Board of Assam, Guwahati, Second edition, 1999, PP. 99-100.
35. *Ibid.* : P. 134.
36. Kalita : 'Opium Prohibition . . . .', *NEIHA-XVI,* P. 187.
37. *Ibid.* : PP. 188-189.
38. *Ibid.* : PP. 185, 187-188.
39. Barpujari (eds) : *Political History . . . ,* P. 133.
40. Barman, S.N. (ed) : *Adhunikatar Agradoot Pandit H. Ch. Barua,* Guwahati, 1996, P. 110.
    Choudhury : 'Bir Bandana . . . .' in S. Barman's (et al), *op. cit.,* P. 64.
    Mills : *op. cit.,* Appendix (J), P. XLIV.
41. *Ibid.* : *op. cit.,* Appendix (J), P. XLIV.
42. Barua : *op. cit.,* PP. 120-121.
    Saikia : *op. cit.,* PP. 214, 218-219.
43. Barua : *op. cit.,* PP. 120-121.
    Saikia : *op. cit.,* PP. 214, 218-219.
44. *Ibid.* : *op. cit.,* P. 220.
45. Kalita : 'Opium Prohibition . . . .' *NEIHA-XVI,* P. 189.
46. *Ibid.* : P. 189.
47. Nehru, J. : 'The Brahmaputra Valley' in A. Bhuyan's (ed), *op. cit.,* P. 375.
48. Bhattacharjee, J.B. : 'Regional Organizations and National Awakening' in A. Bhuyan's (ed), *op. cit.,* P. 94.
49. Barpujari (eds) : *Political History . . . . ,* PP. 157-158.
50. Srinivasa : *op. cit.,* P. 12.
51. Kalita : 'Opium Prohibition . . . .' *NEIHA-XVI,* P. 189.

52. Mookherjee, : 'Peasant resistance and peasant consciousness in colonial
    Mridula India—Subaltern and beyond', *Economic and Political
    weekly*, 8 Oct, 1988, P. 2114.
53. Saikia : *op. cit.*, P. 218.
54. *Ibid.* : P. 220.
55. *Ibid.* : P. 182.
56. Borkataki : *op. cit.*, P. 31.
57. Guha : *Planter Raj* . . . .,PP. 53-54.
58. Sengupta, S.C. : 'The Bengalees in Assam in the 19[th]century', *NEIHA-X*,
    1989, PP. 373-374.
59. Choudhury, P. : *Asamar Saah Banua Aru Ounoish Satikar Bidwan Samaj*,
    Students' Store, Guwahati, 1989, P. 78.
60. Hussain : *op. cit.*, P. 44.
61. Nag, Sajal. : 'Social reaction to bania exploitation' in J. B. Bhattacharjee's
    (ed), *Studies in the Economic History of NEI*, NEHU
    Publications, Shillong, 1986, P. 367.
62. Srinivas : *op. cit.*, PP. 78, 81.
63. Kalita : 'The 19[th]century . . . .' *NEIHA-XV*, PP. 204-205.
64. Tamuli, L.N. : *Bharatar Swadhinata Andolanat Asamor Avadan*, Sept.,
    1988, PP. 110, 121.
65. Kalita : 'The 19[th]century . . . .' *NEIHA-XV*, PP. 204-205.
66. Mills : *op. cit.*, P. 102.
67. Saikia : *op. cit.*, PP. 113, 116.
68. Barpujari (eds) : *Political History* . . . ., PP. 67-68, 102.
69. Kalita : 'The 19[th]century . . . .' *NEIHA-XV*, PP. 203-204.
70. Majumdar : 'Samachar Darpanat Asamar Kotha' in S. Barman's (et al),
    op. cit., P. 145.
71. Barpujari (eds) : *Political History* . . . PP. 150-151.
72. Kalita : 'The 19[th]century . . . .' *NEIHA-XV*, P. 204.
73. Guha : *Planter Raj* . . . ., P. 284.
74. Saha, S. : *1942 struggle – a study of grass root nationalism in the districts
    of Darrang and Nowgong of Assam* (1942-45), NEHU,
    Shillong, 1984, PP. 15-16.
75. Choudhury, : 'Tribals' participation in the nationalist upsurge' in A.
    Medini Bhuyan's (ed), *op. cit.*, P. 296.
76. Goswami, S.D. : 'The nationalist upsurge: its impact on peasants and tea
    garden workers' in A. Bhuyan's (ed), *op. cit.*, P. 189.

77. S a r m a , : 'Peasants uprisings and middle class hegemony: the case of
    Manorama   Assam', *NEIHA–X*, 1989, PP. 328-329.
78. Kalita, R.C.   : 'The Phulaguri uprising of 1861: a peasant mass movement',
                       NEIHA-X, 1989, PP. 310, 324.
    Kalita   : 'The 19[th]century . . . .' *NEIHA-XV,* P. 199.
79. Srinivasa   : *op. cit.,* P. 78.
80. Kalita   : 'The 19[th]century . . . .' *NEIHA-XV,* P. 203
81. Mookherjee   : *op. cit.,* P. 2114.
82. *Ibid.*   : P. 2115.
83. *Ibid.*   : P. 2114.
84. *Ibid.*   : P. 2115.

CHAPTER – FIVE

RAIJ-MELS: MANOEUVRE AND MODUS OPERANDING

A *mel* in Assam was a 'time honoured institution' and a 'recognized feature' of the Assamese social life, for it was the only means through which people could obtain protection from the oppression of the local functionaries.[1] Etymologically, *mel* means a meeting; an assembly of persons coming to decide some questions. The *mel* was a unique feature of the socio-cultural life of the Assamese people since time immemorial. Whenever there was any lapse in social behaviour in the Assamese society, a *mel* was summoned for the redress of the matter. The *mel* was a local judiciary and indeed, a people's court settled disputes at the village level.[2]

Raij-mel was the highest and developed form of the *mel* system. According to Mac Cabe, an English official, *gaon-panchayat* organized with the object of social issue developed gradually and took the name of *Raij-mel* later on. He described the *Raij-mel* as an embodiment of collective strength of the people.[3]

The peasant uprisings of Assam in the late 19th century were the anti-imperialist struggle against the colonial rule. The *Raij-mels,* forming the anti-imperialist struggle, were the outcome of the long drawn-out social customs and traditions of the people of the region, not the sudden outbursts of national feelings.[4] Like the *mels*, the *Raij-mel* also played a conspicuous role in Assam in the 19th century. On many a times when the peasants were circumspected to colonial oppression, people resorted to *Raijmel*. In another word, we can say the *Raij-mel* as the peasants' mobilization campaign. The *Raij-mels* were institutions where the peasants were the most important participating unit.[5]

The history of the peasant uprisings of Assam in the 19th century is synonymous with the *Raij-mel*. The *Raij-mel* appears to have emerged first as a social force of the peasantry in the erstwhile Darrang district during the period of 1707-1769, against the oppressive and unbearable taxes of Lakshmi Nath Singha, the Ahom monarch in 1769. Thereafter, the *Raij-mel* became active again in Darrang in the wake of the fresh outbreak of the *Moamoria* rebellion in the reign of king Gauri Nath Singha. Finally and gradually, the *Raij-mel* became a part and parcel of the social life of the peasantry of Nowgong and Kamrup. The *Raij-mels* emerged as a popular forum among the peasantry of Darrang, Nowgong and Kamrup; and it may be due to the fact that the control of the Ahoms in these districts was not so much rigorous and effective.[6]

II

The peasants-dominated *Raij-mels* were gradually replaced by the middle class-dominated Ryot *sabhas* after1893. Towards the close of the 19th century, the popular *Raij-mels* of Assam gradually merged with the more representative and broad based Ryot *sabhas*.[7] The most prominent among the Ryot *Sabhas* were Tezpur Ryot *Sabha*, Nowgong Ryot *Sabha*, Viswanath Ryot *Sabha*, Saring Ryot *Sabha*, Solaguri Ryot *Sabha*, Ganak Pukhuri Ryot *Sabha*, Na-duar Ryot *Sabha*, Jamuguri Ryot *Sabha*, Chatia Ryot *Sabha* and Helem Kalangpar Baresaharia Ryot *Sabha*. Some of these existed since the sixties of the 19th century, while others in the twenties of the 20th century.[8]

By nature, the *Raij-mels* and the Ryot *sabhas* were anti-imperialist. In the *Raij-mels*, the peasants were more important than the leaders. But in the Ryot *sabhas*, the leadership was more important, and the peasants rarely went ahead of the leaders. Though the organization was named after ryot, it did not represent ryots only but the peasantry in general, as the stratification of peasantry was not uniform. Of course, majority of the members of the Ryot *sabha* were of urban middle class elite.[9]

In areas, where these modern Ryot *sabhas* and associations were in the field, no militant mass struggle on the lines of the *Raij-mels* (1893-94) ever took place.[10] For example, the Ryot *sabhas* which were active in Tezpur, Nowgong and its neighbouring places during 1893-94, did not exert any impact and as a result, the situation did not become hot there due to the liberal leadership of the *sabhas*.[11]

The Ryot *sabhas,* besides its basic objectives, took initiative in other constructive works, like construction of roads and dams, campaign against the evils of opium taking, drinking and gambling among the peasants. The *sabhas* also encouraged education among the illiterate villagers. Several resolutions were also passed by different Ryot *sabhas* demanding free grants of bamboos and thatches to construct their houses, to sanction relief from auctions of their lands for non-payment of revenues, not to allow auction of their houses, cows, bullocks, golden ornaments of the women folk, utensils for non-payment of taxes.[12]

III

The aims of the *Raij-mels* were to place the social and economic problem of the people before the government. The *mels* wanted to safeguard the mutual interest of the peasants and also to protect the peasants from the oppression of the local functionaries, like Marwari traders and *mahajans.* To show the mobility and solidarity of the peasants, irrespective to the caste and creed, was another aim of the *Raij-mels*. Actually, the *mels* redressed the animosity and thus, rebuilt the ethos of greater Assam. The other aims of the *Raij-mels* were not to yield to the government demand and compel the government to reduce the rate of revenue.

The peasants take a great deal of pride in their agriculture. But their pride and prestige was endangered by the colonial apparatus by hiking revenue on their land. The *Raij-mels*, therefore, sought to restore the lost glory of the peasants.

The *Raij-mels* were well organized and well attended, more representative and broad based organizations. They were not planned, rather spontaneous organizations. The main strength and guiding force of the peasants' upheavals of Assam from 1861 to 1894 was the *Raij-mels.* The *Raij-mels* were formed and organized with the people of one tahsil or more than that. Indeed, they were the constellation of heterogeneous assemblies of the villagers. Moreover, the *Raij-mels* were not permanent or regular organizations of the peasantry with its functional continuity. It was convened in times of crisis or emergency when community interests were in jeopardy or required its services.[13]

One noticeable organizational feature of the *Raij-mels* was the *dak-system* and the *lathials*. To carry and convey their orders from village to village, the *mels* appointed its own *dakowals* and organized a corps of *lathials* to resist attachment of property.[14] Its remains expressed that this traditionally organized system had no match to the well-equipped and better organized British machinery, for which its policy and strategy had to meet fiasco at the hands of the colonial power.

To fetch all peasants under one roof so that all remain fastened in one thread, the *melkies* of the *Raij-mels* adopted some strategy. To prevent the peasants from paying the hike-revenue, the leaders sometime put psychological pressure upon the peasantry. Ex-communication and social ostracism was some such strategy, with the help of which they became successful. The embodiment of the order of the *mel* 'if you pay, you are cursed and ex-communicated' created scare in the mind of the ordinary peasants, and for fear of social ostracism, they stopped paying revenue to the government[15] and thus, attempted to collapse the revenue structure of the colonial government. Moreover, the people boycotted Rangia *bazar* by destroying the huts, and made huge loss to the government's revenue.[16] To unite and fasten all the peasants, there was also the fine system. Paying hike revenue to the government was subjected to fine and considered as violation of the verdict of the *mels*. In December, 1892, the tahsils of Pati Darang, Nalbari, Bajali and five other *mauzas* of upper Borbhag and Sarukhetri in their mels resolved and vowed not to yield to the government's demand, and to fine and ostracise those who would pay revenue to the government.[17]

To keep the morale of the peasants unbroken and to decrease the crestfallen among the masses, *mels* were convened secretly at night several times. Indeed, this was done at that time while colonial atrocities went on unabated. The people to evade arrest went underground in the dense forest. For instance, many went underground in the jungle of Sarthebari in 1893-94.[18]

Sometime some secret decisions were taken instantly in the *Raij-mel* at the time of emergency, and to dispatch such secret message, therefore, to far-flung and remote villages, there was the system of *dak*. These *dakowals* carried the messages from one village to another.[19] Faithful were appointed as *dakowals* so that colonial spies could not entice and bribe them.

There were some peasants who for the fear of attachment of their properties wanted to pay their revenue to the government. Still then, there were others who wanted to purchase the auctioned properties of their own men, what had been attached for the failure of payment of revenue arrear. To frighten the both classes of peasants, some *lathials* were appointed.

Sometime, the colonial apparatus engaged some spies to enquire about the modus-operanding of the *Raij-mel*. These spies tried to find out the where-about of the ring leaders and had their hawk-like eyes on their movement. The local leaders, therefore, to get rid of them, shifted their place of halting and venue of *Raij-mel* frequently. Most of the time, it is seen that the *Raij-mel* were convened at *namghars* and *masjid*.

To us, the *melkies* probably selected *namghars* and *masjid* for two reasons: being religious place, the suspicious eyes of the colonial spies would not fall on the *mels*; and it would be much easier for the *melkies* to unite all in such religious places, and swear them in the name of God. Moreover, the leaders of the *mels*, most probably, innovated the idea of mobilizing the public opinion through *naams* (religious songs). For example, in spite of the prohibitory order of McCabe, the Deputy Commissioner of Kamrup, *mels* continued as usual. Stories of *mels* being organized thus, even thereafter, by the Gosains and Pathaks through singing of *naams* popularity called 'rajahuwa naams' (public religious songs) have come down generations after generations. Sindhumal Pathak, a *barpathak* of Sarthebari *panch khel*, seems to have innovated this idea of mobilizing public opinion through *naams*.[20]

Resolutions, mass-petitions and memorandums these are some of the written weapons that the peasants placed before the colonial authority to express their grievance served the peasantry a lot.

One very important and noticeable thing to be mentioned is that sometime decision was made to hold the *mel* for several days. Probably, such decision was taken at a time when the number of the peasants of other far-flung villages were found to be less. For instance, the leaders of the Phulaguri *Raij-mel* decided to hold *mel* for five days so that peasants from far off villages could also attend it. This was done to enable them to take part in the deliberations.

Eric Hobsbaum says that a peasant class cannot really mobilize itself. It is always some leaders who help to raise the consciousness of the peasantry and mobilize them.[21] He also says that the peasants though a potential revolutionary class, are basically a passive class and are need of leadership.[22] Possibly because of this, landlords and influential persons came to take the leadership of the *Raij-mels*. The historians, particularly the imperialist and the nationalist historians have not paid much importance to study the role of the peasants and the workers. They have emphasized to study the history of the Indian masses through the eyes of the elite leadership. In Ahom period, *mels* were organized under the leadership of *kheldars* in Upper Assam. In Lower Assam, it was organized under the leadership of Choudhuries. Choudhuries, Dolois and Gossains were the powerful landlords who presided over the *'mels'*.[23] In colonial period also, the character of leadership did not change altogether and remained almost same like the Ahom period. From the meaning of the term *'Raij-mels'* as well as of its style of functioning, it seems that the leadership of the organization was collective.[24]

R.B.McCabe, the Deputy Commissioner of Kamrup reported that the *Raij-mels* were governed by the Dolois, Gossains and principal landholders; and they were the leaders of the movements. Thereafter, he reported that, in many instances, the leaders of the *mels* were 'dismissed head constables and released convicts.'[25] However, from the report of the government, the real and clear picture of events cannot be had. The peasants themselves also felt no necessity to write the contemporary events due to the lack of their formal education. According to the government report, the leadership of the *Raij-mels* was taken by the Gossains, Dolois and the landowners. But it can be accepted to some extent and at certain level. The leadership of the revolts of Rangia, Lachima, Phulaguri, Nalbari, Barama and Bajali were taken by the oppressed ryots. The Kaivartas, the Tiwas or Lalungs and the Kachari gave the leadership of the revolt of Phulaguri, and some of them even became martyrs. The Martyrs of Patharughat were ordinary peasants. The rebels of Rangia revolt were mainly of Kachari tribes. According to M. Mukherjee, 'the no-revenue movements between 1885 and 1905 were characterized by the leadership of local notables.' One such movement was led by the rural elite in Assam (1893-94).'[26] For example, the men who gave leadership in the *mels* of Sarukhetri were Jogeswar Goswami (Byaskuchi), Bholanath Sarma (Karakuchi), Harakanta Sarma (Helsa), Puspa Kahar (Sarthebari), Abhayram Kalita, Jadu Medhi (Sondhya), Homeswar Talukdar (Balakuchi), Bhakatram Kalita (Nankar Bhoira) and Rupkanta Doloi (Guakuchi). They were all local notables.[27]

The *Raij-mels* of 1861, 1868 and 1893-94 were in similar line with the peasants and tribal revolts in many parts of India. The *Raij-mels* were, by nature, anti-imperialist. McCabe, the Deputy Commissioner of Kamrup, compared the authority of *Raij-mels* to that wielded by the

Vehmgercht (Secret Court) or to come to more modern times by the *Nihilist.*[28]

The nature of the *Raij-mels* was like the village panchayat, but its activities were not confined to the panchayat alone. Sometime, it became like a spokesman not only of the inhabitants of one village but the inhabitants of one or even more tahsils. The authority of the *mel* had a hold in the land where the ryots were more important than the authority of the state. The *Raij-mels* of 1893-94 maintained strict discipline by cursing and ostracizing people who violated the discipline of the *Raij-mels.*[29]

Ultimately, the conservative and parochial character of the *Raij-mels* began to change after the introduction of modern education. The *Raij-mels,* on behalf of the greter interest of the people, raised voice against injustice and thus, indirectly reserved the human rights. Actually, this reveals the judiciary character of the *Raij-mels* and there is no doubt about this. The *mels* considered the augmentation of revenue as an ominous contemplation and a faulty step. Secularism is one of the basic characteristic features of the *Raij-mels.* It had in its fold men from different ethnic groups and religious persuations. Despite having factions and factionalism among them, the peasantry united against the government to show their solidarity and mobility for establishing their rights and liberty through *Raij-mels.*

Differences in the size of land have created diverse agricultural classes in rural society.[30] Inspite of having variations in the peasantry, all united under one banner against the *Raj.* For instance, the Caste-Hindus, the fishermen and the *Lalung* (*Tiwa*) formed the core of the *Raij-mel* at Phulaguri in the district of Nowgong, while the Caste-Hindus from the Brahmin to the lowest Caste-Muslim and the Bodo-Kacharis continued the *Raij-mel* in Darrang and Kamrup, mostly during the period of 1868-94.[31] Thus, the *Raij-mels* was widely horizontal irrespective to caste, creed and community where the masses used to discuss their problems.

The *Raij-mels* of 1861, and the *Raij-mels* of 1893-94 were different in their nature and character. Up to 1880, the peasants had accepted their miseries as their fate, and it was only because of their lack of proper education. But after 1880, the nature of *Raij-mels* began to change. Some educated class emerged in the scene who even took the leadership of the *Raij-mels.* When in 1886, new land laws were introduced in Assam regarding land tenures and *patta* distribution, *mels* of the people were called and from these *mels,* petitions were sent to the government to reconsider the new land laws. Then again in 1893, when land revenue was enhanced, very well argued memorials were sent in the name of the ryots to the Chief Commissioner of Assam and to the viceroy of India.[32]

IV

During the early 35 years of British rule (1826-1860), the *Raij-mels* were the recognized features in the administration of Assam and the authority also viewed them with favour. But being hard-pressed by the defective revenue policy of the government in later period, the peasants of Kamrup, Darrang and Nowgong organized through the *Raij-mels* for the redress of their grievances. The economic discontent aroused the political consciousness amongst the peasantry and the *Raij-mels* motivated them for the revolts right from Phulaguri (1861) till the revolts of Patharughat, Rangia and Lachima (1893-94). The main strength and guiding force of the peasants-uprisings of Assam from 1861 to 1894 was the *Raij-mels*. According to S. D. Goswami, 'the grass-root level mass-organizations like the *Raij-mels* spearheaded the resistance struggle against the repressive and exploitative action of the dominant colonial class and the power'.[33]

Multiplication of taxes was a serious concern to the agricultural ryots. The Assam administration imposed a stamp duty in 1858. Excise duty was already levied at the *sadar* stations of the districts of Kamrup, Darrang and Nowgong. Besides the *jalkar* for fishing in the rivers and *beels*, taxes were also levied on cutting trees, reeds and grazing. In 1852, excise opium was introduced in Assam. Income tax was introduced in Assam in 1861. Fuel was added to the fire when the cultivation of poppy was ceased in Assam in May, 1860. It was, indeed, a major blow to the poppy-growers, particularly, the agriculturists of Phulaguri area in Nowgong district. The area was peopled by the tribals, like the Kacharis and the Lalungs. Actually, the ban on poppy was the breach of privileges which they enjoyed since the time of the Ahoms. By that time, a rumour was surfacing that the government was pursuing a policy of taxes on their houses, *baris* and *paan* cultivation. The process of a license tax, in the meantime, confirmed their apprehension that the cultivation of betel-nut and *paan* be subjected to taxation, which led to holding of *mels* in different places in the periphery of Phulaguri. The peasants of Barpujia, Raha, Kampur, Chapar and Jamunamukh areas assembled in the *Raij-mels* at Phulaguri for having the matter discussed there. The

Raij raised their voice against the imposition of the income tax in the *Raij-mels* and decided to move the matter before the authority. About 1000 ryots as per the decision of the *Raij-mels* came over to the *sadar* court on the 17th September, 1861 to place their grievances before the Deputy Commissioner of Nowgong district. The ryots were not allowed easy passage for their entry into the court. But some of the ryots entered into the Deputy Commissoner's room forcefully. Unfortunately, Lt. Herbert Sconce, the Deputy Commissoner instead of listening to their grievances, treated the matter merely as a law and order problem, and passed orders to detain them in the *thana*. However, they were released by the evening through the mediation of Dhan Sing, a wealthy person of the locality.

On October 9th, some leading persons and the *gaonburhas* of the area submitted to the Deputy Commissioner a memorandum of protest against the ceasing of poppy cultivation and imposition of taxes on their houses, gardens and *paan*. But the Deputy Commissioner did not budge even an inch from his stand and were convinced that they could not have a hearing from him.[34] Finding no ray of hope, they decided to review the tax policy of the government in the *Raij-mels* scheduled to be hold on the 15th October at Phulaguri. The *Raij-mels* were held at the market field situated on the bank of the river Kalang of Nowgong. The *Raij-mels* were held for five days as decisions could not be taken in one sitting. The verdict mooted out was not to pay taxes to be levied on the items.

Acting on an intelligence report, the Deputy Commissioner of Nowgong tried to disperse the *Raij-mels* by deputing a police party under a *daroga* on the 14th October. The party arrived at the site by the 15th October, but failed to curb the *mels*. Another police party was dispatched on the third day but it also met failure. However, interference from the government made the situation volatile leading to the continuation of the proceedings, consequent of which additional groups of *melkies* coming from distant villages made the *Raij-mels* far-flung. In fact, the *Raij-mel* had the sanction of the society where final decision had been taken by the *melkies*. On the 17th October, the *daroga* arrested some leaders to make his attempt successful; but the *melkies* with assistance of the peasants got them released by overpowering the *daroga*.[35]

On direction of the Deputy Commissioner, Lieutenant Singer, the Assistant Commissioner arrived at Phulaguri on the 18th October. He found there a gathering of over three thousand men armed with *lathies* on their hands and *pugris* on the heads. Lt. Singer had mistaken the *lathies* as arms, ordered his police party to disperse the *mels*. He even himself was involved in seizing the *lathies*. As a result, the situation turned violent. Eventually, Singer was beaten to death and his body was thrown into the river Kalang.[36]

The persons involved in the killing were Bahu, Kati Lalung, Thomba Lalung, Jubo Lalung, Mohi Koch and Koli Deka. The Deputy Commissioner sent another police party under a *havildar* on the following day. This party quelled the *Raij-mels* by using fire arms. Several peasants were killed and many others left wounded in the field. Foreseeing the possibility of holding *Raij-mels* over and again, the Deputy Commissioner, accompanied by a party of Assam Light Infantry, marched into Kachuhati, Phulaguri, Nelie and some other places. As a precautionary measure, 41 persons including the sons of the old Lalung Raja were arrested.[37] Nine persons, according to an account, were arrested. Of them, two were banished for 14 years, one was given 7 years rigorous punishment and six were sentenced to transportation for life. It is said in an account that some of the arrested persons were awarded capital punishment; they were Lakshman Singh Deka, Sambor Lalung and Rangbor Deka.[38]

In between the Phulaguri *Raij-mels* of 1861 and the *Raij-mels* of Patharughat, Rangia and Lachima of 1893-94, the peasants of different places of Assam organized their *mels* in different period. For instance, the name of the *Raij-mels* of Patharughat, Bajali, Hadira and Gobindapur of 1869, and Hajo *Raij-mels* of 1890 are worth mentioning

After 1890, William Ward, the Chief Commissioner of Assam, raised the rate of land revenue from 70 to 80 percent in 1892, and the rates were raised in certain cases to 100 percent. The measure was considered to be a foul play on the part of the government. As a consequent, the people decided to take cognizance of the matter in the *Raij-mels*. The *Raij-mels* were held in Rangia and Lachima (erstwhile Kamrup); and Patharughat (erstwhile Darrang). Moreover, the tahsils of Nalbari, Barama, Bajali, Pati Darrang and the mauzas of Sarukhetri and upper Barbhag[39] were also not lagging behind. At Balagaon, a village close to Rangia, a *Raij-mel* was held on the 24th December, 1893. The *mel* dealt with the incidence of the enhanced land revenue on the ryots, and decided not to pay the enhanced rate. The agitated peasants destroyed the huts of the *hat* (market) and looted the shops of the Marwaris on the pretence that their arrival was, mainly, responsible for the hike of revenue.[40]

The no-revenue campaign of Rangia started with the looting of the Rangia *bazaar* in the morning. To discredit the *mel*, the colonial government linked up the *mel* with looting. What the local sources reveal is that Radhanath Barua, the tahsildar of Rangia was an oppressor, and the ryots were, naturally, hostile to him. Moreover, due to the outbreak of *kalazar*, a major chunk of the peasants remained absent from the agricultural field for a certain period of time, which had a devastating effect on agriculture compelling the peasants to take loans from the Marwari money-lenders. The imposition of a market toll on the cash crops irritated the peasants and ultimately, the revenue hike added fuel to the fire. The people out of anger boycotted the *bazaar* by destroying the huts. Boycotting, indeed, was the course of action adopted in the *Raij-mels*.[41]

McCabe, the Deputy Commissioner of Kamrup, on receipt of the information of the proceedings of the *Raij-mels*, deputed Mr. Reilly, the Assistant Superintendent of Police to investigate on the matter.[42] The peasants got scent of it and roughly 2500 to 3000 agitating peasants assembled at Rangia for holding demonstration on the issue. The agitating mob threatened to destroy the post office, *thana, kutcherry* and the tahsildars house. But due to timely intervention of the police, the administration became able to bring the situation under control. But for a number of days, the area remained tensed. Though Reilly could arrest some demonstrators but failed to arrest the *melkies* up to the 5th January, 1894. McCabe proceeded to Rangia and encamped there due to the tensed situation. Another *Raij-mels* were held for reviewing the situation on the 8th January, 1894, and this time, McCabe succeeded in arresting some of the *melkies* involved in the riot of the 24th December.[43]

The news of the arrest of the leaders was circulated to and fro. To make protest of it, *Raij-mels* were held in different parts of the districts of Kamrup and Darrang. On the 10th January, 1894, some peasants came from Betnam mauza of Tamulpur to place their demands before Mccabe. Seeing this, McCabe, on the same day, issued from his Rangia camp an order prohibiting the sitting of *Raij-mels*. A large mob about 2500 to 3000 people encamped in the fields close to the *thana* towards the evening. This large gathering was consisting of the local people and the *melkies* from different mauzas under the tahsils of Rangia. The *melkies* used to come with *lathies* in their hands. McCabe, in order to disperse them, read out his order what the mobs declined to yield. They raised to slogan 'we won't pay the revenue at the enhanced rate.'[44]

The crowd by late evening made proceedings to force the *thana* for getting the prisoners released. When they were trying to make their attempts effective, the Deputy Commissioner then ordered instantly for firing. Finally, he succeeded to arrest and apprehends several persons from among the *Raij*. In the non-official record, more than fifty persons were killed in the firing but official records deny it, and reported that the *Raij* were dispersed without blood shedding.[45]

Mels were held in Nalbari and upper Borbhag mauza under Nalbari revenue tahsil and this can be known form the report of McCabe, the then Deputy Commissioner of Kamrup. A *Raij-mel* was held, according to local source, on the 11th January, 1894 at Raj-Kadamtal of Sandha Paikarkuchi village near Nalbari. The *Raij-mel* at Raj-Kadamtal decided to proceed to Rangia for raising protest before the Deputy Commissioner against the revenue hike on land. But the authority showed indifference to their demand. Rather, some of them were said to have been bulleted by them, though it is difficult to establish due to the lack of recorded data. Rupkanta Doloi hailed from Guakuchi village, was the chief organizer of the *Raij-mel*. The other persons who organized the *mels* were the residents of the nearest villages who attended the *mels* in any capacity.[46]

Raij-mels were held in Bajali also in protest against the revenue hike on land, and therefore, decisions for non-payment of revenue were taken there. The *Raij-mels* issued command to rise against such payment, and the ryots willing to pay were given threatening.[47] Like Bajali, the *Raij-mels* were held in Barama tahsils also with same modus-operanding and with same spirit. The *mels* appointed their own *dakowals* to carry orders from village to village, and organized *lathials* to oppose attachment of property.[48]

From the month of December of 1893, the *Raij-mels* were being held in Sarukhetri mauza. The *mels* continued even after the imposition of prohibitory order by McCabe, the Deputy Commissioner of Kamrup. The local version relating to Sarthebari *Raij-mels,* instead of accepting Lachima as a place of riot of 21st January, 1894, want to establish *Pana-tup* in south Sarthebari as the place of riot. However, the riot was the culmination of a series of *Raij-mels* held in different villages within the periphery of Sarthebari.

The land of Sarthebari was not suitable for wet crops. The revenue-oriented settlement policy conducted in the area was said to have been an unscientific one. The measuring process was also defective. Moreover, the people of the area considered the land revenue as a burden. The Sarthebarians, therefore, organized *Raij-mels* against the revenue-hike and the news of the *Raij-mels* held in some other parts of the district also encouraged them for taking such drive. Decisions were taken in the *Raij-mels* for non-payment of enhanced revenue on land and resistance on its collection. Some of the *melkies* form distant villages, like Chamata and Tapa were also found to have turned up in the *Raij-mels* of Sarthebari. The *melkies* of Sarthebari were Pusparam Kahar, Kanak Kankata Melki, Mulung Tamuly, Japmal Patowary, Sindhumal Pathak, Ghutle Deka, Jadu Choudhury, Bhakatram Member, Bhabna Sadagar, Jina Talukdar and Janaki Talukdar. Amongst the Muslims: Babri Phakir, Bala Phakir, Dhasa Phakir, Mangta Gual, Aghona, Rajat, Powabar Mahajan, Mehbur, Nirmal Phakir, Forester Sayer Ali, Aichena Melki, Lotho Melki, Manik Fakir, Dukho Gual, Mihir Baider and Sambar were present in the *Raij-mels*. About fifty leading Muslims from the nearby villages, like Lachima, Barsala also attended the *Raij-mels*. The peasants from Nasatra, Helacha, Tapabari, Amrikhowa, Byaskuchi *satra* and Namsala also attended the *Raij-mels*. The *Raij-mels* held at the initiative of these leaders decided not to pay enhanced revenue.

On the other hand, the colonial government was bent upon the realization of revenue at any cost, and the agents were, therefore, engaged for that. Holiram Misra, the mandal of Kapla Badesila; Hagura, the *gaonburha* of Lachima; and Dasram Choudhury, the mauzadar of Sarukhetri mauza were trying to collect revenue by intimidation. Of them, some were excommunicated from the society as per the decision of the *Raij-mels*. But inspite of *Raij-mels'* injunction, the mauzadar went to Lachima for collection of revenue. He was accompanied by Holiram Misra, the mandal. Receiving the news, a group of people from Sarthebari rushed to Lachima and assaulted the mauzadar and the mandal.[49]

Sources are silent as to the date of occurrence of the incident. However, in all probability, a great *Raij-mel* was summoned on 21st January, 1894, for reviewing the state of affairs arisen out of the assault on the government agents. The Extra Assistant Commissioner, Sub-Divisional Officer (in-charge) of Barpeta had been to Lachima and encamped there. Madhab Chandra Bordoloi, the then Extra-Assistant Commissioner of Barpeta, tried to mediate for the payment of enhanced revenue. But the *Raij* was stuck to the decision of the *Raij-mel* held earlier. He might have exceeded the limit of exactions which caused excitement among the *Raij* and finally, he was held guilty of going against the interest of the *Raij* and was forced to pay Rs.5.00 as fine besides apologizing for his behaviour. It is said that the *gaonburha* of Lachima had escaped him to Barpeta.[50] Anyway, there is something wrong as to the date and place of occurrence of the incident.

Somehow, McCabe, the Deputy Commissioner of Kamrup, on receipt of the news of incident rushed to the spot by the evening of 24th January,1894. He quickly sent a party of 15 sepoys of the 13th Bengal Infantry and 15 armed police personnel to Lachima. By the next morning, the party arrived at the spot. Measures were taken by the 25th January for the arrest of the ring leaders and finally, 59 were arrested and kept in the temporary lock-up built for the purpose. The *Raij* were greatly ignited at this and thronged to the place to meet in a *Raij-mel*s to decide the course of action. A memorandum was submitted to the Deputy Commissioner signed by 6000 men refusing to pay increased revenue and demanding instant release of the arrested leaders. But the Deputy Commissioner insisted on the government's demand and cautioned the *Raij* against non-payment of revenue and served even *bakijai* notice on it. McCabe ordered a bayonet charge on the *Raij* and dispersed them finally. For the suppression of the *Raijmel*, a section of his police party was dispatched to Barama and Bajali.[51]

A reign of terror was let loose in Sarthebari area. Some of the *melkies* were arrested and some of them were subjected to inhumane torture, viz. putting yoke on the neck to plough in the field of Bainakuchi. Nanda Deka, a man of Sarthebari was dragged to the field for inflicting such torture. Some *melkies* went underground in the jungle for evading arrest. Inspite of this reign of terror, *mels* were held secretly at night several times for keeping the morale of the people unbroken. Anyway, some of the leaders were fined and others were sentenced to imprisonment. Of the fined groups: Atmaram and Chanaram *melkies* were from the village Amrikhowa; and of the imprisonment groups: Pusparam Kahar, Babri Fakir, Jogen Chaudhury, Japmal Patowary and Mulung Kohar were from the village Sarthebari. Some of the *melkies* of the neighbouring villages, viz. Byaskuchi, Amrikhowa, Barkapla, Belbari, Helecha and Bamakhata were also sentenced to imprisonment.[52]

Like the North, Raij *mels* were held in different parts of South Kamrup also in the month of December, 1893 against the enhanced rate of revenue on land which was a matter of great concern to the ryots. The ryots of different tahsils organized *Raij-mels* and decided for non-payment of enhanced revenue. McCabe, the Deputy Commissioner of Kamrup had been to the tahsils of south Kamrup in order to tackle the situation and induced the ryots to accept the increased assessment.[53]

When the *Raij-mels* were held against the enhancement of land revenue, the attempts of the government also went on for its suppression. Police and military were kept on alert so that they could be dispatched at any moment for the suppression of the *Raij-mels*. The *Raij-mels*, as a matter of fact, were escalating in various parts of Pati Darang. Bijoy Choudhury, a man paid Rs.25 as land revenue defying the injunction of the *Raij-mels* which made the situation of Pati Darrang tense. So, a *Raij-mel* was held at Nagaon, Pati Darang to review the situation arising out of the payment of revenue made by Bijoy Choudhury on the 12th December, 1893. Finally, the *Raij-mel* fined him of Rs.25. Fined amount was equal to the amount he paid as revenue to the government on land.[54] A *Raij-mel* was held again in Nagaon, Pati Darang on the 9th January, 1894 where the *Raij* made vow not to give evidence in favour of Bijoy Choudhury. It is said that Choudhury had filed a case in the court against the *Raij-mel* intimidation. As a result, McCabe, the Deputy Commissioner sentenced three leading men one month's rigorous imprisonment. A *Raij-mel* was held at Tengabari, Pati Darang on the 4th January, 1894, and decided not to pay revenue. In the *mels*, the *Raij* determined to take avenge on them who attempted to attach property of the defaulters.[55]

Revenue hike on land in 1892 caused severe resentment in some of the villages of Darrang district. As per the new settlement of land, assessments were augmented in 1892. Land revenues of the district, according to an official record, were augmented from Rs.4,96,682 to Rs.6,48,820 for the financial years of 1892-93 and 1893-94.[56]

As the peasants of the district were not financially viable, increased assessment became their burden. They being immensely dissatisfied, organized *Raij-mels* like the ryots of Kamrup. Therefore, the *Raij-mels* were organized in Kalaigaon, Sipajhar and Mangaldoi tahsils. The *Raij-mels* decided for non-payment of augmented rate of land revenue. The peasants in order to express unity and solidarity, thronged to the *Raij-mel* held at Sipajhar and the decision of the *mel* had been forwarded to the tahsils of Mangaldoi and Kalaigaon. Mr. Ramson, the Sub-Divisional Officer of Mangaldoi out of fear informed the Deputy Commissioner of Darrang about the course of development of the *Raij-mel* and sought measure from going the situation out of control.

Durgaram Choudhury of Sanekuchi village of Nalbari was a *lakhirajdar*, and possessed about 400 *bighas nipsikhiraj* land in Dihina village under Hajo Police Station of Kamrup. The peasants of the village were the ryots of Durgaram Choudhury. But they were not safe under him because they had to give him a major portion of their produce. He very often, used to collect his share forcefully. He became powerful for having the support of the local administration. However, the ryots resorted to a secret *Raij-mel* finding no alternative solutions of their problems. According to the decision secretly taken at the *Raij-mel* of Dihina, Durgaram Choudhury was killed when he went to his zamindari in Dihina on the back of his elephant. Finally, the killers were caught and put to trial in the court. Kania Das and Lakshmi Goswami were awarded life imprisonment, and Mitha Das and Ojan Das, two others were sentenced for two years rigorous imprisonment.[57]

The peasants of the Patharughat tahsil of Darrang district declined to pay the enhanced rate of revenue in accordance of the decision of the *Raij-mel* held in the 26th January, 1894. The tahsildar might have reported it on the same day to Mr. Ramson, the Sub-Divisional Officer of Mangaldoi. On receipt of the telegram from Mr. Ramson; Mr. Anderson, the Deputy Commissioner of Darrang decided to take coercive action and left Tezpur for Patharughat (26th January) being equipped with a body of sepoys and constables under Mr. Barrington, the Superintendent of Police of Darrang. The ryots of Patharughat somehow got scent of it and assembled in a *Raij-mel* on the 28th January, 1894 with a view to placing their demands before the district authorities. The ryots collectively put forward their decisions to the tahsil. They, as a matter of fact, were demanding for the remission of the enhanced rate of land revenue to the rate of the former settlement. Decisions of the *Raij-mels* were circulated throughout the area. In the meantime, J. D. Anderson, the Deputy Commissioner and his party arrived at Patharughat and had spent the night there in the rest house. The Superintendent of Police was engaged to restrain property of the defaulter ryots. Barrington, the Superintendent of Police with a police party and in company of Bhabani Charan Bhattacharyya, the tahsildar of Patharughat tahsil went to attach the property of a default ryot. Knowing this, a group of about 200 peasants came forward to resist it. The peasants advanced to the house where process of attaching property was being started.

The Superintendent of Police having seen it, left off his party with the *havildar* to attach the property and he himself along with the rest marched to halt the incoming of the ryots. The peasants were halted at the point of revolver. The Superintendent of Police, then, made the process of identification of the leading men of the peasants group with the help of the concerned tahsildar and mandals. Of the crowd of peasants, 13 men were identified by the tahsildar. The Superintendent of Police ordered four of them to accompany him and the property of the defaulter ryots was ultimately attached.[58]

The peasants from different localities were in accordance of the decisions of the earlier *Raij-mels*, came to participate in the *Raij-mels* of Patharughat on the 28th January, 1894. According to *Dolipurana*, the leading leaders were: Thetraberia Chaul Bepari, Biyahperia Ganak, Baraberia Jugi, Pradip Patgiri, Baneikuchia Mena, Kaljeria Goria, Tarageya Goria, Sishuram, Amchakaliarama, Narahari Moktar, Bhathirai Gaonburha, Toporam, Dutiram, Buduka, Kamala Mahajan, Umamandal, Patidangia Athia, Ram Chandra Patgiri, Joydhan, Olalhari, Lojoram Gaonburha, Sarumani, Bishnuram Saloi, Kaliram, Rangmena, Ranjit Saloi, Bodharu Koch, Dhaniram, Barlikira and Mihiram. The Koch-Kalita, Hira, Brahmana, Ganak, Suri and the muslims turned up to the *Raij-mels*. By the time, about 2000 peasants were present in the *Raij-mels* to press for the reduction of the enhancement of revenue on land. The Deputy Commissioner was said to have informed the peasants that the re-assessment rates would remain unchanged, except of the rates of *faringati* lands reduced by 10 and 9 *annas* respectively on three classes of *faringati* lands.[59]

Meanwhile, more peasants and ryots were turning up to the field while their demands were turned-down by the Deputy Commissioner. The Deputy Commissioner, then, ordered them to disperse which was defied by them. The situation became so volatile that Barrington, the Superintendent of Police of Darrang had to order his force to disperse the crowd by force. He even ordered to fix bayonets. But, the crowd pressed forward and some of them had even thrown clods of earth and split bamboos. Anderson, the Deputy Commissioner of Darrang, then ordered firing. The mob had to retreat when some of them lay dead and injured. Altogether 15 persons, according to the official record, were killed on the spot, and 37 were injured. According to Dineswar Sarma, 140 peasants were killed, and 150 injured in the fields of Patharughat.[60]

The dead are treated as martyrs of the nation, as they fought for the cause of the peasants of the land. The peasants from Byaspara, Muslimghopa, Dahi, Barkaliajar, Alikahapara, Ghopa, Sarabari, Barampur, Sibikuchi and Pati Darang sacrificed their live for the country.

V

The *Raij-mels* had played a significant role in mobilizing the peasants exclusively against the agrarian policy and the agrarian exploitation conducted by the imperialist ruler and their apparatus. It helped in the growth of consciousness among the masses in the 19th century. According to S. D. Goswami, the main strength and guiding force of the peasant uprisings of Assam from 1861 to 1894 was the *Raij-mels*, which spearheaded the resistance struggle against the repressive and exploitative action of the dominant colonial class and the power.[61]

The *Raij-mels* gave the peasants courage and strength, and the *mels* were the leading and guiding force of the peasant uprisings of Assam. Actually, the *Raij-mels* were the peasant mobilization campaign which mobilized the peasants against the colonial government. The peasants took active part in the *Raij-mels*, hoping that the *mels* would lead them towards right direction giving them respite from the exploitation and burden of revenue. Despite their failure, the *Raij-mels* compelled the colonial government to concede to the partial reduction of the rates of assessment.[62]

Thus, the *Raij-mels* fulfilled the expectations of the peasants. Moreover, by encouraging brotherhood and fraternity among the peasantry, the *Raij-mels* took Herculean step in uniting them against the colonial apparatus. In brief, the *Raij-mels* played a significant role in educating, mobilizing and bringing out the masses into the path of socio-economic and political agitation, leading to the final growth of political consciousness in colonial Assam. In a democracy like India where there is no place for a referendum, people may follow this age-old device of the *Raij-mels* for reviewing the situation arising out of the selfish spirit of the political parties, national or regional, in 'keeping alive democratic ideals for the greater interest of the nation'.[63]

Notes & References

1. Goswami, S.D. : 'Raij versus the Raj: The Nowgong outbreak (1861) in Historical perspective' in J. B. Bhattacharjee's,(ed), *Studies in the Economic History of NE India*, NEHU publications, Shillong, 1986, P. 127.

2. Barman, Santo : *The Raij-mel-A study of the Mel system in Assam*, Spectrum Publications, Guwahati: Delhi, 2005, see 'Preface'.

3. Kalita, R.C. : 'British Amolat Asamor Krishak Bidrohar Patabhumi' in A. Kumar Das & H. Sarma's (eds), *Sarukhetri Raij-mel Satabarshiki Smriti Grantha*, Sarukhetri Raij-mel Smriti-raksha Samit*i*, Baniakuchi, 1994.

4. Barman : *op. cit.*, see 'Preface'.

5. Sarma, Manorama : 'The peasants uprising and middle class hegemony-the case of Assam,' *NEIHA-X*, 1989, P. 328.

6. Kalita, R.C. : 'The 19thcentury peasant movement and the Assamese middle class,' *NEIHA-XV*, 1994, PP. 201-202.

7. Goswami, S.D. : 'The Nationalist Upsurge

8. Saha, Subhash : *1942 Struggle—a study of grass-root nationalism in the districts of Darrang and Nowgong* (M.Phil thesis), NEHU, Shillong, 1984, PP. 83, 85.

9. Goswami : 'Op. cit.' in A. Bhuyan's (ed), *op. cit.,* PP. 187-188.

10. Guha, A. : *Planter Raj to Swaraj* (1826-1947), Tulika Books, New Delhi, 2006, P. 51.

11. Kalita : *op. cit.*, P. 205.

12. Saha : *op. cit.,* PP. 88-89.

13. Kalita : *op. cit.,* P. 203.

14. Barpujari, H.K. (eds) : *Political History of Assam* (1826-1919), Vol. I, Publication Board of Assam, Guwahati, Second edition, 1999, P. 98.

15. : *Letter No. 27, dated the 12thJanuary, 1894 from R. B. McCabe*, Dy. Commissioner of Kamrup to the Commissioner of the Assam Valley District, Proceeding No. 252.

16. Barman : *op. cit.,* P. 78.

17. Barpujari (eds) : *op. cit.,* PP. 96-97.

18. Barman : *op. cit.,* P. 88.

19. Barpujari (eds)   : *op. cit.,* P. 98.
20. Pathak, Moushumi   : 'Peasants' revolt at Sarukhetri-The *Raij-mel*, *NEIHA-XIII*, 2002, PP. 113-114.
21. Nag, Sajal   : 'Religion and ethnicity in class formation
22. *cf* Nag, Sajal   : 'Social reaction to *bania* exploitation, in J. B. Bhattacharjee's (ed), *Studies in the Economic History of N. E. India,* Har Anand Publications, New Delhi, 1994, P. 366.
23 Sarma, Namita   : *The rise and growth of the peasant movement in Kamrup district* (1826-1900), Ph. D Thesis,G. U., Guwahati, 2003.
24. Kalita   : *op. cit.,* P. 202.
25. *cf Ibid.*   : P. 205.
26. Mookherjee, Mridula   : 'Peasant resistance and peasant consciousness in colonial India-Subalterns and beyond' in *Economic and Political weekly,* October 8, 1988, P. 2114.
27. Sarma, Sashi   : 'Raij-mel aru krishak bidroh
28.   : *Letter No. 27, dated the 12th January, 1894 from R. B. McCabe,* Dy. Commissioner of Kamrup to the Commissioner of the Assam Valley District, Proceeding No. 252.
29. Bora, Durgeswar   : 'Raij-mel-Sarukhetri Krishak Bidrohar (1894) Eti Samiksha' in Ajit Kr. Das & H. Sarma's (eds) *Sarukhetri Raij-mel Satabarshiki Smriti Grantha,* Sarukhetri Raij-mel Smriti Raksha Samiti, Baniakuchi, 1994, PP. 13-14.
30. Doshi, S.L. & Jain, P.C. : *Rural Sociology,* Rawat Publications, Jaipur-New Delhi, 2006, P. 175.
31. Kalita   : *op. cit.,* P. 202.
32. Sarma, Manorama   : 'Peasant uprising and middle class hegemony-the case of Assam', *NEIHA-X,* 1989, PP. 327-328.
33. Goswami, S.D.   : '*Raij* versus the *Raj*
34. Allen, B.C.   : *Assam District Gazetteers-Darrang, Nowgong and Kamrup districts,* Shillong, 1905, P. 56.
35. Barman   : *op. cit.,* P. 70.
36. *Ibid.*   : P. 71.
37. *Ibid.*   : PP. 71-72.

38. Kalita : 'The Phulaguri uprising of 1861: a peasant mass movement', *NEIHA-X*, Shillong, 1989, P. 319.
39. Barman : *op. cit.,* P. 77.
40. *Ibid.* : P. 78.
41. *Ibid.* : P. 78.
42. *Ibid.* : Letter No-27 dated the 12th Jan, 1894 from R. B. McCabe, Dy. Commissioner of Kamrup to the Commissioner of the Assam Valley District, Proceeding No. 252, P. 78.
43. Barman : *op. cit.,* P. 79.
44. *Ibid.* : P. 80.
45. *Ibid.* : P. 81.
46. *Ibid.* : P. 82
47. : Sept, 1894 from R. B. McCabe, Dy. Commissioner of Kamrup to the Commissioner of the Assam Valley District. Progs No. 312.
48. *Ibid.* :
49. Barman : *op. cit.,* PP. 85-86.
50. *Ibid.* : P. 86.
51. *Ibid.* : P. 88.
52. *Ibid.* : P. 89.
53. : Letter No. 27, dated the 12th January, 1894 from R. B. McCabe, Dy. Commissioner of Kamrup to the Commissioner of the Assam Valley District, Proceeding No. 252.
54. *Ibid.* :
55. Barman : *op. cit.,* P. 90.
56. Allen, B.C. : *op. cit.*
57. Barman : *op. cit.,* P. 100.
58. *Ibid.* : PP. 92-93.
59. *Ibid.* : P. 94.
60. Nath, Prasanna Kr. : 'Patharughatar Ron' in P. K. Nath's (ed),' *Patharughat*, Sipajhar, Darrang, Assam, 1994, P. 6.
61. Goswami : '*Raij* versus the *Raj* . . . . 'in J. B.'s (ed), ... P. 127.
62. Dutta, K.N. : *Landmarks of the Freedom Struggle in Assam*, Guwahati, 1969, P. 37.
63. Barman : *op. cit.,* P. 130.

CHAPTER – SIX

THE UPRISING: 1861

Southern Central Assam or Nowgong extends from Jagi *chowkey* on the Kalang river on the west to the river Dhansiri on the east is bounded on the north by the Brahmaputra and on the south by Cachar and Jayantia. The Kalang is but a small river, an arm of the Brahmaputra that branches off nearly opposite Biswanath and making a sweep towards the south and west, joins the great river again about 12 miles above Guwahati.[1]

According to J. N. Bhuyan, on the eastern direction of the erstwhile Nowgong was Morikalang Lake. On the west and the south was the river Kalang. *Sahib* graveyard was on the north. In the words of Gunabhiram, Nowgong was a beautiful town just like *Indra Puri*.[2]

Historically famous Phulaguri was within the erstwhile Nowgong in colonial period which is still now within Nowgong. There is a beautiful history regarding the nomenclature of this historical place. After subjugating the Jayantia king Bijoy Manik, the Koch general Chilarai halted and took rest at Raha camp. There, he was given warm welcome by the Phulagurians. The place was abundance with wild and colourful *'Phul'* of various species. Chilarai, being overwhelmed and enchanted at the terrific beauty of the place, asked the congregated to keep the name of the place after the name *'Phul'* as *'Phulaguri.'*[3]

According to some, a good number of tribal people after having cleared the wild flowers and jungles, established there a *'hat'* on the bank of the river Kalong which was known as *'Phulaguri-hat.'*

The importance of Nowgong is enhanced by the fact that there was good water communication between Nowgong and Guwahati. Due to the navigable convenience all throughout the year and more production of various crops, Nowgong became a place of more commercial importance in colonial period.[4] The place was very famous for its agricultural productions. *Ahu, sali* and *bao* rice were extensively cultivated in Nowgong. In 1870-71, rice cultivation covered 78,373 acres, but by 1875-76, it increased by another 38,876 acres. This figure is much lower than 1,31,728 acres shown in the return for the year 1849-50. The formation of the Naga Hills into a separate district and the transfer of some areas to the adjoining district of Sibsagar resulted in the decrease. Indian corn was cultivated but not extensively. The Karbis were the main growers of the crops. Besides rice and Indian corn, various kinds of bean, *matikalai, mug, khesari, musuri* were also grown. Though the cultivation of jute was well-known, it was not a favourite crop among the peasantry. Rhea or China grass was cultivated by certain sections of people who made use of its fibre for fishing-nets.[5]

II

The great upheaval of 1857 had put severe financial strain on the Indian Colonial Government. For undertaking this job of restructuring the Indian finances and to meet the requirements of the British Imperial interest, James Wilson, the Financial Secretary to the Treasury of England had made some financial arrangements which contributed immensely towards the aggravation of the economic position of the peasantry in the country, and this led to the growth of restlessness amongst them in the post-upheaval period (after 1857) in the 19th century. The local authorities in Assam also directed their attention to tapping new sources of revenue with a view to meeting their increasing expenditure. The land tax or revenue and its regular augmentation had become a great source of resentment and irritation among the Indian peasantry, and it was more so in the Brahmaputra valley.[6] The grievances of the peasantry found manifestation in Nowgong in 1861 and 1868-69; and in Kamrup and Darrang in 1893-94.

The peasants coming from different parts of Nowgong assembled at a *namghar* near Phulaguri on the 17th September, 1861, and about 1500 peasants on the same day marched to the *sadar* court in order to get scrapped the anti-ryot policy of the government. They demonstrated peacefully before the Magistrate and placed a petition before him. They made a formal protest against the ban on poppy cultivation and the proposed taxes on their houses, gardens and *paan*. The petition prayed that no further taxes be levied on their *paan* orchards and betel-nuts. The District Magistrate, instead of taking the matter seriously, took it casually and going ahead, he even humiliated them. He dealt with them in provocative and high handed manner. Some had been fined and some others had been detained in the police station by him. The belligerent peasants, therefore, congregated under the shade of three big *ahat* trees on the bank of the river Kalang seeking for retaliation against the government.[7] In that congregation of October, 1861, they, finally, resolved not to pay the taxes and planned ways and means to bring their grievances to the notice of the authorities. The meeting was scheduled to be held for five days at a stretch with a view to enabling participation in the deliberations from distant and the remotest villages. The peasants of Raha, Jagi, Kahighar mauza, Barpujia, Chapari, Kampur and Jamunamukh attended the meeting. It seems that the leaders of the meeting included Sunday and Wednesday within their five days deliberations expecting huge gatherings as that 'two days were the marketing days for the people of Raha and Phulaguri.'[8]

Nearly, 1,000 peasants congregated by 15th October, half of whom were armed with *lathies*. A force was deployed to disperse the meeting but was ended in smoke. By the 17th October, peasants nearly 3,000 to 4,000 had gathered coming from the remotest villages. According to the *Datialia Buranji*, *Panchoraja* (five kings, viz. Sararaja, Kahigharia, Topakuchia, Baropujia and Mikir-raja) and *Satoraja* (seven kings with their areas of jurisdiction: Tetelia, Mayang, Baghara, Ghagua, Sukhnagog, Tarani, Kolbari and Damal) also joined in the revolt against the government [9] as they had also their grievances. Seeing such huge gatherings, police made yet another attempt to disperse and dismantle the meetings and arrested, therefore, some leaders on the same day. But fortunately, the peasants rescued their leaders forcibly and the police, finally, had to leave the spot. Following day, Lieutenant Singer, an English officer came with a force and had interacted with the leading members. Their leader Jati Kalita reiterated their complaints about the ban on poppy cultivation, and apprehension about the tax on the *paan* orchards and income. They also reiterated that they were contemplating devices of placing their complaints to the Apex authorities, since the District Magistrate had expressed his reluctance to hear their grievances. After parleys, Singer ordered the congregated peasants to lay down their arms and disperse. Though some dispersed but many declined to be dispersed. A scuffle ensued where Singer himself attempted to seize the *lathies* in their possession and got himself accidentally killed. Golap Singh, the *daroga* of Raha Police Station was set adrift to Kalang river.[10] The police force, seeing such deteriorating situation, fled in panic.

The news of Singer's death and an intended attack on the town reached Nowgong. Haladhar Barua, the then *daroga* of Nowgong [11] remained alert to cope-up with the situation. The District Magistrate dispatched a small armed force entrenching himself at the Treasury. The force fired on the crowd leading to the death of several. Though the tribal peasants used bows and arrows against the force but they could not defend themselves. The Sepoys of Light Infantry inflicted exactions on the armless peasants. Even women were not spared from their inhuman atrocities. The peasants of Raha and Phulaguri had been forced to supply materials for the Sepoys of Light Infantry.[12]

By 23rd October, normalcy returned at Phulaguri due to arrival of fresh force from Guwahati and Tezpur. Though normalcy returned but everywhere, there prevailed terrific solitude and psycho-phobia. Even dead bodies of the rebel-peasants were burnt secretly by their kith and kins on the bank of a *beel* near Phulaguri. If the bodies of the deceased were identified by the government, they scared, that would add their problem again more violent.[13]

Many peasants lost their lives in the upheaval of Phulaguri, but the colonial machinery kept all the actual record concealed scaring of its intensive reaction.

Forty-one persons including the sons of *Lalung Raja* were arrested in connection with the killings of Lt. Singer. Bahu Kaivarta of Basigpur mauza (Hatigarh) who heated on Singer's head, Rahu Kaivarta, Kati Lalung, Thamba Lalung, Jab Lalung, Katia Lalung, Mohikoch and Koli Deka all were charged in connection of Singer's assassination.[14]

Temporary jails were erected at Raha and Phulaguri with bamboo piles and hundreds of peasants from Phulaguri and the neighbouring villages were kept confined in these jails without providing sheds against sun and rains for months together under tight security guards and without minimum food and clothing.[15] Narsing Lalung and other peasants' leaders, mostly of tribals, were punished with long term imprisonment and transportation.

Hero of Phulaguri revolt was Lakshan Singh Deka of Katahguri. Rongbor Deka hailed from Topakuchi village of Raha was the lieutenant of Lakshan Singh Deka. Changbor Lalung, Bahu Kaivarta, Banamali Kaivarta and Hebera Lalung they were the heroes of Phulaguri revolt.[16]

Anyway, this heroic resistance by the Subaltern group, against the augmenting tax burden and also the bureaucratic red-tapism, is still very much afresh and anew in the folk history of Assam as the *'Phulaguri Dhewa.'*

III

The blood flames and blood drops of Phulaguri revolt is a tragic history written on the unwritten hearts of the Nowgongians, especially, the Phulagurians. Each and every revolution is born out of the womb of injustice, and the revolt of Phulaguri is the reflection of this injustice. The peasants of Phulaguri had fiercely resisted the colonial dominion, and the evils of foreign rule contributed to the culmination of the natural anger which arose out of the experiences of life in the succeeding days. In colonial exploitation system, those who suffered and harassed at best at the hands of the British were the peasants and the subaltern class. That's why, they were the first to react against the colonial government.

The causes, that developed and gave birth to the revolt of 1861, can be categorized into two: *general* and *special causes.*

General causes: It is said that humanitarianism underlaid many of the reforms introduced by the British in the 19th century.[17] But in Assam, we find a complete opposite picture. The government and its apparatus by initiating an endless process of raising revenue demand created tremors and turbulence in the hearts of the peasants what they could hardly forget. They remembered their days under the Ahoms as halcyon days since they had to pay less revenue during their regime.[18]

The peasants of Assam led an independent life in pre-colonial period. Their independent life received tremendous withstand after the introduction of the British rule in their land. The alien government tried to employ them as labourers by imposing heavy tax what the native peasants did not like. The planter community urged the government in 1859 to enhance the land revenue rates so that the poor peasants could be flushed-out of their villages to work for wages on their tea gardens.[19]

Nature's calamities, according to Habib, underlined man's oppression. The heaviest burden that the peasants had to bear was the land tax, an arbitrary confiscation of such a large part of his produce and payment of land tax was the root of all major social conflicts involving the peasants.[20]

In 1861, the government resorted to heavy enhancement of land tax throughout the province, more particularly in the western districts: Kamrup, Darrang and Nowgong. The people of Phulaguri (Nowgong) resisted against this in 1861.[21] According to Kalita, the root cause of the Phulaguri upheaval was economic.[22] Throughout the 19th century, the government had been primarily guided by financial consideration and complete protection of the peasants from the oppression of the government had been a mere dream in Assam.[23]

The colonial government realized Rs.1,55,651 in 1852-53 from land revenue and other taxes, and that too only from Nowgong district.[24] Realization of such a heavy amount and that too only from one specific district bound us to think that probably the government resorted to harsh methods in realizing the revenue resulting the culmination of anger of the peasants of Nowgong.

Instead of criticizing the revenue hike, even the Christian missionaries also supported it. In the issue of November, 1861, it was mentioned in 'Orunodoi' that the rate of revenue in Assam was so light and nominal that such rates could not even be imagined in other provinces of India.[25]

A peasant is always in close contact with his land which survives him. According to Walter Fernandez, land is not merely a source of cultivation or of building in an agrarian economy; it is a sign of a person's social status.[26] The British distorted the so-called social status of people by imposing heavy burden on land. The tribals in Assam, especially, of Nowgong were generally freedom loving people. Their only occupation was agriculture and it is because of that, they, mainly, depended for their mainstay on land. So, whenever the government imposed tax on land, they took it as a challenge to their rights and social status.[27]

The British Government imposed heavy tax burden on the ordinary peasants. But the members of the royal family of *Darrang Raja* when applied for remission, they were exempted from paying the land revenue. The members of the royal family of the *Darrang Raja* failed to pay the revenue even at half rates (1853-54, 1854-55) as fixed earlier and sought, therefore, remission from the government for that. Bolinarayan Konwar, Amritnarayan Bahadoor, Rajooram Konwar and Rajnarayan Konwar were exempted from the payment of revenue. Even government exempted land revenue and money pension to the direct descendants of the Ahom kings.[28] But such type of sympathy and tenderness was not at all shown to the mass people, despite of having their incapability and inability.

The anomalies in the revenue system also created discontentment among the ryots. The manner how settlement in temporarily settled areas was conducted was arbitrary and unjust. The classification of land was neither scientific nor based on actual productivity of the soil.[29] The conduct of the cadastral survey was defective. Monuments of the fields of each mauzas were not carefully and systematically tested. Moreover, objections of the peasants were less discussed and less examined. Surveys were not free from errors.[30]

Cheap price and high revenue also created problem for the people of Assam. The prices of edible goods were cheap and available in Assam in 1876 and 1888. According to Gunabhiram Barua, the price of *jaha*-rice was 4 or 5 paise per seer in erstwhile Nowgong. A family could take the curry of *mowa*-fish at his table by 2 paise. With one hundred rupee, a family could run month happily and even saved from that. The price of 10 seers good quality rice was one rupee at Nowgong *sadar* market in 1875. The price of 8 seers gram or 20 seers *matimah* or 7 seers salt were one rupee.[31] After 12 years also (1887-88) at the same market, 8 seers good quality rice or 16 seers ordinary rice could be purchased at one rupee. Gram 9 seers or *matimah* 15 seers or salt 8 seers could be purchased at one rupee.[32]

There was no dearth and want of food and clothes.[33] If the price of edible goods were cheap and available in 1876 and 1888, then it is quite natural that it was more cheaper in 1860-61. For instance, there were probably no dearths of things at Nowgong in 1860-61. Prices of local commodities were cheap, but on the contrary, the rates of revenues were too high. The relation between the price rate and the revenue rate were centrifugal and centripetal. The government gave them less price for their crops, but collected more from them. There was no conformity and uniformity between give and take, which, finally, gave birth to a wave of resentment.

A peasant takes a great deal of pride in his agriculture. It is the life blood of a peasant. Behind his crop, lies his blood-drop. The colonial government through the maximization of land revenue sucked the blood of the poor peasants. Gandhiji very rightly observed that if villages live, who can perish India and if villages perish, who can save India.[34] The British by discouraging agriculture, sought to destroy the village economy of Assam. They did not encourage traditional agriculture system of

Assam, rather tried to perish it by abolishing the *paik* system so that they could be flushed-out from agriculture to plantation. But the nobles and aristocratic classes did not like its abolition, and took it as an insult to them. For instance, the Brahmana slave-holders of Kamrup even held a protest demonstration and submitted to the authorities a bunch of 1000 petitions seeking permission to retain their slaves and bondsmen.[35]

In ancient and medieval period, our native government gave more importance in agriculture sector. For instance, for the development of agriculture, irrigation had been practised in India from ancient times onwards. Many works of the Mughal emperors on the Ganges and the Jamuna, the inundation canals of Sindh and the tanks, wells and field embankments found everywhere in India[36] show that in ancient times the people of India attached great importance to irrigation. On the contrary, the colonial government showed more apathy in this important sector. As scarcity of water was an impediment of agriculture, the British Government should have given more impetus in this. For the improvement of agriculture, even Mohammad Bin Tughluq in medieval period opened an agricultural department called *'Diwan-i-kohi'*.[37] But the so called modern men with modern outlook and modern technology hardly did such step, what our medieval ancestor did in the 14th century. By establishing Agriculture Technology Development Centre, they could have ameliorated the condition of agriculture.

Cattle are the backbone of Indian agriculture. According to Mills, the cattle of Assam were inferior, and suggested measures to improve the breed of cattle by importing bulls from the North Western province (NWP).[38]. But his suggestions hardly received due attention from the government. The area under cultivation, the nature of the crops grown and the extent of the livestock may be accepted as the best standards of agricultural prosperity. According to Gadgil, livestock is one of the standards of agricultural prosperity.[39] The government by defying these standards, blocked the road of development of agriculture. Unfortunately, the apparatus and process of agriculture throughout the hills and plains remain till date almost the same, except chemical fertilizers and power tillers that have come to be used in a very limited way in some rice fields.[40]

Moreover, to avail the services of credit, marketing services, services relating to seeds, fertilizer, agricultural tools; there was lack of co-operative office. The colonial government remained totally indifferent to them. They cared less for agricultural development of Assam and on the contrary, spent days and nights for tapping new sources of revenues. Inspite of the systematic maximization of revenue, nothing was done to improve the condition of agriculture. Industrial growth and development had no links with the agricultural sector of Assam[41] which finally, invited resentment after resentment in the land.

Phulaguri is situated on the bank of the river Kalang. Kalang, Kapili and Haria these rivers inundated Phulaguri during the flood season. Inspite of her natural abundances, like fishes and tortoises in the *beels* (Jakarua, Rangagada, Bagidowa, Pahupuri and Tap-takarai); deers in the jungles; milk and rice; Phulaguri was not a secured land for agriculture.[42] The rivers made the destiny of the Phulagurians, sometime paupers and sometime princes. Their fate had often been determined by the floods and the cholera epidemic.[43]

Humanitarianism resulted in many administrative measures to fight flood, famine, control epidemics.[44] But thats were on lips and words only. In 1822, there was a wholescale destruction of harvests by locusts in the district of Nowgong resulting scarcity of foods. A second blight was noticed in 1840, and next to that occurred in 1858. The ravage of locusts was aggravated by the appearance of insects as well.[45] Moreover, heavy cattle mortality also deteriorated the economic and agricultural condition of the peasants, but the measures taken by the government was far from satisfactory. They rather invited natural calamities by heavy destruction of forest. As a result, primitive fury of the people burst-out as the time rolled-on.

By introducing the Disaster Management System, Animal Health and Veterinary Centre, Flood Control Department, Meteorological Department, Agriculture Technology Information and Development Centre; the colonial government could have evaded natural calamities to certain extent. More noticeable aspect to be mentioned here is that there was no Crops Insurance System (CIS) to compensate and respite the peasants from the damage of crops caused by locusts, floods and droughts. Disease of men and cattle, calamities of floods and fire, lack of cheap credit facilities, and wiles and artifice of money-lenders contributed to the impoverishment of the peasantry.[46]

By abolishing the slavery and *Paik* system in Assam, the British did a yeoman service to the people of Assam, but they did that only for their parochial interest. Not only that, for the interest of their tea industries, they prepared certain wasteland rules and by such rules, rural cultivators had been displaced from their lands. Moreover, the colonial government leased out to the planters such lands which were actually not wasteland. Land green, rich and thick with natural resources had been besieged by the European planters in the name of wasteland. In Nowgong, some areas covering *sal* trees had been sold as wasteland.[47] The planters even usurped the grazing fields and encroached upon the *jhum* rights of the tribal shifting cultivators.[48]

At the initial stage of the British rule, the people of Assam had good faith on the British and because of this, they showed their catholicity to the government. On mere request, king Purandar Singha even granted to the Assam Tea Company an extensive area near Gabharu hills in 1836 for cultivation of tea, anticipating that in near future, his subjects would be able to reap the benefits of this new enterprise.[49] But his honest anticipation proved wrong in later period.

It remains expressed that the planters formed the largest land owning class in Assam, but this class surprisingly contributed less to the revenue of the state. While the common peasants paid between Rs.1-8 and Rs.3 per acre annually towards the land revenue, the planters held most of their land rent free.[50] The peasants of the province resented against this discrimination which, finally, burst-out as an outbreak in the following days.

The colonial government encouraged migration to remove shortage of labour in their plantation industries. The migrators, at the initial stage, came in small numbers but later on, in large proportion including their children and family, which found expression in the growing population pressure on the land. The population of the Brahmaputra valley, according to an official source, was estimated at 8,30,000 in 1826, and it became 12,00,000 in 1853.[51] This increase served the interest of the planters only, not at all the native cultivators. As a result, indigenous cultivators had expressed their anguish against the authority.

Moreover, due to the rise of tea industries in Assam, flow of labourers began to increase which gave birth to food crisis in the province. As a result, demand for productivity of food-grain increased. To remove the food crisis, the government then relaxed the wasteland rules to encourage cultivators from outside.[52] But government's such drive and strive was not welcome by the native cultivators, as it jeopardized their mainstay. In addition to the inter-state migration, there also started inter-district migration in Assam. For example, the peasants from Kamrup and Darrang migrated to other adjacent districts and marked, thus, their disdain towards the erstwhile social order. Actually, heavy burden of revenue and taxes, and thickly population density compelled them to migrate. Their migration to another district was their silent protest against the *Raj*.[53]

It is said that the *banias* and money-lenders made the people of India poor.[54] The Marwaris during the colonial regime took full advantage of trade and commercial opportunities [55] and thus, they exploited people home and outside. Almost all the trades were solely in the hands of the Marwari traders, but the profits, they earned, were not accumulated in Assam. Almost all profits had been sent and invested to enrich Rajputana, their homeland which can be known from Jenkins' letter to Mills.[56] They came to Assam not to serve the people of Assam. Had they came with that motto, they would not have sent the profits to their homeland, rather invested and spent all that for the development and prosperity of Assam. The exploitation of the peasantry at the hands of the Marwaris and money-lenders shattered the traditional peace and harmony of village life, and created in that place—tension, anger and a smoldering feeling of revenge.

A society steeped in debt is necessarily a social volcano. The cultivators of Assam were born in debt, increased their debt and died in debt.[57] They took loans for various purposes, viz. social ceremonies, productive purposes and improvement of land etc. Social ceremonies, like marriage and *sraddha* accounted for 1/10 to 1/5 of the total loans. Productive purposes, like purchase of cattle, seeds, implements and improvements of land only 15 to 30 percent. Moreover, famines and crop failures were the general causes of loan.[58] The cultivators and the loanees of Assam had to mortgage their movable and immovable property such as land or land documents, ornaments, utensils etc. in exchange of getting loans. Unfortunately, most of the peasant loanees failed to redeem the mortgage and finally, lost their mortgaged property forever.[59]

The cottage industry in India, in the past, had acted as a safety-valve for those depended on agriculture, because it gave a second source of income to the peasants.[60] The British fiscal policy in Assam was directly linked with their commercial programmes in rest of India. In order to achieve this broad objectives in view, the British, in stages, converted Assam into a vast colony. Most of the indigenous institutions were either abolished or recast and certain new arrangements which suited them most were introduced. The abrupt change in policy was bound to create internal instability and social unrest.[61]

Throughout the British rule, India was mercilessly impoverished. Her famous manufactures were ruined and poor artisans and craftsmen were driven-out.[62] The decline of cottage industries deprived the farmers of their subsidiary occupation, thereby, considerably reducing their income and compelling them to take recourse to borrowing. Moreover, due to languishing of trade and handicrafts, and unavailability of cash transactions, it was difficult for the peasants to go to the markets to seek relief. In addition to that, ruin of cottage industries not only created pressure on agricultural land but also made many landless.[63] All this, created conditions for popular protest.

The Alien Government introduced money economy mainly to meet the demand of revenue. They introduced money economy without substantial increase in the existing currency and as a result, its tremendous blow inevitably fell crushingly on the peasants for whom there was no alternative, but to leave their homes with discontent and anguish.[64] The growing monetization economy had induced many peasants to grow more poppy for cash, sometimes even at the cost of other crops which was not a healthy sign for the peasant society.

One important thing to be noticed is that after selling their commodities at the cheap rate in the markets, what remained in their hands that were not enough to pay the revenue at high rate. Moreover, the peasantry was traditionally unaccustomed to this new money taxation system. In addition to that, they got less opportunity to sell their produce in cash whenever necessary. As a result, they could not pay their revenue in time which became arrears causing hardship to them. Finding no alternative, they had to borrow money from the money-lenders which increased their burden of indebtedness. On the contrary, the transaction of the peasants with their money-lenders after the harvest was not better than a distress sale. So, any proposal for augmentation of land revenue by the government made the peasants' blood boil in their veins.[65]

Girded almost on all sides by mountain barrier, Assam remained practically isolated and geography had imposed a formidable barrier on her contact with the rest of the world. The people of this isolated land were happy and led a well contented life as there was no lack of food in the alluvial soil of the Brahmaputra valley. But confrontation started with the arrival of the British into the land. The land abundance in food became the land of scarcity. They held the British responsible for their such pitiable condition as their interest received tremendous withstand at their hands.

It is said that the British judicial system established the principal of equality and created consciousness of positive rights.[66] But their activities revealed their double standard. Slavery, for example, is an extreme form of inequality and because of this, the government abolished *paik* system in Assam. Outwardly, their motive was good but its inner motive was to attract the *paiks* to their tea gardens, and make them their workers, not establish equality in the land at all. Moreover, another example of their bad activities was forcible collection of goods. The servants of the government forcibly took away the goods and commodities of the ryots for a fourth part of their value and by ways of violence and oppressions, they obliged the ryots to give five rupees for goods which were worth but one rupee.[67] Thus, the government exploited and exacted the ryots but they got no justice from the courts, as they were run by their own men. Discrimination and bias-ness in judging the cases were probably the general phenomenon of the day. The Europeans, the rich and well-to-do received justice in the courts. Poor could hardly expect justice from the courts and finally, they had to lose their properties in the name of running the cases due to the excessive demands of fees by the advocates. The ryots of Phulaguri were aware of the injustice done to them by the British and therefore, they became more conscious of their rights.[68]

Slow progress of education might be one of the causes of discontentment of the people. The people of the land neither could compete nor even could apply for the government's posts due to the lack of their educational qualification. Therefore, all the government's posts were got filled-up by the educated immigrants. The illiterate immigrants, on one hand, put pressure on the agricultural lands; and the literate immigrants, on the other, occupied the government's offices. Ultimately, they held the government responsible for this. Illiteracy of the mass people was because of the inadequate number of educational institutions in the villages. The numbers of such institutions were not available even in towns also. As a result, few villagers, therefore, could take the opportunity of this and most of them, on the contrary, remained as illiterate and finally, fell easy prey at the hands of the village *mahajans* and Marwaris.

The success of the Jayantias against the British inspired the peasants of Phulaguri to revolt against them. Nowgong being the adjacent and neighbours of the Jayantias, was the next to revolt against the injustice of the British.[69] Guha says that encouraged and influenced by the

Jayantia revolt, the peasants of Nowgong also started agitation against the authority.[70]

The Ahom kings did not interfere into the internal affairs of the tribal kings and thus, maintained cordial relations with their neighbours. They instead of dissatisfying the tribal kings, made them their part of administration. For example, the Kachari and Jayantia kings were the sentinels of the Ahoms. Making the kings as part of their administration, the Ahoms proved their political shrewdness. The colonial government, on the contrary, eschewed this policy of the Ahoms and started intervening into the internal matters of the tribal kings inviting disdain and resentment against them.[71]

Everything procured from the forest and *beels* by an Assamese peasant in pre-colonial period was free of cost. But all these were brought under assessment during the colonial period. For example, timber, thatch and reeds for the construction of dwelling houses; *beels* for fishing and fodder for domestic animals[72] all brought under assessment. The people reacted against this type of assessment as it created another financial burden on them.

While the people were uttering against the hike of revenue, the Christian missionaries of Assam, on the contrary, were at the same time busy in proselytising the people. During the time of *Durga Puja*, there was huge congregation in Nowgong. The missionaries took full advantage of this distributing some religious pamphlets there. In the pamphlets, it was mentioned that Jesus Christ could save the people from the oppression of the *kala-jar* and earthquake.[73]

The colonial government, instead of rendering medical facilities to the patients during the time of fever, was busy in collecting revenue from the peasants. Similarly, the role of the Christian missionaries was also not satisfactory. They encouraged local people's conversion to Christianity, on one hand and asked them, on the other, to utter the name of Jesus Christ at the time of natural calamities. To them, only Jesus could lighten and heal their miseries and calamities. But the people were not satisfied at this, they rather sought more practical and concrete step from them.

Special Causes: Opium was the most important source of revenue of the province of Assam, next only to land. It was a gold mine for the government.[74] Therefore, to make the opium-eaters totally dependent on the government opium, they were forced to purchase high priced government opium instead of growing it themselves. The government maximized revenue on opium for two reasons: to strengthen their economy; and to force the ordinary people to work in their tea gardens. Opium policy was one of the sources of colonial exploitation in Assam during the British regime.[75]

Britain was the centre of anti-opium agitation at the international level, but their anti-opium agitation manifested their double standard, 'Ram naam' on devil's lips. Probably, opium could have been stamped out completely if the government pursued a more rigorous policy.[76]

Finally, the British abolished poppy cultivation in 1860-61. Prohibitory order of poppy appeared to the illiterate villagers of Nowgong as an infringement upon their social habits and customs. By introducing poppy cultivation in Assam, Capt. Welsh made the independent tribal people of Assam dependent on poppy and brought their physical destruction in the 18th century[77] and economic destruction, thereafter, in the 19th century. Actually, government's prohibitory order was motivated not by humanitarian, but by revenue consideration.

Most of the people did not like opium prohibition. To them, opium cures dysentery and malaria, alleviates pain, gives longevity and livelihood. Moreover, there is no religious bar of taking opium. Rather, opium eaters used to believe that in Satya age, poppy trees were in abundance in the Parijat garden of Lord Indra. He gave this priceless gift to the people of earth.[78] People of religious bent of mind, probably, took the ban as an attack on their religion also. Moreover, already hard hit by the increase of taxation on land, the order of prohibition added fuel to the fire. They scared that they would have to pay dearly for the abkari opium which would compel them to work in the tea gardens of Assam as workers. People, finally, understood that the government's social measures to emancipate the people from effimination, weak, indolent and degradation was just an eye-wash to hood wink the tribal peasants of Phulaguri. Finally, they opposed the ban tooth and nails and girded waist-band on their loins against the government's decision and precipitated the Anglo-Phulagurians enmity in 1861.

The Dravidian system of chewing betel nuts has been widely prevalent in Assam from time immemorial. Regarding the chewing of betel nuts, there are references in the Smriti Sastra and the Kalika Purana. It has great importance even in marriage and worship also. Even a convict could evade and lessen his crime by offering betel nuts to his lord. Moreover, betel nuts determined the social status of the Assamese society.[79] The contemplation of imposition of taxes on the betel nuts and the betel leaf was just like an insult and blow to the social status of the Assamese society. Although the decision to impose tax on *paan* was not taken, it frightened the people more. Henry Hopkinson, the Commissioner of Assam, traced the origin of the outbreak of 1861 on *paan* and betel nuts.[80] Though their fear was more imaginary than real but experiences had convinced them to be alerted and conscious with regard to any rumour emanating from their political masters.[81]

Multiplication of taxes became the matter of serious concern to the agricultural ryots of Assam, specially, the ryots of Nowgong. Tax on the dry crops land, on which linseed and mustard were grown, was enhanced as per the Board of Revenue's estimate to the tune of Rs.11,222 in the district of Nowgong alone in 1861. The peasants of Nowgong openly murmured and all sorts of evil stories were circulated in the villages to increase discontent among the peasants.[82]

Though the income tax did not touch a single agriculturist in Assam and even those who were assessed, the incidence of taxation was extremely trivial. Still its introduction generated misgiving in the minds of the people who were already overburdened with taxes. It was not the amount which mattered the people but the principle of additional taxation. Obviously, this measure shook the confidence of the people who became more and more apprehensive of the next move of the government.[83]

About this time, the Government of India was finalizing the scheme for the introduction of the license tax for collecting forest products. Though the tax was not originally proposed to be extended to Assam, the agricultural community throughout the province was terribly frightened.[84] The news of imposition of income tax and license tax created resentment in the minds of the people of Assam, especially, the people of Nowgong of 1861, it is even confessed by Henry Hopkinson, the Commissioner of Assam. He traced the origin of the outbreak of 1861 on the imposition of taxes on income and forest products.[85]

Except few, most of the people did not get benefit from the policy of David Scott.[86] If it is true, then we can presume that the seed of dissatisfaction was germinated even in the early part of the colonial rule. Moreover, due to the corrupt practices and intrigues of the *amlahs*, and the irregular and undefined additional assessment, the peasants became sick of it.[87] The atrocities of the choudhuries and tahsildars were also responsible for the outbreak of 1861. The announcements of the tahsildars that the property of the defaulter ryots would be seized also created scare and anguish in the minds of the peasants against the government. Tenants suffered lot under the exactions of landowners, mauzadars and choudhuires who were fully guarded by the state machinery.[88] The situation of Nowgong would have been evaded, had the district authorities been really sympathetic towards the difficulties of the common people.

The Phulaguri episode was the culmination of a large number of deep-rooted grievances accentuated by certain acts of omission and commission on the part of Herbert Sconce, the Deputy Commissioner of Nowgong. Had he been a little more tactful and cordial in his approach, and instead of fining and detaining the people so often for making noise in the court, endeavoured to calm their fears by explaining away all their misunderstandings, in all probability the meetings at Phulaguri would never have taken place; the people would have regarded the District Officer as their friend.[89] By his act of imprudence, on the 17th September and the 9th October, Herbert Sconce contributed greatly to transform the excitement of the peasants in to a devastating fire to consume the British rule in the Brahmaputra valley.

Herbert Sconce's order to the *daroga* of the Nowgong *sadar thana* on the 14th October to disperse and arrest the leaders of the *Raijmels,* and the leaders' refusal to disperse and rather continuation of the *mels* abusing and attacking the police party on the 15th October conflagrated the situation.[90] Sir Cecil Beadon, the Lieutenant General of Bengal also pointed his fingers to Herbert Sconce and held him responsible for the volatile situation of 1861. That Herbert Sconce, the Deputy Commissioner of Nowgong was responsible for the outbreak of 1861, it is proved from the sufferings of his punishment. Sconce was demoted to the rank of an Assistant Commissioner and was transferred to the district of Kamrup.[91]

IV

The uprising of the peasants challenged the defensive capability of the British administration in the Brahmaputra valley.[92] Seeing this, the government tried to bring division among the peasantry so that their united efforts could be checked. Ultimately, they became success in their design creating split among the peasantry. Their struggle though did not last for long, basic weakness of it should not be studied in isolation of divisive policies applied by the dominant class and the class power to suppress.

The causes that led to the failure of the revolt of 1861 can be studied in this manner: The peasants of Nowgong used traditional weapons like *daos*, spears, bows and arrows which could not be matched with the superior fire power of the British.[93] Maniram Dewan saw the British might and compared the Indian might inferior to that of the British. The peasants wanted to drive out the powerful British armed with deadly weapons with their bamboo pop guns.[94] The war materials and weapons of Phulaguri revolt were made in the factory of V. V. Kamar, a blacksmith of Molankata of nearby Raha, but they proved to be feeble. Though there were some old guns during the time of the Ahoms, that could not be used against the British as the latter had confiscated them.[95] Two sides confrontation: one numbering only a few led by the whites and assisted by some native represented the administration; and the other in hundreds unarmed poor peasants led by village heads. Under-estimation of the number and power of the British was the main reason that led to the defeat of the Phulagurians. The former in number was lesser than the latter, and the latter thought it as their main strength and even dared to compare their bamboo-sticks equal to that of the British guns. Some even showed their daring-do to flush-out all the British from Phulaguri with their bamboo-sticks.[96]

According to Eric Hobsbaum, the peasantry though a potential revolutionary class, is basically a passive class, and are in need of leadership.[97] Each and every Indian peasant movement produced charismatic leader but the Assam movement none. Lakshan Sing Deka of Katahguri and Rongbor Deka, they could not be matched with the British leaders, and on the arrival of the latter, the former disappeared. As soon as the movement became leaderless, it fizzled out. The roar of the outburst metamorphosed into a quiet bubble.[98] Lack of unity and worth organizers among the leaders, absence of proper leadership, and co-ordination among the tribes proved to be their undoing. Compared to the military skill, efficiency, decision making and adroitness; the local leaders were much more inferior to the alien leaders. Moreover, the peasants of colonial Assam were not well-organized and well-disciplined, and had no any planned or long-termed scheme at their hands. Lack of common cause and different interest among the leaders also brought their downfall. Moreover, most of the time it was found that the revolt became volatile due to the inapt-handling of the readers. Had the leaders become able to show their masses the right way keeping aside violent and volatile means, and pursued, on the contrary, conciliatory and moderate way; probably, then they could have harvested something from the government, but that they could not do. One important thing to be noticed is that most of the traditional leaders of the *Raij-mels* were illiterate. Idea of compromise till then did not develop in their mind, and instead of prayer and petition, they rather prefered to resort violent and aggressive means.

Economy has a great role to play in the revolt but unfortunately, the people of colonial Assam at large, groaned under economic hardship. Probably, because of this, they could not fight a decisive battle against the administration.

It can be inferred that sometime some section of the natives informed the administration regarding the ongoing preparation of the rebels and also about their whereabout which might bring their haste-fiasco. Regarding the decision of the *mels* and place of their sittings, the administration could know more through their espionage system. For instance, while the people assembled at a *namghar* of Phulaguri, the district administration got scent of it through their spies.

Had the land and people's interest been greater than that of the coins, and had there been high morality among the rebel leaders; probably, the alien rulers could not have defeated them so easily. Due to the betrayal and stretching-out their secret hands to the colonial power, the Phulagurians had to witness a crushing defeat at the hands of the whites.

Cruel policy, and rumour and false propaganda from the side of the administration also brought the victory of the British. But the humble and innocent peasants, they did not take asylum to such type false propaganda.

The sharp British intelligence, and instant and timely decision of the Deputy Commissioner and the Superintendent of Police of Nowgong were another cause for the hasty-defeat of the peasants of Nowgong. If sometime the number of troops sent to quell and disperse the *mels* was found inadequate, quickly additional troops was dispatched to the field on the basis of the reports of the intelligence leading to the expedition of the peasants'defeat. For instance, prompt and quick communication of the Deputy Commissioner of Nowgong to the Deputy Commissioner of Darrang and timely arrival of Henry Hopkinson, the Commissioner of Assam with reinforcement from Tezpur to Nowgong precipitated the defeat of the peasants. Emboldened by this, the Deputy Commissioner of Nowgong visited Nellie, Phulaguri, Raha, Kachuhat and several other places and effected the arrest of 41 persons including the sons of the old *Lalung Raja* alleged to have been implicated in the murder of Lt. Singer.[99]

The peasants of Nowgong could not combine to put-up a united front against their common enemy; there were only sporadic outbursts which the administration did not find problem to curb-down. The revolt failed to embrace all sections of the society. Many declined to join the revolt and rather, extended their support to the British. Some had even suspicions on the motives of the rebels. The revolt was highly localized and restricted to some areas, and therefore, many areas remained undisturbed.

The rich peasants, like Bhogram Medhi of Nowgong [100] and others had their status in their societies. They spent their surplus in ornaments, annual feast and marriage ceremonies. The poor, on the contrary, incurred debt and spent money on opium, marriages and purchase of bullocks. Sometime, they even sold their labour as coolies in the tea gardens. Due to economic disparities and enjoying high status, the rich maintained distance with the poor. Though the rich and the poor they both fought together against the British, but how sincerely the rich did fight with the poor against the British, that is under the scanner of suspicion. Probably, their economic and social disparities invited their quick fall.

The period from 1838 to 1893 may also be responsible for the defeat of the Nowgong outbreak of 1861, because, the powerful Ahoms became insignificant and neglected during this period and at the same time, the season of dead march started within them.

The people of some well-to-do families of Assam, probably, had been given some government jobs and this section, therefore, was loyal and acted wholeheartedly for their master and brought, finally, degradation of their own people. Had all sections irrespective to high and low, rich and poor stretched-out their helping hands to the peasants and fought honestly for their common cause, probably, there was a little scope and hope of winning in the battle. Unfortunately, many did not join in the revolt despite having their sympathy due to losing their jobs. Being the ally of the British, some of the mauzadars also stretched-out their helping hand to the government. Moreover, though the landowners joined in the agitation but they did not continue resistance due to fear of loss of properties under attachment order. Indeed, they were the first to retreat.[101]

Ever readiness and ever preparedness also brought victory to the colonial government. Wherever the sepoys went, they went with their fire arms. They were ever ready to face the situation. The rebels, on the contrary, whatever they did, they did that secretly. Moreover, wherever they went, they went with unprepared. Sometime concealing their weapons in their clothes or in the jungles. As a result, the rebels could not use them instantly against the enemies.

Sanskritisation may also be the another cause that led to the defeat of the peasants. Some people who thought their status lower in social hierarchy tried to improve their status by rejecting their traditional style and mode of life. It is because of this, this section began to imitate the British and their culture. Instead of thinking for their own men and society, this section began to think and imitate the culture of the English.

Illiteracy might be one of the causes for their failure. The British they witnessed and experienced some great wars of the world and applied that experience against their enemies in the upheavals of the peasants.

Lack of farsightedness and obstinate nature of the tribal peasants of Phulaguri was also another cause of their fiasco. Whatever decision the peasants took, they took that promptly and haughtily as against the cool, meticulous and contemplated decision of the administration which expedited their fall.

According to Gunabhiram Barua, during the flood-season, there was good water communication system between Guwahati and Nowgong. 'Darrang' and 'Santipur' the two ships introduced the Nowgongians with the outside world, particularly, with the Gauhatians.[102] If it were true, then we can infer that probably the British used land and water route both at the time of the outbreak of 1861, and became able to give a crushing defeat to the rebels.

Firm conviction and rigid determination also helped the British to win over the rebels of 1861. The remark of Henry Hopkinson, the Commissioner of Assam bears the testimony to it. The beginning of a tumult, he once opined, is like the letting-out of water, if not stopped at first, it becomes difficult to stop that afterwards. His conviction helped him to curb the rising tide of 1861, but could not stop it permanently.

Obsolete and traditional mode of peasants' protest had no match with the well-equipped colonial system. It seems that the peasants sometime resorted to artless modes of protest. Jealous gossiping, defamation, tales, nameless sabotage, rumours and nicknames and character assassination all these possibly constituted the symbolic resistance of the peasantry against the administration. Foot dragging, hypocrisy, false submission, desolation, petty thief, pretended ignorance, house-burning [103] were probably resorted by the peasants against the mighty British, which proved futile and evaporated in the long run in front of the gun-fire of the latter. Their language of protest was not the same with that of the British. The British language of protest was guns and brain, but the Phulagurians, on the contrary, fought with passions and emotions. Bombastic words were their main weapons and power. In the October issue of *Orunodoi* in 1861, it has been referred how the leaders gave courage to the local mob. The leaders assured the mob not to scare of colonial guns as they had *barun-baan* to challenge the guns.[104] Emboldened by this, the mob jumped onto the fire and died like moth.

Reinforcement system also helped the British to win over the rebels. In the outbreak of 1861, the Assam Administration deemed it necessary to request the Government of India for increasing the armed forces in the Assam province by the addition of 500 to 800 men, and ultimately, it was recommended.[105] But such step and strive was rarely and hardly seen taken by the native rebels.

V

Traditional leaders mainly the tribals, viz. the Lalungs (Tiwa) and the Kacharis took vital role in the outbreak of 1861. Other non-tribals, viz. the Kaivartas and others also participated in the outbreak of 1861. But the Imperialist and the Nationalist historians, instead of giving importance to study the role of the ordinary peasants and the workers, emphasized to study the history of the masses through the eyes of the elite leadership. Most of the leaders of 1861 were illiterate. But the matter of pride is that the illiterate tribal leaders could resist and fight against the mighty British, though they failed finally.

The Indian elite took up the great task of modernizing their own society.[106] But in Assam, the number of elite was too few in 1860-61, and they were ambivalence towards their own society. The few and new elite who emerged on the scene, had to face opposition from the leaders of orthodox opinion. The latter had the power to fine and excommunicate temporarily or permanently. Excommunication was a serious matter as no member of the caste could have established social intercourse with the excommunicated person and his family. Until the new elite increased substantially in numbers, they were subjected to harassment at the hands of the orthodox. Probably, because of this, they did not come to take the leadership of 1861.

By Nature, the revolt of 1861 was not a freedom movement, and it was organized with the object of compelling the government to yield to the will of the people by the withdrawal of unpopular measures of taxation.[107]

Though there was variation among the peasantry of erstwhile Nowgong in the first half of the 19th century, despite that, they fought together against the colonial British. Their discontentment was confined not lone to them; non-peasantry class also hard-pressed by the measures of the government. For example, the posts and privileges of the *pancho-rajas* (five kings) and the *sato-rajas* (seven kings) were abolished. The mauzas of the mauzadars were also seized by the government.[108]

Moreover, abolition of the *paik* system, plantation and wasteland policy, migration and industrial policy of the British did no good to the people of Assam. Almost all sections in the society were affected by these and took apparently leading role against the government. Ultimately, the revolt assumed mass character.

Compared to the other states of India, the conception of casteism in Assam is more flexible.109 It seems that some of the other higher castes gave up their Sanskritic value in order to have interaction with the lower castes. Possibly because of this, all sections irrespective to caste and creed, high and low, and rich and poor stretched-out their helping hands against the government to show mobility and solidarity for establishing their own rights.

The revolt of 1861, probably because of its localized and sporadic character, was confined only at Phulaguri, Raha and other areas of Nowgong. Entire district was not totally engulfed by its flame.[110]

The absence of intermediaries between the state and the peasantry and persisting clan unity among the peasantry were two major aspects of agrarian social structure that were responsible for the peasants-state direct confrontation.[111] It is because of this, in Assam, it was an open revolt against the government. The '*Amrit Bazar Patrika*' observed in its editorial that in the Deccan, the fury of the ryots was directed against the money-lenders; in Bengal, against the Indigo-Planters in1860; in Pubna, against the zamindars in 1872; but in Assam, it was an open rebellion against the government.[112]

The nature of the peasant revolt in Goalpara is different to some extent from that in Colonial Assam. As against the peasant revolt of 1861, the revolts of the peasants in Goalpara were against the exploitation of the zamindars. The agrarian trouble of Ghurla *parguna* of Gauripur *Raj* Estate was a revolt against the zamindar. The rebellions in Habraghat and Khuntaghat were a clear indication in this context.[113]

Some termed the revolt of 1861 as a less important and mere riot. Some again termed it as the revolt of the tribal alone (Lalung-Kachari's revolt) as no government officials, mauzadars, laskars and businessmen co-operated in this, except the *Lalung Raja*. The *Orunodoi* ridiculed the Phulaguri revolt as the *'kaniar bidroh'* (opium eaters' revolt). Some of the Imperialist historians also termed it in the same tune.[114] The revolt was neither an 'opium eaters' revolt nor a 'tribal revolt,' rather it was the earliest popular revolt of Assam.

Like the Phulaguri resistance of subaltern groups, similar outbreaks were witnessed among the tribals of different parts in the British India. The Kol and Bhumij revolts of 1831-33, the Santhal insurrection of 1855-56, the Birsa Munda uprising of 1899-1900 had stirred the tribal regions outside Assam. Karna is right that the revolt of the Lalungs and the Kacharis in Assam against the British colonial administrators and their Indian troops, police and civilian sub-ordinates was, in the same tradition, of tribal insurrections.[115]

VI

The movement of 1861 failed to achieve its aims and objectives to a great extent. But it germinated the future seed of unrest which culminated after three decades, viz. in 1893-94. The Phulaguri *dhewa* of Nowgong influenced the people of Darrang and Kamrup to take up the cudgels on behalf of the oppressed peasantry.[116] According to Barpujari, though the movement failed but the precedent was not lost upon the people, it was followed up soon-after.[117] The revolt of 1861 inspired the people of other places to revolt against the British. The Nowgong outbreak was not the end, but the precursor of agrarian unrest in Assam.[118]

Due to the increased rate of taxation and exaction of the colonial apparatus, the peasants had to abandon their cultivations. As a result, there emerged stagnation in agriculture. The involvement of the peasants in the *Raij mels* and in the uprisings of 1861, and the peasants' flying

212

to neighbouring villages also resulted bad condition in agriculture. The ryots and the villagers abandoned their villages and took asylum at distant places where they were safe.

As a result of the outbreak of 1861, the gap between the ruler and the ruled widened. The peasants had to lose their bargaining power and thus, chances of removing their grievances lost. The ruled, therefore, developed a deep racial bitterness towards the English ruler and opposed the inferior status granted to them.

As the economy still remained in a state of non-monetization and the money remained a scarce commodity with the people, the suppression of the indigenous production of opium would certainly induce the opium eaters to offer themselves as labourers in the tea gardens of the Europeans.[119]

After 1861, the number of force was increased in Nowgong and its neighbouring areas to strengthen the British control over the land and created, thus, a sense of fear among the restless ryots. The authorities being alarmed at the rapid growth of public awakening often resorted to brutal repression.[120] Moreover, following the Phulaguri episode, the government held enquiries into the affairs and adopted certain measures to remove the apprehension of the people by taking action on the officers found guilty where it was considered necessary.[121]

The administration neither stopped the enhancement of revenue, nor the supply of government opium. They did not give importance on the dissatisfaction of the ryots and kept on collecting high rate of revenue even after 1861. Henry Hopkinson, the Commissioner of Assam proposed in May, 1861 to double the revenues on land to devote the excess to the construction of works of public utility. It was considered, however, inexpedient to enhance the revenue on land as proposed by him. The Secretary of State too, on the recommendation of the Government of India, accorded his approval to the appropriation of 3 percent of the revenues for purpose of local improvement, but the question of increase in assessment was left to the discretion of the Lieutenant Governor of Bengal.[122]

The community worse affected in the outbreak of 1861 was the Lalungs. Other non-Lalung communities were also affected by it.[123] The outbreak of 1861 did not invite any single act of protest from any section of the indigenous population. The participation of the men of the fishing community among others, added strength and widened the mass base of the movement.[124]

The outbreak of 1861 was suppressed ruthlessly. Many became martyrs, many injured and many lost their properties. The suppression of the revolt caused great indignation throughout the province. The resistance movement launched by the *Raij-mels* had its impact throughout the province. The Government of India conceded to the partial reduction of the rates of assessment.

Though quelled with brutal force, the uprising not only exposed the defects of the British rule but also proved beyond doubt that any attempts at socio-economic reconstruction, without corresponding improvement in the moral and material condition of the people, was bound to be abortive.[125]

Though the uprising was not tangibly successful, it reflected the colonial oppression on the peasantry and the determination of the peasantry to combat against the colonial land revenue system.[126]

The government became cruel upon the leaders of the *mels* when they began to raise their voice against the measures of the government. Therefore, sweet relation between the ruler and the ruled turned sour in the later part of their rule.

No event either small or big goes without importance and significance, and the uprising of 1861 is also not exception to that. The significance of the outbreak of 1861 lies in the fact that all sections irrespective to caste, economic position, religion, age and sex united under one roof to combat against the colonial force forgetting factions and factionalism among them. The illiterate tribal peasants gave leadership in the outbreak of 1861 without elite leadership. When the wealthy sections and the government employees tolerated the exploitation of the government and remained silent, the rural people with their *Raij-mels* protested the policy of the government and took the path of revolt. It is not a little matter to be averted. The Colonial consortium could realize the united strength and courage of the peasants in their revolt. This outbreak gave moral strength and courage to the peasants of Darrang and Kamrup in later period, and influenced the future course of action. The peasants were no longer afraid of questioning the government for any injustice done to them. One important and significant aspect to be noticed in the outbreak of 1861 was the participation of the men of the fishing community who gave strength and wide-base to the movement.[127] In spite of having economic and social disparity, the poor peasantry did not revolt against the rich peasantry, may be because of their land, class and cultural affinity. They rather fought jointly and unitedly against the government. Two Tamil peasant castes, the *vellalas* and the *padaiyachis* wanted to be recorded as higher *varna*. The *vellalas* wanted to be called as *vaishyas,* while the *padaiyachis* as *vanniya kula kshatriyas*.[128] But no such upward and upgradation mobility was seen among the Lalung and the Kachari peasants of Phulaguri in 1861.

Unlike some parts of Uttar Pradesh and Rajasthan, the Brahmins were not found working as tenants of the non-Brahmins in Nowgong or in entire Assam. Rather, the Brahmins and the higher castes, they got their land ploughed through their tenants and labourers. But in parts of Uttar Pradesh and Rajasthan, the Brahmins were occasionally found working as tenants of *Rajputs* or *Jat* landowners.[129] Another significant aspect of the revolt of 1861 is that had the peasants of Phulaguri accepted the government's verdict like the ryots of Lakhimpur, Sibsagar, Darrang and Kamrup; then there would have been, possibly, no peasants' revolt in Phulaguri. Their denial to government's verdict gave birth to revolt in Phulaguri.[130] The Phulaguri revolt was not a mere revolt fought in between the ruler and the ruled, it was the first mass-revolt against the colonial government, and was a united effort of the exploited mass for the eradication of their exploitation.[131] Though they failed, significance lies in the fact that the peasants by their revolt wanted to compel the government to yield to the will of the people by the withdrawal of unpopular measures of taxation and colonial exploitation.

Now, there comes the most pertinent question whether the outbreak of 1861 is justifiable or not. Many have given so many opinions and keeping them all in view, we have come to a better justified position on the very issue. The demands of the peasants were real, not sentimental. The burden pressed upon the land was heavier than on land owned by the zamindars in Bengal. So their revolt against the authority would, totally, be justified.

The consumption of opium is bad and injurious to health. Despite that, its sudden prohibition within few months cannot be justified what the people used to consume for several generations. At least for its abolition, it ought to have been the duty of the government to take some short and long-term plan, and also to have them mentally prepared for avoiding this type of drugs.

The colonial government blamed the peasants of Assam exonerating itself for all acts of omission and commission, but the coercive measures undertaken to suppress the popular revolt, could not but, tarnish the fair name of any civilized government.[132] The rightful demands of the ruled placed before the ruler, for compliance and consideration, could not be a crime for using lethal weapons upon them. The so-called civilized colonial government could have discarded the mass-slaughtering with patient hearing adopting give and take policy, instead of shooting and slaughtering the mass people indiscriminately. A black spot on the civilized British Nation, of course, not desired by the British Commons, but by some of their trigger happy cynics without trying to understand the wants of their subjects.[133]

Sir Cecil Beadon, the Lieutenant General of Bengal was convinced that if the ryots had been properly tackled by the Deputy Commissioner of Nowgong by personally meeting and attending to their grievances, they would have, in all probability, peacefully dispersed and accepted the unavoidable financial measures of the government.[134] But his deputation of the police and subsequently of an inexperienced young officer with so small a force and without clear instruction to him was an act of great imprudence.[135]

The revolt of Phulaguri was one of the great events in the history of India, but the matter of regret is that the people of different parts of India know little about this great historic episode. Surprisingly, the people of different districts of Assam, even today, also know little about this historic resistance. Probably, the colonial government had scare of spreading the impact of the revolt on the other parts of the province. If anyhow sometime something leaked, they then tried to show it as the revolt of the few opium eaters only, which is indeed, unfortunate and unjustifiable.[136]

The outbreak of 1861 had a tragic end. The colonial government tried to keep concealed the whole incident in sombre for their vested parochial interest.[137] The countrymen and the outside world were kept in the darkness by keeping the dead buried, but the sins, that could not be!

Notes & References

1. M'Cosh, John : *Topography of Assam*, Logos Press, New Delhi, Second Reprint, 2000, P. 94.
2. Bhuyan, J.N. : 'Gunabhiram Baruar Dinar Nowgong' in J. N. Bhuyan's *Unavimsa Satika—Shristi Aru Chetana*, Lawyers Book Stall, Guwahati, 1998, P. 139.
3. Barua, Abhay : 'Janashrutir Pam Khedi Jagiyal Moujar Rajahgaon Samashtir Naam Itibritta' in Jatin Medhi's (ed), *Phulaguri Dhewar Rengani*, the Reception Committee, 143rd. Anniversary of Phulaguri Dhewa, Phulaguri, Nagaon, 2004, PP. 39-40.
4. M'Cosh : *op. cit.*, P. 94.
5. Saikia, Rajen : *Social and Economic History of Assam* (1853-1921), Manohar, New Delhi, 2001, P. 85.
6. Kalita, R.C. : 'The Phulaguri uprising of 1861: A peasant mass movement', *NEIHA-X*, 1989, PP. 310-311.
7. Nath, Purnakanta : 'Phulaguri Dhewa' in Jatin Medhi's (ed), *op. cit.*, P. 15.
8. Raja, Purnananda : 'Phulaguri Dhewar Para Ajiloike Phulaguri' in Jatin Medhi's (ed), *op. cit.*, P. 19.
9. Raja, Pankaj Kumar : 'Sampritir Saphura: Gosain Uliowar Utshav' in Jatin Medhi's (ed), *op. cit.*, PP. 26-27.
10. Goswami, Indreswar : 'Asamor Pratham Krishak Bodroh—Phulaguri Dhewa' in Jatin Medhi's (ed), *op. cit.*, P. 11.
11. *Ibid.* : P. 10.
12. *Ibid.* : PP. 10-11.
13. *Ibid.* : PP. 11-12.
14. *Ibid.* : PP. 10-11.

15. Kalita : *op. cit.*, P. 319.

16. Deka, Kamal Singh : 'Brihattar Phulaguri Anchalar Dukhuria Chabi' in Jatin Medhi's (ed), *op. cit.*, PP. 29-31.

17. Srinivasa, M.N. : *Social Change in Modern India*, Orient Longman Ltd., New Delhi, 1995, P. 51.

18. Majumdar, P. : 'Samachar Darpanat Asamar Bibaran' in S. Barman's (et al), *Oitihya Aru Itihash*, Journal Emporium, Nalbari, Assam, 2005, P. 145.

19. Guha, A. : *Planter Raj to Swaraj* (1826-1947), Tulika Books, New Delhi, 2006, P. 7.

20. Habib, I. : *Essays in Indian History – towards a Marxist perception*, Tulika Books, New Delhi, 2001, PP. 154-155.

21. Deka, K.C. : 'The martyrs of Assam and the Gohpur episode' in A. Bhuyan's (ed), *Nationalist Upsurge in Assam*, Government of Assam, Guwahati, 2000, P. 359.

22. Kalita, Benudhar : *Phulagurir Dhewa*, Lakheswar Kalita and others, Nowgong, 1961, P. 64.

23. Goswami, S.D. : 'The British Taxation Policy in Assam' in J. B. Bhattacharjee's (ed), *Studies in the Economic History of N.E.India*, Har Anand Publications, New Delhi, 1994, P. 95.

24. Nath, Purnakanta : *op. cit.*, P. 14.

25. *Orunodoi*, Nov., 1861 :

26. Doshi, S.L. & Jain, P.C. : *Rural Sociology*, Rawat Publications, Jaipur and New Delhi, Reprinted, 2006, PP. 105, 144.

27. Choudhury, Medini : 'Tribals' Participation in the Nationalist Upsurge' in A. Bhuyan's (ed), *op. cit.*, P. 296.

28. Saikia : *op. cit.*, PP. 33-34, 37.

29. Barpujari, H.K.(eds) : *Political History of Assam* (1826-1919), Vol. I, Publication Board of Assam, Guwahati, Second Edition, 1999, P. 100.

30. Gait, Sir E. : *A History of Assam*, L. B. S. Publications, Guwahati, Assam, 1984, P. 343.

31. : *The Assam Gazette*, Jan. 1, 1876.

32. : *The Assam Gazette*, Dec. 29, 1888.

33. Bhuyan, J.N. : 'Gunabhiram Baruar Dinar Nowgong' in J. N. Bhuyan's *op. cit.*, P. 145.

34. Doshi & Jain : *op. cit.*, P. 114.

35. Guha : *op. cit.*, P. 9.

36. Desai, S.S.M. : *Economic History of India*, Himalaya Publishing House, Bombay, July, 1990, P. 66.

37. Srivastava, A.L. : *The Sultanate of Delhi* (1206-1526), Agarwala and Company, Agra, 1971, PP. 189-190.

38. Mills, A.J.M. : *Report on the Province of Assam*, Publication Board of Assam, Guwahati, Second Edition, 1984, P. 21.

39. Gadgil, D.R. : *The Industrial Evolution of India*, Delhi, 1982, P. 66.

40. Nath, J.G. : *Agrarian Structure of Medieval Assam*, Concept Publishing Company, New Delhi, 2002, P. 69.

41. Goswami, P. : 'Colonial penetration and the emergence of nationalism in Assam' in A. Bhuyan's (ed), *op. cit.*, P. 18.

42. Raja, Purnananda : *op. cit.*, P. 18.

43. Goswami, S.D. : 'Raij versus the Raj . . . . The Nowgong outbreak of 1861in Historical perspective' in J. B. Bhattacharjee's (ed), *Studies in the History of NE India*, NEHU Publications, Shillong, 1986, P. 127.

44. Srinivasa : *op. cit.,* P. 52.
45. Saikia : *op. cit.,* P. 103.
46. *Ibid.* : P. 110.
47. *Ibid.* : P. 226.
48. Guha : *op. cit.,* P. 12.
49. Saikia : *op. cit.,* P. 181.
50. Goswami, P. : *op. cit.,* P. 15.
51. Barpujari (eds) : *op. cit.,* PP. 59-60.
52. Nag, Sajal : 'The Surma valley Muslims and the Sylhet separation issue' in A. Bhuyan's (ed), *op. cit.,* P. 317.
53. Saikia : *op. cit.,* P. 109.
54. Doshi & Jain : *op. cit.,* P. 120.
55. Srinivasa : *op. cit.,* P. 65.
56. Mills, A.J.M. : *op. cit.,* Para-21, Appendix-B.
57. Ghosh, Lipi. : 'Indebtedness in peasant sector: a study of Assam proper in late 19th century' in J. B. Bhattacharjee's (ed), *Studies in the Economic History of N.E.India,* H.A. Publication, New Delhi, 1994, P. 339.
58. Goswami, P.C. : *The Economic Development of Assam,* Asia Publishing House, Bombay, 1963, P. 60.
59. Saikia : *op. cit.,* P. 117.
60. Kaushal, G. : *Economic History of India* (1757-1966), Kalyani Publishers, New Delhi, Reprint, 1991, P. 180.
61. Goswami, S.D. : 'The British Taxation Policy in Assam' in J. B. Bhattacharjee's (ed), *op. cit.,* P. 95.
62. Kaushal : *op. cit.,* P. 8.
63. Chopra, P.N., Puri, B.N. & Das, M.N. : *A Social, Cultural and Economic History of India,* Vol. III, Mac Millan India Ltd., Madras, 1990, P. 183.
64. Barpujari (eds) : *op. cit.,* P. 15.
65. Saikia : *op. cit.,* P. 105.
66. Srinivasa : *op. cit.,* P. 51.
67. Chopra, Puri & Das : *op. cit.,* P. 167.

68. Goswami, S.D.   : 'Raij versus the Raj: The outbreak of 1861 in Historical perspective' in J. B. Bhattacharjee's (ed), *Studies in the History of NE India*, NEHU Publications, Shillong, 1986, P. 127.

69. Sarma, Sashi   : 'Raijmel Aru Krishak Bidroh: Ati Oitihashik Bisleshan' in K. Kumar Deka's (ed), *Raijmel*, Raijmel Kadamtal Swahid Smriti Sangha, Paikarkuchi, Nalbari, 1996, P. 41.

70. Guha   : *op. cit.*, P. 5.

71. Raja, Purnananda   : *op. cit.*, P. 19.

72. Kalita   : *op. cit.*, P. 311.

73. Bhuyan, J.N.   : 'Gunabhiram Baruar Dinar Nowgong' in J. N. Bhuyan's *op. cit.*, P. 142.

74. Guha   : *op. cit.*, P. 45.

75. Kalita, R.C.   : 'British exploitation in Assam: the opium policy and revenue (1850-94), *NEIHA-XII*, 1991, P. 343.

76. Nehru, J.   : 'The Brahmaputra Valley', Appendix-C (1) in A. Bhuyan's (ed), *op. cit.*, P. 375.

77. Goswami, Indreswar   : *Adha-pora Pandulipi*, Lili Prakashika, Nowgong, 1999, P. 32.

78. Sarma, Benudhar   : *Congressor Kanchiali Radat*, Manuh Prakashan, P. 91.

79. Barua, Dr.Birinchi Kr.   : *Asamor Loka Sanskriti*, Bina Library, Guwahati, 1989, PP. 110-115.

80. Barpujari (eds)   : *op. cit.*, P. 93.

81. Karna, M.N.   : *Agrarian structure and land reforms in Assam*, Regency Publications, New Delhi, 2004, P. 32.

82. Kalita   : 'The Phulaguri uprising of 1861: a peasant mass movement,' *NEIHA-X*, 1989, P. 312.

83. Goswami   : 'Raij versus the Raj . . . . . . ' in J. B. Bhattacharjee's (ed), *op. cit.*, PP. 124-125.

84. Goswami, Dr.Chandana : 'Phulaguri uprising (1861): the first phase of peasant upheaval in Assam,' *ACTA Journal, Vol. XXXI*, Published by Gen. Secretary (ACTA), Guwahati, 2007-2008, P. 91.

85. Barpujari (eds) : *op. cit.*, P. 93.

86. *Ibid.* : P. 19.

87. *Ibid.* : P. 30.

88. Karna : *op. cit.*, P. 31.

89. Goswami : 'Raij versus the Raj . . . .' in J. B. Bhattacharjee's (ed), *op. cit.*, PP. 132-133.

90. Kalita : *op. cit.*, P. 315.

91. *Ibid.* : P. 319.

92. *Ibid.* : P. 320.

93. Bhuyan, A. : 'Introduction' in A. Bhuyan's (ed), *op. cit.*, PP. 2-3.

94. Guha, A. : 'A peep through 19th century Assam-Maniram Dewan' in S. Barman's (et. al), *op. cit.*, P. 357.

95. Kalita, Benudhar : *op. cit.*, P. 72.

96. *Ibid.* : P. 69.

97. Nag, Sajal : 'Social reaction to bania exploitation' in J. B. Bhattacharjee's (ed), *Studies in the Economic History of N.E.India*, Har Anand Publications, New Delhi, 1994, P. 366.

98. Saikia : *op. cit.*, P. 107.

99. Barpujari (eds) : *op. cit.*, PP. 92-94.

100. Saikia : *op. cit.*, P. 94.

101. Guha, A. : *Planter Raj to Swaraj (1826-1947)*, Tulika Books, New Delhi, 2006, PP. 44-45.

102. Bhuyan, J.N. : 'Gunabhiran Baruar Dinar Nowgong' in J. N. Bhuyan's *op. cit.*, P. 141.

103. Saikia : *op. cit.*, PP. 108-109.

104. Kalita, Benudhar : *op. cit.*, P. 68.

 : : Oct. 1861, *Orunodoi.*

105. Kalita : *op. cit.*, P. 321.

106. Srinivasa : *op. cit.*, P. 95.
107. Barpujari (eds) : *op. cit.*, P. 94.
108. Goswami, Indreswar : 'Asamor Pratham Krishak Bidroh' in Jatin Medhi's (ed), *op. cit.*, P. 12.
109. Bora, Dr.Dhrubajyoti : 'Itihashat jaat-pratha: Asamot jaat-paator bhumika' in S. Barman's (et al), *op. cit.*, P. 104.
110. Kalita, R.C. : '19th century peasant movement and the Assamese middle class' *NEIHA-XV*, 1994, P. 199.
111. Karna : *op. cit.*, P. 34.
112. Barpujari (eds) : *op. cit.*, PP. 101-102.
113. Sheikh, Ahijuddin : 'Roots and nature of agrarian unrest—peasant movement in Goalpara', *NEIHA-XIV*, 1993, P. 266.
114. Goswami, Indreswar : *op. cit.*, PP. 1-2.
115. Karna : *op. cit.*, P. 33.
116. Dutta, Anuradha : 'Aspects of growth and development of nationalism in Assam in the 19th century' in A. Bhuyan's (ed), *op. cit.*, P. 63.
117. Barpujari (eds) : *op. cit.*, P. 94.
118. Goswami : 'Raij versus the Raj . . . .' in J. B. Bhattacharjee's (ed), *op. cit.*, P. 134.
119. Kalita, R.C. : 'Opium prohibition and Rai Bahadur J. Barua', *NEIHA-XVI*, 1995, P. 186.
120. Goswami : *op. cit.*, P. 134.
121. Barua, S.L. : *A Comprehensive History of Assam*, Munshiram Manoharlal Publishers Pvt. Ltd., New Delhi, 2005, P. 503.
122. Barpujari (ed) : *The Comprehensive History of Assam*, Vol. V, Publication Board of Assam, Guwahati, 2004, P. 15.
123. Goswami, Indreswar : *op. cit.*, P. 2.
124. Kalita : 'The Phulaguri uprising of 1861: a peasant mass movement' *op. cit.*, P. 321.
125. Goswami : 'The British Taxation Policy in Assam' *op. cit.*, P. 96.

126. Hussain, M.   :   *The Assam movement—Class, ideology and identity*, Manak Publications Pvt. Ltd. in association with Har Anand Publications, New Delhi, First Edn., 1993, P. 41.

127. Kalita   :   *op. cit.*, P. 321.

128. Srinivasa   :   *op. cit.*, P. 100.

129. *Ibid.*   :   P. 70.

130. Kalita, Benudhar   :   *op. cit.*, PP. 59-60.

131. Choudhury, Birajananda   :   *Paradhinatar Para Swadhinataloi*, Himadri Prakashan, Margherita, 1996, PP. 25-26.

132. Barpujari (eds)   :   *Political History of Assam* (1826-1919), Vol. I, Publication Board of Assam, Guwahati, Second Edn, 1999, P. 102.

133. Ali, Dr.M.Abid   :   *Pothorughat—Indianised*, Published by Premananda Sikdar, Mangaldoi, 2007, P. 25.

134. Barpujari (eds)   :   *op. cit.*, P. 93.

135. *Ibid.*   :   P. 93.

136. Kalita, Benudhar   :   *op. cit.*, PP. 72-73.

137. Ali   :   *op. cit.*, P. 26.

CHAPTER – SEVEN

THE YEARS OF UNREST AND IRRITATION: 1862-92

A critical study of the political history of Assam during the period stretching from 1862 to 1892 will tend us to believe that after 1861, there was no outburst of the peasants except a mild bubble in Nowgong in 1868-69. But that does not mean that they reconciled to the British rule. About three decades elapsed without any notable disturbance, despite having enormous scope. The three decades (1862-92) provided the main-strength to the peasant-uprisings of 1893-94 and the freedom struggle in Assam in later period. But in no case, there was a movement in Assam for the freedom of the province from the foreign yoke.[1] It developed in later years. The English educated native did not demand freedom but wanted only the wrongs of the government to be rectified.

In fact, there are several reasons behind this type of conspicuous silence of the common people as well as the leaders. Despite having enormous scope, the peasants and the mass people remained silence during the period of 1862-92. They only wanted change of their master's outlook and behaviour. The people, in general, groaned under economic hardship after 1861 and because of that, they probably could not think of another revolt like 1861. The peasants faced the British might and machinery in 1861, and could not forget that dreadful memory for several decades. They, it seems, never sought its repetition. Moreover, they most probably, considered their traditional mode of warfare inferior to that of the British and waited for the best time to come. After the mutiny of 1857-58, there emerged leadership crisis in Assam. Absence of Maniram Dewan was terribly felt and had there been charismatic leaders like him during this period, probably silence would have been broken. There was also lake of well-organized association to lead the mass people. Though there was *Raij-mel* to mobilize the peasants, despite that, it failed due to the inapt handling of its leaders, as most of them were illiterate and traditional. Ultimately, such condition gave opportunity to the British to be more obstinate to rule the land. The mass people, on the contrary, had no other options but to accept the rule of the British. But wave of ignition continued to blow in their mind silently. The colonial government failed to understand that people die but their protest never.

Unity of action was not yet imagined and probably because of this, they could not unite against the Raj and had to maintain silence. Lack of better substitute was also another cause for their silence. The attempted reforms and reorganization of the administration could not eradicate the evils of the government and their satellites whose interest was more of economic exploitation than of improving the lot of the masses or redress of their grievances. Despite its faults and failures, the masses, in general, accepted the British rule not because that they had love for them, but because that, they could not expect to have better substitute for it.[3]

After 1861, the number of government's force was increased in Assam to cope-up with the situation and it created scare and terror in the minds of the peasants. The government's ever-readiness and ever-preparedness to face any type of situation gave birth crest-fallen in the minds of the peasants.

II

The unrest and irritation blew silently in the minds of the peasants of Assam even after 1861. The causes, that compelled the people to be so, have been termed as *non-dormant* and *dormant*. It remains expressed here that *dormant* and *non-dormant,* both factors were active and alive before 1862 also. The outbreak of 1861 bears the testimony to it. But these factors became powerful, and their vibration and intensity began to augment in unabated manner as the time rolled-on. Ultimately, it invited another series of catastrophe with the wings and feathers of conflagration in Kamrup and Darrang in 1893-94.

Non-dormant factors: The government by raising the revenue demand created terror in the minds of the peasants and infact, the payment of land revenue was the root of all major social conflicts involving the peasants. There was growing spirit of discontent among the people of Assam in consequence of the greatly increased taxation, and all sorts of evil stories were in circulation in the villages to increase their discontent.[4]

One important thing to be noticed is that the planters were the biggest landlords, but the revenue they paid was the lowest. The peasants as they opposed the augmented rate of revenue, the planter-community instead of giving them support, they rather stretched-out their supporting hand to the government as the augmented rate served their purpose. Increased revenue, as they planned, would flush-out the traditional agriculture system and make the indigenous people as their labourers in the tea gardens. The government did not decrease the rate of revenue and rather, tried to convince the people that the increased rate of taxation increase the paying capacity of the people. This type of argument made people volatile.

Moreover, the people of Assam after 1861 understood the real motive of the colonial government behind the ban on the local poppy cultivation. They banned it only for their revenue consideration, not for humanitarian ground at all. Had their motive been humanitarian, they would not have sold their *abkari* opium to the people of Assam. Upto 1861, Nowgong and her surroundings were under the grip of opium. But in course of time, entire Brahmaputra valley including river island Majuli also came under the influence of opium.[5] From 1873 to 1893, the British Colonial Government in Assam sold a total of 31,392 maunds of opium and realized a net price of Rs.3,14,55,576 and a license fee of Rs.47,60,657 from the opium sellers. In this way, they exploited the people of Assam in terms of opium revenue itself to the tune of Rs.3,62,16,233.[6]

Sudden fall of English agriculture from 1875 onwards may be one of the important causes behind the further revenue maximization in their colonies. According to Trevelyan, due to sudden fall of English agriculture from 1875 onwards, catastrophe sets-in in England in the 19th century.[7] Therefore, to restore their economy, they resorted device to augment revenue on land.

Massive fiscal pressure due to the maximization of land revenue led to increasing indebtedness in the villages and caused, therefore, peasants' flight.[8] Actually, the British colonization was mainly responsible for the poverty of Indian peasants. The nature of the British exactions was manifested in the growing pauperization of India.9 Vinoba Bhabe argued that land belongs to God and therefore, it has to be distributed equally. Nehruji also said that land would be justifiably distributed when India would get freedom.[10] Had the colonial government thought like our greatmen and turned their thought into reality, the Indians probably would not have cried for land and therefore, proper justification has been done to them. But that did not happen and as a result of which, the hopes and dreams of the people of India, thus, had been distorted.

The defects of the revenue settlement aroused feelings which often found expression in criminal offences. According to Oliver Mendelsohu and Marika Vicziany, subordinate people gained nothing out of land reforms. Foreign Government implemented no radical land reforms in India.[11] Moreover, the conduct of the Cadastral survey was defective. Field measurements were not carefully and systematically tested. Objections of the peasants were hardly discussed.[12]

Instead of generating structural development, the British agrarian policy pauperized the people and brought their speedy stagnation. Krishna Sarma strongly criticized the agrarian policy of the alien ruler by depicting the miserable condition of the ryots. With the grant of *pattas* for 10,20 and 30 years, the rate of rent revenue went on increasing.[13]

After the Phulaguri uprising of 1861, the land revenue was increased and doubled in 1868. The Settlement Act of 1870 again doubled the rate of revenue and it was increased again in 1883 and 1893.[14] The colonial government squeezed the people in such a manner that there was no fall of land revenue in spite of having epidemic diseases, like Cholera, Small pox and fever in 1879-80 in Goalpara, Kamrup, Darrang and in Nowgong.[15] In the Settlement of 1883, revenue was raised by about 53 percent on the average but in some areas, it was as high as 80 to 100 percent. During the period between 1866 and 1889, the land revenue had more than quadrupled. The peasants began to reel under the increasing burden of land revenue [16] and it affected the agricultural development of the province for the last three decades of the 19th century.

The Assam Land and Revenue Regulations of 1886 was not welcome by the peasants and landlords, as this regulations introduced an elaborate tenancy system which tightened the loopholes and brought all sections under a common code.[17] Great resentment had started in the entire Brahmaputra valley in view of the preparation of this regulations and a public meeting of about 10,000 people at Jorhat on the 2nd June, 1886 had expressed its voices against the measures under the positive role of J.N.Barua.[18]

Resentment and ignition was not confined at Assam alone. It's conflagration spread upto Goalpara which was within the erstwhile Bengal. The ryots of Goalpara also expressed their protest against the government. The government formally extended the application of the Act of 1869 upto Goalpara by the notification of 1892. Unfortunately, privileges granted to the people of Bengal by this Act were not entitled to the people of Goalpara.[19]

The imposition of tax on income created wide spread resentment in the minds of the traders, merchants and the middle class. The government, in addition to that, imposed license tax also for collecting forest products. Agricultural items were also not spared from paying taxes. Moreover, the government brought some revenue free land under assessment. The term of 20 years of revenue free settlement of land with the former *Rajas* of Darrang originated in 1859-60, having expired, the entire land was brought under resettlement.[20] Again, the people grazed their cattle freely on the fields of villages but the government brought these grazing fields also under assessment.[21]

The government cared little for the development of agriculture sector. In spite of the systematic revenue maximization, nothing was done to improve the condition of agriculture. Of course, the British Government showed same apathy towards agriculture in their native land also in the 19th century (from 1875 onward) by divorcing their contact with nature as they did welcome American food to England.[22]

The government instead of developing the rudest implements of agriculture, and conditioning and manuring of fields for better harvest; they cared for collecting revenue. They neglected the irrigation system also. By introducing this, they could have increased the rate of production. Moreover, attempt was hardly made to raise embankments for the protection of crops from the ravages of floods which was of frequent occurrence.

In addition to that, the government hardly showed interest for the development of road and transport that led to the agricultural fields. On the contrary, the public funds were diverted for the interest of plantation. The tea producing districts had a better communication system than that of the non-tea producing ones.[23] The government also remained inactive towards some services, namely credit, marketing services, services relating to seeds, fertilizer and agricultural implements. Ananda Ram Dhekial

Phukan advocated for the importation of foreign technical know-how and pleaded for the establishment of a number of technical schools for the betterment of agriculture.[24] But his cry also became the cry in wilderness. Anyway, by encouraging and developing the agricultural system, the government could have brought green revolution in Assam, but they totally ignored these.

The decisive stage of development of capitalism is imperialism and the only motto of capitalism is to build the mountain of profits. The ryots and the labourers are the creators of all wealth used by men. But the British capitalists did not think for the welfare of these sections even at the time of natural calamities.[25] It is said that humanitarianism resulted in many administrative measures to fight famine and control epidemics, but they were only in name. In colonial period, the natural calamities, like fire, earthquake, drought, floods and cattle disease aggravated the situation of Assam, especially, the condition of peasants became deplorable at that time. Locusts and white-ants also did not lag behind in their destructive operations.[26] For example, broods of locusts were noticed in the districts of Goalpara and Lakhimpur in 1863.[27] Moreover, Lakhimpur was prone to regular and excessive floods. The district of Sibsagar experienced severe drought in 1870 and 1872.[28] But the measures taken by the government was far from satisfactory. In the Brahmaputra valley districts in 1885, cholera claimed 3,411; small pox 936; fever 43,341 and bowl complaints 8,081 lives. The corresponding figures for the same disease in the following year was 15,975.[29] Thus, the public health suffered lot, but the government's apathy further aggravated the situation. The loss of cattle and plough-cattle adversely affected the cultivation and it finally, impoverished the peasants. In 1881-82, a total number of 9,559 heads of cattle perished in Nowgong and 7,098 in Sibsagar. The mortality of cattle in the Brahmaputra valley, according to an official report, was 93,494 in 1883-84; it slightly came down to 91,091 in the following year. After a gap of one year, cattle disease relapsed again and claimed 87,628 heads in 1886-87.[30] But the government's role to eradicate this was not encouraging. The government even paid less respond to the recommendation of the Indian Cattle Plague Commission of 1869.[31] Such type of epidemic could have been averted to some extent, if the government followed its recommendation sincerely. It remains expressed that the government not only showed apathy towards the natural calamities, rather they themselves some time created calamity-like situation. For example, large scale destruction of forest by them also brought catastrophe to agriculture in the name of floods and drought but they did nothing to check them. By constructing embankments, they could have checked the tides of floods to some extent. For example in 1888-89, when a local board grant was needed for the renovation of the Janji bund to protect thousands of acres of paddy land from inundation, there was no response at all.[32] By introducing the crop insurance and credit facility system, the colonial government could have given respite to the people of Assam in the time of natural calamities but no such step was seen taken by the government.

The Assam valley emerged more and more as an important area for commercial exploitation because of its growing tea industry, minerals and timbers.[33] It is because of this, the government cast their covetous eyes on the wasteland of Assam and was allergic to the allotment of the same to the local people. Mills also strongly deprecated the granting of wasteland to the native.[34] The government favoured foreign enterprise, foreign capital and foreign skills. The terms of the wasteland grants were so favourable to the European planters that it tempted them to grab more land than they required. The government by fixing the minimum acreage of land for tea garden at 100 acres discouraged the local planters as they could not dream of such venture. Some could do that only after retirement with their savings. The man with small capital could not do that inspite of having their skills and mind.[35]

The immigration of farmers also created problem for the indigenous farmers. Demand for productivity of foodgrain increased due to the rise of tea industry and labourers, therefore, required for it. The government relaxed the wasteland rule to encourage immigration of farmers as there was scarcity of local labourers, and they were even settled by the planters on their holdings to produce rice.

The government framed certain special rules on behalf of tea cultivation in Assam. In Upper Assam, large areas of land were settled with tea estate owners under Fee Simple Rules of 1862 and 1874. These Fee Simple estates were revenue free and the holders had rights over mines, minerals, forests and fisheries.[36] But such type of revenue free estate was not framed for the indigenous rice cultivation of Assam. It is unfortunate that while the local people paid more and more revenue; the planters, on the contrary, held most of them rent free.

There were some planters whose intention was not to plant the whole area with tea. They most of the time acquired land which contained valuable minerals and timbers. The minerals and timbers, thus acquired, were exported to their homeland and earned, thus, huge profit. The large scale destruction of forest continued in Assam until the Forest Act of 1878 came into force.[37] As a result of the destruction of forest, the economy suffered lot. The timber, firewood, gums and other materials gathered from the forest, possibly, became unavailable due to wanton destruction of forest. The planters carried on their exaction upon the people of Assam in various ways. For example, the local labourers, especially, the Kachari tribe of Darrang district were paid low rate of wages by the European planters which, finally, compelled them to resort to the path of strike for high wages. In 1864, while a free labourer was able to earn a wage of Rs.7 per month, the growing rate in the Assam Tea Company was only Rs.4 to 5. They, therefore, resorted to the path of strike but the authorities quelled them with iron hand. They were tried on the spot by the District Magistrate. While some were imprisoned, some others were dismissed from their services.[38]

The 'Mau' supported the planters on the coolie question, but the Bengal Nationalist Press condemned the planters' exaction on the coolies. The Bengali Brahmo Missionary also condemned it.[39] By abolishing the paik-system, the colonial government did a good service to the people of Assam but that was just an eye-wash and Hippocratic step. Their brutal and diabolic character came to light through their treatment meted-out to the coolies, and Guha terms it as 'the Beasts of a Menagerie.'[40]

Moreover, there was less land available for grazing cattle as all such lands were brought under assessment and purview of wasteland. Sometime, the planters even encroached upon the jhum rights of the tribal farmers. Lands of cultivators were sold as wastelands as it became a easy matter for the European planters.[41] The planters also disrupted the inter-village communications by fencing in portions of existing public roads and denying the rights of way to villages.[42]

Thus, the foreign rulers were not content with merely running the administration. New possibilities were opened up before them by the vast natural resources for exploitation. Political and economic domination were fused leading to complete reduction of Assam to the status of a part of British India. Assam was facing and suffering from the same basic evils of foreign domination as other parts of India did, though there was difference in degrees.[43]

Raw rubber had wide demand in England, Ceylon and Straits settlement, Canada, Australian Commonwealth, France, Japan and the USA.[44] Realizing the commercial importance of these lucrative goods, the colonial government ultimately brought this business in their hands depriving the local rubber cultivators. Unfortunately, the local rubber cultivators could not compete with the colonial men due to their weak money power. Thus, ultimately this business also like the tea went into the hands of the foreigners.

The European employed local labourers in the rubber cultivation of Assam. The Mikirs were paid 8 *annas* per day, the Nepalese and the Assamese were paid Rs.30 and 20 per maund of rubber collected. The Garos were paid 4 *annas* per pound in the first decade of the 19th century. The firms engaged in rubber trade offered advance to the ordinary peasants and others to grow rubber.[45] From this, we come to know that the remuneration and advances paid to the local labourers by the colonial traders were far from satisfactory, but the profits they earned, in return by exporting raw rubbers from Assam at the cost of the blood of the local people, were lot. Thus, appropriation and exploitation to the locals in the name of rubber cultivation continued unabated way.

The advent of the plantation marked the beginning of immigration of labourers as there was shortage of labourers in Assam. But this immigration met the demands and interests of the British planters only. The colonial government enacted a series of legislation from 1863 to 1901 to meet the labour problem in Assam.[46] In 1863, the Transport of Native Labourers Act was passed and it marked the beginning of a tragic chapter of inhuman recruitment and ruthless oppression on millions of indentured labourers imported from different parts of India.[47] Thus, the workers and the peasants both kept-up the smouldering fire of protest and disdain against the British.

The completion and development of the Assam Bengal Railway improved the communication network which facilitated immigration, and the government also took up the issue in right earnest.[48] H.L.Johnson, the Commissioner of Assam adopted some measures in May, 1885 to encourage immigration. The fares of trains and ships were decreased and even land free of revenue was given to them.[49] But unfortunately, such steps were rarely seen taken for the interest of the locals.

In 1853, Mills assessed the total population of Assam proper including Goalpara at above 12 lacs.[50] The population of the Brahmaputra valley was 15 lacs in 1872 and it shot up at 18 lacs in 1881. In 1891, the population figure went above 24 lacs and 76 thousands. It was environmental and medical factors combined with economic forces that generated declining in death rates and increasing in immigration rather than the biological factors, which were generally responsible for the rapid growth of population.[51] The density of population also increased in each districts of Assam due to the rise of population growth decades after decades.[52]

Density of population per sq. mile in the Brahmaputra valley:

District	1872	1881	1891
Kamrup	146	167	164
Darrang	69	80	90
Nowgong	68	82	90
Sibsagar	64	79	96
Lakhimpur	27	40	56

Source: A. Guha's 'Planter Raj to Swaraj', Appendix-3, P. 279.

Initially, the immigrants came in small numbers. So, there was no reaction to it. But when they began to come in large numbers including their families and children, it created pressure upon the land. Moreover, the immigration of landless labourers and cultivators from East Bengal and their habitation in the wasteland of Assam created another problem for the natives. This problem further gave birth to communal and linguistic problem in lather years. The Assamese middle class who were silent on the immigration issue in the initial stage, they also started raising their voice against it towards the end of the 19th century as and when their interest received withstand at the hands of the educated immigrants. In addition to that, the economic condition of the Assamese peasants were also hard-pressed by these. The position of the Assamese in general was being threatened in several parts of Barpeta sub-division by immigrants. Bijni was a clear example of it which was worsely affected.[53]

The immigration posed a serious challenge to race, religion, economy and culture of Assam becoming a source of social conflict and tension in later period. Maniram Dewan even predicted a bad future to the government unless they eschewed the appointment from outside the state.[54] The immigrants had often encroached upon the lands of the indigenous peasants. On the other hand, the indigenous peasants in order to possess cash often sold-off their lands to the immigrants, and wanted the land back later on which the immigrants declined to comply with resulting violent clashes. Again, while the immigrants were settled in the residential areas of the indigenous peasants, even the residential distance were not maintained at that time. The two groups settled in the same vicinity even at the door step of each other.[55] Moreover, importation of skilled labour from outside kicked-out the indigenous labourers and craftsmen.[56] Immigration affected not only one section of the society, others were also terribly affected by its evil effects.

Dormant factors: The British fiscal policy in Assam was directly linked with their commercial programmes in rest of India. In order to achieve commercial program, they in stages converted Assam into their colony. Most of the indigenous institutions were either abolished or recast and certain new arrangements were introduced. The abrupt change created internal instability and this in turn, led to great social unrest.[57] Maniram Dewan, the martyr of 1857's revolt of Assam, was more concerned of the decline of indigenous industries of Assam and had predicted the British a bad future unless they eschewed their industrial policy.[58] Finally, his prophecy arrived at reality.

The colonial rule precipitated the extinction of the village industries gradually and progressively. India was reduced to a position of market for the consumption of goods made in Britain. The colonial government resorted to the policy of *laissez faire,* and in order to flood the Indian markets with machine made goods of Britain, they imposed nominal import duties on the English goods. Again, as a result of the export of Indian raw materials to England, there was lack of raw materials for the local industries. The owners of the local industries criticized this policy of the colonial government. Actually, the colonial policy was designed to facilitate the ruthless exploitation of the people of India. Throughout the British rule, India was mercilessly impoverished, her famous manufactures were ruined, and poor artisans and craftsmen were driven-out.[59]

It was a painful fact that the condition of people became worse under the British rule due to the ruin of village industries, as they acted as safety valve for those dependent on agriculture. It gave people, especially, to farmers a second source of income. Its decline deprived the farmers of their subsidiary occupation and considerably reducing their income and compelling them to take recourse to borrowing.[60]

It remains expressed that the decline of the crafts was neither sudden nor totally unexpected. The commercial treaty of 1793 between Gaurinath Singha, the Ahom king and the East India Company gave the first blow on the traditional crafts of Assam.[61]

The peasants had to suffer a lot due to languishing of trade and handicrafts of Assam. The cash was unavailable in day to day transactions and because of this, it was difficult for them to go to the markets to seek relief. The decline of cottage industries augmented pressure of population on agriculture leading to the inevitable sub-division and fragmentation of the peasants' holdings. The growth of population hastened this process. The fragmentation of lands resulted in the limitless growth of uneconomic holdings leading to the birth of poverty. Moreover, the ruin of village industries threw not only vast numbers on agriculture, but also created many landless rural labourers.

The *Asom Dipak*, a monthly journal published from Majuli, pleaded with the public in November, 1876 to patronize native manufacture and suggested remedies against the crippling effect of the imported goods. It called for the formation of trading companies by the Assamese, patronization of Assamese shops and use of articles against the foreign ones.[62] But unfortunately, the government was not at all concerned of that which, finally, aggravated the matter in further-days.

Indebtedness from which the peasant had not even a remote hope of escape turned him into a medieval serf, dishonest debtor, an inefficient farmer, thriftless head of the family and an irresponsible citizen. A society steeped in debt is necessarily a social volcano. Discontent between the classes is bound to arise smouldering discontent which is always dangerous.[63] Social ceremonies, like marriage and *sraddha* accounted for 1/10 to 1/5 of the total loans and productive purposes, like purchase of cattle, seeds, implements and improvement of land only 15 to 30 percent. Famines and crop failures were the general causes of loan.[64]

The peasants of Assam in colonial period took loan from the Marwari *mahajans* as there were none to compete with them in this field, and this gave them chances to exploit the natives. They gave money to the natives either on interest or on mortgaged of their properties. Thus, the people fell in the trap of rural indebtedness. According to the census report of 1891, there were 1,793 money-lenders in the Brahmaputra valley. Of them,1,211 were in Kamrup alone.[65]

The money-lending class gave money in advance to the peasants for which interest rate was 37 to 75% per annum for small loans. In larger transactions where a mortgage was given upon movable property, its rate was 12 to 20%. As regards paddy loans, there was a peculiar system that a man borrowing before the harvest had to pay double at the time of harvest.[66]

The perpetual direct exploitation of the peasants led to a very high degree of rural indebtedness, like transfer of landed property from cultivating classes to non-cultivating classes, rise of a wage earning landless peasant class and the creation of near famine like condition by seizing harvest against loans and hoarding of food-grains.[67]

Moreover, the exaction of exorbitant rates oppressed the peasants heavily. In order to meet the high demand of revenue, the peasants perpetually remained indebted to the local money-lenders. Many of them lost their lands to these greedy money-lenders for the inability to pay back the borrowed amount. Thus, the cultivators had to die in debt.[68]

Anyway, due to the increasing trends and rates of rural indebtedness and the exploitation of the money-lenders to the peasants shattered the traditional peace and harmony of village life, and created in its place tension, anger and a smouldering feeling of revenge.

Like the British, the Marwaris also took full advantage of trading and commercial opportunities in Assam. They carried on their trade in Assam even before the British and exploited the Assamese through their trade. They had sweet relation with the British and latter had even imported some of them from Marwar and gave them employment as mauzadars what Maniram Dewan protested tooth and nail.

The Marwaris gave cash as advance to the peasants as against interest or the pledged crops or mortgaged of their assets. The peasants after harvests had to pay more crops to the Marwaris as against the few advance. The people had to give one *dun* to the Marwari *mahajans* after harvest. But their *dun* was not of 3 seers, it contained more than that. More tragic was the fact that if even the debt was repaid, they did not strike-off the name of the borrowers from their *khatas*; even the amounts remained there forever. Manipulation and interpolation of such amounts often occurred in their *khatas* what even Rai Bahadur Nilambar Dutta, a planter from Dibrugarh also opined.[69] Thus, once a person signed in the long red book and obtained a loan, he was doomed.

The government employees were also not spared from the exactions of the Marwari *mahajan*. The clerks, for example, when they laid their hands on the monthly salary, the Marwari money-lenders would snatch all of it against the loans they provided. The clerks, when they entered home with empty handed, their wives would inform them that not a single grain of food left at home. The clerks finding no other alternative, had to go back again and requested the same Marwari money-lenders for loans.[70] Thus, caught in a vicious circle of intensified exploitation, the people started agitating not only against the colonial government but also against the Marwari *mahajans,* as they had monopolized the internal trade and exploited the people through usury.

Sometime, the Marwari even indulged in slave trade. They sent their agents for collection of elephants and rubber, and resorted to undue excesses on the tribal people of the hills.[71] The Marwari dealers bought tusks from the tribal hunters at cheap rate and sold them in Calcutta at high rate, and thus, earned lots of profit.[72] By establishing a network of trade connection with Calcutta, as remarked by one Lakheswar Barthakur, the Marwaris exported valuable materials to Calcutta through the river and earned lot.[73]

The trade being solely in the hands of the Marwari traders, the profits mostly went to enrich Rajputana, their homeland as they did not accumulate this profit in Assam.[74] They, except few, came to Assam to exploit the natives, not to assimilate with the Assamese.[75] Had they desired, they could have merged with the Assamese society by inter-marrying with the Assamese. Except few, they did not do that, probably, due to having their racial arrogance. If the colonial conditions were responsible for the thorough impoverishment of India, it was the Marwaris and their doings that pushed it to further predicament.[76]

In addition to the exploitation of the British and the Marwari traders, some locals were also responsible for the exploitation and exactions upon their own people. Statistics since 1862 to 1900 shows a general rise in prices of essential commodities. Taking full advantage of the situation and the hardship of the masses; the landlords, the mauzadars and the *gaonburhas* always took the opportunity to snatch-away the ryot's last hold of land at the cheapest rate in the name of helping them.[77] Local people, like the *Telis, Johlas, Kabuliala,* the government stamp-vendors, clerks and pleaders were also engaged in money-lending business.[78] The severity of such exploitation is beautifully depicted by J.P.Agarwala in his famous creation '*Lovita*'. The cultural icon in his play mentions that not only the colonialists but along with them collaborationist mauzadars and the village headmen were also responsible for the exploitation of their own men.[79]

The remote control of British India was controlled from Britain. Britain being a colonial country believed in the policy of expansion and exploitation. For expansion, they adopted certain tools, viz. subsidiary alliance and doctrine of lapse. On the contrary, they prepared and framed wasteland rule, tax and revenue rule, export-import and industrial policy for exploitation. These were formulated and given shape by their colonial bureaucrats who neglected the interest of the ruled. The colonial bureaucrats spent public and private funds both mainly for the tea plantation and gave more impetus, especially, to the planters. For the cultivation of new staples, they even granted them leases on very favourable terms. The wasteland rules were prepared for their people's interest, and hardly encouraged local and traditional crops. They framed revenue and agrarian policy for their people's interest.

Elite immigrants from outside Assam became the eye-sore for the upper middle classes of Assam, as the former held almost all the departments.[80] The upper class did not like this and held the bureaucrats responsible for their such condition. To them, behind the root of all evils, the hands of the *amlah's* were there.

The colonial bureaucrats created stable and loyal rural gentry that could be relied upon as a strong ally of the administration. For instance, mauzadars were placed for revenue collection and they were succeeded to the offices by one of their families. Due to their hereditary position, they could exploit people generation after generation and thus, created fear in the minds of the ryots. The threatening and menace of the tahsildars also created scar in their minds. The announcement of the tahsildars that the properties of the defaulter ryots would be confiscated made them worry and disappointed all through-out the years.

Not only the people of Assam, but some of the British officials also realized the corrupt practices and intrigues of the *amlahs* in revenue affairs which was founded upon on no certain data. Moreover, irregular and undefined additional assessments created resentment in the minds of the ryots. Absence of decentralization of power was also one of the reasons of such condition prevailed in colonial India. Jorhat *Sarbajanik Sabha* criticized the concentration of all powers in the hands of Chief Commissioner of Assam.[81] T.C.Robertson, an English official of colonial Assam also mentioned the corrupt practices of the bureaucrats in four decades of the 19th century, which turned into its worst forms towards the close of the 19th century.[82]

The commercialization of agriculture kicked-out the barter economy and placed money economy in its place, but the peasantry was traditionally unaccustomed to this new system. The people faced lots of problem due to the introduction of this new system. Currency was not available at that time. Introduction of money as the medium of exchange without substantial increase of currency created problem for them. They had no other alternative either to leave their land or to take loan from the money-lenders. Thus, indebtedness of the peasants began to grow.

Moreover, this system developed at a time when there existed no trade by which people could dispose of their commodities. There were no markets in close proximity and because of this, they got less opportunity to sell their produce in cash whenever necessary. As a result, they could not pay their revenue in cash to the government in time which, finally, worsened their relation with the authority.

That the intention of the government behind the introduction of the money economy was revenue, people could understand that in later period. The government, no doubt, might have some motives, but if they showed least interest for the common people, probably, grievances against the government would have been reduced to some extent. But they did not do so which ultimately invited wide spread resentment in their mind against the government.

The British talked of the principle of equality [83] but their activities revealed their double standard. Slavery is an extreme form of inequality and the government by abolishing the *paik* system of Assam did a yeoman's service for the people of the province. But behind this abolition was their commercial interest, not at all establishing equality among the people.

The people under the colonial government got no justice against exploitation and extortion due to discriminatory and biasness of the European judges. For example, the servants of the government forcibly took away the goods of the ryots by ways of violence.[84] The ryots, they sought justice against this but failed, as the courts were run by the government judges. Only the white and the men of well-to-do families got justice in the courts. The legal system gave fillip to the rich to oppress the poor. Not only that, some sections of the society even lost their movable and immovable properties in running the cases in the courts. As a result, the ordinary people suffered lot at the lower levels of police, judiciary and general administration. Moreover, sometime people were given heavy punishment in their lesser crime. For example, the Deputy Commissioner of Nowgong in 1870, gave two men six months imprisonment for their light crime, though it was reduced to three months later on.[85] One important thing to be mentioned here is that there was no equal distribution of land. The European planters' grabbed more land than the local planters. Even the government machinery helped the former and made certain rules for their benefit. The government did nothing for the welfare of the peasants of Assam. Seeking and demanding more revenue from the peasants without doing any duty for them was another form of injustice and exploitation. Though the peasants sought justice from the court but their attempt failed. As a result, sometime peasants' fury burst-out and found expression in criminal offences.[86]

The British after the revolt of 1861 introduced the Indian Penal Code system in Assam. Former judicial system was abolished without taking approval of the local people. The *cutcherry* buildings were constructed in the towns, and *munshiffs* and *amins* were appointed there. The people, however, were not acquainted with the *Sadar Diwani Adalat* and *Sadar Nizamat Adalat* which created another problem for them.[87]

In addition to that, the legal procedure was defective. Anandaram Dhekial Phukan wrote in 1853, 'under the present judicial system of the province, a party how trivial so ever may be, the nature of his complaint can never obtain relief without submitting to a vexatious and harassing course of procedure, extending from at least six months to an unlimited length of time.' Anyway, the new judicial system run by the European machinery contributed to the sufferings of the mass people. The aim of the government was good, but it did no good to the people. It reduced vast masses to poverty; many even left Assam for Bhutan when their last hopes of remedy were cruelly belied by the government machinery. Further, those in charge of dispensing justice were mostly corrupt combined with rude behaviour towards the people.[88]

Humanitarianism resulted in many administrative reforms, like founding of schools, colleges and orphanages.[89] But it cannot be accepted. Had it made the colonial government to establish schools and colleges, probably, there would have been no dearth of such institutions in Assam. Probably because of this, the process of growth and development of the educated middle class was slow in Assam compared to Bengal.[90]

The number of educational institutions during the colonial period was few, and that too were constellated in the towns only. As a result, poor sections of the society mainly from the villages could not go to the towns to take their education there. Actually, they were kept black-out of the light of education. Taking full advantage of their illiteracy, the village money-lenders mainly the Marwari *mahajans* exploited them in inhuman manner.

The colonial government was least interested in spreading and disseminating education among the mass people of Assam which resulted in the birth of a discouraging number of educated in the land. The circumstances, at a time, deteriorated in such a way that the government had to import educated people from outside Assam with a view to filling-up the governmental posts in various departments of Assam. The colonial government reserved all the high appointments in India for their own nominees seeking a lucrative career in the East. The colonial British by exploiting and appropriating the Assamese people, checked their natural development.[91] As a result, material and intellectual prosperity of the regions received tremendous setback.

When the government started the process of elimination of the *paiks*, the process of assimilation between the rich and the poor had started. The people through-out Assam thought that elimination of the *paik* would narrow down the gap between the rich and the poor. But these were all just eye-wash. Despite the elimination of the *paiks*, the condition of the coolies of the tea-gardens of Assam was the worst form of serfdom. Thus, miseries and agonies of the masses continued to increase as the time rolled-on.

The role of the Christian missionaries was also not encouraging. They gave importance on conversion, and showed more addiction to their own Christian religion. The government also encouraged them on the issue of conversion, as they all belong to same religion. But, on the other hand, the government neglected the study of the *satras*. Like their Christian religion, they should have given same impetus to other religions and their institutions also, specially, to the *satras*.

While the people of Assam were suffering from the diseases of different type, the colonial government like Nero, (The Roman emperor who was fiddling when Rome was burning) instead of rendering medical facilities to the victims, was busy in collecting revenue and encouraging missionaries to proselyte native to Christianity. They sought healing of the victims by uttering the name of Jesus Christ. During the time of *Durga puja*, there was huge congregation in Nowgong. The Christian missionaries taking full advantage of it, arrived there and had distributed some pamphlets, relating to Christianity. In the pamphlets, it was mentioned that Jesus Christ could heal the victims and the patients from the clutches of fever and natural calamities.[92] The people, however, were not satisfied at this, and sought practical and remedial step to eliminate these.

From 1886 to 1892, different Associations and *Rayat Sabhas* from the Brahmaputra valley took part in the sessions of the Indian National

Congress without fail held in Calcutta, Madras, Allahabad, Bombay, Calcutta, Nagpur and Allahabad; and placed their various demands to the government. Satyanath Bora represented the Nowgong *Rayat* Association, Calcutta in 1886; Lakshmikanta Barkakati represented the Tezpur *Rayat Sabha*, Madras in 1887; Ghanashyam Barua represented the Nowgong Rayat Association, Allahabad in 1888 and Haridas Roy from Dibrugarh took part in the Bombay session in 1889.[93] But their participation bore no fruits, as the government was least concerned of their demands. Being dissatisfied at this, they did not participate in the further sessions held in 1893 and 1894; and stretched-out their helping hands and minds to the peasants of Assam in their revolts in that years. Thus, the dormant and non-dormant, both factors kept the environment of colonial Assam hot and volatile all through-out the years stretching from 1862 to 1892. Actually, these three decades prepared the ground reality of the outbreaks of 1893-94.

III

The revolt of 1861 created a vast gap between the ruler and the ruled; and it began to unabate as the time rolled on. Suspicion, enmity, disdain and belligerent tendency developed on both sides. The ruler, gradually, started to increase the number of their forces to avert any further revolts in the coming days, and created, thus, a sense of fear in the minds of the restless ryots. The *Raij-mels* also remained silent for some time for the fear of the colonial government.

The ruled, on the contrary, developed a deep racial bitterness towards the ruler during this period, and opposed the inferior status that was granted to them. The peasants had to lose their bargaining power after 1861, and the chances of getting their grievances, thus, were removed. Finally, the people organized at grass-root level against the government, and the government also remained stony hard to divide the masses. After 1861, the colonial government learnt that until and unless the voices of the people were crushed and silenced, their existence in Assam would bound to be menaced and jeopardized. They, therefore, became alert and firm to suppress the voices of the people at any cost. The mass people also, on the contrary, prepared themselves against the government but waited for better opportunity to come.

Following the Phulaguri uprising of 1861, the government held enquiries and adopted certain measures to remove the apprehension of the people by taking action on the guilty officers, but did not stop the enhancement of land revenue. The people were firm not to pay the enhanced rate of revenue, on one hand and the government, on the other, was also adamant to collect that at any cost, even by using force if needed. As a result, confrontation and enmity developed. The relation between the ruler and the ruled started deteriorating in Nowgong, Kamrup and Darrang in comparison to the other districts of Assam. Denial to accept the government's verdict gave birth to anguish and enmity in these three districts in later period.

The years of 1862-92 may be termed as the years of peasants' unrest and it is proved from their *mels* held in the different districts of Assam, especially, in Kamrup and Darrang. The aggrieved, the Hindus and the Muslims, both met in their *mels* and protested against the increased revenues on land. From the early 1869, the *mels* were frequently held at Patharughat of Mangaldoi sub-division of erstwhile Darrang; and at Gobindapur, Hadira and Bajali in the north of the district of Kamrup. When the year of 1869 was a blessing for the mankind (as M.K.Gandhi was born in that year); the burden of revenue, on the contrary, was doubled in Assam in that same year.

The *Raij-mel* of Phulaguri had far reaching impact on the minds of the people of Assam as they were becoming discontented with the fiscal policy of the colonial government. Surprisingly, the authority, instead of paying attention to the impact of the Phulaguri *Raij-mel*, was trying to enhance the rates of revenue even after that. The rates of revenue were doubled in 1869. At the time of making the revenue rate double in 1869, they did not consider even for once the backward state of agriculture of Assam. The ryots of Patharughat were the first to react it, and the *Raij-mels* were held at different villages in protest against the enhancement of land revenue. Colonel Comber, the Deputy Commissioner; Driberg, the Sub-Divisional Officer and the District Superintendent of Police, they all rushed to Patharughat. The officers were besieged on the very night by a disorderly mob at Patharughat but fortunately, no extreme measures were resorted to on either side. The officers were said to have been shut in a bungalow at Patharughat.[94] The impact of revenue hike was seen among the peasants of Nowgong also in 1869, as the government ignored their capacity and capability.

Against the enhancement of land revenue, the peasants of different parts of the erstwhile district of Kamrup were found to have been aggrieved; and as a result of which, the *Raij-mels* were summoned for the discussion on the issue. The *Raij-mels* were frequently held at Bajali, Hadira and Gobindapur from the early part of 1869. The *mels* decided not to pay the enhanced revenue and also for its remission. Despite the scanty of source materials of the *Raij-mels*, it is said that Mr.Campbell, the Sub-Divisional Officer of Barpeta, received information that a *Raij-mel* was held at Gobindapur to protest the augmented rates of land revenue towards the end of January, 1869. Mr.Campbell directed the Police Inspector of Barpeta to enquire instantly about the proceedings of the *Raij-mels* and also to furnish the names of the prominent leaders. The Police Inspector rushed to the spot but could not disperse the mob as his party was consisted of a few men with muskets. It is said that the party had to quit the place under the cover of darkness. The Inspector, of course, collected the names of some *melkies* but failed to forward to the higher authority the details of the *Raij-mels*. Major Agnew, the Officiating Commissioner, expressed his anguish and condemned the Inspector for his failure and directed him to take coercive action for quelling the *Raij-mels*. As a result of the stern action of the government, the *Raij-mels* could not be held regularly. But that did not end the discontent of the peasants, and the practice of holding the *Raij-mels* went on, though not regularly.[95]

In spite of the ignition among the peasantry, the colonial government was pursuing its revenue enhancement policy slowly and steadily. In 1870, the government decided for settlement of all kinds of land, and imposed rents accordingly. Actually, they did this in order to make sure the quantum of revenue collection. The peasants were forced to pay rent for the surplus and fallow lands which they enjoyed revenue free. Thus, there was augmenting resentment against the revenue measures of the alien government. After two decades, in May, 1890, the *Raij-mels* were held again in different tahsil areas of Hajo. The leaders of the *Raij-mels* decided not to pay rent of land which compelled the acting Deputy Commissioner of Kamrup to come to Hajo on the 27th May, 1890 probably for pursuing the peasants to pay revenue. The Superintendent of Police also accompanied him. The Deputy Commissioner and Superintendent of Police's arrival at Hajo indicate that the situation was tense there. Babu Uday Chandra Barua, the tahsildar of Hajo was said to have issued the list of defaulters. He was assisted by the *gaon-burhas*.

Barua, the tahsildar, might have been menaced for his attempt to collect land rent. The Acting Deputy Commissioner on tour, it is said, was assailed, probably for his act of mediation which forced the Deputy Commissioner to go to the place of occurrence on the June7. He was accompanied by an Acting Judge. Anyway, on the June12, the case was tried and the accused were sentenced to six months imprisonment.[96]

In 1892, the people of Patidarang, Nalbari, Barama, Bajali and also other five mauzas of upper Barbhag and Sarukhetri in their *mels* decided not to give revenue to the government.

Actually, though there was no occurrence of movements of serious nature during this period (1862-92), yet cold wave of protest and ignition blew in the minds of the people silently all through-out the years. This period, indeed, prepared the ground-road for the outbreaks which culminated in Kamrup and Darrang in 1893-94.

Notes & References

1. Barpujari, H.K. (eds) : *Political History of Assam*, Vol. I, Publication Board of Assam, Guwahati, Second Edition, 1999, Preface-xii.

2. Barua, S.L. : *A Comprehensive History of Assam*, Munshiram Manoharlal Publishers Pvt. Ltd., New Delhi, 2005, P. 507.

3. Barpujari (eds) : *op. cit.*

4. Barpujari, H.K. : *The American Missionaries and N.E. India* (1836-1900), Delhi, 1986, P. 94.

5. Nath, Dambarudhar : 'Satradhikar's role in national awakening' in A. Bhuyan's (ed), *National Upsurge in Assam*, Govt. of Assam, Guwahati, 2000, P. 136.

6. Kalita, R.C. : 'Opium Prohibition and Rai Bahadur J.N.Barua', *NEIHA-XVI*, 1995, P. 187.

7. Trevelyan, G.M. : *English Social History*, Orient Longman Ltd, Mumbai, 2001, PP. 552-553.

8. Sarma, R.S. : *Indian Feudalism* (A.D. 300 to 1200), Mac Millan India Ltd., Madras, Reprinted, 1996, P. 267.

9. Bhattacharjee, J.B. : 'Trade and Colony—the British Colonization of N.E. India', *NEIHA*, Shillong, 2000, PP. 2-3.

10. *cf.* Doshi, S.L. & Jain, P.C. : *Rural Sociology*, Rawat Publications, Jaipur, New Delhi, 2006, PP. 137-138.

11. *cf. Ibid.* : PP. 117-118, 120.

12. Gait, Sir E. : *A History of Assam*, L. B. S. Publications, Guwahati, Assam, 1984, P. 343.

13. : *Krishna Sarma's Diary*, A. P. Board, Guwahati, 1972, P. 249.

14. Choudhury, Anil Roy : 'Asamot Praja-Abhyutthan

15. Saikia, Rajen : *Social and Economic History of Assam* (1853-1921), Manohar, New Delhi, 2001, PP. 86-87.

16. Goswami, S.D. : 'The Raij-mels

17. Saikia : *op. cit.*, P. 108.

18. Kalita : *op. cit.*, P. 184.

19. Guha, A. : *Zamindarkalin Goalpara Jilar Artha Samajik Avastha—Eti Oitihasik Drishtipat*, Natun Sahitya Parishad, Guwahati, 2000, P. 43.

20. Saikia : *op. cit.*, PP. 86-87.

21. Guha, A. : *Planter Raj to Swaraj* (1826-1947), Tulika Books, New Delhi, 2006, PP. 74-75.

22. Trevelyan : *op. cit.*, PP. 552-553.

23. Hussain, M. : *The Assam Movement—Class, Ideology and Identity*, Manak publications Pvt. Ltd. in association with H. A. Publications, New Delhi, 1993, PP. 44-45.

24. Barpujari (eds) : *Political History of Assam*, Vol. I, P. B. of Assam, Guwahati, Second edition, 1999, PP. 121-122.

25. Srinivasa, M.N. : *Social Change in Modern India*, Orient Longman Ltd., New Delhi, 1995, P. 52.

26. Saikia : *op. cit.*, P. 226.

27. Hunter, W.W. : *A Statistical Account of Assam*, Vol. I, P. 370, Vol. II, PP. 70-71.

28. *Ibid.* : Vol. I, PP. 54, 258., Vol. II, P. 71.

29. : *Report on the Administration of Land Revenue*, 1886-1887.

30. : *Report on the Administration of Land Revenue*, 1881-82, 82-83, 83-84, 84-85, 85-86, 86-87 (1881-87), Shillong, 1881.

31. Saikia : *op. cit.*, PP. 87-88

32. Guha : *op. cit.*, P. 27

33. Bhattacharjee : *op. cit.*, P. 54

34. Mills : *Report on the Province of Assam*, Publication Board of Assam, Guwahati, Second Edition, 1984, P. 16.

35. Saikia : *op. cit.*, P. 228.

36. Karna, M.N. : *Agrarian Structure and Land Reforms in Assam*, Regency Publications, New Delhi, 2004, PP. 25-26.

37. Saikia : *op. cit.*, PP. 226-227.

38. Guha : *op. cit.*, P. 13.

39. *Ibid.* : P. 53.

40. *Ibid.* : P. 35.

41. *Ibid.* : PP. 12,34.

42. *Ibid.* : P. 12.

43. Barooah, D.P. : 'The rebellion of 1857 and its impact on Assam' in A. Bhuyan's (ed), *op. cit.*, P. 42.

44. Purkayastha, S. : 'Rubber trade and cultivation in Assam during the colonial period', *NEIHA—XVI*, 1995, PP. 204, 207.

45. *Ibid.* : P. 208.

46. Gait : *op. cit.*, PP. 360-361.

47. Barua : *op. cit.*, PP. 506-507.

48. Hilaly, Sarah : 'Railways in Assam and immigration of peasants in the colonial period', *NEIHA—XXII*, 2001, P. 227.

49. Gohain, H. (eds) : *Asom Andolon—Pratishruti aru Phala Shruti*, Banalata, Guwahati, 2007, P. 18.

50. Mills, A.J.M. : *op. cit.*

51. Goswami, H. : *Population trends in the Brahmaputra valley*, Mittal Publications, New Delhi, 1985, P. 176.

52. Guha : Appendix—3, *op. cit.*, P. 279.

53. Sarma, N. : *The rise and growth of the peasant movement in Kamrup district between 1826-1900* (Ph. D. Thesis) G. U., Guwahati, 2003, P. 77.

    Mahanta, A. : 'Planter Raj to Swaraj—Eti Paryalochana' in S. N. Barman's (et-al), *Oitihya aru Itihash*, Journal Emporium, Nalbari, 2005, P. 266.

54. Barpujari (eds) : *op. cit.*, PP. 67-68.

55. Nag, S. : 'Religion and ethnicity in class formation

56. Guha : *op. cit.*, P. 68.

57. Goswami, S.D. : 'The British taxation policy in Assam' in J. B. Bhattacharjee's (ed), *Studies in the Economic History of NE India*, Har Anand Publications, New Delhi, 1994, P. 95.

58. Barpujari (eds) : *op. cit.*, PP. 67-68.
59. Kaushal, G. : *Economic History of India* (1757-1966), Kalyani Publishers, New Delhi, Reprint, 1991, P. 8.
60. *Ibid.* : P. 180.
61. Saikia : *op. cit.*, P. 226.
62. *Ibid.* : P. 74.
63. Kaushal : *op. cit.*, P. 183.
64. Goswami, P.C. : *The Economic Development of Assam*, Asia Publishing House, Bombay, 1963, P. 60.
65. Guha : *op. cit.*, P. 39.
66. Ghosh, Lipi : 'Indebtedness in peasant sector
67. Nag, S. : 'Social reaction to bania exploitation' in J. B. Bhattacharjee's (ed), *Studies in the Economic History of N. E. India*, NEHU publications, Shillong, 1986, P. 365.
68. Ghosh : *op. cit.*, P. 339.
69. *Ibid.* : P. 342.
70. Nag : *op. cit.*, PP. 367-368.
71. Bhattacharjee : *op. cit.*, P. 87.
72. Saikia : *op. cit.*, P. 57.
73. Ghosh : *op. cit.*, PP. 340-341.
74. *Ibid.* : P. 340.
75. M'Cosh, John : *Topography of Assam*, Logos press, New Delhi, Second Reprint, 2000, PP. 25-26.
76. Nag : *op. cit.*, P. 365.
77. Saha, S : *1942—struggle—a study of grass root nationalism in the districts of Darrang and Nowgong* (M. Phil dissertation), NEHU, Shillong, 1984, P. 75.
78. Ghosh : *op. cit.*, P. 341.
79. Saha : *op. cit.*, P. 76.
80. Barpujari (eds) : *op. cit.*, P. 61.
81. *Ibid.* : P. 159.
82. *Ibid.* : P. 30.
83. Srinivasa : *op. cit.*, P. 51.
84. Chopra, P.N., Puri, B.N. & Das, M.N. : *A Social, Cultural and Economic History of India*, Vol. III, Mac Millan India Ltd., Madras, 1990, P. 167.

85. Bhuyan, J.N. : 'Purnananda Sarma Baruar Katha' in J. N. Bhuyan's, *Unavimsa Satika: Shrishti aru Chetana*, L. B. Stall, Guwahati, 1998, P. 130.

86. Barooah, D.P. : *op. cit.*, P. 41.

87. Goswami, I. : *Adhapora Pandulipi*, Lili Prakashika, Nowgong, 1999, P. 34.

88. Barooah : *op. cit.*, P. 41.

89. Srinivasa : *op. cit.*, P. 52.

90. Saikia : *op. cit.*, P. 168.

91. Gohain, Hiren : *Asomiya Jatia Jivanat Mahapurushiya Parampara*, L. B. Stall, Guwahati, 1990, Aag-katha.

92. Bhuyan, J.N. : 'Gunabhiram Baruar Dinar Nowgong' in J. N. Bhuyan's *op. cit.*, P. 142.

93. Guha : *op. cit.*, P. 284.

94. : *Assam Secretariat Proceedings* for Sept. 1894, bearing on the Rangia, Lachima and Patharughat riots . . . . Proceeding No. 320.

95. Barman, Santo : *The Raij-mel—A Study of the Mel System in Assam*, Spectrum Publication, Guwahati, Delhi, 2005, PP. 74-75.

96. *Ibid.* : PP. 75-76.

CHAPTER – EIGHT

THE UPRISINGS: 1893-94

Kamrup in colonial period was bounded on the west by Goalpara, on the north by Bhutan, on the south by the Khashi hills, on the east (north of the Brahmaputra) by Darrang and (South of the Brahmaputra) by Nowgong. Describing the revenue system of Kamrup, M'Cosh says, 'the *zillah* of *Kamroop* is divided into 54 *Pergunnahs*, 5 *Deshes*, 9 *Dwars* and 7 *Choumooas* and these when large are subdivided into *Talooks* and *Mouzahs*, with a still further distinction into *Kiraj* and *Lakiraj* lands; *Kiraj* being applied to lands assessed to full amount and *Lakiraj* to privileged lands which are assessed at a low rate.'[1] The soil of the most part of the Brahmaputra valley is composed of rich black mould. The Brahmaputra may be called great drain of Assam.[2]

In Kamrup, all the three varieties of rice, like *ahu, bao* and *sali* were cultivated. Due to available production of rice, it was comparatively cheaper in Kamrup. In 1878, 14 *seers* rice could be purchased for a rupee.[3] Other crops included mustard seed, *til, matikalai, mug, masuri,* hemp, jute and sugarcane. In Kamrup, cultivation of rice was common to every family engaged in agriculture. The area of rice cultivation was started to have increased by 27% in between 1850 and 1875. The exact return for 1875-76 showed that out of 4,50,792 acres under cultivation, 3,42,481acres or more than 76% was covered by rice; 24,363 acres by other food grains; 55,335 by oil seeds; 3,391 by sugarcane; 2,351 by cotton; 4,515 by tea and 19,352 by other crops.[4]

Northern Central Assam or Darrang lies entirely on the north bank of the Brahmaputra. She is separated from Kamrup on the west and from

Na-duar on the east; on the north, she is bounded by Bhutan and the land of the Akas and the Daphlas; and on the south by the Brahmaputra.[5]

Sali rice was the staple crop in Darrang and *ahu* occupied a small percentage of cultivable lands. For Sixteen years (1850-1866), there was a gradual increase in the area under rice cultivation. In 1850, it covered 1,45,109 acres of land and by 1866, it registered a downward trend. In 1870, the area under rice cultivation was recorded 2,11,023 acres; the figures further went down to 1,82,172 acres in 1875. The approximate area under different crops in 1874-75 was: rice cultivation occupied 1,82,172 acres; mustard 3,644 acres; sugarcane 1,126 acres; *matikalai* 1,828 acres; *mug* 955 acres; *til* 116 acres; cotton 850 acres and jute 184 acres only.[6] It remains expressed that rice was costlier in Darrang and Lakhimpur. In Kamrup and Nowgong while 14 and 13 *seers* rice were obtainable for a rupee in 1878; on the contrary, 10 and 9 *seers* rice could be purchased for a rupee in Darrang and Lakhimpur in the same year.[7]

II

The impending enhancement of land revenue rates under the new settlement of 1892 led to a widespread discontentment in the minds of the peasants of the Brahmaputra valley. The Chief Commissioner who was on a tour to the Brahmaputra valley in the winter of 1892, received complaint from the ryots that they were unable to pay the enhanced land revenue as they had to pay the government an exorbitant price for opium. The Jorhat *Sarbajanik Sabha* also protested the government policy by holding a series of meetings from the October, 1892 to the Feb, 1893.[8]

The new settlement fixed the land value and the rate on the basis of the population density and the demand for land in each village. Initially, in the Brahmaputra valley, the revised rates involved an enhancement of 53 percent on average but in many villages, it was as high as 70 to 100 %. The Chief Commissioner, though in the beginning declined to pay any attention to the complaints of the ryots, finally, he passed orders to reduce the increased rate to an average 37%. But the ryots were not satisfied at this and demanded postponement of the collection even at that reduced rate until the last orders of the Government of India on the pending appeals were received. The Chief Commissioner was reluctant to any such postponement.

The people of Kamrup and Central Assam organized themselves once more against the government's move and convened *mels* to decide upon their fate with 'no-rent campaign.' According to Guha, the demand for enhanced land revenue would push them further into the grip of the Marwari traders to get advances for paying the land revenue, and caught, thus, in a vicious circle of intensified exploitation, they started agitating not only against the government but also against the Marwari traders.[9] Kalita also says that regular enhancement of land revenue and tax had become a great source of misery and discontentment among the peasantry in India, and it was more so in the Brahmaputra valley.[10]

The peasants when (again after 1861) found the government ruthlessly imposing higher rates of assessment, rose in rebellion towards the close of the 19th century inviting a series of potests beginning with December, 1893. If Nowgong led the way of peasant unrest via the Phulaguri of 1861, then the turn of Kamrup and Darrang was the next to take-up the cudgels on behalf of the oppressed peasantry of Assam via the Rangia and the Lachima uprisings of Kamrup, and the Patharughat uprising of Darrang.

For nearly three decades after 1861, outwardly there was no movement in Assam except a bubble in 1868-69. But the whole course altered in 1892, when Sir William Ward, the Chief Commissioner of Assam, augmented the rates of revenue on land in the new settlement to 70 to 80% and sometime even 100%. Finally, the simmering discontent of the people took terrific turn against this assessment in Kamrup and Darrang in 1893-94.

It is noteworthy to mention that despite the decreasing production rate of crops, there was no respite from the proposed rate of assessment on land. Even going ahead, the colonial apparatus forcibly realized taxes from the impoverished peasantry. Seeing such deplorable and awkward position of the people, the *keyas* intensified their exploitation scale and the people fell in their trap. The people, finally, understood the motives of the *keyas* and started to ventilate their grievances not only against the government but also against them. The looting of the Rangia *bazaar* by a crowd of 200 to 250 people, mostly of Kacharis on the morning of the Dec 24, 1893 is the clear example of this.[11]

In the evening of the 24th Dec, when the peasants returning from Belagaon *mel* near Rangia, they gutted-down the huts at the Rangia *bazaar* and threatened a *keya* shopkeeper that his shop would be looted on the 30th December as their presence had increased the revenue burden on land.[12] They considered the traders to be in hand in glove with the British.

On the 30th December, 1893, there was a massive gathering at Rangia where about 2500 to 3000 people participated. This massive gathering held demonstration all the night and threatened destruction of the *thana*, post-office and the tahsildar's bungalow. The people of Rangia had their tremendous disdain towards Radhanath Barua, the tahsildar of Rangia. Almost all the people of seven mauzas of Rangia tahsil (East and West Badigog, East and West Barbhag, Kaurbaha, Panduri, East Cutcherry Mahal) never forgot his exaction, and he was, finally, targeted by them.[13] Threatening of destruction of *thana*, post-office and the tahsildar's bungalow was taken seriously by the government, and armed-police was summoned later to stop it but failed completely.

On the 6th January, 1893, R.B.McCabe, the Deputy Commissioner of Kamrup arrived at Rangia with a police party under Padmaram Kachari, the *daroga*[14] and arrested some persons alleged to have been implicated in the incident of the 24th Dec, 1893. The arrests, however, did not prevent the people from further attacks. On the 10th to the 17th Jan, 1894, a large crowd of about three thousand gathered at near Rangia *thana*. The castes and tribes, like the Koch, Kalita, Saloi, Kaivarta, Namasudra, Nath, Napit, Sonari, Baishya, Bania, Bodo-Kacharis and the muslims coming from far flung vllages assembled at Kadamtal-Pandarthan and took decision, and then began to march towards Rangia. The tribal farmers along-with their counterparts of other communities also took part in it.[15]

They with cries 'we won't pay at the increased rate', started coming closer to Rangia *thana*. They were asked by the Deputy Commissioner to disperse, but refused his order and even dared to release forcibly of their comrades Praneswar Goswami (Kon), Abhay Choudhury, Kirti Lahkar, Joltiram Kalita, Muktaram Bayan Kalita, Rahmat Khalipha and Parashuram Baro who were detained and locked-up at the time of submitting memorandum to the Deputy Commissioner. For taking part in the *mel*; Joltiram Kalita, a mandal of Batakuchi, was dismissed from his service.[16]

Disobedience of order compelled McCabe to open fire on the gatherings which forced them to retreat. In response to the violent outbursts, the colonial government effected a reign of terror. There were huge casualties in Rangia upheaval but the numbers, that were shown, were too few. Hiding the actual numbers and the fact was an easy matter for the colonial government. Finally, notices were issued for the maintenance of peace and harmony; and the leaders of the affected areas were appointed as the special constables. A detachment of the 44th Gurkha Rifles and the Volunteer Force were requisitioned to suppress the defiant people. All licensed guns in Rangia, Barama, Nalbari and Bajali tahsils were seized.[17]

The *mels* at Patidarang, Nalbari, Barama, Bajali, Hajo, Tamulpur and under Sarukhetri mauza were banned. However, the situation in the northern Kamrup did not change and the ryots continued to decline to pay the enhanced rent by organizing *mels* at Pandarthan of Nalbari. As a result, out of the total revenue demand of 10.5 lakhs in the Barpeta subdivision, not more than 1.5 lakhs could be collected.[18]

Moreover, the *mels* were said to have appointed their own *daks* to carry out their dictates from one village to another, and organized *lathials* to resist attachment of assets. As a result, the *ryots* were placed in between the edges of blade and fire.

In spite of government's ban, the *mels* continued in some part of northern Kamrup, like Sarukhetri mauza. The people from all walks of life: the ryots, bell-metal artisans, *chahuas*, brahmins, muslims, *satriya gosains* and the villagers from the entire Sarukhetri mauza assembled at Panagaon-*tup*, a mound like area between Lachima and Sarukhetri on the Jan, 1894. Lachima is a village under Sarukhetri mauza and the river Alpa flows between Lachima and Sarthebari. The villages Sarthebari, Karakuchi, Gomura, Palla, Namsala, Helsa, Bengapara, Baniakuchi, Haldhibari, Kapla, Byaskuchi, Majdia, Belbari, Baghmara, Lachima and Amrikhowa all were under erstwhile Sarukhetri mauza. In the Panagaon-tup; Jogeswar Goswami, the *satradhikar* of Byaskuchi *satra*, presided over the *mel*.[19] It remains expressed that altogether 140 muslim inhabitants from Lachima, Panagaon and Sarthebari took active part in the *mels*, and by their participation, they sacrificed lot for the cause of Sarukhetri. Babari Fakir was their prominent leader.[20]

Enhancement of revenue in 1892 by 70 to 80% and sometime even at 100% made the situation of entire northern Kamrup volatile as it was the highest of the districts of the Assam province. On the January, 1894 when the people assembled at Panagaon-*tup*, there they decided not to pay the enhanced rate of revenue to the government. To them, in lieu of settling the land and calculating the revenue from each assessee, it was in reality 'tekeli-bhanga' (jar-breaking) over their heads.[21]

In the meantime, on the 21st January, 1894, when Dasaram Choudhury, a mauzadar along with Haliram Misra, a mandal of the area, reached Kapla near Lachima in the Sarukhetri mauza of Kamrup to collect revenue, the peasants declined to comply with the order. But when they insisted on forcible collection of revenue, a group of ryots assaulted the mauzadar and the mandal both. Again M.C.Bordoloi, an Extra-Assistant Commissioner was fined of Rs.5/ for his ill behaviour towards the *mels*. Seeing all this, the Sub-Divisional Officer ordered the police to break the *mel* which further excited them. The administration apprehended 75 persons finally in connection with the incidents. Arrested persons were Ananta Dev Goswami, Debi Nath Sarma, Makuram Talukdar (90 years), Mangalram Talukdar (96 years), Achyutananda Goswami (70years), Sampadram Deka (40 Years), Yogeswar Goswami (65 years, Byaskuchi) and Pusparam Kahar (60Year, Sarthebari).[22] But soon they were forcibly released. Realizing the gravity of the matter, the Deputy Commissioner himself arrived at Lachima, and 59 leaders were arrested by the 25th Jan, 1894 and were compelled to construct a temporary lock-up for themselves.[23]

About six thousand people in the same evening drew them near the Deputy Commissioner's camp and placed a mass petition for the release of the detained persons. But their petition was turned-down and forced to dispose when a bayonet charge was ordered.

The people who suffered a lot on behalf of the people of Sarukhetri were Jaycharan, Simbhu and Dandi of Baghmara; Leita Pitharam, Mitharam Aklu, Puspa Adhikari, Saona, Bansita Kankata, Kala Das Dehi, Dharani Mahanta, Gauri Rajot and Bolu of Kapla; Akalosa and Uma Jagatsa of Lachima; Yogeswar Goswami of Ranga; Kalduma of Byaskuchi; and Mangala Kahar and Puspa Kahar of Sarthebari.[24]

January 28, 1894 is a dark and black spot in the history of the British rule in India, and it cannot be obliterated easily. It is a black day not only for the *Patharughatians,* but also for the people of the Brahmaputra valley where about 140 innocent peasants embraced bullets on their breasts. Determined to crush the movement, the belligerent Deputy Commissioner of Darrang arrived at Patharughat with a force. The people who had gathered in thousands in anticipation of his arrival, sat down on the field facing the rest-house where he encamped. He first ordered them not to hold any *mels* and warned of the inevitable consequences of denial to it. In spite of his threats, the *mel* declined to disperse until and unless their honest demands were solved. A bayonet charge and volleys of firing followed, causing deaths and injuries to many. According to official source, the number of dead was 15, wounded

37; but the number was much higher than that. Lieutenant Berrington who carried the order of firing and was on the spot, reported that it was impossible to ascertain the exact number of casualties. Special constables were ordered to persuade the ryots to take their comrades to Mangaldoi dispensary.[25] This reveals that the number of wounded was heavier. It is said that altogether 140 people died at patharughat. The name of 64 had been traced-out and of them,7 were muslims.[26]

Eventually, they had to meet defeat before the power of arms of the British, though they resisted till last with cheering slogans '*Jai Hari*', '*Allah-Ho-Akbar*', and answered back by throwing bamboo sticks and clods of earth to their enemies. The rebels, however, could not keep up their heroic resistance movement for long in the face of unprotected and naked repression of the colonial guns. The ryots were tortured and their assets were seized and looted. Ultimately, they had to surrender before the government's demand by paying enhanced revenue.[27] '*Dolipuran*', a semi-contemporary Assamese metrical work by Narottam Das provides a description of the upheaval of Patharughat.

III

In colonial exploitation system, those who suffered and harassed at best at the hands of the British were the subaltern groups. That's why, they were the first to react against it. The causes, that led to the outbreaks of 1893-94, can be categorized into two: the common and general causes; and the uncommon and immediate causes. The causes, that generally found similar with the outbreak of 1861, are termed as the *common and general,* and the others, on the contrary, are termed as the *uncommon and immediate.*

Common and the general causes: The heaviest burden that the peasants had to bear was the land tax which was the root of all major social conflicts. The fiscal policy of the government was the cause of great social tension in Assam. In the fast changing situation, the peasants were forced to live in the most dissipated manner and in the absence of any comprehensive plan to mitigate their growing grievances, their conditions worsened with the progress of the British rule. Frequent enhancement of land revenue added fuel to the fire.[28]

The colonial government, by initiating an endless process of raising revenue demand, created scare in the minds of the peasantry. Moreover, the people could hardly forget the exactions of the chaudhuries and the tahsildars, and their thundering voice, 'if you do not pay, your property will be attached.'

The government by imposing high rate of revenue upon the land, not only made the people poor but also distorted their hope, dream, social status and glorious traditions. Enhancement had become a great source of irritation and dissatisfaction among the peasantry of the Brahmaputra valley. According to Sarkar, it provoked a different type of rural protest in the districts of Kamrup and Darrang of Assam in 1893-94.[29]

The excessive zeal, shown by the local authorities in improving the revenues of the government, caused considerable hardship, irritation and resentment to the ryots and it, finally, compelled them to take law in to their own hands. The reassessment was made on the basis of a new classification of the soil, and the manner how the rates were doubled in some cases, could not but arouse suspicion in the minds of the unsophisticated ryots that the government was out to fleece them.[30]

The Assam Land and Revenue Regulations of 1886 introduced an elaborate tenancy system, and it tightened the loopholes and brought all and sundry under a common code. The traditional landed gentry though secured concessions but they did not welcome the Regulations. These disgruntled men were waiting for a chance to wreak vengeance on the government and instigated the peasantry to move forward. The peasantry could not ignore them as they were their source of credit in the villages.[31] The condition of the peasantry worsened very much in 1891 onward due to the further rise of the prices of *abkari* opium.[32]

In 1893, when the Resettlement of Assam Valley was made again and revenue was raised from 70 to 80 percent and in some cases to 100 percent, people through-out the valley protested against this measure, and sent memorandum even to the Chief Commissioner. But the administration put a deaf ear to it.[33]

There are also some other exceptional aspects which ignited peoples' mind. The members of the royal family of the Darrang *Raja* and some of the direct descendants of the Ahom *Raja* were exempted from the payment of revenue when they had sought remission for that to the government. Though this is not directly related to the outbreaks of 1893-94 but indirectly it made people ignited. If the Royal family could be exempted from the payment of revenue in spite of having their capacity comparatively to those of the peasants, why not to them? Moreover, they did not want remission; they wanted only minimization of revenue rate. Again, the planters were the biggest land-holders at that time, but the revenue they paid was the lowest. It ignited the minds of the small land-holders and compelled them to come in to direct clash with the big.[34]

The priority of the government was always on quicker and larger collection of revenue rather than on increased production and efficient distribution. Encouragement was rarely given to induce the ryots to extend and improve their holdings. Complete protection of the peasants from the oppression had been a mere dream in Assam under the British.[35] The British revenue reforms and their agrarian policy did not do any good to the peasants. The present agrarian problem of rural India is the outcome of the colonial policy adopted by the British.[36]

Krishna Sarma strongly criticized the agrarian policy of the colonial government by depicting the wretched condition of the ryots. With the grant of *pattas* for 10, 20 and 30years, the rate of land revenue went on augmenting which aggravated further the condition of the rural peasants.[37] Moreover, the peasants' complaints were hardly discussed and examined.[38]

The revenue policy of the government dissatisfied the people of colonial Assam. Arbitrary and unjust settlement, and classification of land was neither based on scientific nor on actual productivity of the land. In addition to that, no permission was required for transfer of land during the Ahom regime, but now they could not transfer their land without the prior permission of the Deputy Commissioner. The number of *pattas* had been multiplied and the ryots, therefore, had to bear extra-stamp duty for that. The ryots of Assam under the British rule were neither land-holders nor tenants'at-will, and their leases could be cancelled on breach of any of the conditions.[39]

The Secretary to the Government of Bengal concluded that the imposition of numerous fines and taxes on the people was a major cause of the revolt.[40]

The middle class, merchants and traders did not welcome to the government's move of the imposition of taxes on their income; rather they opposed it. But the government was indifferent to them. The government, even going ahead a step, imposed license tax for collecting forest products. Some agricultural items were also not spared of paying taxes. In addition to that, the people in pre-colonial period, grazed their cattle freely and openly under the sky, but the government brought these grazing fields also under assessment.[41]

The tea plantation industry was one of the sources of colonial exploitation in Assam.[42] The plantation industries gave birth to two classes in Assam: the capitalists and the workers. The workers were mostly belongs to the Kachari tribe of Kamrup district.[43] The local labourers, especially, the Kachari tribe of Kamrup and Darrang worked in the tea gardens, but they were paid low rate of wages which compelled them to resort to the path of strike for high wages. In 1864, while a free labourer was paid as wage Rs.7 per month, the going rate of wages in the Assam Tea Company was only Rs.4 to 5 per month. They, finally, resorted to strike against this disparity but were dealt with badly. The planters made the worst use of semi feudal methods of reducing the condition of the labourers to a kind of serfdom.[44]

Sometime, by selling cultivators' land as wasteland to the tea companies, another way of exploitation was perpetrated. In Kamrup, some forest land had been made over to the Lower Assam Tea Company as wasteland. In Darrang and Nagaon also best *sal* trees areas had been sold as wasteland.[45] By purchasing the forest land at a nominal and cheap rate in the name of wasteland, they, thus, exploited the natural resources of the province.

The area of wasteland in the Assam province was so large that no necessity had till then arisen for checking the freedom of the ryots to transfer their land.[46] But the matter of concern was that towards the close of the 19th century, the freedom of the peasants had been checked. The government, for example, by encroaching upon the *jhum* rights of the tribal shifting cultivators,[47] checked their freedom.

The settlement of wasteland, especially, in Kamrup and Darrang was loudly decried by the mauzadars while the ryots had complaints of false measurements and exactions. The chaudhuries of Kamrup were dissatisfied with the operation of Captain Dalton's arrangements regarding wasteland.[48]

Two very important things to be noticed are that while the common peasant paid between Rs.1.8 and Rs.3 per acre annually as the land revenue, the planters held most of their land rent-free.[49] The other thing to be noticed is that due to the rise of the tea industry in Assam, the demand for productivity of foodgrain increased giving impetus to the importation of immigrant labourers from Bengal, who, finally, settled on their holdings.

Each and every family of Assam was engaged in agriculture, and it provided them almost all the necessaries that required for leading a happy and prosperous life. They cultivated rice, pulses, fruits and vegetables to supply their tables; mustard to light their houses; and silk and cotton to provide their garments. But there was no improvement of ploughs, harrows, hoes and spades, the breed of cattle, seeds and plants. Truly speaking, the government totally neglected this. In Assam, unfortunately, industrial growth and development had no links with the agriculture sector.[50] By bringing the vast area under cultivation, improving the nature of crops and extent of the livestock; the colonial government could have fetched revolutionary change in agricultural sector. The apparatus, and the process and methods of agriculture through-out the regions, hills and plains both, remain till date almost same. There were no available irrigation facility and fertilizer-application system in colonial period. To avail the services, namely the credit and marketing, there was lack of co-operative offices in Assam.[51] By introducing the Agriculture Technology Information and Development Centre, Animal Health Care Centre, Meteorology Department and Disaster Management System; the colonial government could have fetched green revolution in agriculture sector, but they dashed all the hopes of the people to the ground.

Disease of men and cattle; calamities, like floods and fire; lack of cheap credit facilities and wiles of moneylenders contributed to the impoverishment of the peasantry. In 1891-1901, many Kachari people had to migrate from Kamrup and Mangaldoi, and worked as tea labourers to get respite of the *kala-azar*.[52] As a result, the production of agriculture dwindled. It again aggravated when the Bhutias carried on their atrocities to the people of North Kamrup. Many people abandoned Kamrup, and took asylum in Darrang. It added fuel to the fire when Sir William Ward augmented the rate of revenue in 1891.[53]

The government by adopting certain measures could have checked the inter-districts migration. But due to lack of far-sightedness or interest, it expedited further resulting in tremendous set back to agriculture. Heavy cattle mortality also deteriorated their condition. Moreover, the peasants produced only for their annual need. Scarcely there was a surplus for sale or for rainy season. Their condition became bad in the event of failure of crops due to drought or floods. There was no crop insurance system to compensate the peasants from the damage of crops. As a result, their condition deteriorated more and more at the time of natural calamities.

Forests are a handmaid to agriculture as it influences climate, rain-fall, water supply, flood-control, soil erosion and fertility of the soil.[54] The British Government, though they reserved forest land in the name of wasteland, but conservation was not their intention. Their covetous eyes were only on the rich natural resources of the forests. They exported forest products by carrying on their wanton destruction of forest. Destruction of forest invited bad impact on climate whose impact directly fell on agriculture, resulting floods and drought. The government was directly or indirectly responsible for that, but they kept one eye closed at the time of natural calamities and kept another open for the realisation of revenue.

The advent of the plantation met only the demands and interests of the British planters, but the burden of these immigrant labourers fell on the agricultural land of Assam. By enacting a series of legislations from 1863 to 1901, and completing the Assam Bengal Railway, the colonial government tried to meet their labour problem. But these immigrated labourers created multi-dimensional problem. All sections were terribly affected by its evil effect. Due to the incentive of the government, the population of Assam increased from 12 lacs in 1853 to 24 lacs and 76 thousands in 1891. The immigrants of Assam became a source of social tension in later period of the 19th century. Kamalakanta Bhattacharyya, through his poem 'udgoni' (inspiration), therefore, appealed to the Assamese to shed-off their lethargy, and take lessons from the humiliations they were being subjected to.[55]

The people of Assam had to confront lots of problem due to the introduction of money economy. Currency was not available at the time of introduction of money economy, and introduction of money as the medium of exchange without substantial increase of currency created problem for them. The peasants had to walk long distances for two or three days to get their goods converted into cash.[56] Sometime for cash, they had to sell their land or to take loan from the money-lenders. Moreover, money economy was introduced at a time when there existed no trade to dispose of their goods. As a result, they could not pay their revenue in cash to the government in time. The rural peasants of North Kamrup and Mangaldoi faced lots of problem in adjusting with the new system, as they got less scope to sell their goods in cash.

The decline of village industries deprived the rural people of their subsidiary occupation, thereby, compelling them to take recourse to borrowing.[57] The ruin of village industries invited pressure of population on agriculture leading to the fragmentation of the peasants' holdings. The decline of cottage industries also created a vast numbers of landless rural labourers.[58] India was mercilessly impoverished through-out the British rule, and her famous manufactures were ruined, and the poor artisans and craftsmen were driven-out.[59] The abrupt change of their industrial policy created internal instability leading to great social unrest.[60]

The peasants in colonial period took recourse to borrowing, generally, during the time of famine and failure of crops. Social ceremonies also compelled them to take loans.[61] Indebtedness made their position like medieval serfs. According to the Census Report of 1891, there were 1,793 money-lenders in the Brahmaputra valley and of them, 1,211 were in Kamrup alone.[62] The loanees, they had to mortgage their movable or immovable properties, like land or land documents, ornaments and utensils as against the loan. According to Kaushal, a society steeped in debt is necessarily a social volcano which is always dangerous.[63]

The people of Assam, once upon a time, led a happy and contended life. But their halcyon days disappeared. Their once food-abundance land transmuted to the land of scarcity and poverty. Freshness and moistness disappeared from the land, and dryness appeared on the scene. The people held the British and the outsiders responsible for their such miserable and deplorable condition.

Abolition of the *paiks* by the British was good, and the people in general appreciated their humanitarian, holistic and equalitarian approach. But, finally, people understood their double standard. The *paiks* and labourers who welcomed the initiatives of the government at its initial stage, started to express their anguish in later period when they were forced to work in their gardens; on the contrary, the aristocrats and nobles who enjoyed the services of the *paiks* and maintained their royal standard, they also started to ventilate their grievances when they were deprived of their privileges. They were joined by the Brahmins and the Mahantas of Kamrup.[64]

The lease system introduced by them irritated the indigenous people of Assam. The land of Assam, according to the people of Assam, belongs to them. To them, foreign government had no authority to give lease right to the native, as the latter themselves were the owners of the land.[65]

The role of the Christian missionary was also not satisfactory. Their duty ought to have been to ask the government for rendering relief and medical facilities to the victims at the time of natural calamities. But they only insisted on conversion. So, the people placed them also in same line with the government.

The British judicial system established the principle of equality.[66] But it cannot be accepted wholly. For instance, the government eradicated slavery system in Assam to attract the freed people towards their tea gardens. In addition to that, the servants of the colonial government forcibly took away the goods of the ryots and the merchants for one fourth (1/4) of their value; and by ways of violence and oppression, they obliged the ryots to give five rupees for governments which were worth but one rupee.[67] In this way, the government machinery exploited and squeezed the ordinary peasants.

Nepotism, discrimination and bribes these engulfed the surroundings of the courts at that time, and the hope for getting justice from the courts was just like cry in the wilderness. Judiciary and police system were inactive and helpless to save the ryots from the exactions and extortions of the foreign apparatus.[68] The courts and legal system, it seems, encouraged the rich to oppress the poor.

The *banias* and money-lenders of India made her people poor.[69] During the British rule, the Marwaris took advantage of trading and commercial opportunities not only in their home regions but also outside.[70] The exploitation of the peasantry at the hands of the *keyas* and the local traders shattered the peace and harmony of village life. Statistics since 1862 to 1900 shows a general rise in prices of essential goods. Taking advantage of the situation, the *keyas* and the local money-lenders snatched away the ryots' last hold of land at a cheaper rate in the name of helping them.[71] Bhattacharyya, through his poem '*purnimar ratiloi chai*' (looking at the night of full moon) described how the Marwaris trapped the innocent and simple Assamese by their sweet and soft words, and made them sign in their *khatas*.[72] Years after years, the ryots had been pledging their crops to the Marwari traders. The demands for enhanced land revenue pushed them further in to their grips. Thus, caught in a vicious circle, the ryots started agitating against the Marwari traders also.[73] The *Marwaris* earned huge profits in Assam, but the profits, thus, earned were sent to Rajputana to enrich their land.[74] Like the Marwari traders, local traders also exploited their people. For example, the ryots of Kamrup were exploited not only by the Marwaris and foreign rulers, they were equally exploited by the local traders.[75] But surprisingly, the local people did not express their grievances against them.

Uncommon and immediate causes: The causes, which were not found similar with the outbreak of 1861, are termed as uncommon and immediate causes. The highhandedness of Radhanath Tahsilder was mainly responsible for the revolt of Rangia. Unlike the tahsilders of Kamrup, he supported the revenue hike and even encouraged the Deputy Commissioner of Kamrup in this drive. Those who could not pay their revenue in time, they were even forced to render their physical labour at his residence. Even the widows of the peasants were not spared and had been compelled to render their services at his residence from dawn to dusk. The mandals and *gaonburhas*, they had to give bribes to the tahsildar, what they did not like. So, almost all sections had their disdain towards him.[76] Inhuman exactions of Radhanath Barua compelled the peasants of Rangia to react against him.

The impending enhancement of land revenue rates under the new settlement, as notified in 1892, led to a widespread dissatisfaction that rocked the rural society. The ryots complained that as they had to pay the government an exorbitant price for opium, they were unable to pay the enhanced land revenue. The revised rates in the Brahmaputra valley, initially, involved an enhancement of 53 percent on average; but in many villages, it was as high as 70 to 100 percent and the highest was in Kamrup. Though the rates was reduced, finally, to an average 37 percent, but the ryots demanded postponement of the collection even at that reduced rate until the final orders of the Government of India, on the pending appeals, were received. The Chief Commissioner disallowed any such postponement which led to organize the peasant through the *Raij-mel*, and decided upon a no-rent campaign.[77]

The authority with the intention of increasing the amounts of revenue made settlement of the infertile lands also in the name of the local people. Where local people were in the mood of surrendering their lands to the government to get rid of taxes, the news of settlements of infertile lands in their name, added fuel to the fire. The people began to term it as '*tekeli bhonga piyal*' (jar breaking settlement). What the local people felt was that in lieu of settling the land and calculating the revenue from each assesses, it was in reality, '*tekeli bhanga*' over their heads. Yogeswar Goswami of Byaskuchi *satra* and other prominent persons of the locality protested it, and decided to launch no-revenue campaign leading to the arrest of several persons and their lodging up in temporary lock-up.[78]

M.C.Bordoloi, the Extra-Assistant Commissioner of Barpeta Sub-division came to the *mels* as a government representative. The peasants requested him for the remission and exemption of revenue. But he was more adamant even to listen to their problems, and threatened and behaved them like beasts. His rude and harsh behaviour, therefore, compelled the *Raij* to be ignited.[79]

Assault on the mandal and the maujadar by the people of Lachima was also responsible for the revolt of Lachima of 1893-94.The situation could have been evaded, if not, minimized its intensity to certain extent, had the people of Kapla village refrained from assaulting on the mandal and the maujadar on the 21st Jan, 1894. Assault on them, however, made the situation conflagrable leading to the arrest of several persons and their lodging up in temporary lock-up.[80]

In 1893, the land of Sarukhetri mauja was surveyed. According to the survey, the lease was given for non-arable land, and as a result, people had to pay revenue for their non-arable land also. Formerly, there was an advantage that if a cultivator neither cultivated a land nor gave revenue to the government, then the lease-holder could surrender his land to the government. But the survey of 1893 wiped-out this system, forbidding the people to surrender their arable and non-arable land even at the time of their worst financial condition. Some time, of course, they could do so at the cost of giving bribe to the mandals. Ultimately, all this gave birth to widespread dissatisfaction in the minds of the lease-holders of land.[81]

Das Ram Choudhury, the maujadar and Hali Ram, the mandal gave more importance in collecting revenue. They were the sincerest servants of the governement, and always cried for their master. Their collection nature became so much dreadful that whenever they visited the houses of peasants of Lachima for collecting revenue, the sound of crying of the house-holders rocked the sky. Their rapaciousness sometime even went beyond imagination. They seized ornaments, utensils, cattle and even the cloth of hand-looms. Finally, disdain and anguish penetrated in people's mind against them. Rent became the talk of the day, wherever and whenever two or three people assembled.[82]

Banning of the *Raij-mels* by R.B.McCabe, the Deputy Commissioner of Kamrup, neither could solve the problem of the government nor the peasants. The government by its ban tried to curb the rising tide of the *mels* but failed. The banning made the people belligerent, and took it as their prestige question. The Deputy Commissioner became adamant to curb the *mels,* and the people also, on the other hand, became obstinate not to be banned. In spite of his order, the *mels* declined to be banned, and continued to be as active as before at Nalbari, Barama and Bajali. Finally, this gave birth to confrontation between the government and the ryots, as both sides were firm in their determination and deliberations.

The uprisings of 1893-94 failed, but it had challenged the defensive capability of the colonial government. Use of traditional weapons as against the modern weapons was the main reason of the defeat of the peasants of Kamrup and Darrang. The peasants of Rangia, Lachima and Patharughat used traditional weapons, like spears, bows, arrows and *daos* as against the modern weapons of the British. Their weapons could not be compared with that of the British. The peasants sought to vanquish the mighty British with their bamboo pop-guns. The peasants of Patharughat failed as they fought pitched-battle with the help of their fish-spears, branches of trees, bamboo sticks and clods of earth. They cast these as missiles on the gunmen. While the arms men of the colonial power fought with their dresses and shoes, the peasants fought with their scanty wearing, barefoot and bare-hand.

Underestimation of the power and number of the British was the main reason that led to the hasty defeat of the peasants of Kamrup and Darrang.

The seize of license guns was one of the causes of their quick defeat. The people of Kamrup could have used their guns, had their guns not been seized by the government. All license guns in Rangia, Nalbari, Barama and Bajali tahsils, the storm centres were seized following the order of R.B.McCabe, the Deputy Commissioner of Kamrup.[83]

Lack of unity and worth organizers among the local leaders, and absence of proper leadership precipitated their haste defeat. Compared to the military skill, efficiency, decision making and adroitness, the local leaders were inferior to the colonial leaders. They had no any planned and long-termed scheme at their hands. Lack of common cause and different interest among the leaders brought their downfall. They failed to show the peasants the right way to fight. They could have gained something from the government by pursuing conciliatory and moderate ways. Idea of compromise, probably, did not develop till then in their mind, and most of the time, the revolts became conflagrable due to their inapt-handling.

R.B.McCabe, the Deputy Commissioner of Kamrup, became successful in winning some of the leaders to his side.[84] Probably, he enticed them by fulfilling their parochial interest. Moreover, by appointing the rebel leaders as constables at the disturbed areas, the power of the rebels was weakend. Thus, the shrewd and astute British could create division among the leaders.

Most of the time, it was found that the leaders of the *mels* had no control upon their people. For example, Kan Goswami appealed to the people not to give high revenue to the tahsildar of Rangia. Though, initially, his appeal was welcome, but finally, it was dashed to the ground by Rudra Sarma of Septi.[85] In addition to that, the leaders of Patharughat wanted to resist those who would be paying revenue to the government. From this, it can be inferred that, probably, somebody wanted to pay revenue to the government defying the order of their leaders which proves their weak control upon their people.

The people of Assam, at that time, groaned under economic hardship and probably, because of this, they could not fight a decisive battle against the administration.

The strong espionage system also helped the government in curbing the tide of the revolt. The administration could know about the rebel leaders, and of their *mels* through their spies. Some native also informed the government about the rebels, and their whereabouts. As a result, their secrecy leaked. Unfortunate is that, the native betrayed the native only for coins, and dug, thus, their own grave-yards.

Rumour, false propaganda from the side of the government also brought success to the government. On the other hand, the innocent peasants, they did not resort to such policy.

The strong British intelligence, and quick and timely decision of the Deputy Commissioner and the Superintendent of Police brought easy victory for the government. The government could collect secret information of the rebel leaders and of their sitting of the *mels,* through their intelligence and could, thus, take haste decision. If sometime, the number of troops sent to quell and disperse the *mels* was found short, immediately additional troops was sent on the basis of the reports of the intelligence. For instance, the situation of Lachima became tense following the assault on the mandal and the maujadar on the 21st Jan, 1894, but timely arrival of R.B.McCabe, the Deputy Commissioner of Kamrup, at Lachima on the 24th Jan, 1894 saved the situation from being conflagrated.

The quick and prompt decision of J.D.Anderson, the Deputy Commissioner of Darrang, to open fire on the mob who continued to approach towards him in spite of his order to leave the place, resulted scores of them lay dead and wounded along the Mangaldoi road. His instant decision brought victory to the government, on one hand, and defeat of the peasants of Patharughat, on the other.

The uprisings of 1893-94 were confined at the two districts only. Moreover, the entire Darrang and Kamrup districts, especially, South Kamrup were not conflagrated by their flame. The revolts were highly localized, and restricted to some areas only. Many areas remained undisturbed, so, the administration found no problem to curb them. Sporadic outbursts helped the government to quell the uprisings instantly.

The uprisings failed to embrace all sections of the society. Had all sections, irrespective to high and low, rich and poor, governmental and non-governmental employees stretched-out their helping hands to the peasants, and fought sincerely for them, probably, there was scope of lasting the revolts for more time. Many did not help the peasants in spite of having sympathy due to losing their jobs. For example, Sonaram Talukdar, a school teacher had been discharged from his job due to his taking part in the *Raij-mels,* and even his primary school of Byaskuchi was also banned. This, however, created scare in the minds of others, and therefore, remained silent.[86]

Some sections supported the peasants but they did not stretch-out their helping hands to them. For instance, an unknown Barua of Jayantipur told Kan Goswami, Rahmat Khalipha and Abhay Choudhury that he would not go openly against the government.[87] Moreover, the incident of Lachima and Patharughat failed to stir the imagination of the educated minds.[88] In addition to that, though all peasants fought together, their social and economic disparity also created division among them. The rich peasants, how sincerely they did fight with the poor, that is under scanner.

Some of the leaders did not join openly against the British in spite of having their grievances against them. These disgruntled men were waiting for a chance to wreak vengeance on them. The uprisings of 1893-94 gave opportunity to this section who wasting no time, began to instigate the peasants to move forward. The peasants could not ignore their leaders' command as they were the source of credit in the villages. They appeared as saviours, but they were the first to retreat.[89] In the face of government repression, the peasantry stood their ground, made sacrifices, but the leaders betrayed them and disappeared. Their proxy resistance broke-down.[90]

Ever-preparedness and ever-readiness also brought victory to the British Government. They were ever ready to face any type of situation. The rebels, on the other hand, whatever they did, did that secretly. Ever-preparedness and ever-readiness-was not found in them.

269

As against the cool, meticulous and contemplated decision of the administration, the rebel leaders took prompt and haughty decision which precipitated their ruin.

The British administration always resorted to well-equipped strategy and manoeuvre. But the peasants' mode of protest was obsolete and outdated. Defamation, nameless sabotage, tales, jealous gossiping, rumours, character-assassination and nicknames these were, probably, the symbolic resistance of the peasants against the government.[91] Foot dragging, house burning, hypocrisy, petty theft these were, probably, resorted by the peasants which, finally, evaporated in front of the gun-fire of the government. The British language of protest was guns and brains. But the peasants of Kamrup and Darrang fought with their passions and emotions. Their main weapons were their bombastic words. The leaders assured the mob not to scare of colonial guns, and emboldened by this, the mob jumped onto the fire like moth, and brought their ruin.

To bring all under one roof, the leaders of the *mels* resorted to some psychological strategies, like blessings and cursings. But, how did such strategy act, it cannot be said. Had the *mels* adopted some better, practical and well-equipped strategy to unite their men, probably, they could have won. Their utopian, traditional, obsolete and superstitious strategy brought their ultimate failure.

Awkward position might also be responsible for making the condition of the peasants unstable and fragile. The ryots were in between two fires. If they supported the government, they were socially ostracized, and if supported the society, their property was seized. They, therefore, felt unstable, insecure and nervous.

Put ban on the *mels* on the 10th Jan, 1893, by R.B.McCabe, the Deputy Commissioner of Kamrup, gave birth to crestfallen in the minds of the peasants. The ban disheartened and dejected their mind. They, probably, began to think that if the government could put ban on the *mels*, it was too easy for the administration to quell them personally. So, ultimately, it resulted in their degradation.

IV

Almost all the movements from below, leadership is ostensibly provided by elite elements. The uprising of Maharastra in 1879 was led by Vasudeo Balvant Phadke, an English educated; the Deccan riots of

1875 was led by better off sections of the peasantry and in Maharastra, the Poona *Sarvajanik Sabha* took the dominant role encouraging peasants to resist payment of revenue from 1896 to 1900. In the famous Indigo revolt of 1859, the leadership came from the zamindari-based intellectuals, Calcutta educated *mukhtars* or attorneys and journalists. In Champaran in 1917, school teachers and members of urban intelligentsia also provided leadership. In Kheda and Bordoli of Gujarat, the leadership came from the upper castes *patidars* and brahmins. In the Tebhaga movement of Bengal (1946-47), initiative was clearly taken by the upper caste leadership of the Communist Party and *Kishan Sabha*. The peasant movements of Mewar (1913) and Durbhanga (1919-20) were also led by the men of same categories.[92] The no-revenue movements between 1885 and 1905 were characterized by the leadership of local notables. The no-revenue movements in Assam were led by the rural elite in 1893-94.[93]

There are two sets of leaders in Assam in 1893-94: one traditional and the other, new elite. As the Assamese middle class began to emerge as the most dominant class in the society, it not only changed the leadership of the peasant movements, but also brought a change in the nature of the movements. The peasants, finally, lost its own leadership, and accepted the leadership and ideas of the most dominant class.[94]

The non-cultivating classes, like the Brahmins, Gosains, Mahantas and Dolois apparently took the initiative and a leading role in the revolts of 1893-94. But, it was the poor peasantry and other sections of the rural poor including artisans who gave it a militant character.[95] For example, Pusparam Kahar, a plebian bell-metal artisan of Sarukshetri, is still remembered in the folk memory of Kamrup for his role in the revolt of Lachima of 1893-94. The other example of emergence of leadership (outside Assam) from below is that of Birsa Munda, the son of a share—cropper.[96] Moreover, R.B.McCabe, the Deputy Commissioner of Kamrup, reported that in addition to the Dolois, Gosains, Mahantas and principal land-holders; others who gave leadership were the dismissed head constables and released convicts.[97]

V

Basically, the insurrections of 1893-94 were secular in character, as all sections irrespective to castes and creeds, rich and poor, high and low united and fought against the colonial government.

The revolts of 1893-94, by nature, were not freedom movement. They were no-rent campaigns, organized with the object of compelling the government to yield to the will of the people by the withdrawal of unpopular measures of taxation. Compared to the Phulaguri upheaval of 1861, the no-rent agitations of 1893-94 were more organized and disciplined, though they failed. Regarding the outbreaks, it can be said that, they were not sudden and sporadic outbursts at all. The revolts of 1893-94 were mass revolts as all sections cultivating and non-cultivating, peasantry and non-peasantry took part in them. Despite having economic and social disparity and variations among the peasantry, all peasants rich and poor fought jointly against the *Raj*. Non-peasantry classes, like the Dolois, Gosains, Mahantas, Brahmins, artisans, local planters, local traders also hard-pressed by the measures of the government.[98] Abolition of posts and privileges, plantation and waste-land policy of the government, migration and industrial policy and various kinds of taxes made them vexed, and ultimately, the revolts assumed mass character by their participation. Flexibility in Assamese society also contributed lot to unite them together. De-sanskritization also helped lot to assume the revolts a mass character, as many higher castes gave-up their sanskritic value in order to have interaction with the lower castes. Thus, all joined hands together to show mobility and solidarity for establishing their own rights.

It remains expressed that the leaders of different Associations and *Rayat Sabhas* of the Brahmaputra valley took part in the sessions of Indian National Congress from 1886 to 1892. But, when their participation bore no fruits, then, they also stretched-out their helping hands to the peasants, boycotting the sessions of Indian National Congress in 1893 and 1894.[99]

By nature, the revolts of 1893 and 1894 were the peasants and state direct confrontation. The absence of intermediaries between the state and the peasantry was mainly responsible for the peasants and state direct confrontation. The fury of the ryots was directed against the money-lenders in the Deccan; against the Indigo planters in Bengal in 1860; against the zamindars in Pubna in 1872; but in Assam, they were an open rebellion against the government in 1893-94.[100]

VI

After 1894, there was no outburst of peasants in Assam. But that does not mean that they reconciled to the British rule. As a result of 1893-94's revolt, consciousness and awareness increased in Assam. In fact, they provided the main strength to the freedom struggle in Assam in further days.[101] The martyrdom of the peasants of Patharughat, Rangia and Lachima is the bench-mark in the history of struggle for freedom of India.

As a result of increased taxation, peasants abandoned cultivation leading to the stagnation in agriculture. Due to the involvement of the peasants in the *Raij-mels* and their flying to the neighbouring villages due to the increasing pressure of revenue, production of goods began to decrease resulting famine like situation in Assam.

The cleft between the ruler and the ruled widened after 1893-94. Suspicion, enmity and racial bitterness developed between them. The number of colonial forces was increased to strengthen the British control over the province so that further revolts could be averted and evaded in Assam.

The *Raij-mels* were suppressed ruthlessly which caused great indignation through-out the province. Finally, the Government of India had to concede to the partial reduction of the rates of assessment. At last, the government realized the folly of using force on an unwilling people, and communicated its decision of further diminishing the rates of revenue to 32.7% and also limiting the increase on an individual holding to about 50% on the previous rental.[102] The reduction of the land revenue, ultimately, by the British Government speaks for itself the success of the peasants' revolts, and it contributed enough groundwork to the national movement of India in later period.

The peasants' movements did not remain confined to the rural areas alone, gradually, the urban elite also began to make a united front with the proprietary peasants on all common issues against the rulers.[103]

As a result of the outbreaks of 1893-94, the twinkling sounds of the bell metal industry of Sarukhetri mauza was silenced. Annual Sarthebari *Sabha* was closed down for three years as a mark of homage to the martyrs who fought for noble cause.[104] Many became martyrs, many injured and many lost their properties as a result of the outbreaks of Kamrup and Darrang.

The revolts of 1893-94 failed, but they inspired the people of other places to revolt against exploitation in future. They also made an impact on the contemporary Assamese society.

The prices of goods in Assam in the 19th century was cheaper. But due to the augmantation of the government revenue on the *hats*, that also began to increase. The villagers, when they instead of bringing their produced goods for selling at *hats*, began to exchange that at their villages, it brought bad effects upon the government's *hats*. Many *hats* collapsed as a result of this.[105]

The no-rent campaigns of 1893-94 were no more successful than other resistance movements of its kind, if far reaching changes in the agrarian structure are taken as the exclusive criterion.[106] Despite that, they received adequate media coverage, and the matter was raised even in the Imperial Legislative Council by Rashbihari Ghose.

The impact of the revolts of 1893-94 fell in Sibsagar also. At a public meeting, the inhabitants of the district vehemently resented the sudden increase of land revenue.[107]

Though the lower strata of the peasantry had nothing in comparison to the dominant land owning caste, in spite of that, they did not revolt against them. Rather, forgetting their social and economic disparity, fought together under one roof against their common enemy, the British.

The revolts of 1893-94 failed, but it is a matter of great pride that the peasants of Assam, at least, became able to defend themselves against the mighty British. It is also because of their movements, the rate of revenue was reduced to 53% first and finally, to 32.7%. The revolts of 1893-94 may not be famous like the chivalrous and gallant deeds of Mangal Pandey or Lakshmi Bai; nevertheless, how the peasants of those regions fought against the mighty British, it is a rare instance in the history of India. Whatever might be the result of the revolts of 1893-94, the colonial government could realize the united strength and might of the peasants in their revolts.

The revolts of 1893-94 paved the way for organized challenge to the British rule. It heralded the beginning of a new era of peasant awakening in Assam by effectively upholding the value and utility of organized resistance to governmental injustice.[108] Though the cultivating and non-cultivating classes took part in the revolts of 1893-94, it was the rural poor who gave them militant character.

One noticeable aspect is that, in spite of Government of India's abatement order of revenue, the order of abatement did not reach Assam soon, due to the red-tapism of the colonial bureaucrats.[109] But, the cool and calm peasants, they did not resort to the path of revolt against the authority still then, in spite of having all reasonable scope and ground. It substantiated the patience of the peasants.

The revolts of 1893-94 were guided by reasons, not by passions and emotions. The peasants reacted and fought against exploitation and injustice; not for their rights, privileges and social status. 'The Indian Nation' on the 1st April, 1894, regarded the demands of the Raij-mels as real, not sentimental. According to the paper, the demand of revenue was heavier in Assam than in Bengal.

Though quelled with brutal force, the uprisings not only exposed the defects of the British rule, but also proved beyond doubt that any attempt, at socio-economic reconstruction without corresponding improvement in the moral and material condition of the people, was bound to be abortive. What was needed in Assam was the infusion of energy and enterprise into individual character, not malicious disregard for the problems of the ryots.[110]

The peasantry and the workers, who constituted the majority of the Indian masses, had showed their historic resentment against the government in 1893-94 without waiting for elite leadership, though the latter also, finally, took role in that.

As against the brahmins of Uttar Pradesh and Rajasthan who were occasionally found working as tenants of Rajputs and Jat landowners,[111] the brahmins of Assam, on the contrary, got their land ploughed by others. The brahmins of Assam in colonial period were high and educated class, and gave even the leadership in the outbreaks of 1893-94.

Unlike the two Tamil peasants' castes, the *vellalas* and the *padaiyachis* who wanted to be recorded as higher *varnas,* like the *vaishyas* and the *vanniyakula kshatriyas*; [112] there was found no such upward caste mobility among the peasants of Assam.

A most important value of westernization is humanitarianism which means welfare of all human being. Equalitarianism and secularism are both included in humanitarianism.[113] Significantly and surprisingly, the government neglected all these human values; otherwise, there would have been no revolts in 1893-94. When most of the educated and well-to-do sections of the society tolerated the exploitation of the government and remained silent, the illiterate rural masses protested the policy of the government, and had taken the path of revolts. It is, really, an important and laudable aspect to be noticed.

In the revolts of 1893-94, we find some important things. Some of the higher castes gave up their Sanskritic value (De-Sanskritisation) in order to have interaction with the lower castes. For example, we can mention the name of Jogeswar Goswami of Byaskuchi who in spite of his high position in the society, mixed up with the masses in general.

Significantly, the peasants of Assam of 1893-94 gave importance only on their economic problems, forgetting their religious and community bar. The muslims of Assam took a leading role in 1893-94. For example, they took a vital role in the revolt of Patharughat of 1893-94, maintaining and upholding their legacy of enmity that their ancestors had against the British. Of the 140, who died in 1894 at Patharughat, 64 had been identified. Of them, 7 were muslims. In addition to that, the main leader of the Panatup-*mels* of Lachima was Babri Phakir.[114]

The revolts of 1893-94 were a dispute between the ruler and the ruled. The colonial government blamed the peasants of Assam exonerating itself for all acts. They kept concealed all these acts only for their own colonial interest. The dead were buried, but how the sins could be!

The demands of the peasants were real, and the burden pressed upon the land was heavier even than in Bengal. So, their movements against the authority could, totally, be justified. But, late arrival of abatement order of revenue could not be justified. The rightful demand of the peasants, placed before the authority for compliance and consideration, could not be a crime using lethal weapons on them. The colonial government could have evaded the mass slaughtering with patient consideration adopting give and take policy instead of shooting and slaughtering the mass people whimsically. A black spot on the civilized British nation, of course, not desired by the British Commons, but caused by some of their trigger happy cynics without trying to understand the wants of their subjects.[115]

Notes & References

1. M'Cosh, John : *Topography of Assam*, Logos Press, New Delhi, Second Reprint, 2000, PP. 84, 121.
2. *Ibid.* : PP. 5-6.
3. *cf.* Saikia, Rajen : *Social and Economic History of Assam* (1853-1921 Manohar, New Delhi, 2001, Table—3.5, P. 110.
4. Hunter, W.W. : *A Statistical Account of Assam*, Vol. I, Reprint, Delhi, 1990, PP. 45-46.
5. M'Cosh : *op. cit.*, P. 93.
6. Saikia : *op. cit.*, P. 85.
7. *Ibid.* : P. 111.
8. Guha, A. : *Planter Raj to Swaraj* (1826-1947), Tulika Books, New Delhi, 2006, P. 41.
9. *Ibid.* : P. 42.
10. Kalita, R.C. : 'The Phulaguri uprising of 1861
11. Guha : *op. cit.*, P. 42.
12. Barpujari, H.K. (eds) : *Political History of Assam* (1826-1919), Vol. I, Publication Board of Assam, Guwahati, Second Edition, 1999, P. 97.
13. Kakati, Mayaram : 'Asamiya Terasa Sanat Rangia' in Pabin Kalita's (ed), *Rangia Raij-mel*, Raij-mel Krishak Martyrs Memorial Committee, Rangia, 2005, P. 3.
14. Anonymous : '1894 Sanar Rangia' in P. Kalita's (ed), *op. cit.*, PP. 69-70.
15. Deka, M.Kr. : 'Rajkadamtalar Oitihya—Bartaman aru Bhabisyat' in K. Kr. Deka's (ed), *Raij-mel Kadamtal*, Swahid Smriti Sangha, Paikarkuchi, Nalbari, 1996, PP. 10-11.
    Choudhury, Medini : 'Tribals' participation in the nationalist upsurge' in A. Bhuyan's (ed), *Nationalist Upsurge in Assam*, Government of Assam, Guwahati, 2000, P. 296.
16. Anonymous : '1894 Sanar Rangia' in P. Kalita's (ed), *op. cit.*, PP. 69-70.
17. Karna, M.N. : *Agrarian structure and land reforms in Assam*, Regency Publications, New Delhi, 2004, P. 38.
18. *Ibid.* : PP. 38-39.

19. Pathak, Moushumi : 'Peasants' revolt at Sarukhetri—the Raij-mel', *NEIHA—XXIII*, 2002, P. 113.

20. Barua, R. Hussain : 'Krishak Bidroh aru Asamar Musalman' in K. Kr. Deka's (ed), *op. cit.*, P. 17.

21. Pathak : *op. cit.*, PP. 112-113.

Sil, Upen : 'Namani Asamor Brihattam Raijmel—Panagaonar Tup' in A. Kr. Das & H. Sarma's (eds), *Sarukhetri Raijmel Satabarshiki Smriti Grantha*, Sarukhetri Raijmel Smriti Raksha Samiti, Baniakuchi, 1994.

22. Bora, Durgeswar : 'Raij-mel

23. Karna : *op. cit.*, P. 39.

24. Sil : *op. cit.*

25. Barpujari (eds) : *op. cit.*, PP. 99-100.

26. Hussain : *op. cit.*, P. 17.

27. Karna : *op. cit.*, PP. 39-40.

28. Goswami, S.D. : 'The British Taxation Policy in Assam' in J. B.'s (ed), *Studies in the Economic History of NEI*, Har Ananda publications, New Delhi, 1994, P. 96.

29. Sarkar, S. : *Modern India* (1885-1947), Mac Millan, Delhi, Reprint, 2008, P. 53.

30. Barpujari, H.K. (ed) : *The Comprehensive History of Assam*,Vol.V, Publication Board of Assam, Guwahati, 2004, PP. 34-35.

31. Saikia : *op. cit.*, P. 108.

32. Guha : *op. cit.*, P. 41.

33. Bose, M.L. : *Development of Administration in Assam*, Concept Publishing Company, New Delhi, 1985, P. 59.

34. Karna, M.N. : 'Historical Studies in the Agrarian Problems of North East India', *NEIHA—VII*, 1986, P. 393.

35. Goswami : *op. cit.*, P. 95.

36. Doshi, S.L. & Jain, P.C. : *Rural Sociology*, Rawat Publications, Jaipur, New Delhi, 2006, P. 119.

37. *Krishna Sarma's Diary*, Assam Publication Board, Guwahati, 1972, P. 249.

38. Gait, Sir E.A. : *A History of Assam*, L. B. S. Publications, Guwahati, Assam, 1984, P. 343.

39. Barpujari (eds)   : *Political History of Assam*, Publication Board of Assam, Guwahti, 1999, P. 100.

40. Guha   : *op. cit.*, P. 6.

41. *Ibid.*   : PP. 74-75.

42. Kalita, R.C.   : 'British exploitation in Assam

43. Sarma, N.   : *The rise and growth of the peasant movement in Kamrup district* (1826-1900), Ph. D thesis, G. U., Guwahati, 2003, P. 34.

44. Guha   : *op. cit.*, P. 13.

45. Saikia   : *op. cit.*, PP. 226-227.

46. Allen, B.C.
     Allen, C.G.H.
     Gait, E.A. &
     Howard, H.F.   : *Gazetteer of Bengal and NEI*, Mittal Publications, New Delhi, 2001, P. 105.

47. Guha   : *op. cit.*, P. 12.

48. Mills, A.J.M.   : *Report on the Province of Assam*, Publication Board of Assam, Gauhati, Second Edition, 1984, PP. 13-14.

49. Goswami, P.   : 'Colonial penetration and the emergence of nationalism in Assam' in A. Bhuyan's (ed), *op. cit.*, P. 15.

50. *Ibid.*   : P. 18.

51. Bhalla, G.S.   : *Condition of Indian Peasantry*, National Book Trust of India, New Delhi, First Edition, 2006, P. 7.

52. Guha   : *op. cit.*, PP. 31-32.

53. Kalita, Mohan Ch.   : 'Raij-mel' in Pabin Kalita's (ed), *op. cit.*, P. 29.

54. Desai, S.S.M.   : *Economic History of India*, Himalaya Publishing House, Bombay, July, 1990, P. 70.

55. Nag, Sajal   : 'Social reaction to bania exploitation' in J. B.'s (ed), *Studies in the Economic History of NEI*, NEHU Publications, Shillong, 1986, P. 67.

56. Guha   : *op. cit.*, P. 7.

57. Kaushal, G.   : *Economic History of India* (1757-1966), Kalyani Publishers, New Delhi, Reprint, 1991, P. 180.

58. Chopra, P.N.   : *A Social, Cultural and Economic History of India*, Vol. III, Mac Milan India Ltd., Madras, 1990, P. 183.

Puri, B.N. &
Das, M.N.

59. Kaushal : *op. cit.*, P. 8.
60. Goswami, S.D. : *op. cit.*, P. 95.
61. Goswami, P.C. : *The Economic Development of Assam*, Bombay, 1963, P. 60.
62. Guha : *op. cit.*, P. 39
63. Kaushal : *op. cit.*, P. 83.
64. Saikia : *op. cit.*, P. 39.
65. Raja, Purnanada : 'Phulaguri Dhewar Para Ajiloike Phulaguri' in J. Medhi's (ed), *Phulaguri Dhewar Rengani*, Receiption Committee, 143rd Anniversary of Phulaguri Dhewa, Phulaguri, Nagaon, 2004, P. 19.
66. Srinivasa, M.N. : *Social Change in Modern India*, Orient Longman Ltd., New Delhi, 1995, P. 51.
67. Chopra, Puri & Das : *op. cit.*, P. 167.
68. Sarma, N. : *op. cit.*, P. 41.
69. Doshi & Jain : *op. cit.*, P. 120.
70. Srinivasa : *op. cit.*, P. 65.
71. Saha, Subhas : *1942-struggle*
72. Nag : *op. cit.*, P. 367.
73. Guha : *op. cit.*, P. 42.
74. Ghosh, Lipi : 'Indebtedness in peasant sector
75. Sarma, N. : *op. cit.*, P. 41.
76. Kakati : *op. cit.*, P. 3.
77. Guha : *op. cit.*, PP. 41-42.
78. Deka, Rajendra Nath : 'Swadhinata Sangramat Sarukhetrir Avadan' in A. Kr. Das & H. Sarma's (eds), *op. cit.*, P. 24.
79. Deka, Dr.K.B. : *Alpar paror biplab*, Kalindi Prakashan, Sarthebari, Barpeta, 1995, P. 10.
80. Barpujari (eds) : *Political History of Assam*, P. 98.
81. Sil : *op. cit.*
82. *Ibid.* :
83. Guha : *op. cit.*, P. 43.
84. Barua, S.L. : *A Comprehensive History of Assam*, Munshiram Manoharlal Publishers Pvt. Ltd., New Delhi, 2005, P. 504.
85. Kakati : *op. cit.*, P. 14.

86. Deka, Bhabananda : 'Britishar Biruddhe Asamot Pratham Gana Andolan' in A. Kr. Das and H. Sarma's (eds), *op. cit.*, P. 96.
87. Kakati : *op. cit.*, P. 5.
88. Saikia : *op.cit*, P. 107.
89. *Ibid.* : P. 108.
    Guha : *op. cit.*, PP. 44-45.
90. Saikia : *op. cit.*, P. 108.
91. *Ibid.* : PP. 108-109.
92. Mookherjee, Mridula : 'Peasant resistance and peasant consciousness in Colonial India—Subalterns and beyond' in *Economic and Political Weekly*, Oct. 8, 1988, PP. 2114-2115.
93. *Ibid.* : P. 2114.
94. Sarma, Manorama : 'Peasant uprisings and middle class hegemony
95. Guha : *op. cit.*, P. 44.
96. Mookherjee : *op. cit.*, P. 2114.
97. Kalita, R.C. : 'The 19th century peasant movement and the Assamese middle class', *NEIHA—XV*, 1994, P. 205.
98. Karna : *Agrarian Structure and land reforms in Assam*, P. 36.
99. Guha : *op. cit.*, P. 284.
100. Barpujari (eds) : *op. cit.*, PP. 101-102.
101. Saikia : *op. cit.*, P. 109.
102. Goswami, S.D. : 'The Raijmels
103. *Ibid.* : P. 306.
104. Pathak : *op. cit.*, P. 115.
105. Kalita, Mohan Ch. : *op. cit.*, P. 30.
106. Karna : *op. cit.*, P. 40.
107. Barpujari (eds) : *op. cit.*, PP. 100-101.
108. Goswami : *op. cit.*, P. 306.
109. Barpujari (eds) : *op. cit.*, P. 101.
110. Goswami : The British taxation policy in Assam in J. B. Bhattacharjee's *op. cit.*, P. 96.
111. Srinivasa : *op. cit.*, P. 70.
112. *Ibid.* : P. 100.
113. *Ibid.* : P. 51.
114. Barua, R. Hussain : *op. cit.*, p.17.
115. Ali, Dr. M. Abid : *Pothorughat—Indianised*, Published by P. Sikdar, Mangaldoi, 2007, p. 25.

CHAPTER – NINE
CONCLUSION

A peasant is one who tills and works on land for agriculture, and lives in village. Want, deprivation and exploitation began to give him problem as the time rolled on. As a result, there broke out revolution in his mind. The peasant revolt and the agrarian revolt, both go hand to hand, and each seeks to redress particular grievances. The present problem of peasant of rural India is, mainly, the outcome of the colonial policy adopted by the British in Pre-Independent India. The peasant revolt is, mainly, a revolt born out of agrarian problem, and in course of time, it becomes a part of social movement.

Tapping of new sources of revenue to meet the increasing expenditure of the colonial government after 1857 prepared the background of the revolt of Nowgong of 1861. Frequent enhancement of land revenue even after 1861, apathy to develop the traditional agriculture system and to fight the natural calamities, and the discriminating waste-land and plantation policy—all these gave birth to the background of the series of peasant protests in Kamrup and Darrang in 1893-94.

Large scale of land grants in ancient periods brought problem in the South in between the 6th and the 9th centuries. The *Kalabhras* revolted against the landed brahmanas of Tamilnadu in the 6th century. Same problem arose in Garhwal in the 9th century. In the 11th and 12th centuries, we also find the same problem in Andhra and Karnataka against the landlord brahmanas. Some time, heavy and excessive tax burden also invited resentment. For example, we can mention the name of the Kaivartas of North Bengal who revolted against heavy taxation in the 11th century.

In ancient time, we also find some different nature of peasant protest in India. To take the advantage of royal visit for lodging complains, and self-immolation against the exploitation of landlords are some of the nature of peasant protest in 7th century. For example, the peasants lodged their complaint to Harsha, when he along with his army was passing through the countryside in the 7th century. In South India, we find an example of a girl who registered her protest against the landlord by throwing herself from the temple tower.

In medieval period, we find the improvement in agricultural tools and methods due to the intrusion of Islam in to India. Surprisingly, the land tax was no longer seen in the form of tribute. But its imposition remoulded peasants' relation with their superiors, and failure to pay the taxes was subjected to raids and enslavement. A triangular relationship came to exist among the peasantry, the zamindars and the ruling class in medieval period. The ruling class and the zamindars, both exploited the peasants at that time.

We also find the peasant protest against the oppression of the landlords in the Chola period in the first half of the 13th century. The revolt in the Doab in 1330 was the result of excessive revenue demand by Muhammad Bin Tughluq. The Sultan quenched his thirst by killing and blinding the *khots* and the *muqaddams*. But what is noticeable on his part is the opening up of an agriculture department known as *'diwan-i-kohi'*. Sometime, the increasing fiscal demands on the peasantry, and the imposition of *jizya* from the *parganas* of Mughal North India in medieval period also aggravated the condition of Indian peasantry.

In 17th century, we also find two peculiar peasant protests in Khuntaghat, situated on the south bank of the river Brahmaputra and within the erstwhile district of Goalpara. One occurred in 1614-16, under the leadership of Sanatan Sarkar against the abduction of daughters and sons of the peasants, and forcible collection of revenue from them. Another occurred in 1621, against the capturing of elephants by the Mughal Government, and thereafter, sentenced to death and whipped to some elephant drivers by the government. Unlike the ancient period, the peasants of medieval India sometime revolted for the possession of ponds and tanks also, as they were the great sources of irrigation at that time. The chief of Hanche died fighting the people of Kerehalli for a pond in 1212.

From 1763 to 1900, there broke out a series of peasant protests in India. Most of them were tribal by nature. The rebellions of Sanyasi, Chuar and Ho, Pagalpanthis, Bhils, Ahoms, Khasis, Kols, Santhals, Mundas, Gond and Khonda Dora—almost all of them were tribal revolts by nature.

We also find some major peasant revolts in India in the 19th and the 20th centuries. When some of them were directed against the British planters; some others were against the zamindars, talukdars, jagirdars and deshmukh; some revolted against the Marwari and Gujarati money-lenders, whereas some others again revolted against the excessive land revenue demanded by the government. Sometime, rural indebtedness and large scale alienation of agricultural land to non-cultivating classes also led to the peasant protest. Again, sometime peasants' primitive fury burst-out when the government declined to remit land revenue due to the failure of crops. By annihilating the big farmers, landlords and the jagirdars; some sections of peasants even wanted to alter the picture of their entire society. Sometime, the revolution assumed communal colour. For example, we can mention the name of the Moplah revolt of 1921. But such example is rare to be seen in Assam.

Some major peasant revolts of India of 19th and 20th centuries are: Indigo revolt of Bengal, Pabna and Bogra revolt of East Bengal, Maratha revolt, unrest of Punjab, Champaran struggle of Bihar, Kheda Satyagraha of Gujarat, Raebareilly and Faizabad revolt of Uttar Pradesh, Mewat revolt of North Central India, Moplah revolt, Bordoli Satyagraha of Gujarat, Telengana revolt of Andhra Pradesh and Naxalbari revolt of Darjeeling. All these revolts broke out in between 1858-1967.

Like the peasant revolts of India, we also find some peasant revolts beyond the periphery of India, and most of them were against the excessive and heavy land revenue demands of the manorial lords. The peasant insurrection in Merovingian time (579) was directed against the excessive tax burden of Chilperich. The insurrection in Carolingian time (841-843) was against the Frankish type of feudal rule. The peasants of Stellinga in Saxony took the initiative of this Carolingian insurrection. Some of the major peasant revolts of the world which find place are: the revolts of Flanders (1323-1328), France (1358), Germany (later Middle Age), South West Germany (1370-1383), England (1381), Germany (1525), China (1851-1864), Swing riots of England (1830-1831) and Japan (during the Tokugawa period, 1603-1867).

In the study, some peculiar aspects come to our notice. In ancient time, our peasants revolted against our native rulers. But in medieval and modern time, we find most of the rulers were either the Muslim or the Europeans, against whom our peasants fought for due.

In ancient time, the numbers of peasant protests were few. But they began to increase in medieval time, and again multiplied in modern time. Want, exploitation and deprivation might be the causes behind them. In ancient and medieval time, people paid their revenue in kind and cowrie. But, with the advent of the British in India, it transformed and transmuted in to cash.

In ancient time, what we find, the taxes and the revenues realized from the people were invested either in the philanthropic purposes of the land or spent in wars. But in medieval and modern period, most of the Muslim and the European rulers were found to have invested most of their collected revenues for the welfare of their native lands: either Middle East or Europe. There was huge drain of wealth from India in medieval and modern period. The nature of peasant protest in ancient and medieval India was somewhat different from that of the modern time. Possession of tanks and ponds, self-immolation and royal visit—these are rare to be found in modern time, what the people of ancient and medieval India adopted for the means of irrigation, against the oppression of landlords and *bhogpatis*.

The British agrarian policy was, mainly, responsible for the revolts of 1861 and 1893-94. Initially, in the wake of turmoil and disturbances; the people of Assam received the British rule with much enthusiasm. But all belied later on, as the colonial rulers introduced substantial changes in agrarian class relations. The introduction of new agrarian system did not generate any structural development, rather accelerated the process of pauperization and rapid stagnation. Some even strongly criticized the agrarian policy of the colonial government by depicting the deplorable condition of the farmers. The conduct of the cadastral survey was so erroneous that these were always confronted with numerous objections. The measurements of the fields of each mauza were not carefully and systematically tested. The peasants' complaints were hardly discussed and examined. Introduction of money economy and commercialization of agriculture also gave them trouble, as they were not acquainted with that changed system.

The revenue policy of the government dissatisfied the people. In addition to arbitrary and unjust settlement, classification of land was neither scientific nor based on actual productivity of the soil. Moreover, formerly the ryots were the owners of their land, but now they could be ejected from their land on the breach of conditions of lease. Formerly, they could transfer their land, now required permission from the Deputy Commissioner. Former single *patta* had been multiplied for which the ryots had to bear extra stamp duty. The government classified and increased the rate of revenue on land at a time when productivity of the soil was considerably declining. Even the rate of revenue was not reduced during the time of natural calamities. With every assessment, the alien rulers used to augment the rate without caring for low productivity and yielding. The nature of British exactions pauperized the people of Assam. Imposition of new taxes, like stamp duty, license fee for collecting forest products and grazing fee for grazing cattle—invited widespread resentment against the alien government. The waste-land rule, migration and plantation policy, apathy of the government towards the development of agriculture and fighting the natural calamities, and the decline of cottage industries due to the industrial policy of the government—invited widespread dissatisfaction among the people of Assam.

Exploitation and extirpation continued in unabated manner. Anyway, due to the agrarian policy of the British, the economic condition of almost all sections of peasantry started deteriorating during the second half of the 19th century which, finally, culminated in Assam in 1861 and 1893-94.

The middle class of Assam, though an outcome of the colonial regime, had their inspiration from their neighbouring Bengal. Under the colonial shade, a new Calcutta-oriented Assamese middle class developed in the late 19th century. Like the Indian middle class of the 19th century, this newly emerged middle class of Assam also expressed their deep loyalty to the colonial government, and wanted change in their societies under colonial tutelage.

Regarding their role and participation in the peasant uprisings of 1861 and 1893-94; we can say that the middle class of Assam had no role in the uprising of 1861, as they till then did not emerge as a class in the province. They emerged and developed as a class in Assam towards the eighties of the 19th century. They took a vital role in the uprisings of 1893-94. The middle class of Assam were divided in to several sections regarding their role and participation in the peasant uprisings of Assam. Some section supported the British Government, and wanted change under them. This section never supported the peasants and their problems. They even ridiculed them, and remained silent on the questions of revenue, migration, plantation and waste-land policy of the government. There were again some section who wanted to bring change in their society. This radical section raised their voice against exploitation and extirpation, and opposed the government on the questions of plantation, waste-land, migration and revenue. This section gave their wholehearted support to the peasants in their movements against the government. There was again some section who had their loyalty towards the government, but did not go openly due to the scare of fine and excommunication from their orthodox leaders. Still then, there were others who had their sympathy to their rebel peasants, but did not stretch-out their helping hand to them due to the scare of the government machinery. They scared if they supported them, the government would give them additional revenue pressure and terminate them from their jobs. Some section observed neutrality during the time of the peasant uprisings of Assam. Some even instigated the government and the peasants, both against each other, and wanted to have the gain from the both. Anyway, the middle class of Assam though divided into several sections and factions, in spite of that, they gave their physical and moral supports to the rebels, as they were also hard pressed by the imposition of income tax by the government. They even assumed leadership in 1893-94. But it was the lower class peasantry who gave the peasant uprisings a militant character.

During the early 35 years of the British rule (1826-1860), the *Raij-mels* were the recognized features in the administration of Assam, and the authority also viewed them with favour. But, enmity cropped-up between the administration and the *Raij-mels* when the latter began to motivate the peasants of Nowgong, Kamrup and Darrang—right from the Phulaguri (1861) till the revolts of Patharughat, Rangia and Lachima (1893-94). The main strength and guiding force of the peasant uprisings of Assam from 1861 to 1893-94 was the *Raij-mels*. They played a significant role in mobilizing the peasants exclusively against the agrarian policy of the British. They helped the masses for the growth of consciousness among them in the 19th century. The *Raij-mels* gave the peasants courage and strength, and spearheaded them against the repressive colonial class. The peasants also took active part in the *mels* hoping that the *mels* would lead them towards the right direction. The *mels* also tried their level best to fulfill their aspirations. Finally, we can say that though the *Raij-mels* played a significant role in the peasant movements of Assam in 1861 and 1893-94, and tried to bring out the masses in to the path of socio-economic and political agitation and compelled the government to concede to the partial reduction of the rates of assessment, despite that, they failed ultimately.

Application of old strategy and manoeuvre as against the modern strategy of the British; traditionally organized system as against the well organized system of the British; illiterate and half-literate traditional leaders as against the highly qualified leaders—brought failure to the *Raij-mels*. Traditional and out-dated weapons expedited their fiasco at the hands of the sophisticated weapons of the colonial government.

Another noticeable thing that we come across is the relation between the *Raij-mels* and the peasant movements of Assam. The peasant movements became strong and powerful there where the influence of *Raij-mels* was strong. Due to the strong existence of the *Raij-mels* in Kamrup and Darrang, the vibration of the peasant movements was powerful there.

The places where there were no existences of *Raij-mels*, we find no peasant movements there. The *Rayat sabhas* or the *Sarbajanik sabhas* were there in lieu of the *Raij-mels*. These *sabhas* tried to solve the problem of the peasants through prayer and petition to the government. They believed in compromise formula what the leaders of the *Raij-mels* could not even think of. In addition to that, these *sabhas* were run by the educated middle class, and probably because of this, the peasants of that place did not accept militant path, and solved their problems through negotiation.

In the *Raij-mels* of 1826-1870, the influence of literate and educated person was weak. May be because of less number of educated or scare of taking the leadership from the hands of the dominant orthodox class. Their existence, probably, began to increase in between 1870 and 1880. More or less, the relation between the government and the *Raij-mels* was good till 1860. After that, enmity cropped-up between them which, finally, estranged their relation.

The prohibition of opium in 1860-61, and the imposition of various taxes on betel nut, betel leaf, income, forest products and on water at the same time was, mainly, responsible for the outbreak of 1861 in Nowgong. Had there been no prohibition of opium in 1860-61, probably, there would have been no outbreak at Phulaguri in 1861. Opium prohibition acted as nucleus and others as electron and proton. Other causes which expedited the speed of outbreak were: land revenue policy of the colonial government, government's apathy towards agriculture development and fighting the natural calamities, waste-land rules and planters' exactions, migration, atrocities of the Marwaris and the money-lenders, rural indebtedness, ruin of cottage industries and problems of adjustment with the new money economy. In addition to them, comparative scarcity, injustice, lack of minimum education, success of the Jayantias against the British, interference of the British into the internal affairs of the tribal kings and role of the Christian missionaries also contributed lot for the outbreak of 1861.

The peasants of Phulaguri fought against the British exploitation but ultimately met failure. The root causes of their failure are: use of traditional weapons, lack of charismatic leaders, economic hardship, betrayal of some sections, greed for coins, false propaganda from the side of government, sharp British intelligence, prompt and quick decision of the Deputy Commissioner and the Superintendent of Police of Nowgong, sporadic outbursts, poor peasants doubt on rich peasants regarding their sincere participation, aloofness of some sections, ever readiness and ever preparedness of the British Government in curbing the revolt, lack of farsightedness and obstinate nature of the tribal leaders, firm conviction and strong determination of the British, obsolete mode of protest, reinforcement system of the government and lack of compromise formula—all these accelerated their process of failure.

Though some non-tribal people also took part, mainly, the tribal people took the vital role in the outbreak of 1861. The role of the middle class was extremely weak, as they still then was in embryonic stage due to the slow progress of education. The *Raij-mels* led by the traditional rural leaders took leading role in it.

By studying the nature of the outbreak of 1861, we come to the point that it was a mass movement as all sections, rich and poor, high and low, took part in it. All classes, like nobles and aristocrats, brahmins, Mahantas, Gosains, Dolois, Lalungs, Kacharis and Kaivartas were hard pressed by the policy of the colonial government. Due to the participation of all classes, it assumed, finally, the mass character.

The outbreak of 1861 was not a freedom movement, it was a movement against exploitation of the colonial government and therefore, emancipation from that. The revolt was localized and sporadic in character. In addition to that, it was a direct confrontation between the state and the people.

It was neither a tribal's revolt nor an opium eaters' revolt by nature. Non-tribal and non-opium eaters also took part in it. Ultimately, it assumed the character of a popular movement.

The revolt of 1861 germinated the future seed of unrest, and influenced the people of Darrang and Kamrup to take-up the cudgels on behalf of the oppressed ryots. As a result of their revolt, there emerged stagnation in agriculture. The gap between the ruler and the ruled widened, and the number of colonial force was increased. The revolt of 1861 also induced the opium eaters to work as labourers in the tea gardens of the British. In addition to that, the authority neither decreased the rate of revenue nor the supply of the government opium. The *Lalung* community was worse affected by the revolt of 1861.

Many became martyrs, many injured and many lost their properties. The outbreak of 1861 reflected the colonial oppression on the peasantry, on one hand and determination of the peasantry to fight against the government, on the other. The outbreak also proves one thing that any attempt, at socio-economic reconstruction without corresponding improvement of the people, was bound to be abortive. Significance of the outbreak of 1861 was that the illiterate tribal peasants gave leadership in it without the elite leadership.

The colonial government could realize the united strength and might of the peasants. It also encouraged the peasants of Darrang and Kamrup, and influenced the future course of action.

The Phulaguri revolt was not a mere revolt of local nature fought in between the ruler and the ruled, it was the first mass-revolt fought against the colonial government. Though they failed, by the outbreak of 1861, they wanted to compel the government to yield to the will of the people by the withdrawal of unpopular measures of taxation and colonial exploitation.

One exceptional aspect of this outbreak is that Lakhimpur, Sibsagar, Kamrup and Darang all the districts accepted the government's verdict of prohibition of opium, except Nowgong. So, only Nowgong had to witness the outbreak in 1861. But the entire area of Nowgong was not engulfed by its flame. Only Phulaguri, Raha and its neighbouring areas were engulfed by it.

During the peasants' unrest of three decades (1862-1892), there was no outburst of the peasant movement, except some mild bubbles in 1868-69. Roughly speaking, there prevailed silence only for three decades. But that does not mean that they reconciled to the British rule. They, probably, maintained silence during this period. Economic hardship, leadership crisis, lack of well-organized association, dreadful memory of 1861, lack of unity of action, lack of better substitute, increasing number of colonial forces after 1861—all these compelled them to observe silence for three decades.

Though they maintained silence, still then, wave of ignition and irritation blew in their minds. Frequent enhancement of land revenue, imposition of tax on income, license tax on forest products, tax on agricultural goods, apathy towards agricultural development, indifferent towards natural calamities, encouragement of foreign enterprise, foreign capital and foreign skill, more interest on plantation than on cultivation, government's allotment of waste-land to the European planters depriving the same to the local planters, control over rubber-cultivation depriving the local rubber cultivators, immigration problem—all these ignited the people openly. These issues made them wild and provocative. In addition to these issues, there were some others which made them worried and frustrated. Decline of cottage industries, exactions of the Marwari and *mahajans*, rural indebtedness, red-tapism of the colonial bureaucrats, no ray of hope of justice against colonial exploitation, double standard equality, less interest of the government in spreading education among the masses, neglected attitude of the government towards the *satras*, role of the Christian missionary in proselytisation to the local people—these issues also made the people alerted and awakened. As a result, gap and cleft between the ruler and the ruled began to unabate, and this finally, gave birth to suspicion, enmity and hatred in them as the time rolled on. The people again began to organize their *Raij-mels* in different districts of Assam, and thus, created awareness against the British. Ultimately, their patience lost and culminated in 1893-94.

From our study, we come to know that there was no movement of serious nature in between the 1862-92. The causes, why the movement of serious nature did not occur for three decades in Assam, may be because of scare of the British might and power, scare of losing lives, economic hardship and seize of properties by the government. Finally, we come to know that atrocious nature of Radhanath Barua, the tahsildar of Rangia; revenue augmentation in 1892, settlement of infertile lands in the name of local people, survey of 1893 and abolition of surrender of land, rude behaviour of M.C.Bordoloi, the Extra-Assistant Commissioner of Barpeta sub-division and his denial of peasants' request for remission of revenue; assault on the mandal and maujadar on the 21st Jan,1894 at Lachima; rapacious and avaricious nature of mandal and maujadar, banning of the *Raij-mels* by R.B.McCabe, the Deputy Commissioner of Kamrup—these are, mainly, responsible for the outbreaks of 1893-94. In spite of their decisive battle against the colonial ruler, they failed in their revolts in 1893-94. Use of traditional weapons, under-estimation of the power and number of the British, seize of license guns by the government, lack of unity among the local leaders, creation of division among the peasantry, weak control of the leaders upon the people, economic hardship, strong espionage system of the government, false propaganda from the side of the government, strong decision, sporadic outburst, failure to embrace all sections of the society, retreat of some of the leaders at the peak time of outbreaks, ever readiness of the government against the rebels, cool and meticulous decision of the administration, obsolete and outdated strategy of the local leaders—these factors contributed immensely for the failure of the revolts in 1893-94.

We also come to know that there were two sets of leaders in 1893-94: one, the traditional and the another, the new elite. The middle class of Assam emerged as a powerful class from the seventies of the 19th century, and from then on, they started to take dominant role in the revolts. But, it is an established fact that the common peasants gave the revolts a militant character.

The insurrections of 1893-94 were, basically, secular in character. In the revolt of Moplah of 1921, many Hindus had been killed, many temples had been sacked and many had been converted to Muslims. But in Assam, we find a complete opposite picture. Here, the Hindus and the Muslims, both fought together against the British. By nature, it was not a freedom movement. In addition to that, the revolts of 1893-94 were mass revolts, as all sections took part in them. Moreover, the outbreaks of 1893-94 were the peasants and the state direct confrontation.

Though the outbreaks met failure, despite that, they had great result and impact. They paved the way of greater dimension in future. They generated and germinated the future seed of freedom movement. Due to the involvement of the peasants in the outbreaks, stagnation started in agriculture. The outbreaks also widened the cleft between the ruler and the ruled. As a result, the number of colonial forces was increased, and the Government of India had to concede to the partial reduction of the rates of assessment. The outbreaks also gave death blow to the bell-metal industry of Sarukhetri mauza. Many became martyrs, many injured and many lost their properties due to the outbreaks of 1893-94. The outbreaks inspired the people of other places to revolt against exploitation in future. The prices of goods began to increase after the outbreaks of 1893-94. Many *hats* collapsed as a result of the outbreaks of 1893-94.

The significance and importance of the outbreaks of 1893-94 is that, in spite of having disparity among the peasantry, they fought together against the colonial government. The government could realize the united strength of the peasants in their revolts. The revolts heralded the beginning of a new era of peasant awakening in Assam. One very important thing is that though the cultivating and non-cultivating classes took part in the revolts of 1893-94, the rural and poor cultivating classes only gave them militant shape. The revolts proved the patience of the peasants, when the abatement order of revenue did not reach Assam soon. In spite of having all probability, they remained silent at that time. The peasants, what we find, revolted against exploitation and extirpation, not for their rights, privileges and social status. Their demands were real, not sentimental. Significance of these revolts is also that when the well-to-do and educated sections of the society remained silent and tolerated the exploitative nature of the government because of their vested interest, the poor peasantry themselves took-up the cudgels against the government. The religious and community bar could never prevent the peasants from uniting together against the government. The Hindus and the Muslim, both united under one roof, and fought against their common enemy in 1893-94, which is rare in history.

Rural people's response to the whites rule was good at the initial stage of their rule, as the former expected more from the latter. That's why, they did not want freedom from them. They only wanted freedom from exploitation. Till then from 1826 to 1885, they did not want freedom. When their hope and expectation belied, cry for freedom started to conceive in their minds slowly and gradually in further years.

Some other aspects of our study is that after 1870, England met severe financial crisis. Probably because of this, they wanted to strengthen their economy by increasing the rate of revenue in India and in their colonies of the world. Had they compromised in the case of revenue, probably, further outbreaks after 1861 could have been either evaded or restricted to some extent.

There was no uniformity in between the production, distribution and collection system. The government cared little for production and distribution system, they only cared for collection. As a result, their economy sounded, and local economy, on the contrary, impoverished.

After 1874, the people of England divorced their relation with nature. They showed their apathy towards agriculture due to the floods of American goods in England. Goods of free trade engulfed the English market, and probably because of this, the English Government showed their little interest towards agriculture at their home and in colonies.

One significant aspect of the outbreaks of 1893-94 was that the Muslim of Assam took a leading role in it. The Hindus and the Muslim, both fought together against the British at Patharughat and Lachima, and the revolts, therefore, assumed a secular character in Assam. In the revolt of Moplah of 1921, the rebels slaughtered 500 Hindus, sacked 100 temples and converted 2500 Hindus to Muslim; but the Hindus and the Muslim of Assam, on the contrary, demonstrated their unity twenty-seven years back.

The higher caste, what we find, interacted with the lower caste in Assam. Yogeswar Goswami of Byaskuchi maintained good relation with the lower caste people. Many high caste rebel leaders sat together with the lower caste people in the *Raij-mels*.

Another exceptional aspect what we find is that unlike the brahmins of Assam, the brahmins of Uttar Pradesh and Rajasthan ploughed and worked under the Rajputs and the Jats. In Assam, we find completely a different and opposite picture, where the brahmins got their land ploughed by others.

We find rare example of upward caste mobility in Assam in 1893-94, unlike the *vellalas* and the *padaiyachis*, the two tribes of Tamilnadu.

The new elites at their initial stage, probably, had to face opposition from the leaders of orthodox opinion, as they had the power to fine and excommunicate. Possibly because of fear and scare, they were ambivalence towards their own society.

From our study, some new areas and directions have come to notice which give us lots of curiosity and there is possibility of huge scope for further research in these. There were no revolts in the erstwhile districts of Assam in 1861 after the prohibition order of opium, why then it occurred only in Nowgong. There were no records of revolts in Assam in 1893-94 after the revenue hike in 1892 except some mild bubbles, why only in Kamrup and Darrang. The British exploited the people of Assam, that's why, they revolted against the British, but why did the native not revolt against the native, when they were exploited by them. There were economic and social disparities among the peasantry of Assam. In spite of that, what were the secret forces that united them together against the government. The Marwaris exploited the people of Assam and earned, thus, lot from Assam, but why they did invest their profits only in Rajputana, their homeland, discarding Assam. What were the internal causes that forced the colonial government to increase revenues year after year in spite of knowing its bad consequences. The relevance of the *Raij-mels* in present day context also needs further study. Furthermore, the two peasant uprisings of the Khuntaghat *pargana* of the Brahmaputra valley of 17th century: the revolts of Sanatan Sardar and the *Hathikheda,* deserve and wait to be explored further in a critical and historical perspective.

BIBLIOGRAPHY

SOURCE: THE PRIMARY

Accounts & Reports of Foreign Travellers:

Hamilton, Francis Buchanan	:	*An Account of Assam* (collected in between 1807-1809), S. K. Bhuyan (ed.), Guwahati, Second Edition, 1963.
Hunter, W. W.	:	*A Statistical Account of Assam,* Vol. I, Reprint, Delhi, 1990.
Hunter, W. W.	:	*A Statistical Account of Assam,* Vol. II (published first in 1879), Delhi, 1982.
M'Cosh, John	:	*Topography of Assam,* Logos Press, New Delhi, Second Reprint, 2000.

Buranji (Assamese):

Barua, Gunabhiram	:	*Asam Buranji,* Guwahati, Reprint, 1972.
Barbarua, Srinath Duara	:	*Tungkhungia Buranji,* S. K. Bhuyan (ed.), Guwahati, Second Edition, 1964.
Bhuyan, S. K. (ed.)	:	*Deodhai Asam Buranji,* Guwahati, Reprint, 1962.

Bhuyan, S. K. (ed.) : *Satsari Asam Buranji* (collection of seven old chronicles), Guwahati, Second Edition, 1964.

Bhuyan, S. K. (ed.) : Jayantia Buranji, Guwahati, Second Edition, 1964.

Bhuyan, S. K. (ed.) : *Kamrupar Buranji,* Guwahati, Second Edition, 1958.

Charit-puthi:

Lekharu, U. C. (ed.) : *Katha Guru Charit,* Nalbari, 15th Edition, 1987.

Chronicle (English):

Barua, Rai Sahib G. C. (trans. & edited) : *Ahom Buranji,* Guwahati, Reprint, 1985.

Gazetteers:

Allen, B. C. : *Assam District Gazetteers—Darrang, Nowgong and Kamrup districts,* Shillong, 1905.

Allen, B. C., : *Gazetteer of Bengal and North East India,*

Allen, C. G. H., Mittal Publications, New Delhi, 2001.

Gait, E. A. & Howard, H. F. Hunter, W. W. : *The Imperial Gazetteer of India,* Vol. IV & VI, Calcutta, 1879.

—*The Assam Gazettes,* Jan 1, 1876 & Dec 29, 1888.

Periodicals:

Asam Bandhu   :   Barua, Gunabhiram (published and edited in 1885-86) compiled and edited by N. Saikia, Guwahati, 1984.

Orunodoi   :   A monthly magazine, compiled and edited by M. Neog, Guwahati, 1983.

Proceedings/Official records:

- *Assam Secretariat Revenue Proceedings, A, Sept, 1890.*
- *Revenue and Agriculture Deptt. Proceedings, March, 1893.*
- *Assam Secretariat Proceedings, Sept, 1894 bearing progs. Nos. 252, 312 and 320 on the Rangia, Lachima and Patharughat Riots.*
- *Letter No. 27, dtd. the 12th Jan, 1894 from R. B. McCabe, the Deputy Commissioner of Kamrup to the Commissioner of the Assam Valley districts, No. 252*

- *Letter No. 312, dtd. the Sept, 1894 from R. B. McCabe, the Deputy Commissioner of Kamrup to the Commissioner of the Assam valley districts.*
- *The Assam Land Revenue Manual,* Vol. I, Calcutta, 1896, Shillong, Reprinted, 1965

Reports and Records:

Mills, A. J. M.   :   *Report on the Province of Assam,* Publication Board of Assam, Guwahati, Second Edition, 1984.

Pemberton, Capt. R. B.   :   *Report on the Eastern Frontier of British India,* DHASA, Guwahati, Reprint, 1966.

- *Report on the Administration of Revenue in Assam, 1874-1905, 1912-1922.*
- *Report on the Administration of Land Revenue, 1879-80,* Shillong, 1881.
- *Assam Valley Re-assessment Report, 1892-93.*

SOURCE: THE SECONDARY

Books (*English*):

Alam, M. & : *The Mughal State: 1526-1750,* Oxford University

Subrahmanyam, S. (eds.)
Press, New Delhi, 2008.

Agarwal, A. N. : *Indian Agriculture,* Vani Educational Books, New Delhi, 1980.

Ali, Dr. M. Abid : *Pothorughat-Indianised,* P. Sikdar, Mangaldoi, 2007.

Banerjee, A. C. : *A new history of medieval India,* S.Chand & Company Ltd.

Banerjee, B. & Singh, K. : *Middle class people and rising prices,* Prakashan Kendra, Lucknow, 1997.

Barman, Santo : *The Raijmel—A Study of the Mel System in Assam,* Spectrum Publication, Guwahati, Delhi, 2005

Barooah, D. P. : *Aspects of the history of Assam,* Darbari Prakashan, Kolkata, 2002.

Barpujari, H. K. : *The American missionaries and NE India, 1836—1900,* Delhi, 1986.

Barpujari, H. K. (eds.) : *Political History of Assam, 1826-1919,* Vol. I, Publication Board of Assam, Guwahati, Second Edition, 1999.

Barpujari, H. K. (ed.) : *The Comprehensive History of Assam,* Vol. II, Publication Board of Assam, Guwahati, First Edition, 1992.

Barpujari, H. K. (ed.) : *The Comprehensive History of Assam,* Vol. V, Publication Board of Assam, Guwahati, 2004.

Barpujari, H. K. : *Assam in the days of the Company (1826-1858),* NEHU Publication, Shillong, 1996.

Barua, Hem : *The Red River and the Blue Hill,* L. B. Stall, Gauhati, Assam, Revised, 1962.

Barua, S. L. : *A Comprehensive History of Assam,* Munshiram Manoharlal Publishers Pvt. Ltd., New Delhi, 2005.

Bhalla, G. S. : *Condition of Indian Peasantry,* National Book Trust of India, New Delhi, First Edition, 2006.

Bhattacharjee, J. B. (ed.) : *Studies in the Economic History of North East India,* H. A. Publications, New Delhi, 1994.

Bhattacharjee, J. B. (ed.) : *Studies in the Economic History of North East India,* NEHU Publication, Shillong, 1986.

Bhattacharjee, J. B. : *Trade and Colony—the British Colonization of North East India,* NEIHA, Shillong, 2000.

Bhuyan, A. (ed.) : *Nationalist Upsurge in Assam,* Govt. of Assam, Guwahati, 2000.

Bhuyan, S. K. (ed.) : *Kamrupar Buranji,* Calcutta, 1930.

Bhuyan, S. K. : *Studies in the History of Assam,* Guwahati, 1965.

: *Lachit Barphukan and his times,* Gauhati, 1947.

Biswas, G. R. : *Peasant Movement in North East India,* 1946-50, Regency Publications, New Delhi, 2002.

Bose, M. L. : *Development of Administration in Assam,* Concept Publishing Company, New Delhi, 1985.

: *Social History of Assam,* Concept Publishing Company, New Delhi, 2003.

Chandra, Bipan	:	*India's struggle for Independence, 1857-1947,* Penguin Books, New Delhi, 1998.
Chopra, P. N.,	:	*A Social, Cultural and Economic History of*
Puri, B. N. & Das, M. N.	:	*India,* Vol. III, Macmillan India Ltd, Madras, 1990.
Choudhury, K. A.	:	*Ancient Agriculture and Forestry in Northern India,* Bombay, 1977.
Das, A. N.	:	*Agrarian unrest and socio-economic change, 1900-80,* Manohar, Delhi, 1983.
Desai, S. S. M.	:	*Economic History of India,* Himalaya Publishing House, Bombay, July, 1990.
Dhanagare, D. N.	:	*Peasant Movements in India, 1920-50,* Oxford University Press, Bombay, Calcutta & Madras, 1983.
Digby, William	:	*Prosperous British India,* Sagar Publications, New Delhi, 1969.
Doshi, S. L. & Jain, P. C.	:	*Rural Sociology,* Rawat Publications, Jaipur, New Delhi, 2006.
Dutta, K. N.	:	*Landmarks in the Freedom Struggle in Assam,* Guwahati, 1958 & 1969.
Gadgil, D. R.	:	*The Industrial Evolution of India,* New Delhi, 1982
Gait, Sir E.	:	*A History of Assam,* L. B. S. Publications, Guwahati, Assam, 1984.
Goswami, H.	:	*Population trends in the Brahmaputra valley,* Mittal Publications, New Delhi, 1985.
Goswami, P. C.	:	*The Economic Development of Assam,* Asia Publishing House, Bombay, 1963.
Guha, A.	:	*Assamese peasant society in the late 19th century: structure and trend,* Centre for Studies in Social Sciences, Callcutta, Aug, 1979

	:	*Medieval and Early Colonial Assam,* K. P. Bagchi and Co., Calcutta, New Delhi, 1991.
	:	*Planter Raj to Swaraj,* 1826-1947, Tulika Books, New Delhi, 2006.
Habib, Irfan	:	*Essays in Indian History: towards a Marxist Perception,* Tulika Books, New Delhi, 2001.
	:	*A People's History of India—Indian Economy, 1858-1914,* Tulika Books, New Delhi, 2007.
Hussain, M.	:	*The Assam Movement—Class, Ideology and Identity,* Manak Publications Pvt. Ltd. in association with H. A. Publications, New Delhi, 1993.
Jaiswal, Suvira	:	*The Origin and Development of Vaishnavism,* Delhi, 1967.
Jha, D. N.	:	*Ancient India in Historical Outline,* Manohar, New Delhi, Reprinted, 2001.
Josh, Bhagwan & Joshi, Sashi	:	*Struggle for Hegemony in India, 1920-47,* Sage Publications, New Delhi.
Karna, M. N.	:	*Agrarian Structure and Land Reforms in Assam,* Regency Publications, New Delhi, 2004.
Kaushal, G.	:	*Economic History of India (1757-1966),* Kalyani Publishers, New Delhi, Reprint, 1991.
Keswani, K. B.	:	*Modern India (1819-1964),* Himalaya Publishing House, New Delhi, First Edition, 1990.
Krishna Sarma's Diary	:	Assam Publication Board, Guwahati, 1972.
Maiti, P.	:	*Studies in Ancient India,* Kolkata, 2007.
Mukherjee, P.	:	*History of India,* Calcutta.
Nath, J. G.	:	*Agrarian Structure of Medieval Assam,* Concept Publishing Company, New Delhi, 2002.

Rosener, Werner : *Peasant in the middle ages,* Polity Press, Cambridge, 1996.

Roy Choudhury, S. C. : *Modern India,* Surjeet Publications, New Delhi.

Saikia, Rajen : *Social and Economic History of Assam (1853-1921),* Manohar, New Delhi, 2001.

Sarkar, Sumit : *Modern India* (1885-1947), Macmillan, Delhi, Reprint, 2008.

Sarma, Manorama : *Social and Economic Change in Assam: Middle Class Hegemony,* Ajanta Publications, New Delhi, 1990.

Sarma, R. S. : *Aspects of Political Ideas and Institutions in Ancient India,* Delhi, 1959.
: *Indian Feudalism, AD 300-1200,* Macmillan India Ltd., Madras, Reprinted, 1996.
: *India's Ancient Past,* Oxford University Press, New Delhi, 2008.

Sarma, S. N. : *A Socio-Economic and Cultural History of Medieval Assam* (*1200-1800AD*), Gauhati, 1989.

Sequeira, G. & Quadros, S. : *History of Ancient India-I,* J. J. Publications, Mangalore, First Edition, 2001.

Sertsova, A. : *What is Revolution?* Progress Publishers, Moscow, 1986.

Shishkina, V. & | Yakovleva, L.

Singh, A. K. : *History of Far-East in modern times,* Surjeet Publications, New Delhi.

Srinivas, M. N. : *Social Change in Modern India,* Orient Longman Ltd., New Delhi, 1995.

Srivastava, A. L. : *The Sultanate of Delhi* (*1206-1526*), Agarwala & Company, Agra, 1971.

Stein, Burton : *Peasant, State and Society in Medieval South India,* Oxford University Press, Delhi, 1999.

Thakur, V. K. &	:	*Peasant in Indian History-I,* Janaki Prakashan, Aounshuman, A. (eds.) Patna, New Delhi, 1996.
Tripathy, R. S.	:	*History of Ancient India,* Motilal Banarsidass, Delhi, Reprinted, 1987.
Trevelyan, G. M.	:	*English Social History,* Orient Longman Ltd., Mumbai, Indian Reprint, 2001.

Thesis unpublished (Ph. D. & M. Phil.) :

Saha, Subhash	:	*Grassroot Nationalism—A Study of Mass Resistance in the Districts of Darrang and Nowgong of Assam, 1937-1947* (Ph. D. Thesis), NEHU, Shillong, 1989.
Saha, Subhash	:	*1942-Struggle—A Study of Grassroot Nationalism in the Districts of Darrang and Nowgong* (M. Phil), NEHU, Shillong, 1984.
Sarma, N.	:	*The rise and growth of the peasant movement in Kamrup district, 1826-1900* (Ph. D. Thesis), G. U., Guwahati, 2003.

Books (Assamese):

Barkataki, S.	:	*Asomiya—Madhyashreni,* Navajeevan Prakash, Guwahati, 2000.
Barman, S. (et al)	:	*Oitihya aru Itihash,* Journal Emporium, Nalbari, 2005
Barman, S. N.	:	*Adhunikatar Agradoot Pandit H.Ch. Barua,* Guwahati, 1996.
Barua, Birinchi Kr.	:	*Asamar Loka Sanskriti,* Bina Library, Guwahati, 1989.
Bhuyan, J. N.	:	*Unavimsa Satika: Shrishti aru Chetana,* L. B. Stall, Guwahati, 1998.

Choudhury, Birajananda : *Paradhinatar Para Swadhinataloi,* Himadri Prakashan, Margherita, 1996.

Choudhury, Prasenjit : *Asamor chah banua aru ounoish satikar bidwan samaj,* Students' Store, Guwahati, 1989

Gohain, Hiren : *Asamiya Jatia Jivanat Mahapurushiya Parampara,* L. B. Stall, Guwahati, 1990.

Gohain, Hiren (eds.) : *Asom Andolan—Pratishruti aru Phalashruti,* Banalata, Guwahati, Second Edition, Dec., 2007.

Goswami, Indreswar : *Adha-Pora Pandulipi,* Lili Prakashika, Nowgong, 1999.

Guha, A. : *Jamidarkalin Goalpara Jilar Artha-Samajik Avastha: Eti Oitihashik Dristipat,* Natun Sahitya Parishad, Guwahati, 2000.

Kalita, Benudhar : *Phulaguri Dhewa,* Lakheswar Kalita and others, Nowgong, 1961.

Sarma, Benudhar : *Congressor Kanchiali Radat,* Manuh Prakashan.

Tamuli, L. N. : *Bhartar Swadhinata Andolanat Asamor Avadan,* Sept, 1988.

Drama (*Assamese*):

Deka, K. B. B. : *Alpar Paror Biplab* (a social drama), Published by Kalindi Prakashan, Sarthebari, Barpeta, 1995.

Articles (*English*):

Alam, M. : 'Aspects of Agrarian Uprisings in North India in Early 18th century', in M. Alam & S. Subrahmanyam's (eds.) *The Mughal State, 1526-1750,* Oxford University Press, New Delhi, 2008.

Barman, S.	:	'Christian missionaries and the 19th century Santhals migration to Assam', *NEIHA-XXVIII*, 2007.
Barooah, D. P.	:	'The Rebellion of 1857 and its impact on Assam', in A. Bhuyan's (ed.) *Nationalist Upsurge in Assam*, Govt. of Assam, Dispur, Guwahati, 2000.
Bhattacharjee, J. B.	:	'Regional Organizations and National Awakening', in A. Bhuyan's (ed.) *Nationalist Upsurge in Assam*, Govt. of Assam, Dispur, Guwahati, 2000.
	:	'The Eastern Himalayan Trade of Assam in the Colonial Period', in J. B. Bhattacharjee's (ed.) *Studies in the Economic History of North East India*, Har Anand Publications, New Delhi, 1994.
Bhuyan, A.	:	'The Non-Co-Operation Stir in Assam', in A. Bhuyan's (ed.) *Nationalist Upsurge in Assam*, Govt. of Assam, Dispur, Guwahati, 2000.
Chandra, S.	:	'The Mughal State—Review of the crisis of the Jagirdar's system', in M. Alam & S. Subrahmanyam's (eds.) *The Mughal State, 1526-1750*, Oxford University Press, New Delhi, 2008.
Choudhury, M.	:	'Tribals' Participation in the Nationalist Upsurge', in A. Bhuyan's (ed.) *Nationalist Upsurge in Assam*, Govt. of Assam, Dispur, Guwahati, 2000.
Dasgupta, Keya	:	'Industrialization in the Brahmaputra valley (1881-1921)', in J. B. Bhattacharjee's (ed.) *Studies in the Economic History of North East India*, Har Anand Publications, New Delhi, 1994.

	: 'Coming of tea in the Brahmaputra valley: Changes in pattern of trade', in J. B. Bhattacharjee's (ed.) *Studies in the Economic History of North East India,* Har Anand Publications, New Delhi, 1994.
Das, Pramodanand	: 'Tribal peasantry in Bihar: a structural analysis', in V. K. Thakur & A. Aounshuman's (eds.) *Peasants in Indian History-I,* Janaki Prakashan, Patna and Delhi, 1996.
David, B.Vasantharaj	: 'Integrated Management of Pests and Diseases', in *the Hindu—Survey of Indian Agriculture,* 2008.
Deka, K. C.	: 'Assam and the Gohpur episode', in A. Bhuyan's (ed.) *Nationalist Upsurge in Assam,* Govt. of Assam, Dispur, Guwahati, 2000.
Dutta, A. K.	: 'The Background of National Awakening in Upper Assam', in A. Bhuyan's (ed.) *Nationalist Upsurge in Assam,* Govt. of Assam, Dispur, Guwahati, 2000.
Dutta, Anuradha	: 'Aspects of growth and development of nationalism in Assam in the 19th century', in A. Bhuyan's (ed.) *Nationalist Upsurge in Assam,* Govt. of Assam, Dispur, Guwahati, 2000.
Gautam, Bhadra	: 'Two Frontier Uprisings in Mughal India', in M. Alam & S. Subrahmanyam's (eds.) *The Mughal State, 1526-1750,* Oxford University Press, New Delhi, 2008.
Ghosh, Lipi	: 'Indebtedness in peasant sector: a study of Assam proper in late 19th century', in J. B. Bhartacharjee's (ed.) *Studies in the Economic History of North East India,* Har Anand Publications, New Delhi, 1994.

Goswami, Chandana	:	'Phulaguri Uprising (1861): The first phase of peasant upheaval in Assam', *ACTA Journal,* Vo.l. XXXI, Published by General Secretary, ACTA, Solapara, Guwahati, 2007-08.
Goswami, Priyam	:	'Colonial Penetration and the Emergence of Nationalism in Assam', in A.Bhuyan's (ed.) *Nationalist Upsurge in Assam,* Govt. of Assam, Dispur, Guwahati, 2000.
	:	'Opening up of Nambor forest for settlement—A missed opportunity', *NEIHA-XXIII,* 2002.
Goswami, S. D.	:	'The nationalist upsurge: Its impact on peasants and tea garden workers', in A. Bhuyan's (ed.) *Nationalist Upsurge in Assam,* Govt. of Assam, Dispur, Guwahati, 2000.
	:	'Raij versus the Raj: The Nowgong outbreak (1861) in Historical perspective', in J.B. Bhattacharjee's (ed.) *Studies in the Economic History of NEI,* NEHU Publications, Shillong, 1986.
	:	'Revenue reorganization of Assam under David Scott', *NEIHA-I,* 1980.
	:	'The Raiimels: their historic role in peasant movements of Assam', *NEIHA-X,* 1989.
	:	'The British taxation policy in Assam', in J. B's (ed.) *Studies in the Economic History of North East India,* Har Anand Publication, New Delhi, 1994.
	:	'Revenue settlement in the hill districts of Assam—A study of the house tax', in J. B. Bhattacharjee's (ed.) *Studies in the Economic History of NEI,* NEHU Publications, Shillong, 1986.

Gough, Kathlene	:	'Indian peasant uprising', in *Economic and Political Weekly*, Vol. IX, Special number, Aug, 1974
Guha, A.	:	'Saga of the Assamese middle class (1826-1921)-A review article', *NEIHA-XXIII*, 2002.
	:	'A peep through 19th century Assam: Maniram Dewan', in S. Barman's (et al) *Oitihya aru Itihash*, Journal Emporium, Nalbari, 2005.
	:	'Land rights and social classes in medieval Assam', in *Indian Economic and Social History Review*, Sept, 1966.
Hilaly, Sarah	:	'Railways in Assam and immigration of peasants in the colonial period', *NEIHA-XXII*, 2001.
Jain, V. K.	:	'Dynamics of Hydraulic Activity and Agrarian Formation during the Mauryan and Post-Mauryan period', in V. K. Thakur & A. Aounshuman's (eds.) *Peasant in Indian History-I*, Janaki Prakashan, Patna, New Delhi, 1996.
Jha, D. N.	:	'Land Revenue in India', in R. S. Sarma's (ed.) *Historical Studies*, Delhi, 1971.
Jha, Hetukar	:	'Understanding peasant—Its low classness', in V. K. Thakur and A. Aounshuman's (eds.) *Peasant in Indian History-I*, Janaki Prakashan, Patna, New Delhi, 1996.
Kalita, B. C.	:	'Administrative Units of NEI—A Geographical Note', in *The North Eastern Geographer*—Vol. XII, Nos. 1 & 2, 1980.
Kalita, R. C.	:	'The Phulaguri uprising of 1861: A peasants mass movement', *NEIHA-X*, 1989.
	:	'British exploitation in Assam: The opium policy and revenue (1850-1894)', *NEIHA-XII*, 1991.

	:	'The 19th century peasant movement and the Assamese Middle class', *NEIHA-XV*, 1994.
	:	'Opium Prohibition and Rai Bahadur J. N. Barua', *NEIHA-XVI*, 1995.
Karna, M. N.	:	'Historical studies in the agrarian problems of North East India', *NEIHA-VII*, 1986.
Liu Xinru	:	'Some Kharosthi records concerning irrigation co-operatives in the Kushana period', in V. K. Thakur and A. Aounshuman's (eds.) *Peasant in Indian History-I*, Janaki Prakashan, Patna, New Delhi, 1996.
Mookherjee, Mridula	:	'Peasant resistance and peasants consciousness in colonial India-Subalterns and beyond', in *Economic and Political Weekly*, Oct 8, 1988.
Nag, Sajal	:	'The Surma valley Muslims and the Sylhet separation issue', in A. Bhuyan's (ed.) *Nationalist Upsurge in Assam*, Govt. of Assam, Dispur, Guwahati, 2000.
	:	'Religion and ethnicity in class formation: Aspect of peasants class composition in colonial Assam in the context of Communalism', *NEIHA-V*, 1984.
	:	'Social reaction to Bania exploitation', in J. B. Bhattacharjee's (ed.) *Studies in the Economic History of North East India*, Shillong, 1986.
	:	'Economic roots of the regional capitalist class: A study of the primitive accumulation of the Marwari community in Colonial Assam', in J. B. Bhattacharjee's (ed.) *Studies in the Economic History of North East India*, Har Anand Publications, New Delhi, 1994.

Nath, Dambarudhar : 'Satradhikar's role in national awakening', in A. Bhuyan's (ed.) *Nationalist Upsurge in Assam,* Govt. of Assam, Dispur, Guwahati, 2000.

Nehru, Jawahar Lal : 'The Brahmaputra valley', in A. Bhuyan's (ed.) *Nationalist Upsurge in Assam,* Govt. of Assam, Dispur, Guwahati, 2000.

Pande, Rekha : 'Writings on peasant in medieval India: A historiographical critique', in V. K. Thakur and A. Aounshuman's (eds.) *Peasant in Indian History-I,* Janaki Prakashan, Patna, New Delhi, 1996.

Parasher, Aloka : 'Writings on villages and peasants in early India: Problems in historiography', in V. K. Thakur and A. Aounshuman's (eds.) *Peasant in Indian History-I,* Janaki Prakashan, Patna, New Delhi, 1996.

Pathak, Moushumi : 'Peasants' revolt at Sarukhetri—The Raijmel', *NEIHA-XXIII,* 2002.

Purkayastha, Sudesna : 'Rubber trade and cultivation in Assam during the colonial period', *NEIHA-XVI,* 1995.

Rana, R. P. : 'Was there an agrarian crisis in Mughal North India?', in Prabhat Patnaik's (ed.) *Social Scientist,* Tulika, New Delhi, Nov-Dec, 2006.

Saha, Subhash : 'Capital Labour relations: A study of tea plantation in Assam (1835-1926)', in J. B. Bhattacharjee's (ed.) *Studies in the Economic History of North East India,* Har Anand Publications, New Delhi, 1994.

Saikia, Anand : 'The British land revenue policy in Assam—Its impact upon peasantry', in J. B. Bhattacharjee's (ed.) *Studies in the Economic History of North East India,* NEHU Publications, Shillong, 1986.

Sarma, G. P. : 'The Assamese Literature and the Nationalist upsurge', in A. Bhuyan's (ed.) *Nationalist Upsurge in Assam,* Govt. of Assam, Dispur, Guwahati, 2000.

Sarma, Manorama : 'Peasant uprisings and middle class hegemony: The case of Assam', *NEIHA-X,* 1989.

: 'Class formation in Assam: The agrarian sector', (1911-1947), *NEIHA-XII, 1991.*

Sen, Ranjit : 'The peasant question in Bengal in the second half of the 19th century—A note on the marginal peasants', in V. K. Thakur and A. Aounshuman's (eds.) *Peasant in Indian History-I,* Janaki Prakashan, Patna, New Delhi, 1996.

: 'General pattern of revenue maximization in Bengal (including Lower Assam) in the18th century', in J. B. Bhattacharjee's (ed.) *Studies in the Economic History of North East India,* NEHU Publications, Shillong, 1986.

Sengupta, S. C. : 'The Bengalees in Assam in the19th century', *NEIHA-X,* 1989.

Sheikh, Ahijuddin : 'Roots and nature of agrarian unrest—Peasant movement in Goalpara', *NEIHA-XIV,* 1993.

Siddiqui, M. H. : 'History and society in a popular rebellion—Mewat (1920-33)', in Kumkum Roy's *Past in the Present,* ASC, JNU, New Delhi, 2001.

Smith, W. Cantwell : 'Lower class uprisings in the Mughal empire', in M. Alam & S. Subrahmanyam's (eds.) *The Mughal State, 1526-1750,* Oxford University Press, New Delhi, 2008.

Thakur, V. K.

: 'The peasant in early India: Problems of identification and differentiation', in V. K. Thakur and A. Aounshuman's (eds.) *Peasant in Indian History-I,* Janaki Prakashan, Patna, New Delhi, 1996.

Articles (*Assamese*):

Anonymous

: '1894 sanar Rangia', in P. Kalita's (ed.) *Rangia Raijmel,* R. K. M. M. Committee, Rangia, 2005.

Barman, Santo

: 'Zamidarkalin Goalpara Jilar Artha Samajik Avastha: Eti Mulyayan', in S. Barman's (et al) *Oitihya aru Itihash,* Journal Emporium, Nalbari, Assam, 2005.

Barua, Abhay

: 'Janashrutir Pam khedi Jagiyal Mouzar Rajahgaon Samashtir Naam Itibritta', in J. Medhi's (ed.) *Phulaguri Dhewar Rengani,* Reception Committee, 143rd Anniversary of Phulaguri Dhewa, Phulaguri, Nagaon, 2004.

Barua, R. Hussain

: 'Krishak Bidroh aru Asamor Musalman', in K. Kr. Deka's (ed.) *Raijmel,* R. K. S. S. Sangha, Paikarkuchi, Nalbari, 1996.

Bhuyan, J. N.

: 'Asom Bandhu aru Asamor Samasamayikata', in J. N. Bhuyan's *Unavimsa Satika: Shrishti aru Chetana,* L. B. Stall, Guwahati, 1998.

: 'Gunabhiram Baruar Kathin Sabdar Rahasya Byakhya', in J. N. Bhuyan's *Unavimsa Satika: Shrishti aru Chetana,* L. B. Stall, Guwahati, 1998.

	: 'Gunabhiram Baruar Dinar Nowgong', in J. N. Bhuyan's *Unavimsa Satika: Shrishti aru Chetana,* L. B. Stall, Guwahati, 1998.
	: 'Purnananda Sarma Baruar Katha', in J. N. Bhuyan's *Unavimsa Satika: Shrishti aru Chetana,* L. B. Stall, Guwahati, 1998.
Bora, Dhrubajyoti	: 'Itihashat Jaat-Pratha: Asamot Jaat-Paatar Bhumika', in S. Barman's (et al) *Oitihya aru Itihash,* Journal Emporium, Nalbari.
Bora, Durgeswar	: 'Raijmel-Sarukhetri Krishak Bidrohar (1894) Eti Samiksha', in A. Kr. Das & H. Sarma's (eds.) *Sarukhetri Raijmel Satabarshiki Smriti Grantha,* Sarukhetri Raijmel Smriti Raksha Samiti, Baniakuchi, 1994.
Choudhury, Prasenjit	: 'Bir-bandana aru bouddhik byadhi: Ounoish satikar Asom aru baopanthi itihash-sarsar eti dish', in S. Barman's (et al) *Oitihya aru Itihash,* Journal Emporium, Nalbari.
Deka, Bhabananda	: 'Britishar biruddhe Asamot pratham gana andolan', in A. Kr. Das & H. Sarma's (eds) *S. R. S. S. Grantha,* S. R. S. R. Samiti, Baniakuchi, 1994.
Deka, Kamal Singh	: 'Brihattar Phulaguri anchalar dukhuria chabi', in J. Medhi's (ed.) *Phulaguri Dhewar Rengani,* Reception Committee, 143rd Anniversary of Phulaguri Dhewa, Phulaguri, Nagaon, 2004.
Deka, M. Kumar	: 'Rajkadamtalar oitihya—Bartaman aru bhabisyat', in K. Kr. Deka's (ed.) *Raijmel,* Kadamtal Swahid Smriti Sangha, Paikarkuchi, Nalbari, 1996.

Deka, Rajendra Nath : 'Swadhinata sangramat Sarukhetrir avadan', in A. Kr. Das & H. Sarma's (eds.) *Sarukhetri-Raijmel Satabarshiki Smriti-Grantha*, Sarukhetri Raijmel Smriti Raksha Samiti, Baniakuchi, 1994.

Goswami, Indreswar : 'Asamar pratham Krishak bidroh', in J. Medhi's (ed.) *Phulaguri Dhewar Rengani*, Reception Committee, 143rd Anniversary of Phulaguri Dhewa, Phulaguri, Nagaon, 2004.

Hussain, Haidar : 'Daas-prathar nirlajja parisangkha', in *Sambhar*, a weekly magazine of an Assamese daily *Asomiya Pratidin*, Guwahati, March 22, 2009.

Kakati, Mayaram : 'Asamiya terasa sanat Rangia', in P. Kalita's (ed.) *Rangia Raijmel*, R. K. M. M. Committee, Rangia, 2005.

Kalita, Mohan Ch. : 'Raijmel', in P. Kalita's (ed.) *Rangia Raijmel*, R. K. M. M. Committee, Rangia, 2005.

Kalita, R. C. : 'British amolat Asamar Krishak bidrohar patabhumi', in A. Kr. Das & H. Sarma's (eds.) *Sarukhetri Raijmel Satabarshiki Smriti-Grantha*, Sarukhetri Raijmel Smriti Raksha Samiti, Baniakuchi, 1994.

Mahanta, Arpana : 'Planter-Raj to Swaraj: Eti paryyalochana', in S. Barman's (et al) *Oitihya aru Itihash*, Journal Emporium, Nalbari, 2005.

Majumdar, Paramananda : 'Samachar Darpanat Asamor katha', in S. Barman's (et al) *Oitihya aru Itihash*, Journal Emporium, Nalbari, 2005.

Nath, Prasanna Kr. : 'Patharughatar Ron', in P. Kr. Nath's (ed.) *Patharughat*, Sipajhar, Darrang, Assam, 1994.

Nath, Purna Kanta : 'Phulaguri Dhewa', in J. Medhi's (ed.)
Phulaguri Dhewar Rengani, Reception
Committee, 143rd Anniversary
of Phulaguri Dhewa, Phulaguri,
Nagaon, 2004.

Raja, Pankaj Kumar : 'Sampritir saphura: Gosain uliowar
utshav', in J. Medhi's (ed.) *Phulaguri
Dhewar Rengani,* Reception
Committee, 143rd Anniversary
of Phulaguri Dhewa, Phulaguri,
Nagaon, 2004.

Raja, Purnananda : 'Phulaguri Dhewar para ajiloike
Phulaguri', in J. Medhi's (ed.)
Phulaguri Dhewar Rengani, Reception
Committee, 143rd Anniversary
of Phulaguri Dhewa, Phulaguri,
Nagaon, 2004.

Roy Choudhury, Anil : 'Asamot praja abhyutthan: Ounoish
satika', in P. Kr. Nath's (ed.)
Patharughat, Sipajhar, Darrang,
Assam, 1994.

Roy Choudhury, Anil : 'Nava-vaishnava Satrar artha-samajik
dis: Eti samiksha', in S. Barman's
(et al) *Oitihya aru Itihash,* Journal
Emporium, Nalbari, 2005.

Sarma, Dr. Debabrata : 'Saotal Gana-sangramor Itihash', in
Khiren Roy's (ed.) *Asomiya Khabar,*
Guwahati, 6th Feb, 2008.

Sarma, Sashi : 'Raijmel aru Krishak bidroh: Eti
oitihashik bisleshan', in K. Kr. Deka's
(ed) *Raijmel,* Raijmel Kadamtal
Swahid Smriti Sangha, Paikarkuchi,
Nalbari, 1996.

Sil, Upen : 'Namani Asamor brihattam
Raijmel-Panagaonar Tup', in A. Kr.
Das & H. Sarma's (eds.) *Sarukhetri
Raijmel Satabarshiki Smriti-Grantha,*
Sarukhetri Raijmel Smriti Raksha
Samiti, Baniakuchi, 1994.

Magazines/Journals (English):

- *ACTA Journal*, Vol. XXXI, General Secretary, ACTA, Guwahati, 2007-2008.
- *The Hindu-Survey of Indian Agriculture*, 2008.
- *The Historical Studies*, R. S. Sharma (ed.), Delhi, 1971.
- *Indian Economic and Social History Review*, Sept, 1966.
- *Journal of Historical Research*, Dibrugarh University.
- *North Eastern Geographer*, Vol. XII, Nos. 1 & 2, 1980.
- *Social Scientist*, Vol. XXXIV, Prabhat Patnaik (ed.), Tulika, New Delhi, Nov-Dec., 2006.
- *The Past in the Present*, Kumkum Roy (Course Co-ordinator), Academic Staff College, JNU, New Delhi, 2001.

Proceedings of North-East India History Association (English):

Volums. I. (1980), V. (1984), VII. (1986), X. (1989), XII. (1991), XIV. (1993), XV. (1994), XVI. (1995), XXII. (2001), XXIII. (2002) and XXVIII. (2007)

Magazine (Assamese):

Sambhar	:	A weekly magazine of *Asomiya Pratidin* (An Assamese Daily), Guwahati, 2nd March, 2009.

Souvenirs (Assamese):

Das, A. Kr. &	:	*Sarukhetri Raijmel Satabarshiki Smriti-Grantha*, Sarma, H. (eds.) Sarukhetri Raijmel Smriti Raksha Samiti, Baniakuchi, 1994.

Deka, K. Kr. (ed.)   :   *Raijmel,* Raijmel Kadamtal Swahid Smtriti Sangha, Paikarkuchi, Nalbari, 1996.

Kalita, P.   :   *Rangia Raijmel,* R. K. M. M. Committee, Rangia, 2005.

Medhi, J. (ed.)   :   *Phulaguri Dhewar Rengani*, Reception Committee, 143rd Anniversary of Phulaguri Dhewa, Phulaguri, Nagaon, 2004.

Nath, Prasanna Kr. (ed.)   :   *Patharughat*, Sipajhar, Darrang, Assam, 1994.

Weekly (English):

- *Economic and Political Weekly,* Vol. I & IX, Special numbers 32-34, Aug, 1974.
- *Economic and Political Weekly*, Oct. 8, 1988.

Newspapers (*Assamese*):

Hussain, Haidar (editor)   :   *Asomiya Pratidin*, Guwahati, 22nd March, 2009

Dr. Roy, Khiren (editor)   :   *Asomiya Khabar*, Guwahati, 6th February, 2008.